TRANSNATIONAL NARRATIVES AND REGULATION OF GMO RISKS

This book employs transnational legal analysis as a methodological framework to deconstruct narratives on agricultural biotechnologies from within, across and beyond the nation state level.

The book frames the transnational conundrum of genetically engineered organisms against the background of hegemonic and counter-hegemonic narratives and two ideal regulatory models: evidence-based and socially acceptable risk approaches. The analysis cuts across US law, EU law, the WTO Agreement on Sanitary and Phytosanitary Measures and hybrid standards, exploring relevant regulatory frameworks and case law.

The book demonstrates that both transnational narratives are socially and politically constructed, and neither ideal regulatory model can lay claim to neutrality and objectivity. It argues that regulatory choices are always, directly or indirectly, informed by non-scientific normative frames. Three factors determine the threshold of legally relevant adverse effects: recourse to more or less prudential approaches to risk assessment, regulatory focus on 'sound science' or on multiple forms of uncertainty, and the extent to which regulators prioritise the cost-benefit effectiveness of risk governance measures, as opposed to pursuing enhanced protection and considering other legitimate factors.

The regulation of agricultural biotechnologies thus becomes a lens through which to investigate the underlying value systems, goals and far-reaching implications of transnational discourses on the governance of uncertain risks. Against this backdrop, the normative strand of analysis points to the limited ability of science and procedural deliberation to generate authentic agreement and to identify normatively legitimate solutions, in the absence of pre-existing shared perspectives.

Transnational Narratives and Regulation of GMO Risks

Giulia Claudia Leonelli

•HART•
OXFORD • LONDON • NEW YORK • NEW DELHI • SYDNEY

HART PUBLISHING
Bloomsbury Publishing Plc
Kemp House, Chawley Park, Cumnor Hill, Oxford, OX2 9PH, UK
1385 Broadway, New York, NY 10018, USA
29 Earlsfort Terrace, Dublin 2, Ireland

First published in Great Britain 2021

A catalogue record for this book is available from the British Library.

Library of Congress Cataloging-in-Publication data

Names: Leonelli, Giulia Claudia, author.

Title: Transnational narratives and regulation of GMO risks / Giulia Claudia Leonelli.

Description: Oxford ; New York : Hart, 2021. | Based on author's thesis (doctoral - King's College London). | Includes bibliographical references and index.

Identifiers: LCCN 2021032666 (print) | LCCN 2021032667 (ebook) | ISBN 9781509937387 (hardback) | ISBN 9781509954445 (paperback) | ISBN 9781509937370 (pdf) | ISBN 9781509937394 (Epub)

Subjects: LCSH: Genetically modified foods—Law and legislation.

Classification: LCC K3927 .L46 2021 (print) | LCC K3927 (ebook) | DDC 344.04/232—dc23

LC record available at https://lccn.loc.gov/2021032666

LC ebook record available at https://lccn.loc.gov/2021032667

ISBN: HB: 978-1-50993-738-7
ePDF: 978-1-50993-737-0
ePub: 978-1-50993-739-4

Typeset by Compuscript Ltd, Shannon

Ai miei genitori

ACKNOWLEDGEMENTS

This monograph draws on my PhD thesis, winner of the Elsevier Prize for Outstanding Doctoral Work (year 2018). I thank my PhD supervisor, Professor Peer Zumbansen (Transnational Law Institute, King's College London; Faculty of Law, McGill), for accepting to supervise my project. At the time, I was in the third year of my PhD and preparing to change research area. I thank him for believing in my project and for taking me on as one of his supervisees.

I thank Federico Ortino and Michael Schillig (King's College London) for their continued friendship and support throughout the years, including the very difficult years of my PhD. I also thank Jan Oster (Leiden University) and Christopher Townley (King's College London) for their support and their generous help. I wish to thank Professor Alan Minuskin (Boston College) for being the best and nicest teaching auditor that one could wish for, and for his support throughout the years. Further, I thank Dr Jennifer Neller for the amazing job she has done editing the draft monograph and for her thoughtful comments and feedback.

Finally, I want to wholeheartedly thank my PhD examiners, Professor Christian Joerges (Hertie School of Governance, Berlin) and Dr Patrycja Dabrowska-Klosinska (Queen's University Belfast; Warsaw). I don't think I could have possibly been luckier in the choice of the examiners. I thank Dr Dabrowska-Klosinska very much for her support, including for deciding with Professor Joerges to nominate my PhD thesis for a prize. But more than anyone else, I wish to thank Professor Joerges for his continued support, extremely generous help, and encouragement. To him goes the biggest thanks of all. I will always be grateful for all his help.

TABLE OF CONTENTS

1

Introductory Overview: Transnational Narratives, Evidence-Based and Socially Acceptable Risk Approaches, Normative Analysis

An analysis of different approaches to risk regulation and opposed transnational narratives on agricultural biotechnologies and their uncertain risks lies at the heart of this book. Three analytical strands are tied up and set within a unitary framework as the enquiry of the book unfolds: these are methodological, institutional and normative strands of analysis. This introductory chapter provides an overview of these three strands of enquiry. The first section sketches out the broader picture, providing some background on genetically engineered organisms and demarcating the analytical scope of the book. The second section turns to methodological aspects. The methodological framework applied in the book and the relevant analytical implications are then illustrated in greater detail in the second chapter.

The third section, on the other hand, takes a closer look at the institutional strand of enquiry. The book deconstructs the hegemonic and counter-hegemonic transnational narratives on agricultural biotechnologies and their uncertain risks against the backdrop of two ideal approaches to risk regulation: evidence-based and socially acceptable risk models.[1] It examines the two approaches and their specific implications by focusing on relevant governance frameworks, regulatory categories and case law in the field of agricultural biotechnologies. The analysis cross-cuts different legal systems, where the hegemonic and counter-hegemonic narratives on genetically engineered organisms are embedded. The third section explores the rationales, premises and characteristics of these two diametrically opposed ideal regulatory models, anticipating the findings of the book.

[1] On 'socially acceptable risk' approaches, see GC Leonelli, 'The Fine Line between Procedural and Substantive Review in Cases Involving Complex Technical-Scientific Evaluations: Bilbaína' (2018) 55 *CML Rev* 1217; GC Leonelli, 'The Glyphosate Saga and the Fading Democratic Legitimacy of EU Risk Regulation' (2018) 25 *Maastricht Journal of European and Comparative Law* 582; and GC Leonelli, 'The Perfect Storm: GMO Governance and the EU Technocratic Turn' in M Peeters and M Eliantonio (eds), *Research handbook on EU Environmental Law* (Edward Elgar, 2020). The origins of the terminology of 'evidence-based' risk governance are uncertain; for its use, see inter alia A Alemanno, annotation of Case C-77/09, *Gowan Comércio Internacional e Servicos Lda* v. *Ministero della Salute*, EU:C:2010:803, (2011) 48 *CML Rev* 1329.

Finally, the fourth section focuses on the normative strand of enquiry. From this angle of analysis, the book investigates the extent to which the two opposed transnational narratives and ideal regulatory models may be reconciled, by identifying an agreeable and normatively legitimate solution to transnational regulatory conflicts. The book takes into consideration modern science-centred and legal procedural paradigms, questioning the ability of science and of deliberative practices to generate authentic agreement and build consensus in the face of scientific complexity and intense political and socio-economic controversies. The transnational conundrum of agricultural biotechnologies thus becomes a lens through which irreconcilable perspectives on risk regulation and their broader implications are investigated.

The book draws the conclusion that transnational conflicts on agricultural biotechnologies cannot and should not be solved. Diametrically opposed perspectives on whether, how and why uncertain risks ought to be regulated should merely coexist. Further, the failure of deliberation and legal proceduralisation in the field of agricultural biotechnologies is the starting point for a set of broader considerations. If, as the book suggests, successful *procedural* deliberation largely *results from* specific *substantive* preconditions, notably pre-existing shared perspectives, values and goals, the focus should ultimately shift from modern procedural analysis, which seeks to construct legitimate solutions to increasingly complex regulatory conflicts, to a post-modern substantive deconstruction of regulatory approaches and their underlying premises, goals and impacts.

I. The Broader Picture: Agricultural Biotechnologies and Transnational Controversies

Genetic engineering techniques have evolved considerably since the 1970s, when the first advances in recombinant DNA (rDNA) mediated gene transfer, or genetic modification, took place.[2] Transgenesis, ie 'traditional' genetic modification by means of inserting foreign DNA, has been largely replaced by different techniques. A whole range of new breeding techniques ('NBTs') inducing genetic mutations has been developed throughout the years. These include both techniques that involve genome editing, such as CRISPR-Cas9 technology, TALENs and Zinc Finger Nucleases technology, and techniques that do not involve genome editing, such as RNAi technology, agroinfiltration, epigenetic approaches and oligonucleotide-directed mutagenesis.[3]

[2] See the overview in ch 3, section I.

[3] For a general (pro-biotechnology) overview, see www.geneticliteracyproject.org/ and www.nbtplatform.org/. For a thorough but not entirely up to date overview, see European Scientific Advice Mechanism, High Level Group of Scientific Advisors, *New Techniques in Agricultural Biotechnology* (2017).

Genetic mutations through NBTs often target the same traits that were selected by means of transgenesis, with a view to achieving the same or similar goals. In this sense, at least at the current stage, the picture has largely remained unchanged; the advantages or disadvantages associated with organisms engineered by means of NBTs are not remarkably different from the ones of 'traditional' genetically modified organisms ('GMOs').[4] As to their uncertain public health and environmental risks, the scientific community has acknowledged the increased target precision of NBTs; yet, uncertainty persists as to the potential effects and risks of off-target interferences, unintended mutations, the disruption of different gene sequences and repeated small alterations through the application of one technique or more techniques simultaneously.[5] At a general level, yet again at the current stage of technical-scientific knowledge, the uncertain environmental and public health risks at issue do not appear to be significantly different from the ones at stake in the case of 'traditional' GMOs.[6]

Further, the scope of application of genetic engineering techniques has considerably expanded. Throughout the years, these techniques have been used to engineer crops, bacteria and microorganisms, animals, insects or (in a specific and highly controversial case) human beings; genetically engineered crops can be used as food and feed or for industrial or pharmaceutical purposes.[7] NBTs have also been used in the medical field. Taking this complex picture into consideration, it is ultimately unsurprising that different legal systems have varied in their approaches to (old and new) genetic engineering techniques. Different definitions of 'genetic modification', 'GMOs' or 'genetic engineering'[8] and different regulatory categories[9] coexist across different legal systems.

The analytical scope of the book is broader and at the same time more circumscribed than the title might, at first sight, suggest. On the one hand, the book takes into consideration more than 'traditional' GMOs; the analysis encompasses recent

[4] See below, in this section.

[5] See inter alia European Scientific Advice Mechanism, High Level Group of Scientific Advisors (n 3) 62 ff; the Statement on New Genetic Modification Techniques of the European Network of Scientists for Social and Environmental Responsibility ('ENSSER'), available at www.ensser.org/publications/ngmt-statement/, and RA Steinbrecher, 'Genetic Engineering in Plants and the New Breeding Techniques ('NBTs'): Inherent Risks and the Need to Regulate' [2015] *Econexus Briefing*.

[6] See below, in this section; however, see also the final considerations in ch 7, highlighting that the overall picture might change as technical-scientific knowledge evolves and the specific applications of these technologies develop.

[7] For further information on different applications, see www.geneticliteracyproject.org/. On the first and highly controversial application of CRISPR-Cas9 to human beings, see the interview to the co-discoverer of CRISPR technology and Nobel Prize winner Professor Jennifer Doudna, at www.issues.org/wp-content/uploads/2020/04/37-39-Doudna-Spring-2020-ISSUES.pdf.

[8] See ch 3, on the US approach to 'traditional' GMOs and to NBTs; chapter 4, on the EU legislative definition of 'GMOs' and its broader scope of application to organisms obtained through NBTs; chapter 5, on the 2000 Cartagena Protocol on Biosafety to the Convention on Biological Safety and terminology of living modified organisms ('LMOs'); and chapter 6, on the relevant definitions under the Codex Alimentarius Commission system.

[9] eg see ch 3 for the regulatory categories of 'plant pests' and 'plant-incorporated protectants', and ch 4 for reference to 'GMOs as or in products' and 'GM food and feed'.

regulatory developments and reforms relating to products obtained through the application of NBTs. For this reason, while the title refers to the familiar notion of 'GMOs', the book uses the more accurate terminology of 'genetically engineered' organisms ('GE organisms'). On the other hand, the scope of the analysis is limited to agricultural biotechnologies, with a focus on the cultivation of GE crops and the marketing of GE food and feed varieties. Other applications of GE techniques are not taken into consideration. Further, as the title makes clear and as already mentioned at the beginning of this chapter, the book focuses on the governance of agricultural biotechnologies and their *uncertain risks* from a *risk regulation* perspective. The specific governance approaches, regulatory categories and notions analysed throughout the book belong to the field of risk regulation. Different regulatory aspects or policy debates are only taken into account in so far as they are relevant to the enquiry into transnational narratives on GE organisms and their uncertain risks.

Upon these preliminary clarifications, the rest of this section endeavours to sketch out the broader picture on agricultural biotechnologies and identify the main issues at stake in this complex regulatory area. This paves the way for the threefold analysis of the following sections. The commercialisation of GE products started in the mid-1990s. In 2018, GE crops were grown in 26 countries; the cultivation and marketing of GE organisms is entrenched in several countries, the object of a blanket ban in a few countries, and stringently regulated in other jurisdictions.[10] Genetic mutations target specific traits, associated with agronomic or quality characteristics. GE crops have so far been engineered to achieve herbicide or multi-herbicide resistance, pesticidal traits, disease resistance, tolerance to environmental stresses, delayed ripening or bruising, enhanced nutritional qualities or a lack of specific toxins and allergens.[11] In the vast majority of cases, from the origins of transgenesis until nowadays, GE crops have been engineered to be herbicide or multi-herbicide resistant; these are also the most commonly farmed GE varieties.[12]

Like in other highly controversial areas of risk regulation, uncertainties and scientific inconclusiveness primarily surround the existence and nature of specific adverse effects, rather than the characterisation of the relevant risks.[13] Starting with environmental effects, uncertainty surrounds the possibility, extent and potential impacts of hybridisation, crop to crop gene flow and any adverse effects that these could have on biodiversity and specific ecosystems.[14] Similar considerations apply to the impact on non-target organisms of pest-resistant GE crops; in

[10] See the data in Brief 54-2018 of the International Service for the Acquisition of Agri-Biotech Applications ('ISAAA'), available at www.isaaa.org/resources/publications/briefs/54/executivesummary/default.asp.

[11] See ch 3, section IV in particular.

[12] See data available on www.isaaa.org/default.asp.

[13] See below, section III.

[14] For an analysis, see chs 3 and 4.

this specific case, the relevant risks are characterised and deemed to be negligible in many jurisdictions.[15] As to the public health adverse effects of GE food, the possibility that GE varieties may trigger allergic reactions has been debated for years.[16] The potential effects of (copiously) spraying herbicide or multi-herbicide resistant GE varieties with the relevant herbicide(s) and other maintenance pesticides have also come under close scrutiny.[17] As explained in the third section of this chapter, persisting uncertainty as to the potential adverse effects posed by GE organisms is evaluated and taken into consideration in different ways under different regulatory models. Different inferences are drawn from the available scientific evidence; further, as the book shows, the very framing of the relevant scientific questions varies considerably. The importance of the public health and environmental interests at issue and the magnitude and pervasiveness of potential indirect or long-term adverse effects makes scientific evaluations in this field even more controversial.

An analysis of the other factors at stake in this field makes the picture increasingly complex. Like in other contentious areas of risk governance, these factors play a prominent role. At a general level, in national and transnational trade circles, GE products are of considerable interest in light of the potential profits to be generated from their market entrenchment. Advocates of agricultural biotechnologies argue that GE organisms yield wide-reaching environmental and social advantages, resulting from an alleged reduction in the use of herbicides and insecticides,[18] an alleged increase in agricultural productivity and a reduction of costs for both farmers and consumers.[19] From this position, by increasing total agricultural production while lowering costs, GE organisms can serve the purpose of feeding an expanding global population, tackling starvation and achieving food security in developing and less developed countries.[20] Further scientific-technological advances in the field are also portrayed as the way forward to grow nutritionally enhanced or vitamin-fortified GE varieties as well as climate resilient GE crops, which have recently gained increased visibility.[21] On these grounds, to summarise, GE organisms have come to be associated with significant technical-scientific as well as socio-economic opportunities.

[15] See ch 3.

[16] On the question of allergenicity and other public health risks, see, eg, ch 4, section V.

[17] ibid. Herbicide-resistant crops have often been engineered to be resistant to glyphosate-based herbicides; for this reason, the debate on glyphosate and its uncertain public health risks is also connected to the one on agricultural biotechnologies. On glyphosate, see Leonelli, 'The Glyphosate Saga and the Fading Democratic Legitimacy of EU Risk Regulation' (n 1).

[18] Due to their herbicide resistance and pesticidal traits, respectively.

[19] See www.geneticliteracyproject.org/ and www.isaaa.org/default.asp.

[20] For a reference to President GW Bush's famous criticism of the EU precautionary approach to GE organisms on these specific grounds, see M Pollack and G Shaffer, *When Cooperation Fails. The International Law and Politics of Genetically Modified Foods* (OUP, 2009) 116.

[21] See A Saab, *Narratives of Hunger in International Law. Feeding the World in Times of Climate Change* (CUP, 2019).

This perspective is disputed by different stakeholders in several jurisdictions. These actors consider the cultivation of GE crops to be environmentally unsustainable; in this respect, stakeholders have pointed to increased herbicide resistance of weeds, as a result of the copious spraying of herbicide resistant GE crops,[22] and to the impact on ecosystems of GE crops with pesticidal traits. The contention that agricultural biotechnologies result in increased productivity and greater yields is also disputed, especially in the debate on climate resilient crops.[23] At a broader level, stakeholders and social movements influenced by the food sovereignty philosophy have challenged the argument that agricultural biotechnologies will help achieve food security, emphasising distributional issues and questions of access to food.[24] From a similar perspective, they have argued that nutritionally enhanced or vitamin-fortified GE varieties have failed to deliver on their promises. Ultimately, these constituencies contend that agricultural biotechnologies have only yielded benefits to biotech corporations, which profit from intellectual property law protection.[25]

Yet, there is more to the debate on agricultural biotechnologies. Public opinion, public perception of risk and cultural and ethical considerations have played an important role.[26] The same is true of public interest in high levels of food quality.[27] Coexistence measures, which allow the cultivation of GE, conventional and organic crops alongside each other, are difficult and costly to set in place. Their effectiveness across different geographic areas varies considerably. The limited effectiveness of coexistence measures results in the ubiquitous adventitious presence of GE components in seeds, crops and food.[28] Where the uncertain risks posed by GE varieties are considered too high to be acceptable, stakeholders have then come to indirectly identify a public health and consumer protection dimension in the governance of coexistence, as if these measures were proper risk management measures.[29] Without doubt, ineffective coexistence measures can affect consumer choice and the economic viability of conventional and organic

[22] See inter alia data made available by the Non-GMO Project, www.nongmoproject.org/; GM Watch, www.gmwatch.org/en/; Slow Food International, www.slowfood.com/; and Greenpeace US, www.greenpeace.org/usa/. Increased herbicide resistance has resulted in an increased use of herbicides, changes in the specific herbicides used, and the development of multi-herbicide resistant GE crops.

[23] See Saab, *Narratives of Hunger* (n 21).

[24] See ch 6.

[25] See ch 6. The same macro-corporations holding patents for GE crops also trade in herbicides to which GE organisms have been engineered to be resistant. On intellectual law property protection, see inter alia Saab, *Narratives of Hunger* (n 21).

[26] See, eg, ch 4, section VI.C. On this point, see inter alia M Echols, 'Food Safety Regulation in the European Union and the United States: Different Cultures, Different Laws' (1998) 4 *Columbia Journal of European Law* 525; and D Vogel, *The Politics of Precaution. Regulating Health, Safety and Environmental Risks in Europe and the United States* (Princeton University Press, 2012).

[27] See ch 6.

[28] See ch 3.

[29] Rather than measures put in place to avoid contamination. See ch 4, section VI.B (albeit with reference to the alleged environmental protection dimension of coexistence measures).

agriculture, due to cross-contamination. All in all, the economic costs of managing coexistence are too often borne by conventional and organic farmers.[30] Thus, the main point of controversy is the impact of the entrenchment of agricultural biotechnologies on different agricultural models.

Against this backdrop, and to draw some conclusions, two aspects in the case of GE organisms are particularly relevant from a risk regulation perspective. The first is that uncertainties and scientific inconclusiveness primarily surround the existence and nature of specific adverse effects, rather than the characterisation of the relevant risks. This makes the scientific dimension of the regulatory conundrum highly contentious. Second, the availability of more demonstrably sustainable alternatives to GE organisms, controversies as to the socio-economic advantages that GE products may yield and the clash between different long-term visions for the agricultural and food system make this case even more controversial. These specific dimensions re-surface in the third and fourth sections of this chapter, which respectively focus on the institutional and normative strands of enquiry of the book.

II. The Methodological Framework: Transnational Legal Analysis and Transnational Narratives

The journey of transnational legal studies started with Philip Jessup's famous Storrs Lectures.[31] Since then, transnational law has increasingly come to be associated with *hybrid* standard-setting and norm-making by *non-state actors and bodies* operating *beyond* the nation state level. As chapter two explains, transnational legal theory captures the partial unravelling of the nation state and the shifting balance of power at times of globalisation. As non-state actors are increasingly involved in regulatory governance, new patterns of norm-making are established and the resulting regulatory systems come to interact with both national law and other positive legal regimes. In this sense, transnational law and the socially constructed transnational space are neither public nor private, neither national nor international.[32] Indeed, transnational regulatory governance develops and unfolds across territorial levels and societal forms of organisation, engaging different actors within different sites of norm-making.

[30] See ch 3. Further problematic aspects, such as herbicide drift associated with the cultivation of herbicide resistant GE crops, may come into play. The recent high profile 'Dicamba' litigation in the US has put this issue in the spotlight; see *National Family Farm Coalition and Others v Environmental Protection Agency*, No 17-70810 (9th Circuit 2020).

[31] PC Jessup, *Transnational Law. Storrs Lectures in Jurisprudence at Yale Law School* (Yale University Press, 1956).

[32] P Zumbansen, 'Neither Public Nor Private, National Nor International: Transnational Corporate Governance From a Legal Pluralist Perspective' (2011) 38 *Journal of Law and Society* 50.

On these grounds, transnational legal theorists have traditionally carved out a circumscribed focus of analysis for transnational legal studies. First, a distinction is usually drawn between national law, other positive legal systems, including public international law, and transnational law.[33] Transnational regulatory standards do interact with other legal regimes; the Codex Alimentarius Commission's standards, taken into consideration as a 'benchmark' for WTO law purposes under the Agreement on the Application of Sanitary and Phytosanitary Measures ('SPS Agreement'), are one of the most famous examples.[34] Further, transnational regulatory standards are 'recursively'[35] interpreted, applied and enforced across territorial levels and jurisdictions; to provide an example, transnational standards might be incorporated in contracts concluded at the national level and be interpreted and enforced in national courts. Nonetheless, *hybrid* transnational law is usually distinguished from *positive* (national, international or supra-national) legal regimes. Second, transnational law is regarded as a self-standing, albeit hybrid, 'field' or 'quasi-field' of law; most transnational legal theorists have so far explored the 'transnationalisation' of entire areas of law and regulation.[36]

From a 'traditional' transnational legal perspective, the 'transnational' regulation of the uncertain risks posed by GE organisms would only encompass regulatory standards enacted by market actors, NGOs and agencies operating beyond the nation state level. This book takes a different view and puts forward an alternative understanding of 'transnational law' and 'transnational legal analysis'. For the purposes of this book, 'transnational law' is understood as a social reality and a social product of globalisation, rather than as a self-standing 'field' or 'quasi-field' of law.[37] 'Transnational law' is thus defined as the composite and highly complex *regulatory infrastructure* underpinning globalisation flows; a regulatory infrastructure which all legal categories, starting from the traditional notions of 'national' and 'international' law, fail to capture. Consequently, the 'transnational' regulation of GE organisms and their risks is understood as the regulatory infrastructure underpinning the asymmetric globalisation of agricultural biotechnologies. Such regulatory infrastructure results from the coexistence and interaction of transnational discourses on GE organisms and the governance of the uncertain risks that they may pose. More specifically, it is the social product and social reflection of two conflicting, hegemonic and counter-hegemonic transnational narratives.

Clearly, transnational narratives and discourses do not exist in a social vacuum; nor do they emerge out of thin air. They originate from different regulatory sites and are socially and politically constructed *from within*, *across* and *beyond* the

[33] This, however, does not always happen; see ch 2, part 1.

[34] See chs 5 and 6.

[35] See inter alia TC Halliday, 'Recursivity in Global Norm Making: A Socio-Legal Agenda' (2009) 5 *Annual Review of Law and Social Sciences* 263; and TC Halliday and G Shaffer, 'Transnational Legal Orders' in TC Halliday and G Shaffer (eds), *Transnational Legal Orders* (CUP, 2015).

[36] See ch 2, part 1.

[37] See also GC Leonelli, 'The Postmodern Normative Anxiety of Transnational Legal Studies' in P Zumbansen (ed), *The Oxford Handbook of Transnational Law* (OUP, 2021).

nation state level.[38] From this perspective, the regulation of agricultural biotechnologies *within* specific national and regional jurisdictions, or under international or supra-national legal regimes (*across* the nation state level), has been just as relevant to the construction of transnational narratives as hybrid standard-setting by actors operating *beyond* the nation state. National, supra-national and international legal systems coalesce to frame transnational discourses on agricultural biotechnologies and feed into the 'transnational' regulatory infrastructure. In this sense, the book shows that transnational legal narratives do not necessarily originate beyond the nation state level or beyond positive, formalised systems of law; nor should they be automatically associated with hybrid standard-setting by societal actors, in line with the traditional focus and object of enquiry of transnational legal studies.

As chapter two explains in greater detail, transnational legal analysis is employed in the book as a *methodological framework* to deconstruct transnational narratives on agricultural biotechnologies from within, across and beyond the nation state level. The application of this methodological framework postulates a focus on *transnationally relevant* legal systems; these are the norm-making sites where transnational narratives have originated and where they have been shaped, reshaped, challenged or reinforced. On these grounds, the book uses transnational legal analysis to *interrogate* transnationally relevant regulatory frameworks and case law, with a view to *deconstructing* opposed transnational narratives on GE organisms and risk regulation and uncovering their rationales, policy goals, underlying values and implications.[39] The examination of hegemonic and counter-hegemonic narratives unfolds across three analytical dimensions; these are defined as 'extra-territoriality', 'legal pluralisation', and 'legal hybridisation'.[40]

The introductory section in each substantive chapter focuses on the application of the methodological framework, addressing four interconnected questions. The first question relates to the narrative under analysis throughout the specific chapters. The third chapter (US law), fifth chapter (SPS Agreement) and first part of the sixth chapter (Codex Alimentarius Commission) focus on the hegemonic narrative on GE organisms and risk governance. The fourth chapter (EU law) and second part of the sixth chapter (standard-setting by NGO actors), on the other hand, engage with the counter-hegemonic narrative.

The second question focuses on the transnational relevance of the legal systems under analysis throughout the chapters. In other words, it addresses the reasons why these legal systems are the object of analysis and describes how the hegemonic or counter-hegemonic narratives have been constructed, reinforced or challenged within these legal systems. The US system is the legal order where the

[38] ibid. For the use of very similar terminology, albeit in a different theoretical context and with a different meaning, see TC Halliday and G Shaffer, 'With, Within and Beyond the Nation State: The Promise and Limits of Transnational Legal Ordering', in P Zumbansen (ed), *The Oxford Handbook of Transnational Law* (n 37).

[39] See also Leonelli, 'The Postmodern Normative' (n 37).

[40] ibid.

transnational hegemonic narrative on GE organisms originated. Categories and regulatory notions which were first developed and employed in US risk governance have become a constituent part of hegemonic discourses on risk regulation; thus, US regulatory categories have clear transnational relevance. This reflects the logics of *extra-territoriality* at times of globalisation, whereby national and regional legal systems have unprecedented extra-territorial impact and national or regional legal categories have increased transnational relevance and application. On these grounds, the third chapter deconstructs the hegemonic narrative on GE organisms and risk governance *from within* the US national legal system.

The fourth chapter focuses on EU law. From a methodological perspective, this legal system cuts across the two dimensions of *extra-territoriality* and *legal pluralisation*. First, if analysed as a regional system, the EU legal regime is the site where the counter-hegemonic narrative on GE organisms has been constructed. For this reason, just like in the case of US regulation, EU regulation of agricultural biotechnologies has had an important transnational impact. Second, as a supra-national system in its own right, the EU legal regime impacts on EU Member States. This adds a further layer of analysis, as the EU and EU Member States have repeatedly clashed on regulatory implementation matters in the field of agricultural biotechnologies. The fourth chapter thus deconstructs the counter-hegemonic narrative on GE organisms and risk governance *from within* the EU regional legal system and *across* the nation state (ie EU Member State) level.

The fifth chapter turns to the SPS Agreement. The interpretation and application of the Agreement provisions has had a significant impact on the transnational debate on GE organisms; more specifically, it has considerably strengthened the hegemonic discourse on agricultural biotechnologies and regulation of their uncertain risks. The fifth chapter examines the hegemonic narrative and its far-reaching implications by analysing the WTO law regime, *across* the nation state level (*legal pluralisation*). Finally, the sixth chapter encompasses an analysis of the Codex system and hybrid regulatory standard-setting by non-profit NGO actors (*legal hybridisation*). Both sites of norm-making have transnational relevance. On the one hand, the Codex standard-setting system has strengthened transnational evidence-based discourses on risk governance and agricultural biotechnologies. On the other hand, NGO actors have directly challenged the hegemonic narrative on GE organisms and defended counter-hegemonic discourses. The sixth chapter thus engages in a further deconstruction of the hegemonic and counter-hegemonic narratives, *beyond* the nation state level.

The final questions addressed in each chapter partially overlap. How has the examination of these transnationally relevant legal systems helped deconstruct the hegemonic and counter-hegemonic narratives on GE organisms, casting light on their rationales, underlying value systems, goals and implications? And how has the analysis of these legal systems helped deconstruct transnational discourses on the regulation of uncertain risks, more generally? The answer to these questions is part of the institutional findings of this book, anticipated in the third section of this chapter.

To draw some preliminary considerations on the methodological strand, this book takes a perspective which distinguishes it from other studies on transnational law and transnational legal theory. First, it does not frame transnational law as a discrete and self-contained 'field' or 'quasi-field' of law. In this sense, for the purposes of the present analysis, the traditional transnational focus on societal actors and standard-setting bodies operating beyond the nation state level is considered insufficient to fully understand socio-legal ordering at times of globalisation. This narrower focus neglects regulatory layers which are integral to the social construction of transnational discourses and fails to capture how they influence the dynamics of transnational juridification.

Second, it casts light on the value of transnational legal analysis as a methodological framework. The contextualised analysis of different legal orders does not aim to compare and contrast them; nor is the enquiry anchored to any such legal system. In other words, the legal systems under analysis are not quite relevant in and of themselves. Rather, the analysis shows that elements of these legal orders have transnational relevance and a transnational impact, in so far as legal categories, notions and regulatory approaches embedded in these legal orders have become part of transnational narratives.

Finally, the book transposes 'methodological transnationalism'[41] into the practice of legal analysis. By deploying transnational legal analysis as a framework, the analysis cuts across different territorial levels, forms of societal organisation, legal systems and regulatory fields. From this viewpoint, this book applies 'methodological transnationalism' to a specific regulatory question within a discrete area of regulatory governance.

III. The Institutional Strand of Analysis: Transnational Narratives on GE Organisms, Ideal Regulatory Models and Different Forms of Uncertainty

This book frames the conundrum of agricultural biotechnologies against the backdrop of two diametrically opposed, hegemonic and counter-hegemonic, transnational legal narratives on GE organisms and uncertain risks. The two narratives are directly connected to two ideal regulatory models in the field of risk governance: evidence-based and socially acceptable risk approaches. The institutional strand of analysis thus deconstructs the characteristics and implications of the hegemonic and counter-hegemonic narratives by conducting an analysis of evidence-based and socially acceptable risk approaches. The enquiry focuses on legal frameworks, regulatory categories and case law, cutting across transnationally relevant legal systems.

[41] For use of this terminology, see P Zumbansen, 'The Incurable Constitutional Itch: Transnational Private Regulatory Governance and the Woes of Legitimacy' in M Helfand (ed), *Negotiating State and Non-State Law. The Challenge of Global and Local Legal Pluralism* (CUP, 2015).

The book concludes that both hegemonic and counter-hegemonic transnational narratives, and both evidence-based and socially acceptable risk models, are socially and politically constructed. Both pursue specific goals, reflect specific value systems and have specific implications. On these grounds, neither can lay claim to neutrality and objectivity.

Under the hegemonic narrative on risk governance, uncertain risks *must* be taken as long as the potential adverse effects of a product or process have not been conclusively established[42] or in so far as this regulatory choice proves economically cost-benefit effective.[43] Under the counter-hegemonic narrative, risk managers are called upon to make a *convincing case* that uncertain risks are socially acceptable and worth taking, affording due consideration to the intended level of protection in the field, the specific values at stake, the pervasiveness of the potential effects and any relevant other legitimate factors.

The burden of proof shifts under the two narratives. Under the hegemonic narrative, the presumption is that uncertain risks *should* be run unless a product or process has been proven to be unsafe, or to the extent that this choice responds to economic cost-benefit analysis; in the second scenario, risk regulation comes into play where the probability of occurrence of adverse effects and their severity is such that not regulating would not be economically cost-benefit effective. Overall, a product or process should be regulated in so far as this conforms to a cost-benefit calculus. Under the counter-hegemonic narrative, risks *should not* be taken unless, in the face of persisting scientific uncertainty, a product or process has been proven to be sufficiently safe. The determination that a product or process is safe enough for any connected risks to be socially acceptable lies at the heart of the counter-hegemonic narrative.

In turn, the two transnational narratives are directly connected to the dichotomy of evidence-based and socially acceptable risk approaches to the governance of uncertain risks.[44] As the following sub-sections illustrate, evidence-based models postulate recourse to a sound science approach to risk assessment, a focus on sound science and reliance on cost-benefit analysis. Conversely, socially acceptable risk approaches postulate a prudential approach to risk assessment and allow regulators margins of manoeuvre to take persisting scientific uncertainty, the pursuit of enhanced levels of protection, the tenets of the precautionary principle and other legitimate factors into account.

Evidence-based and socially acceptable risk approaches are ideal regulatory types, set along a spectrum of differential regulatory implementation.[45] In this

[42] ie, where uncertainty persists as to the existence of a causal link between the (potentially hazardous) characteristics of a product or process and specific adverse effects, or as to the actual materialisation of a risk. See below, in this section, for a detailed explanation.

[43] ie, in cases where hazards and risks have been conclusively proven and characterised. See below, in this section, for a detailed explanation.

[44] See above, n 1.

[45] A specific caveat applies. Borrowing the words used by Fisher in her discussion of procedural Rational-Instrumental and Deliberative-Constitutive paradigms and setting them in the different

book, they are not regarded as approaches that regulators rigidly follow in practice. Rather, they provide a conceptual framework to explain regulatory divergencies, in circumstances where different approaches to risk assessment are adhered to, diverging levels of protection are pursued, and different non-scientific factors feed into the determination of the intended level of protection and threshold of acceptable risk. As the book shows, the two ideal types are informed by different rationales and based on the application of different regulatory categories. No national or regional system of risk governance is entirely based on one or the other model across each and every field of regulatory action; nor is each and every regulatory framework perfectly aligned with one or the other paradigm.[46] Further, regulatory implementation may vary considerably. Regulatory frameworks reflecting an evidence-based approach may be implemented in such a way as to accommodate the pursuit of enhanced levels of protection, for instance through recourse to prudential risk assessments, while regulatory frameworks drawing on socially acceptable risk approaches may be implemented in an evidence-based manner.[47] Legal categories and concepts also vary from jurisdiction to jurisdiction, so that at times they can hardly be compared.

However, it is fair to acknowledge that different legal regimes and different regulatory frameworks are largely *informed* by one or the other ideal model. This emerges very clearly from the specific case of GE organisms. Opposed transnational narratives on agricultural biotechnologies, reflecting the clash between evidence-based and socially acceptable risk approaches, have been socially and politically constructed within specific legal systems. In the case of transnational discourses on GE organisms, as the book illustrates, we ultimately witness a polarisation at the two ends of the regulatory spectrum. This reflects a quasi-perfect adherence to the two ideal types.

Under the hegemonic narrative on GE organisms, and in accordance with evidence-based models, the uncertain risks posed by agricultural biotechnologies must be taken. This regulatory choice draws on sound science and is perfectly respondent to cost-benefit analysis. Reliance on socially acceptable risk approaches, by contrast, has (so far) largely resulted in the determination that the same risks are neither socially acceptable nor worth taking, considering the complex scientific, political and socio-economic picture illustrated in the first section. This determination is reflected in the counter-hegemonic narrative on agricultural biotechnologies. On these grounds, transnational narratives on GE organisms and the contentious issues at stake in this regulatory field provide a unique opportunity to deconstruct the nature and implications of the two ideal regulatory types.

context of substantive evidence-based and socially acceptable risk approaches, the ideal regulatory models under examination in this book are not 'reified and fixed realities'; rather, they represent 'polar and incommensurable opposite understandings' of risk governance. See E Fisher, *Risk Regulation and Administrative Constitutionalism* (Hart Publishing, 2007), 27 and 28.

[46] See, eg, ch 3 for an examination of how different US regulatory agencies follow slightly different approaches in the governance of the uncertain risks posed by GE organisms.

[47] See ch 4 for the latter scenario.

The book argues that the determination of the threshold of *legally relevant* adverse effects, ie the threshold which will trigger regulatory intervention, is never a matter of 'pure' science.[48] Rather, this determination results from three different factors. The first factor is adherence to more or less prudential approaches to risk assessment.[49] This is a matter of risk assessment policy and impacts on the *evidence base* that regulators draw upon. As acknowledged since the famous 1983 US National Research Council 'Red Book', policy judgments are embodied in risk assessment.[50] The selection of specific scientific literature, 'hard' data, assumptions and models involves so-called 'science-policy choices', which will influence the final results of a risk assessment.[51]

The second factor is the extent to which regulators adhere to sound science, understood in this book as conclusive scientific proof of the existence of hazards and risks, or focus on scientific insufficiency or relevant uncertainties. This aspect concerns the *inferences* that regulators draw from the available scientific evidence, in the face of persisting uncertainty.[52] As expressly recognised by the scientific community, 'because all assessments of scientific data are subject to uncertainties and because scientific knowledge is incomplete, it is possible for different analysts to arrive at different interpretations of the same set of data'.[53]

The adoption of more or less prudential approaches to risk assessment and the variable extent to which different forms of uncertainty are taken into account, as the book shows, are influenced by specific *normative frames*. Recourse to less prudential (sound science) approaches to risk assessment and adherence to sound science are economically cost-benefit effective and *indirectly* reflect the pursuit of a cost-benefit effective level of protection. Prudential approaches to risk assessment

[48] For the first suggestion that the determination that a risk exists 'cannot be a matter of pure science', developed through an analysis of the logical structure of risk findings and an examination of the logical relationship between available scientific evidence and findings of risk, see V Walker, 'The Myth of Science as a "Neutral Arbiter" for Triggering Precautions' (2003) 26 *Boston College International and Comparative Law Review* 197, 198 ff; reference to this sentence and terminology is borrowed from this author. On the socially embedded nature of science, and on the co-production of science and social order, see first and foremost S Jasanoff, *The Fifth Branch: Science Advisers as Policy-Makers* (Harvard University Press, 1990); S Jasanoff (ed), *States of Knowledge: the Co-Production of Science and Social Order* (Routledge, 2004); S Jasanoff, *Designs on Nature. Science and Democracy in Europe and the United States* (Princeton University Press, 2005); and S Jasanoff, *Science and Public Reason* (Routledge, 2012).

[49] The terminology of 'prudential' risk assessment is borrowed from European Commission, COM(2000)1 Final, *Communication from the Commission on the Precautionary Principle*, 12, section 5. For a similar focus on different approaches to risk assessment, see also Walker, 'The Myth of Science' (n 48).

[50] National Research Council, *Risk Assessment in the Federal Government: Managing the Process* (National Academies Press, 1983), the 'Red Book', 28 ff. See also Jasanoff, *The Fifth Branch* (n 48); Jasanoff, *Science and Public Reason* (n 48).

[51] National Research Council, *Science and Judgment in Risk Assessment* (National Academies Press, 1994), the 'Blue Book', 27 ff; National Research Council, *Science and Decisions: Advancing Risk Assessment* (National Academies Press, 2009), the 'Silver Book', 43 to 45.

[52] See also Jasanoff, *Science and Public Reason* (n 48); Walker, 'The Myth of Science' (n 48).

[53] 'Silver Book' (n 51), 30.

and regulatory focus on persisting uncertainty, by contrast, are not cost-benefit effective and *indirectly* reflect the pursuit of high(er) levels of protection and consideration of other legitimate factors.

The third and final factor consists in the *level of protection* that regulators are *directly* pursuing. In cases where hazards and risks have been conclusively established, the determination of the threshold of probability of occurrence of adverse effects triggering regulatory intervention will vary in accordance with the intended level of protection. On the one hand, regulators might pursue a cost-benefit effective level of protection, whereby adverse effects should not be 'unreasonable' or 'excessive' taking into consideration the economic costs of regulation and the economic benefits associated with the relevant (hazardous) product or process. On the other hand, regulators might choose to pursue enhanced levels of protection, taking factors other than economic cost-benefit effectiveness into consideration. These specific aspects are illustrated in greater detail in the following sub-sections.

Against a backdrop of scientific dispute, then, regulatory conflicts in the field of risk governance do not relate to issues of 'pure' science; nor are they triggered by allegedly non-scientific precautionary measures. In the face of scientific complexity and multiple uncertainties, sound science will not necessarily yield factually 'correct' answers. The same applies to the 'best' and 'most reliable' science, assuming that it can be identified at all. The boundaries between facts and values thus fade in the field of risk regulation.[54] Even in cases which are relatively uncontroversial in scientific terms, and regardless of how small uncertain risks may be, science can tell us nothing of the acceptability of a risk; the determination that a risk is worth taking and should be taken is always, unavoidably, informed by normative considerations surrounding the intended level of protection and all relevant stakes. Science therefore does not quite lie at the heart of risk regulation disputes. What is truly controversial is recourse to different approaches to risk assessment, the set of inferences that regulators draw from the available scientific evidence, and the level of protection and specific goals that they pursue.

Science can be more or less disputed, and uncertainty more or less pervasive. The level of public health and environmental protection pursued in different jurisdictions may vary to a greater or lesser extent. Further, the overarching tenets of the precautionary principle and the relevant social or distributional factors at stake, as opposed to considerations surrounding the cost-benefit effectiveness of risk regulation, may be more or less prominent in specific regulatory fields. This will impact on the level of controversy, when different regulatory approaches are being adhered to. In this sense, each case and each controversy in the field of risk regulation is unique. Yet, different normative frames and perspectives are always, *directly* or *indirectly*, at the centre of disputes in risk governance.

[54] For a fascinating account, see SO Funtowicz and JR Ravetz, 'Science for the Post-Normal Age' (1993) 25 *Futures* 739.

Controversial risk governance cases such as agricultural biotechnologies or residues of hormones in meat, where science cannot provide conclusive proof of specific adverse effects and public opinion, social and distributional factors are prominent, are often analysed through the prism of the 'science' versus 'politics' dichotomy.[55] These analyses are based on a watertight distinction between technical expertise and politics, objective 'facts' and subjective 'values'. 'Science' is usually associated with 'sound science', neglecting the reality of scientific pluralism or suggesting that sound science is 'better' science. Sound science is then deemed to be the 'correct' basis for decision-making. Further, it is considered value-neutral. Clearly, in the face of scientific complexity and persisting uncertainty, the former assumption is open to dispute. As to the latter point, these accounts fail to acknowledge that recourse to sound science approaches and adherence to sound science are not neutral and objective. The assumption that sound science approaches *must* be relied on and that sound science *must* be adhered to is indirectly informed by non-scientific evaluations surrounding the cost-benefit effectiveness of the intended level of protection, if not directly driven by economic imperatives. As the book shows, sound science cannot be equated to 'pure' science: facts and values are intertwined in the field of risk governance. On these grounds, as the next subsections illustrate in greater detail, the book rejects the 'science' versus 'politics' dichotomy and reframes risk governance controversies in terms of a clash between evidence-based and socially acceptable risk approaches.

A. Mapping Different Forms of Scientific Uncertainty

The starting point of the analysis is the broader picture of scientific uncertainty in the field of risk regulation. The notion of 'risk assessment' refers to the technical-scientific evaluation of uncertain risks, conducted by experts.[56] 'Risk management', on the other hand, involves a decision as to whether and how to regulate uncertain risks, weighing alternative policy and regulatory options.[57] The process of risk assessment is divided into different stages: hazard identification, hazard

[55] For a critique of this dichotomy and an acknowledgment that all decision-making unavoidably results from a mix of facts and values, science and politics, see for instance Fisher, *Risk Regulation* (n 45), 246. However, Fisher does not set regulatory conflicts against the backdrop of different substantive approaches; rather, from a procedural perspective, she considers that 'disputes over standard-setting and risk appraisal in risk regulation are disputes over administrative constitutionalism'. See n 45, 5. For a critique of the 'illusory separation between values and science' in the field of risk regulation, see also M Lee, 'Beyond Safety? The Broadening Scope of Risk Regulation' (2009) 62 *Current Legal Problems* 242; M Lee, *EU Regulation of GMOs* (Edward Elgar, 2008), 39 ff and 80 ff; and M Lee, *EU Environmental Law, Governance and Decision-Making* (Hart Publishing, 2014), 249 ff.

[56] eg, see Codex Alimentarius Commission, *Procedural Manual*, 27th edn (Joint FAO/WHO Food Standards Programme, 2019), 128.

[57] ibid. In risk regulation systems informed by socially acceptable risk approaches, risk management functions are usually allocated to political authorities rather than technical regulatory agencies; for more details, see chs 3 and 4.

characterisation, exposure assessment and risk characterisation.[58] Uncertainties can surface throughout each and every stage. This book categorises different forms of uncertainty under four broad categories, defining them as *hazard-related* uncertainties, *stricto sensu* matters of *scientific uncertainty* and *scientific ignorance*, *risk-related* uncertainties and *methodological* uncertainties.[59]

A 'hazard' is defined as a biological, chemical or physical agent with the potential to cause adverse effects.[60] *Hazard-related* uncertainties may surround inconclusive scientific proof of the existence of a causal link between the (potentially hazardous) characteristics of a product or process, on the one hand, and adverse public health or environmental effects, on the other. GE organisms are a good example; hazard-related uncertainties surface in respect of the possibility and potential effects of hybridisation and crop to crop gene flow, the resulting impact on the environment and biodiversity, or potential food safety issues or allergic reactions to GE food. The potential development of antibiotic resistance due to the use of antibiotics as growth promoters in livestock,[61] or inconclusive scientific proof of the adverse public health effects of residues of hormones in meat,[62] are other prominent examples. Confounding factors will often come into play in these cases.[63]

Hazard-related uncertainties may also emerge throughout the hazard characterisation stage; these uncertainties relate to the nature and the severity of the specific hazards at stake. For instance, extrapolations from the findings of animal studies and their applicability to humans are a source of uncertainty.[64] Further, variability will come into play. This may depend on endogenous or exogenous factors and is an 'inherent characteristic of a population, inasmuch as people vary substantially in [...] their susceptibility to potentially harmful effects [...]'.[65] Specific constituencies will be more vulnerable than others to the effects of exposure to specific hazards. These forms of uncertainty or variability can be addressed through the application of quantitative uncertainty analysis ('QUA'), safety factors, expert judgement and assumptions.[66] More specifically, 'defaults' consist of

[58] Codex Alimentarius Commission (n 56), 128.

[59] For different categorisations of forms of scientific uncertainty, see inter alia SO Funtowicz and JR Ravetz, *Uncertainty and Quality in Science for Policy* (Kluwer, 1990), 17 ff; Walker, 'The Myth of Science' (n 48), 105 ff; and A Klinke and O Renn, 'A New Approach to Risk Evaluation and Management: Risk-Based, Precaution-Based and Discourse-Based Strategies' (2002) 22 *Risk Analysis* 1071.

[60] Codex Alimentarius Commission (n 56), 128. The definitions enshrined in the Procedural Manual expressly refer to the risk analysis process as relating to food safety issues, in accordance with the Codex Commission's regulatory remit. However, they have broader relevance in that they refer to transnationally established regulatory notions.

[61] In EU case law, for instance, see Case T-13/99, *Pfizer Animal Health SA* v *Council*, EU:T:2002:209, and Case T-70/99, *Alpharma* v *Council*, EU:T:2002:210.

[62] See ch 5, sections II, III and VIII.A.

[63] ibid.

[64] 'Silver Book' (n 51), 43. See below in this section on dose-response assessments and relevant uncertainties.

[65] ibid 6.

[66] 'Silver Book' (n 51), 7 and 32.

inference guidelines and scientific assumptions selected among a set of available options.[67]

Stricto sensu matters of *scientific uncertainty* and *scientific ignorance* largely involve hazard identification and hazard characterisation, as well. At their core lies the question of whether persisting uncertainty or scientific ignorance as to the characteristics of a product or process have been dispelled in so far as technically possible. Recourse to comparative assessments, as opposed to all-encompassing risk assessments, exemplifies different approaches to *stricto sensu* matters of scientific uncertainty in the governance of GE organisms.[68]

The next step consists in analysing the notion of a 'risk'. A 'risk' is a function of the probability of occurrence of adverse effects and the severity of these effects, consequential to exposure to a hazard.[69] *Risk-related* uncertainties may emerge at the exposure assessment and risk characterisation stages. The former involves a qualitative or quantitative evaluation of exposures, and is usually fraught with uncertainties. It is undertaken through the development of exposure scenarios; these draw on measured exposures or on modelled estimates. Usually, models play a key role. Risk characterisation, the final stage, consists in the qualitative or quantitative estimation of the probability of occurrence and severity of known or potential adverse effects, as resulting from exposure to a hazard.[70]

Several forms of risk-related uncertainty will emerge. First, these may relate to the qualitative or quantitative evaluation of exposures in real life conditions. The efficacy of relevant risk management measures will also come into play. Pesticidal products offer some good practical examples. Operator exposure to pesticides is affected by the efficacy of risk management measures as well as by climatic, environmental and geomorphological conditions. The same is true for plant or animal exposures to residues of pesticidal products.[71]

Another source of uncertainty stems from multiple exposures. Aggregate effects are the result of exposures to the same substance from different sources, whereas cumulative effects result from exposures to different substances sharing a common mode of action (mechanism of toxicity).[72] Variability (in exposures) will also come into play at the exposure assessment stage; in other words, the range of exposure is variable in different cases, in different contexts and in different population groups. For instance, taking pesticidal products into consideration, dietary exposures to residues of pesticides in food largely vary, on the basis of a plurality of

[67] ibid 99ff, for an overview of these different strategies.

[68] In this respect, see ch 3 and 4.

[69] Codex Alimentarius Commission (n 56), 128.

[70] ibid.

[71] See GC Leonelli, 'Judicial Review of Compliance with the Precautionary Principle from *Paraquat* to *Blaise*: Quantitative Thresholds, Risk Assessment and the Gap between Regulation and Regulatory Implementation' (2021) 22 *German Law Journal* 184.

[72] For a detailed overview, see the 'Silver Book' (n 51), 213 ff.

factors. Again, these forms of uncertainty or variability may be addressed through the application of safety factors, expert judgement or specific models.

Turning to the final stage of risk characterisation, available evidence may in some cases be regarded as insufficient for the purposes of a reliable qualitative or quantitative estimation of the probability of occurrence of adverse effects and their severity. Diverging data may also cast doubt on the possibility of adequately characterising risks. This might result in the decision to ban a product, or apply stringent risk management measures.[73] The pathway by which a risk may materialise can also be disputed. For instance, this form of uncertainty emerges from cases relating to the entry, establishment and spread of pests or diseases.[74]

To conclude, *methodological* uncertainties specifically arise from the application of different casual relationships, methods and models for the purposes of the assessment of hazards and risks. These may yield very different results. For example, the hazardous characteristics of a product may be proven *in vitro*; however, conclusive proof *in vivo* may be missing.[75] The relevance of methodological uncertainties emerges very clearly in the field of the regulation of chemicals, where the application of different models can have a remarkable impact on the evaluation of hazards and classification of chemical substances.[76]

Importantly, methodological uncertainties may also surface when dose-response assessments are conducted. A dose-response assessment is the determination 'of the relationship between the magnitude of exposure (dose) to a chemical, biological or physical agent and the severity and/or frequency of associated adverse [...] effects (response)'.[77] Linear or threshold models may be employed; threshold models can also be based on different approaches. Linear models are premised on the assumption that no threshold exists below which adverse effects will not occur. Upon identification of a point of departure ('POD'),

[73] On EU case law involving bans or stringent risk management measures in the field of pesticidal active substances, as a result of the regulatory determination that the relevant scientific evidence is insufficient for the purposes of an adequate characterisation of the relevant risks, see GC Leonelli, 'Acknowledging the Centrality of the Precautionary Principle in Judicial Review of EU Risk Regulation: Why It Matters' (2020) 57 *CML Rev* 1773.

[74] See ch 5, sections IV, V and VI. See also ch 3, for examples in the field of governance of GE organisms.

[75] See ch 5, section VIII.A.

[76] For a very clear example in the field of chemicals, see the analysis in Leonelli, 'The Fine Line between Procedural and Substantive Review' (n 1). For an analysis of the implications of recourse to different models and an argument in favour of greater transparency in the selection and application of specific methods, see P Pascual, W Wagner and E Fisher, 'Making Method Visible: Improving the Quality of Science-Based Regulation' (2013) 2 *Michigan Journal of Environmental and Administrative Law* 429. Fisher et al acknowledge that this does not address substantive issues (ie 'science-policy choices'); see 434 and 435. In this sense, by following a procedural approach and by focusing on questions of transparency, the authors start from the implicit assumption that a 'correct' answer (ie the application of 'better' methods) may be procedurally identified, persisting uncertainty and scientific complexity notwithstanding.

[77] Codex Alimentarius Commission (n 56), 129.

the relevant risks are assumed to decrease linearly as the dose decreases.[78] Taking into consideration low doses, regulators will determine the threshold of probability of occurrence of adverse effects which they deem 'negligible'. Under threshold models, by contrast, the assumption is that a threshold below which effects will not occur (or are very unlikely to occur) may be identified. This is the reference dose (RfD) or reference concentration (RfC) value for a hazardous substance, which may be calculated on the basis of a No-Observed-Adverse-Effect Level ('NOAEL') or, in the majority of cases, on the basis of a Lowest-Observed-Adverse-Effect Level ('LOAEL') or Benchmark-Dose-Lower-Confidence Limit ('BMD').[79] Use of different data, assumptions and safety factors, combined with the application of different models, will yield different results. Bearing this picture in mind, how do evidence-based and socially acceptable risk models approach and frame questions of scientific uncertainty and complexity?

B. The Hegemonic Transnational Narrative and Evidence-Based Paradigms

As anticipated, ideal evidence-based models postulate recourse to a *sound science approach* to risk assessment and regulatory focus on *sound science*. Starting from the latter notion, for the purposes of the analysis in this book, 'sound science' is associated with positive and conclusive scientific proof of the existence of a hazard and pathway for the materialisation of a risk. As the book illustrates, scientific inconclusiveness as to the existence of a hazard and *stricto sensu* uncertainties are regarded as 'theoretical uncertainty' in legal systems informed by the evidence-based paradigm.[80] The same applies to uncertainties surrounding the existence of a risk, when a pathway for its materialisation cannot be positively established.[81]

Symmetrically, adherence to sound science will hardly result in a determination that the available scientific evidence is insufficient for the purposes of an adequate evaluation and characterisation of the relevant risks.[82] In other words, it is irrelevant whether more (or more reliable) evidence and data could be gathered in the future, as technical-scientific knowledge develops; regulatory intervention should be based on what has been positively proven at the current stage of knowledge. In this sense, a presumption of scientific 'sufficiency' applies. Nor is the existence of diverging data and bodies of scientific opinion likely to be relevant, in so far as majority opinion is usually taken into account.

[78] 'Silver Book' (n 51), 127.

[79] See US Environmental Protection Agency, *Guidelines on Conducting a Human Health Risk Assessment*, available at www.epa.gov.

[80] See ch 3, section V.A; and ch 5, sections II, III, VII and VIII.A.

[81] See ch 3, section V; and ch 5, sections IV, V and VI.

[82] See, eg, ch 5, sections V, VI, VII and VIII.A.

The notion of a 'sound science approach' to risk assessment is more encompassing in its scope, and relates to specific ways in which risk assessors deal with multiple forms of uncertainty and variability. As already explained, policy judgments are inherent to risk assessment. The selection and application of specific data, models and methods involve 'science-policy choices' and will have an impact on the final results of a risk assessment. Reliance on a sound science approach to risk assessment may be reflected in recourse to specific models for hazard identification and for hazard characterisation, specific forms of probabilistic modelling as regards the assessment of potential exposures, the application of specific safety factors to address variability, and reliance on specific defaults, assumptions and forms of expert judgments.

In the face of scientific complexity, it would be useless to try and identify specific pre-determined elements which make a risk assessment 'sound', rather than 'prudential'. Clearly, this will depend on a plurality of factors. Nonetheless, it is important to highlight that sound science approaches to risk assessment reflect a specific understanding of uncertainty and variability; these are considered manageable, objectively quantifiable and reducible.[83] Erring on the side of precaution and potentially over-estimating risks through recourse to prudential approaches is thus unwarranted from an evidence-based perspective.[84] Where regulatory frameworks provide for a streamlined process, limited to an evaluation of data provided by market applicants and excluding a *stricto sensu* authorisation process, the adoption of prudential approaches to risk assessment is even less likely.[85] At a general level, reliance on 'regulatory science', as opposed to 'research science',[86] tips the balance in favour of sound science approaches.

Recourse to sound science approaches to risk assessment and adherence to sound science will result in a specific *evidence base* and specific *inferences* being drawn from the available data. If compared with prudential approaches to risk assessment and regulatory focus on multiple forms of uncertainty, sound science approaches and adherence to sound science clearly relieve market actors from regulatory burdens and economic costs. More specifically, as the analysis of this book shows, they *indirectly* respond to the tenets of economic cost-benefit analysis.[87]

In cases where hazards and risks have been conclusively established, then, economic cost-benefit analysis will come into play *directly*. In these cases, it is impossible to determine a point where the probability of occurrence of adverse

[83] For a similar point, albeit from a procedural perspective and focusing on the 'Rational-Instrumental' paradigm, see Fisher, *Risk Regulation* (n 45), 29 and 33.

[84] This does not imply that, in the face of persisting uncertainty and variability, such approach is 'correct' or 'better' than a prudential one; see below, in this section.

[85] See ch 3, section V.

[86] ibid. On the notions of 'regulatory science' and 'research science' see Jasanoff, *The Fifth Branch* (n 48).

[87] See the analysis in ch 3, sections V, VI and VII. See also how cost-benefit considerations influence the extent to which products, processes and activities are tested: see ch 3, section V.A.

effects is zero. In many cases, it will also prove impossible to identify a threshold of exposure below which adverse effects are expected to be very unlikely.[88] In this context, how to determine the *legally relevant* threshold of probability of occurrence of adverse effects, and how to decide whether the potential adverse effects and their consequences are 'acceptable' or 'negligible'? How to decide whether regulatory action should be taken at all, how to devise risk reduction strategies, and how to enact risk mitigation measures?

As an ideal regulatory model, the evidence-based paradigm postulates that risks should only be regulated in so far as this choice is cost-benefit effective. Regulatory measures in the field of risk governance, at a general level, are bound to be cost-benefit effective; in other words, the level of protection pursued by regulators shall be economically cost-benefit effective. Risks should be taken in so far as the economic costs associated with regulatory intervention or the economic benefits of a product or process outweigh the expected environmental or public health benefits of regulation. Risk regulation thus comes into play to the extent that the expected adverse effects, as evaluated in the light of what has been positively proven and established, are 'unreasonable' or 'excessive'; the legally relevant threshold of adverse effects should be determined through the application of economic cost-benefit analysis.

This goal may be reflected in legislative or regulatory measures, which set out the scope of application of risk governance frameworks and the relevant arrangements.[89] However, it may also emerge directly in the context of product authorisations and risk mitigation measures. In the latter case, the public health and environmental benefits associated with potential regulatory measures are computed from the results of risk assessment.[90] A fully-fledged application of economic cost-benefit analysis does not simply focus on the cost-benefit effectiveness of *alternative risk management measures*, adopted to meet a specific intended level of protection. Rather, it targets the cost-benefit effectiveness of the *level of*

[88] See above, sub-section A; in any case, the determination of any such threshold will still be fraught with uncertainty. Variability will also come into play.

[89] See ch 3, section VI, for considerations surrounding economic cost-benefit effectiveness in regulatory frameworks in the field of governance of GE organisms. For an example of a legislative provision influenced by evidence-based approaches and considerations surrounding economic cost-benefit effectiveness, see also the stipulation under the US Federal Insecticide, Fungicide and Rodenticide Act that the US Environmental Protection Agency shall register a pesticide if it has, inter alia, determined that '[…] (C) it will perform its intended function without *unreasonable adverse effects* on the environment; and (D) when used in accordance with widespread and commonly recognised practice it will not generally cause *unreasonable adverse effects* on the environment' (emphasis added); see 7 USC, s 136a(c)(5). For the definition of 'unreasonable adverse effects' on the environment, see 7 USC, s 136(bb): the term means '(1) any *unreasonable risk* to *man* or the *environment*, taking into account the economic, social and environmental costs and benefits of the use of any pesticide, or (2) a human dietary risk from resides that result from a use of a pesticide in or on any food inconsistent with the standard under section 346a of Title 21' (emphasis added). Under 21 USC, s 346a(b)(2)(A)(ii), the standard is the one of a 'reasonable certainty that no harm will result from aggregate exposure to the pesticide chemical residue […]'.

[90] See for instance the 'Silver Book' (n 51), 50.

protection pursued by regulators,[91] underpinning the identification of a *cost-benefit effective threshold of probability of occurrence of adverse effects.*[92]

Chapters three (US governance of GE organisms), five (SPS Agreement) and six (Codex Alimentarius Commission) explore the regulatory categories, underlying value systems and overarching goals of evidence-based approaches, against the specific backdrop of the transnational controversy on GE organisms; as already explained, evidence-based models are clearly connected to the hegemonic narrative on agricultural biotechnologies. The analysis shows that, in contexts of scientific complexity and scientific pluralism, sound science approaches to risk assessment and adherence to sound science can neither be considered 'better' than prudential approaches and a focus on uncertainty, nor 'correct' or universally valid. Crucially, evidence-based models cannot lay claim to neutrality and objectivity. Far from being neutral and objective, as the book demonstrates by analysing the governance of GE organisms, the assumption that sound science approaches to risk assessment *must* be adhered to and sound science *must* be relied on is informed by non-scientific considerations surrounding the economic cost-benefit effectiveness of risk regulation. And indeed, in regulatory systems influenced by evidence-based paradigms, these non-scientific considerations are expressly taken into account in cases where hazards and risks have been scientifically established.

On these grounds, the book moves on to uncover the specific implications of dominant transnational discourses on the regulation of uncertain risks, highlighting their strengths and weaknesses. First, the deconstruction of US governance of GE organisms shows that evidence-based models are associated with a technocratic approach to risk regulation, wherein both risk assessment and risk management functions are allocated to regulatory agencies. Public opinion and public perception of risk are considered immaterial to 'objective' decision-making. Second, by relying on a sound scientific evidence base, by focusing on sound science and by employing cost-benefit analysis, regulators will ultimately identify a baseline threshold of safety.[93] For this reason, unlike socially acceptable risk approaches,

[91] It is in this spirit, to provide a practical example, that the 'Silver Book' recommends the use of linear rather than threshold models. 'Because [the reference values identified through threshold models] do not quantify risk for different magnitudes of exposure but rather provide a bright line between possible harm and safety, their use in risk-risk and risk-benefit comparisons and in risk management […] is limited' (8). '[Threshold models] are inadequate for cost-benefit analyses or for comparative risk analyses. [They] do not provide a basis for formally quantifying the magnitude of harm at various exposure levels. […] The approach remains one of defining a [reference value] without any sense of the degree of population risk reduction that would be found in moving from one dose to another dose. A probabilistic approach […] would be much more useful in cost-benefit analysis' (133). This perfectly reflects evidence-based approaches and reliance on economic cost-benefit analysis.

[92] If the analysis is conducted through the lens of proportionality, a maximalist application of economic cost-benefit analysis does not simply target the necessity of risk management measures, but their *stricto sensu* proportionality (ie their cost-benefit effectiveness). On the applications of the principle of proportionality in judicial review of EU risk regulation, see Leonelli, 'Acknowledging the Centrality of the Precautionary Principle' (n 73).

[93] See the detailed analysis in ch 3, sections VI and VII.

evidence-based models do not allow the pursuit of enhanced levels of protection. Further, the application of cost-benefit calculus to a sound scientific evidence base, in conditions of scientific uncertainty, is liable to reduce the overall level of public health and environmental protection. This will be particularly problematic in cases where uncertainties are underestimated at the risk assessment stage and reliance on sound science is misplaced, or where the relevant economic stakes are high.[94]

Finally, other legitimate factors such as the availability of less hazardous alternatives, or a long-term vision for the development of more sustainable approaches in specific sectors, are beyond the radar of evidence-based risk regulation. The same applies to the evaluation of the broader (qualitative) socio-economic advantages and disadvantages of a product or process and the distributional stakes of risk regulation; in other words, consideration of which stakeholders will bear the costs and which constituencies will reap the benefits of the decision to take uncertain risks.[95]

However, evidence-based models also yield benefits. As the analysis of US governance of GE organisms illustrates, adherence to evidence-based risk regulation maximises aggregate wealth by relieving market actors from economic burdens and costs. This facilitates the exercise of individual trade rights and fosters technological-scientific innovation. Similar considerations ensue from the analysis of disputes brought under the SPS Agreement. Chapter five points to the repeated attempts by the WTO Panels and Appellate Body to identify a standard of review within the spectrum from deference to de novo review, taking a closer look at the *EC – Biotech* dispute.[96] In the absence of any objective, self-standing criteria of 'pure' science, the evidence-based interpretation of the SPS Agreement provisions and adherence to *de novo* review draw on the mere acknowledgment that, in the face of ubiquitous uncertainties and scientific pluralism, a deferential reasonableness review would afford Members the opportunity to defend virtually *any* SPS measure. This would be irreconcilable with the rationale and overarching goal of the system: trade liberalisation. In other words, it would undermine any attempt at transnational regulatory convergence in SPS regulation. This casts further light on the implications of the evidence-based narrative on GE organisms, and risk governance more generally. Not only do evidence-based approaches, as illustrated in the third chapter, pursue aggregate wealth maximisation; they are also linked to transnational regulatory convergence and trade liberalisation. This connection is explored in further detail in chapter six.

Evidence-based models thus result in a *double* economic dividend. The exercise of individual (trade-related) rights lies at the core of this ideal regulatory type.

[94] ibid.

[95] See ch 3, sections VI and VII. For sociological accounts on the distributional implications of risk governance, see inter alia U Beck, *Risk Society. Towards a New Modernity* (SAGE, 1992); and U Beck, *World at Risk* (Polity Press, 2009).

[96] *EC – Measures Affecting the Approval and Marketing of Biotech Products*, Panel Report (adopted 21 November 2006) WT/DS291, WT/DS292, WT/DS293 (*EC – Biotech).*

On these grounds, the deconstruction of evidence-based models throughout the analysis of US law, the SPS Agreement and the Codex Commission shows what lies underneath the hegemonic narrative on GE organisms and regulation of uncertain risks. As chapter seven concludes, the hegemonic narrative on GE organisms and hegemonic discourses on the governance of uncertain risks are hegemonic *because* they yield a double economic dividend.

C. The Counter-Hegemonic Transnational Narrative and Socially Acceptable Risk Approaches

Socially acceptable risk approaches postulate a *prudential* risk assessment. Further, under this ideal model of risk governance, regulators are *not* bound to adhere to *sound science*. They may take into account uncertainties as to the existence of a causal relationship between the characteristics of a product or process and adverse effects, where the latter effects can neither be conclusively established nor excluded. Uncertainties surrounding the actual materialisation of a risk may also be taken into consideration. In a similar vein, in the face of scientific complexity, regulatory action may be warranted where the available evidence is deemed insufficient for a reliable characterisation of risk.

All in all, uncertainty and variability have a completely different value under evidence-based and socially acceptable risk models; this is reflected in the gap between sound scientific and prudential risk assessments. A prudential risk assessment will expressly disclose uncertainties emerging from each and every stage of the assessment process; these uncertainties should be taken into due consideration for the purposes of drawing any relevant scientific inferences. Further, when 'science-policy choices' are required, it will involve the selection and application of prudential models, methods, assumptions and safety factors. These will yield very cautious estimates, usually by taking into consideration worst case scenarios, and may thus over-estimate the relevant risks.[97] Matters of *stricto sensu* uncertainty and scientific ignorance should also be adequately dealt with. For this purpose, prudential risk assessments should be comprehensive, take into account potential long-term or indirect risks, and strive to dispel scientific uncertainty in so far as is technically possible with the current stage of knowledge.

The allocation of risk management functions and final decision-making powers to political authorities, rather than technical-regulatory agencies, is typical of legal systems informed by socially acceptable risk approaches.[98] This acknowledges that more than (allegedly objective) scientific matters are at stake in risk

[97] See for instance *Communication from the Commission on the Precautionary Principle* (n 49), 28, Annex III. For a more detailed overview, see ch 4. On prudential safety factors and prudential expert judgement, see for instance the analysis in ch 5, sections V and VIII.B.

[98] See chs 3 and 4.

governance, and that normative frames and judgments play a crucial role in this field. One relevant implication is that political risk managers may disregard the positive results of a risk assessment, reaching the conclusion that uncertain risks are not socially acceptable. This might occur where a risk assessment is perceived as being insufficiently prudential; in this case, political risk managers can refer to alternative studies, assessments and data to substantiate their position. It might also happen where, taking into consideration the available evidence and the level of protection pursued in the field, risk managers draw different inferences as to the acceptability of the relevant risks. For instance, they may point to the scope of persisting uncertainty and the severity of the potential adverse effects, taking the view that the relevant risks are not socially acceptable in the specific field at issue. As already mentioned, disagreements need not stem from reference to a different evidence base. The very same scientific evidence can be differently interpreted and thereby become an object of controversy.

Turning to a more specific analysis of risk management and the extent to which uncertainties may be taken into account, socially acceptable risk approaches postulate that regulators may take *precautionary action*, where warranted. Where uncertainties persist as to the existence and nature of a hazard or the materialisation of a risk, or scientific data is considered insufficient or unreliable, a product may be subject to stringent risk mitigation or may not be authorised at all.[99] Different definitions and understandings of the precautionary principle coexist across legal orders. At a general level, under a baseline understanding, the precautionary principle stipulates that a lack of scientific proof of adverse effects should not prevent regulators from taking action.[100] For the purposes of the analysis of this book, the precautionary principle is analysed within the specific legal orders that are relevant to the deconstruction of transnational narratives on GE organisms.[101] Considerations surrounding the specific values at stake, the pervasiveness of the potential adverse effects or any long-term public health or environmental impacts fall under the scope of the precautionary principle. As the book shows, the determination that uncertain risks may not meet the intended level of protection in a specific field underlies recourse to the precautionary principle.[102]

A prudential approach to risk assessment and a focus on different forms of uncertainty, as opposed to sound science approaches to risk assessment and adherence to sound science, *indirectly* reflect the pursuit of a higher than cost-benefit effective level of protection and consideration of other legitimate factors. And indeed, under socially acceptable risk approaches, regulators may *directly* choose to pursue *enhanced* rather than cost-benefit effective levels of protection,

[99] For a plurality of examples, see the analysis in Leonelli, 'Acknowledging the Centrality of the Precautionary Principle' (n 73).

[100] For the same understanding, see Fisher, *Risk Regulation* (n 45).

[101] See ch 4 on EU law, and ch 5 on the SPS Agreement, including an analysis of different references to the precautionary principle under public international law and the 2000 Cartagena Protocol on Biosafety to the Convention on Biological Safety.

[102] See chs 4 and 5, and Leonelli, 'Acknowledging the Centrality of the Precautionary Principle' (n 73).

in cases where hazards and risks have been established. For instance, they may decide to minimise exposures to hazardous substances[103] or set a presumption that no safe level of exposure can be determined for highly hazardous substances.[104] At a general level, the pursuit of enhanced rather than cost-benefit effective levels of protection is bound to result in very different regulatory outputs. The threshold is much higher than the one of 'unreasonable' or 'excessive' adverse effects.[105]

All in all, under socially acceptable risk approaches, economic considerations are only one and not necessarily the most important factor to be taken into account at risk management level. As explained above, regulators may choose to take precautionary action when uncertain risks may not meet the intended level of protection in a specific field; clearly, regulatory focus on persisting uncertainty and recourse to the precautionary principle do not comply with the tenets of cost-benefit analysis. Further, when determining the intended level of protection and

[103] For an example of a regulatory framework which pursues enhanced levels of protection and aims to minimise exposures, see EU regulation of pesticidal active substances under Regulation (EC) 1107/2009/EC of the European Parliament and of the Council of 21 Oct 2009 Concerning the Placing of Plant Protection Products on the Market and Repealing Council Directives 79/117/EEC and 91/414/EEC, [2009] OJ L309/1 ('PPP Regulation'). Article 4(2), read in conjunction with Annex II, stipulates that the residues of representative plant protection products (PPPs) containing an active substance, consequent on application consistent with good plant protection practice and having regard to realistic conditions of use, must not have *any harmful effects* on human health, animal health and groundwater, and *any unacceptable effects* on the environment. Pursuant to Art 4(3), representative PPPs containing an active substance must not have *any immediate or delayed harmful effects* on human health and animal health, directly or indirectly, *no immediate or delayed effects* on groundwater and *no unacceptable effects* on the environment. This higher threshold as regards the intended level of protection is reflected, inter alia, in the identification of Acceptable Operator Exposure Levels ('AOEL') for representative PPPs and Acceptable Daily Intakes ('ADIs') for residues of pesticides in food, under Annex II; these are considerably higher than the transnational baseline, as the aim is to minimise exposures to hazardous pesticidal substances. Further, when Maximum Residue Levels ('MRLs') are set for pesticide residues complying with the ADI, the minimum level of application (and residues) necessary for a PPP to be effective on a crop in accordance with good agricultural practice will be taken into consideration to set the MRLs. This also reflects the pursuit of enhanced levels of protection and the intention to minimise exposures.

[104] For an example, see the EU hazard-based cut-off criteria in regulation of pesticidal active substances. In the case of highly hazardous active substances, a (rebuttable) presumption applies that no safe level of exposure can be determined, and that these active substances shall not be approved at EU level; see Art 4 and Annex II of the PPP Regulation. See also ch 5, section VIII.A, on regulation of hormones administered as growth promoters and regulation of genotoxic substances.

[105] For instance, compare US and EU regulation of pesticidal substances and the different 'benchmarks' set with reference to the intended level of protection; see nn 89, 103 and 104. Even in cases where uncertainties are not salient, reference to enhanced or cost-benefit effective levels of protection will still result in different regulatory outputs, reflecting a different balance between economic and non-economic factors. See also ch 3, sections V, VI and VII. It is worth noting that, in cases where hazards and risks have been conclusively proven, systems informed by socially acceptable risk approaches are often alleged to regulate on the grounds of 'hazards' rather than 'risks'; see, eg, R Lofstedt, 'Risk versus Hazard. Regulating in the 21st Century' (2011) 2 *European Journal of Risk Regulation* 149. In fact, divergences in regulatory standards across different systems stem from reliance on *more or less prudential approaches* to risk assessment, a different focus on persisting *uncertainties*, and the decision in specific legal regimes to minimise exposures and pursue *enhanced* levels of protection, regardless of considerations surrounding economic cost-benefit effectiveness and regardless of whether adverse effects are deemed 'negligible' in other jurisdictions. On this point, see Leonelli, 'Judicial Review of Compliance with the Precautionary Principle' (n 71).

threshold of socially acceptable risk in a specific field, regulators may take *other legitimate factors* ('OLFs') into account.[106] OLFs encompass public opinion, considerations as to the availability and practical efficacy of alternative risk management measures, the specific advantages and disadvantages associated with the decision to take uncertain risks, and distributional stakes. Distributional concerns relate to the distribution of (economic and social) costs and benefits across different constituencies, as opposed to the criterion of aggregate wealth maximisation underpinning cost-benefit analysis.

Considerations as to the substitution of products or processes with less hazardous alternatives,[107] a long-term vision for the development of more sustainable approaches in specific sectors[108] and questions surrounding the socio-economic advantages or disadvantages of a product or process[109] are also part of OLFs. To summarise, the evaluation of OLFs may be defined as the qualitative equivalent of quantitative cost-benefit analysis. OLFs will feed into the determination of the threshold of socially acceptable risk. For instance, the acknowledgment that more sustainable alternatives are available or the conclusion that the socio-economic advantages associated with a product or process are limited will influence the decision as to how high the intended level of protection should be, and how low the corresponding threshold of socially acceptable risk should be.[110]

One further consideration and clarification ensues from this brief overview. Socially acceptable risk models neither aprioristically pursue a zero-risk threshold,

[106] For references to OLFs and their role in risk management, see inter alia Codex Alimentarius Commission (n 56), 125 (Section IV, Risk Analysis, Working Principles for Risk Analysis for Application in the Framework of the Codex Alimentarius, para 28); Codex Alimentarius Commission (n 56), 245 (Appendix: General Decisions, Statements of Principle Concerning the Role of Science in the Codex Decision-Making Process and the Extent to Which Other Factors Are Taken into Account); see also *Communication from the Commission on the Precautionary Principle* (n 49), 19, sub-section 6.3.4, and the detailed analysis in ch 4, section III.

[107] For examples of regulatory provisions informed by socially acceptable risk approaches, see the comparative assessment procedure under EU regulation of pesticidal active substances, Art 50(1) of the PPP Regulation; and the substitution principle enshrined in Art 55 of Regulation (EC) 1907/2006 of the European Parliament and of the Council of 18 December 2006 concerning the Registration, Evaluation, Authorization and Restriction of Chemicals (REACH), Establishing a European Chemicals Agency (ECHA), amending Directive 1999/45/EC and repealing Council Regulation (EEC) 793/93 and Commission Regulation (EC) 1488/94 as well as Council Directive 76/769/EEC and Commission Directives 91/155/EEC, 93/67/EEC, 93/105/EC and 2000/21/EC, [2006] OJ, L396/1 (hereafter, 'REACH Regulation').

[108] In this respect, see for instance the European Commission's 'Farm to Fork' Strategy enacted under the European Green Deal: COM(2020)381 Final, *Communication from the Commission to the European Parliament, the Council, the European Economic and Social Committee and the Committee of the Regions. A Farm to Fork Strategy for a Fair, Healthy and Environmentally-Friendly Food System*. See also Directive 2009/128/EC of the European Parliament and of the Council of 21 Oct 2009 Establishing a Framework for Community Action to Achieve the Sustainable Use of Pesticides, [2009] OJ, L309/1.

[109] For examples of regulatory provisions influenced by consideration of socio-economic OLFs, encompassing more than cost-benefit effectiveness, see, eg, the specific procedure of Art 50(2) of the PPP Regulation, and references to the availability of 'suitable alternative substances or technologies' in the socio-economic procedure provided for under Art 60 of the REACH Regulation.

[110] See ch 4. For an argument in favour of greater consideration of OLFs under risk regulation, see first and foremost Lee, 'Beyond Safety?'; and Lee, *EU Environmental Law* (n 55).

nor necessarily advocate the lowest possible threshold of risk.[111] Rather, what is distinctive about socially acceptable risk models is that prudential approaches to risk assessment should be followed and more than sound science and cost-benefit analysis *may* be taken into consideration. This means that high risks might be socially acceptable in some instances, while comparatively lower risks might not be acceptable and worth taking in other instances. The other distinctive feature of the approach, as the unfolding of the analysis will show, is that the threshold of acceptable risk must be socially and politically agreeable. The acknowledgment that different risk governance measures reflect different normative perspectives shines through this regulatory model; for this very reason, risk regulation should reflect societal views on the acceptability of uncertain risks.

The counter-hegemonic narrative on the uncertain risks posed by GE organisms clearly reflects transnational discourses on socially acceptable risk. Chapters four (EU law) and six (hybrid regulatory standards) deconstruct the rationale, regulatory categories and broader implications of socially acceptable risk discourses, against the background of the controversy on agricultural biotechnologies. The analysis shows that the attempt to strike a different balance between individual rights and collective interests, and the possibility for the latter dimension to prevail, lies at the heart of socially acceptable risk models. In this sense, the thread is a focus on collective values, including public health, environmental, socio-economic and distributional stakes. Beyond the boundaries of national or regional jurisdictions, adherence to socially acceptable risk approaches goes hand in hand with a defence of legal and value pluralism in the regulation of uncertain risks. As chapter six shows, counter-hegemonic discourses also challenge the assumption that aggregate wealth maximisation, pursued through the application of economic cost-benefit analysis, results in positive spill-overs and benefits civil society at large.

In this light, just like evidence-based models, socially acceptable risk approaches have strengths and weaknesses. They reinforce political and democratic legitimacy in the field of risk governance, enable regulators to pursue enhanced levels of protection, regardless of whether adverse effects are deemed 'negligible' or 'acceptable' in other jurisdictions, and account for OLFs. However, they may be economically inefficient and stifle innovation.

Clearly, they are neither value-neutral nor objective. The choice to rely on prudential risk assessments and focus on persisting uncertainties incorporates a normative non-scientific component. However, the same is true of the assumption that sound science approaches and sound scientific evidence must be adhered to. Indeed, the very assumption that political or social OLFs are irrelevant to establish

[111] For the general assumption that this is bound to occur in regulatory systems where the precautionary principle (or 'strong' versions of the principle) may apply, and that the precautionary principle is inherently paralysing and leads in no direction at all, see C Sunstein, 'Beyond the Precautionary Principle' (2003) 151 *University of Pennsylvania Law Review* 1003; and C Sunstein, *Laws of Fear. Beyond the Precautionary Principle* (CUP, 2005). For a more recent defence of cost-benefit analysis, see C Sunstein, *The Cost-Benefit Revolution* (MIT Press, 2018).

the acceptability of 'small' or 'big', 'unlikely' or 'likely' risks is an artificial discourse informed by economic considerations. Symmetrically, in cases where hazards and risks have been established, taking OLFs and enhanced levels of protection into account for the purposes of setting the threshold of acceptable risk entails non-scientific evaluations. Nonetheless, the same is true of the application of economic cost-benefit analysis. To summarise, the pursuit of enhanced levels of protection and the evaluation of OLFs are just as non-scientific as the direct or indirect pursuit of cost-benefit effective levels of protection.

Against this overall backdrop, the deconstruction of socially acceptable risk models throughout the analysis of EU law and regulatory standards enacted by NGO actors sheds light on the counter-hegemonic narrative on GE organisms, counter-hegemonic discourses on the governance of uncertain risks and their specific implications. This sub-section concludes the introductory overview of the institutional strand of enquiry of the book. The next and final section of this chapter turns to the normative aspects of the analysis.

IV. Normative Analysis: Modern Paradigms and Post-Modern Deconstruction of Regulatory Approaches

Deconstructing the hegemonic narrative on the governance of GE organisms casts light on the connections between evidence-based approaches to risk regulation and a double economic dividend. By contrast, an acknowledgment of the value-laden nature of any regulatory choices in the field of risk governance, a defence of legal and value pluralism and the possibility (if not the attempt) to strike a different balance between individual trade rights and collective stakes lie at the heart of socially acceptable risk approaches, which underpin the counter-hegemonic narrative. This is the starting point for a set of normative reflections on the legitimacy of the dynamics of transnational juridification. Here, the ability of *modern* science-centred or procedural deliberative paradigms to identify agreeable solutions to complex regulatory conflicts comes into play.

The normative strand of analysis enquires into the legitimacy of the governance of agricultural biotechnologies at a transnational level. How can regulatory conflicts over GE organisms be solved, reconciling diametrically opposed transnational discourses, and which normative yardsticks may be relevant to this end? From the transnational angle of analysis, the logics of power and socio-legal ordering at times of globalisation unfold beyond the traditional 'inter-governmental' paradigm, which centres on state sovereignty and public international law, and beyond the 'trans-governmental' dimension, which focuses on the rise of networks of technical experts. This triggers a set of questions on how to structure a normative enquiry beyond state sovereignty and technocracy.[112]

[112] See ch 2, part 2.

From a normative theoretical perspective, the Conflicts Law framework[113] offers a way forward towards safeguarding the legitimacy of law at times of globalisation. As explained in detail in chapter two, Conflicts Law theory aims to procedurally construct law's legitimacy by re-coupling law and politics beyond the normative vacuum of transnational legal studies. From this vantage point, it explores the potential for the solution of transnational legal conflicts through *procedural* political deliberation, by *procedurally* balancing regulatory harmonisation and legal and value pluralism, and by *procedurally* re-embedding societal governance and self-governance. As the second part of the second chapter explains, these three dimensions correspond to three constellations of regulatory conflict: horizontal, vertical and diagonal.

The unfolding of the analysis of the book shows that, in the field of agricultural biotechnologies, these transnational conflicts are destined to remain unsolved. The book analyses whether procedural political deliberation might solve the transatlantic horizontal conflict on GE organisms,[114] the failed attempts to solve EU-wide horizontal and vertical regulatory conflicts,[115] the vertical conflict underlying the *EC – Biotech* dispute[116] and conflicts triggered by hybrid standard-setting regimes.[117] None of these regulatory conflicts have been satisfactorily solved. The book thus reaches the conclusion that reconciling the hegemonic and counter-hegemonic narratives on GE organisms through the procedural resolution of transnational regulatory conflicts is an impossible endeavour. Conflicts Law is bound to fail.

This triggers a set of broader considerations on the ability of modern *science-centred* and *procedural deliberative* paradigms to construct normatively legitimate solutions in controversial cases. The analysis is conducted by reference to, and within the specific boundaries of, the field of risk regulation and the controversy on agricultural biotechnologies. Both science-centred and procedural deliberative accounts belong to or are influenced by the modernist tradition. Both are rooted in a rationalist vision of reality. Procedural deliberative paradigms encompass a focus on science, analysing its role in the solution of regulatory conflicts. However, this is set against the broader backdrop of political deliberation, which includes attempts to achieve procedural agreement by reconciling different normative perspectives and political, socio-economic and cultural stakes.[118] Science-centred accounts, in

[113] For applications of the framework at the transnational level, see inter alia C Joerges, PF Kjaer and T Ralli, 'Conflicts Law as Constitutional Form in the Post-National Constellation' (2011) 2 *Transnational Legal Theory* 153; and C Joerges, 'A New Type of Conflicts Law as the Legal Paradigm of The Post-National Constellation' in C Joerges and J Falke (eds), *Karl Polanyi, Globalisation and The Potential of Law in the Transnational Markets* (Hart Publishing, 2011). See in detail ch 2, part 2.

[114] See ch 3.

[115] See ch 4.

[116] See ch 5.

[117] See ch 6.

[118] Among authors influenced by this tradition, see Fisher, *Risk Regulation* (n 45); M Weimer, *Risk Regulation in the Internal Market. Lessons from Agricultural Biotechnology* (OUP, 2019); P Dąbrowska Klosinska, 'EU Governance of GMOs: Political Struggles and Experimentalist Solutions?' in CF Sabel and J Zeitlin (eds) *Experimentalist Governance in the European Union* (OUP, 2010).

contrast, put the accent on technical-scientific elements and postulate that (sound) science provides the means of solving conflicts and disagreements.[119]

Starting from the latter accounts, the book takes the view that science, in and of itself, can hardly generate any form of agreement. Consensus can hardly be built by focusing solely on scientific matters and by seeking to identify the 'best' and 'most reliable' science. In the face of scientific complexity and persisting uncertainty, the 'best' science may not provide factually 'correct' answers: as already explained, the boundaries between facts and values thus fade in the field of risk governance. Even in cases which are relatively uncontroversial in scientific terms, science can tell us nothing of the acceptability of uncertain risks. Ultimately, science can neither provide a single 'valid' answer, nor a universally agreeable one. The modern myth of science's neutrality and objectivity is untenable in the field of risk regulation.[120]

As illustrated in detail in the third section of this chapter, where different approaches are being followed, science will be evaluated through different lenses. Normative frames unavoidably come into play, and science cannot square the circle. Nor can any objective and self-standing criteria of 'pure' science solve disputes, as the slippery slope of procedural versus substantive review of risk regulation clearly shows.[121] In fact, as the book illustrates through specific examples, the very framings of the relevant scientific questions are hardly reconcilable where different approaches are being adhered to.

Science-centred accounts eschew normative elements from their analysis. Yet, 'pure' science is nothing more than an ideal notion in the field of risk regulation.[122] In fact, science-centred accounts usually point to *sound science approaches* to risk assessment and adherence to *sound science* as a way to solve conflicts. This reflects the hegemonic transnational narrative on risk regulation and evidence-based models; however, it does not provide a normatively legitimate solution.

Finally, making scientific methods more transparent and accessible[123] is often regarded as key to solving risk regulation disputes. Yet, as illustrated in the third section, different approaches to risk assessment may be more or less prudential and yield different results. In cases of persisting uncertainty and in the face of scientific complexity, different models and diverging bodies of scientific opinion will always coexist. Improved transparency throughout the risk assessment stage will facilitate communication in procedural terms; however, it will not make the choice to employ one model, assumption or safety factor rather than another satisfactory

[119] Among authors influenced by this modernist strand of thought, see inter alia C Sunstein, *Laws of Fear* (n 111); M Pollack and G Shaffer, *When Cooperation Fails* (n 20); JB Wiener et al (eds), *The Reality of Precaution. Comparing Risk Regulation in the United States and Europe* (Routledge, 2011); in a similar perspective, albeit not directly dealing with risk regulation issues, see A Alemanno and JB Wiener, 'The Future of International Regulatory Cooperation: TTIP as a Learning Process Toward a Global Policy Laboratory' (2016) 78 *Law and Contemporary Problems* 101.

[120] See first and foremost Jasanoff, *The Fifth Branch* as well as Walker, 'The Myth of Science' (n 48).

[121] See ch 5, and Leonelli, 'Acknowledging the Centrality of the Precautionary Principle' (n 73).

[122] See Jasanoff, *The Fifth Branch* as well as Walker, 'The Myth of Science' (n 48).

[123] See, eg, Pascual, Wagner and Fisher, 'Making Method Visible' (n 76).

if the final findings are bound to vary. Nor will it make the decision to consider specific data and disregard other evidence satisfactory if hazard-related or risk-related uncertainties persist and the underlying normative premises diverge, or generate any agreement where different levels of protection are being pursued by regulators.[124] As for top-down coordination and convergence in technical-scientific matters, by means of harmonising technical-scientific protocols, this comes with a set of implications. Ultimately, it implies adherence to a specific approach to risk assessment, which could be more or less prudential. Yet again, this is not likely to be agreeable to all parties. Nor will it necessarily do justice to a prudential, cautious approach to risk assessment.

On these grounds, science has a limited role to play for the purposes of generating genuine agreement and identifying legitimate solutions in controversial cases. As explained in the third section, regulatory conflicts in the field of risk governance do not relate to issues of 'pure' science. All in all, reference to scientific matters can only be expected to make a substantial contribution in cases which are uncontroversial. Where uncertainties are very low and scientific agreement very solid, mere reference to scientific matters *may* be sufficient to build consensus.[125]

Procedural deliberative accounts, by contrast, are more encompassing. As anticipated above, they enquire into the ability of actors to identify procedural criteria for the solution of regulatory conflicts by engaging in rational deliberative practices. The relevant criteria will vary in accordance with the specific conflict constellations at stake;[126] however, technical-scientific *as well as* political and socio-economic factors must be taken into due consideration with a view to successfully addressing contentious cases. To put it differently, (authentic) deliberation is structurally different from 'technocratic deliberation'[127] and adherence to sound science. Unlike science-centred models, procedural deliberative accounts acknowledge that normative disagreements play a key role in regulatory conflicts, including in the field of risk regulation. Therefore, normative factors must be adequately addressed for the ultimate solution to be legitimate.

As explained in the second part of chapter two, legal proceduralisation lies at the heart of deliberative accounts. The analysis thus consistently focuses on procedural governance arrangements, procedural deliberative dynamics and the margins for a procedural construction of agreeable legal solutions. The book reaches the conclusion that the *procedural* struggle to identify concerted and normatively legitimate solutions through deliberation *can* work. However, it will only work where a set of pre-existing *substantive* conditions are met. Broadly speaking, and having regard to the field of risk regulation, specific scientific preconditions can

[124] See, eg, the analysis in ch 4, section V.

[125] Even though normative perspectives, values and the specific level of protection pursued by regulators may still result in different determinations as to the acceptability of a risk and different regulatory outputs.

[126] See ch 2, part 2.

[127] For use of this terminology, see Pollack and Shaffer, *When Cooperation Fails* (n 20).

facilitate procedural agreement; as already mentioned, where uncertainties are very low and scientific agreement is very solid, consensus will generally be easier to build.[128] More importantly, pre-existing and shared substantive perspectives, value systems and goals will facilitate deliberative practices and the identification of legitimate solutions.

Where similar approaches along the spectrum from evidence-based to socially acceptable risk models are being employed, and the same goals are being pursued in a specific regulatory area, reaching an agreement will be possible. Where different regulatory approaches are being followed, yet perspectives, values and goals are shared in the context of a specific regulatory field, agreement will also be possible. In other words, in so far as the normative premises of the relevant actors are similar, different approaches to the governance of uncertain risks can yield similar results at the implementation stage. Other variations could be sketched out, referring to alternative scenarios where a viable intermediate solution might be identified along the regulatory spectrum: for instance, where similar regulatory approaches are employed but the perspectives of the actors involved and the goals pursued partially diverge. In every case, shared substantive perspectives, value systems and objectives will play a crucial role in ensuring that political processes are *truly* deliberative and that they result in the identification of normatively legitimate solutions. Ultimately, shared values and perspectives will result in similar approaches to risk assessment, similar inferences being drawn in a context of disputed science and a similar level of protection being pursued.

In the case of GE organisms, these substantive preconditions are lacking. The two transnational narratives on agricultural biotechnologies and the governance of their uncertain risks are irreconcilable; the polarisation between evidence-based and socially acceptable risk approaches is clearer than in any other case in the field of risk regulation. Scientific disagreements as to the uncertain risks posed by GE organisms are intense; the relevance of *stricto sensu* uncertainties and hazard-related uncertainties in this regulatory field, where science is often unable to establish a causal link with specific adverse effects, adds a further layer of complexity and controversy. Moreover, OLFs have a unique prominence in this field. The debate on the socio-economic advantages and disadvantages of GE organisms and on the distributional implications of different regulatory approaches has reached unprecedented levels of disagreement.

The failure of procedural deliberation and legal proceduralisation in the field of agricultural biotechnologies thus illustrates the irreconcilable tensions between technocratic evidence-based models of risk governance, the double dividend of aggregate wealth maximisation, transnational regulatory convergence and trade liberalisation, and radically different perspectives on legal pluralism, sustainability and collective and distributional stakes. The book thus draws the conclusion that transnational conflicts on agricultural biotechnologies cannot and should not be

[128] However, see the caveat in n 125.

solved. Diametrically opposed perspectives on whether, how and why uncertain risks ought to be regulated[129] should merely coexist. It acknowledges that fully-fledged transnational conflicts in politically charged fields cannot be completely resolved; nor should they be solved at all costs. To attempt to do so would be counterproductive. Focusing on procedural aspects or pursuing unsatisfactory procedural compromises will either exacerbate conflicts or be ineffective. In either case, regulatory conflicts are bound to persist and re-surface.

On these grounds, the book offers an alternative reading of the margins within which a normatively legitimate solution to complex regulatory conflicts can be constructed. Ultimately, it concludes that successful *procedural* deliberation largely *results from* pre-existing shared perspectives, values and goals. These are the *substantive* preconditions mentioned above in this section. In this sense, the success of truly deliberative practices is a procedural reflection of pre-existing substantive factors and conditions; conversely, a failure of deliberation is a procedural reflection of an unbridgeable normative gap. Normative premises, value systems and objectives need not be perfectly aligned for deliberative processes to yield positive results. Yet, a common substantive background and some unity of intent must exist.

Overall, the book suggests that modern procedural deliberative accounts have put too much faith in the ability of *rational communicative processes* to produce shared substantive values and identities and thereby underpin social integration. The book concludes that a different analytical balance should be struck in evaluating the dialectics of substantive vis-à-vis procedural, material vis-à-vis communicative, political and socio-economic vis-à-vis rational-deliberative, and objective vis-à-vis inter-subjective factors.[130] Deliberative and communicative processes do not exist in a political, socio-economic and cultural vacuum;[131] the assumption that any conflict can (and should) be procedurally solved is a legacy of modern, rationalist paradigms.

This has three implications. First, from this perspective, the focus should shift from procedural governance arrangements and procedural dynamics to substantive regulatory approaches and their underlying value systems and goals. This can pave the way for an enquiry into the substantive preconditions for genuine political agreement. In this sense, a modern *construction* of potential solutions by

[129] In this perspective, see Lee, 'Beyond Safety? The Broadening Scope of Risk Regulation' (n 55), with a particular focus on the socio-economic and distributional implications of risk governance.

[130] See also ch 7. See J Habermas, *Communication and the Evolution of Society* (Beacon Press, 1979), in particular 106 ff., 111 ff. and 142-142. Ultimately, what underpins long-lasting societal integration or, in Habermasian terms, a 'life-world'? Can consciousness and communication underpin effective societal integration, or does social existence determine consciousness and communication? Does societal integration ultimately rely on *material* and *objective* factors, or on *procedural* and *inter-subjective* elements? On these points, see also Leonelli, 'The Postmodern Normative' (n 37).

[131] M Everson, 'The Limits to the Conflicts Law Approach: Law in Times of Political Turmoil' (2011) 2 *Transnational Legal Theory* 271.

means of procedural practices and interactions should be preceded and complemented by a post-modern *deconstruction* of substantive regulatory patterns. In the book, the latter form of analysis is conducted throughout the institutional strand of enquiry: this part of the analysis deconstructs the nature of the hegemonic and counter-hegemonic narratives, and the specificities of evidence-based and socially acceptable risk approaches, as embedded in the relevant regulatory systems.

Second, deconstructing substantive regulatory approaches sheds light on their implications and broader impact, together with the overarching policy goals that they pursue. This deconstruction process helps to pinpoint the relevant issues at stake and what different forms of agreement would entail. As rightly noted, a procedural focus on governance arrangements and deliberative practices can obscure the substantive political and socio-economic issues at stake; in this sense, and in so far as agreement is framed and pursued as a 'goal', modern procedural deliberative accounts incorporate a technocratic element.[132] Further, if legal analysis loses track of the relevant values at stake, mere technocratic agreement could end up being mistaken for a successful deliberative outcome.[133]

Third, and finally, the book concludes that modern procedural paradigms face unprecedented challenges in the transnational, post-modern reality. If legal proceduralisation fails to solve transnational legal conflicts and identify normatively legitimate solutions, a turn back to legal materialisation and the construction of substantive normative arguments could then be the only way out of the post-modern normative conundrum.

The next chapter provides a more detailed overview of the methodological framework and normative background of the book. Some final considerations on the institutional, methodological and normative strands of enquiry are then sketched out in the concluding chapter.

[132] ibid.

[133] See ch 3, section VIII; and ch 4, sections VIII and IX.

2

Methodological and Normative Aspects: Transnational Legal Analysis as a Methodological Framework and the Limits of Legal Proceduralisation

The current legal and regulatory landscape is less 'global' and more 'transnational' than ever. In the face of increasing economic interconnectedness and demographic, information and media flows, law keeps on undergoing far-reaching transformations; yet, powerful centrifugal forces push against any form of further and deeper integration, structural legal ordering and 'hard' legalisation. This has resulted in increased legal fragmentation and asymmetry. As the WTO legal system partially unravels, trade and investment agreements proliferate, commercial arbitration thrives, public international 'hard' law languishes and even the European legal integration project faces unforeseen challenges, the law governing the 'global community', assuming that any such community exists, hardly qualifies as 'global' law.

While the political events and societal developments of the past years need not be unequivocally interpreted as a triumph of nationalism and nation state sovereignty, they have shattered the illusion that economic globalisation, regulatory convergence and legal integration come at no cost. Unsurprisingly, then, any projects for systematic and 'deeper' legal integration have come to a halt, and the 'global' law agenda has retrenched. What we are left with is 'transnational' socio-legal ordering. In this sense, the trajectory, validity and normative legitimacy of transnational law are, more than ever before, topical issues.

This triggers a plurality of methodological as well as normative considerations. The first methodological reflection centres on the notion of 'transnational law' and its nature. A set of normative questions follow suit. In the face of asymmetric 'transnational' dynamics of legalisation and juridification, how can intractable regulatory conflicts be legitimately solved? How are we to carve out a normative dimension of enquiry, and will law's normative legitimacy underpin long-lasting dynamics of societal integration beyond the nation state level? From this perspective, a methodological and a normative component coexist in the definition of 'transnational law'.

This chapter is divided into two parts. The first part lays out the methodological framework applied to the analysis of the book. Section I provides a broad overview of Law and Globalisation and transnational legal studies, describing the origins and foundations of transnational legal theory and emphasising its specific characteristics. Sections II and III analyse Transnational Legal Ordering and Transnational Legal Pluralism theory, respectively, explaining the differences between these two approaches and illustrating the alternative framing of 'transnational law' and 'transnational legal analysis' put forward in this book. Section IV concludes the first part of the chapter by providing a more detailed insight into the deployment of transnational legal analysis as a methodological framework, explaining how this will be applied to the enquiry into the governance of GE organisms.

The second part of the chapter, on the other hand, focuses on the normative dimension of analysis. Section V starts by exploring the normative conundrum of transnational legal studies. Section VI turns to an analysis of Conflicts Law theory, explaining why this theoretical approach offers a way forward for attempts to construct a normative discourse on law's legitimacy at times of globalisation. Sections VII and VIII anticipate the conclusions of the book, casting some light on the limits of modern, rationalist paradigms in the post-modern landscape and pointing to the complex relationship between substantive and procedural analysis.

Part 1. Transnational Legal Analysis as a Methodological Framework

I. Law, Globalisation and Transnational Law

Every field of law and legal analysis has had to confront the challenges posed by global interdependencies. In this sense, it is hard to identify any areas of legal enquiry which have not been impacted by the unfolding of globalisation. However, a preliminary distinction must be drawn between, on the one hand, accounts of how specific fields of law respond to global challenges and seek to tackle the externalities of globalisation, and, on the other hand, legal theoretical strands exploring the transformations of law at times of globalisation. This section focuses on the latter legal theoretical bodies of research. While the overview is by no means all-encompassing, it endeavours to map and single out some of the most prominent research strands in this very rich debate.

At one end of the spectrum lie accounts of law driven and oriented by public law, encompassing Global Constitutionalism and Global Administrative Law ('GAL'). Under Global Constitutionalism, the search for a 'global' legal order goes hand in hand with the 'upwards rescaling' of a constitutional framework at the global level. Global Constitutionalism refers 'to the continuing, but not linear, process of gradual emergence and deliberate creation of constitutionalist elements in the legal order by political and judicial actors'.[1] In the face of these developments, lawyers have enquired into the legal and judicial dynamics which may underpin and foster the constitutionalisation of the international legal order, while political scientists have engaged with a transposition of democratic theory beyond nation state boundaries. Thereby, different strands of Global Constitutionalism theory have advocated the advent of a Global Demos and World State,[2] the constitutional nature of the UN Charter,[3] the rise and entrenchment of cosmopolitanism and cosmopolitan citizenship,[4] a democratic turn within global governance[5] or a quasi-constitutionalisation of the law of the international community.[6]

In a different vein, albeit from an equally public law-centred perspective, GAL theory has focused on the cross-national development and application of regulatory standards in the field of administrative law. In this light, it has endeavoured to investigate the normative legitimacy of the expanding body of GAL[7] through the identification and application of procedural principles, including publicity and transparency, reason-giving, participation requirements, legal accountability, liability and review of administrative action.[8] On these grounds, both Global Constitutionalism and GAL theory have applied a substantive or procedural, 'thick' or 'thin' transposition of nation state-based categories to the analysis of the 'global' space.

Second, we find legal pluralist accounts of law 'beyond constitutionalism',[9] or in 'the twilight of constitutionalism'.[10] Works in this research strand explore the strain

[1] A Peters, 'The Merits of Global Constitutionalism' (2009) 16 *Indiana Journal of Global Legal Studies* 397. See also A Peters, 'Are We Moving Towards Constitutionalization of the World Community?' in A Cassese (ed), *Realizing Utopia: The Future of International Law* (OUP, 2012).

[2] O Höffe, *Democracy in an Age of Globalization* (Springer-Verlag, 1999).

[3] B Fassbender, 'Rediscovering a Forgotten Constitution: Notes on the Place of the UN Charter in the International Legal Order' in JL Dunoff and JP Trachtman (eds), *Ruling the World? Constitutionalism, International Law and Global Governance* (CUP, 2009).

[4] See inter alia D Held, *Cosmopolitanism* (Polity Press, 2010).

[5] D Archibugi, M Koenig-Archibugi and R Marchetti (eds), *Global Democracy. Normative and Empirical Perspectives* (CUP, 2012); D Archibugi, *The Global Commonwealth of Citizens. Towards Cosmopolitan Democracy* (Princeton University Press, 2008).

[6] See inter alia N Walker, *Intimations of Global Law* (CUP, 2015); JL Dunoff and JP Trachtman, 'A Functional Approach to International Constitutionalization', in Dunoff and Trachtman (eds), *Ruling the World?* (n 3).

[7] See inter alia B Kingsbury, N Krisch and R Stewart, 'The Emergence of Global Administrative Law' (2005) 68 *Law and Contemporary Problems* 15; N Krisch, 'Global Administrative Law and the Constitutional Ambition' in P Dobner and M Loughlin (eds), *The Twilight of Constitutionalism?* (OUP, 2010); C Harlow, 'Global Administrative Law: The Quest for Principles and Values' (2006) 17 *European Journal of International Law* 187; S Cassese (ed), *Research Handbook on Global Administrative Law* (Edward Elgar, 2016).

[8] See, eg, the overview in B Kingsbury, 'The Concept of 'Law' in Global Administrative Law', *NYU Working Paper no 29/2009*, 22 ff.

[9] N Krisch, *Beyond Constitutionalism. The Pluralist Structure of Postnational Law* (OUP, 2010).

[10] Dobner and Loughlin (eds), *The Twilight of Constitutionalism?* (n 7).

and progressive unravelling of hierarchical, positive legal ordering at national and international levels, against the backdrop of law's increasing fragmentation at times of globalisation.[11] However, theorising legal pluralism in the post-national legal universe and acknowledging that national constitutionalism is nowadays part of a much more encompassing and complex legal picture does not entail embracing a 'global' or 'transnational' law perspective. 'The fact that both [national and international] layers interact and perhaps even function in similar ways […] suggests taking the different layers into view together as an object of study, but not necessarily drawing them into one as a matter of legal theory.'[12] Indeed, many scholars on the legal pluralist side of the debate have not sought to frame the transformations of law within a 'global' or 'transnational' legal paradigm.

Halfway between these accounts and a fully-fledged analysis of 'transnational' law, we see bodies of research engaging with global legal pluralism.[13] Yet again drawing on legal pluralism, but with a distinctive sociological, socio-legal or legal anthropological approach, we find scholars investigating the societal logics driving globalisation and the underpinning legal-regulatory apparatus. On the sociological side of the debate, Saskia Sassen has famously analysed globalisation as the ubiquitous product of cross-border global assemblages of territory, authority and rights ('TARs').[14] From a similar perspective, De Sousa Santos has argued that transnational legality as inter-legality results from the mutual interactions of 'globalised localism' and 'localised globalism'.[15]

These sociological or socio-legal accounts highlight how the logics driving globalisation and transnational juridification are in fact structured *within* as well as beyond the nation state; this perspective shifts the focus away from the alleged marginalisation, shrinking or 'hollowing out'[16] of the nation state, to illuminate how structured spheres of societal activities at the national and local levels coalesce and drive globalisation processes. Thus, increasingly de-territorialised spaces of societal interaction, such as global capital markets,[17] cross-cut territorial boundaries and testify 'how the triad of territory, authority, rights is inescapably subjected

[11] See also M Koskenniemi, 'The Fate of Public International Law: Between Technique and Politics' (2007) 70 *MLR* 1; M Koskenniemi and P Leino, 'Fragmentation of International Law? Post-Modern Anxieties' (2002) 15 *Leiden Journal of International Law* 553.

[12] Krisch, *Beyond Constitutionalism* (n 9) 11.

[13] See for instance PS Berman (ed), *Oxford Handbook of Global Legal Pluralism* (OUP, 2020); M Helfand (ed), *Negotiating State and Non-State Law. The Challenge of Global and Local Legal Pluralism* (CUP, 2015).

[14] S Sassen, *Territory, Authority, Rights. From Medieval to Global Assemblages* (Princeton University Press, 2006); S Sassen, 'The Places and Spaces of the Global: An Expanded Analytic Terrain', in D Held and A McGrew (eds), *Globalization Theory. Approaches and Controversies* (Polity Press, 2007).

[15] B De Sousa Santos, *Toward a New Legal Common Sense: Law, Globalization and Emancipation* (Butterworths, 2002).

[16] See RAW Rhodes, 'The Hollowing Out of the State: The Changing Nature of the Public Service in Britain' (1994) 65 *Political Quarterly* 138.

[17] See, eg, S Sassen, 'The Embeddedness of Electronic Markets: The Case of Global Capital Markets' in K Knorr Cetina and A Preda (eds), *The Sociology of Financial Markets* (OUP, 2005).

to [...] processes of de-assembling and re-assembling'.[18] From different socio-legal or legal anthropological perspectives, other scholars have also enquired into the logics shaping globalisation and legalisation beyond the nation state.[19]

Finally, and before the detailed analysis of Transnational Legal Ordering and Transnational Legal Pluralism theory, this section will spend a few words on the origins and scope of 'transnational legal studies', as a discrete area of legal enquiry. The origins of transnational legal studies are acknowledged as lying in systems theory and the theorisation of a 'World Society' beyond the familiar boundaries of the nation state and of politically structured national societies.[20] While it is certainly true that not all transnational legal scholars draw on systems theory, the roots of the notion of 'transnational law' lie there. More precisely, 'transnational law' evolved from the original transposition of systems theory to legal analysis; this dates back to enquiries into the Lex Mercatoria (Law Merchant) from the late 1980s onwards. The dispute centred on the nature of this de-territorialised body of law, cross-nationally developed and applied by non-state, private actors.[21]

This form of enquiry was then pushed further to encompass the analysis of new private regulatory regimes, unfolding beyond the nation state. The logics of functional differentiation of the 'World Society' and corresponding challenges posed to law and legal unity, in the face of the proliferation of sites of norm-making, were famously captured by the analysis of the 'Global Bukowina'[22] and ubiquitous regime collisions.[23] The hybridisation of the category of law, resulting from the entrenchment of private regulatory standard-setting regimes, added a further level of complexity to this picture. The law of the 'World Society' was neither enacted by the nation state nor anchored to the national level; further, it consisted of hybrid forms of regulatory governance and norm-making.

The original systems theory analysis of law later evolved into the theorisation of societal constitutionalism. This has set hybrid societal regulation and self-regulation at the centre of the enquiry, defending the intrinsic normative value of these 'constitutional fragments'.[24] However, systems theory investigations

[18] P Zumbansen, 'Transnational Legal Pluralism' (2010) 10 *Transnational Legal Theory* 141, 182.

[19] See inter alia KE Davis, A Fisher, B Kingsbury and SE Merry (eds), *Governance by Indicators. Global Power Through Quantification and Rankings* (OUP, 2012); SE Merry, 'New Legal Realism and the Ethnography of Transnational Law' (2006) 31 *Law and Social Inquiry* 975.

[20] See below, section III, for a more detailed overview.

[21] See inter alia G Teubner, 'Introduction to Autopoietic Law' in G Teubner (ed), *Autopoietic Law: A New Approach to Law and Society* (Walter De Gruyter, 1987); G Teubner, *Law as An Autopoietic System* (Blackwell, 1993).

[22] G Teubner, 'Global Bukowina: Legal Pluralism in the World Society' in G Teubner (ed), *Global Law Without a State* (Aldershot, 1997).

[23] For a first reference see Teubner, *Law as An Autopoietic System* (n 21); for the development of the notion, see A Fischer-Lescano and G Teubner 'Regime-Collisions: The Vain Search for Legal Unity in Fragmentation of Global Law' (2004) 25 *Michigan Journal of International Law*, 999.

[24] See G Teubner, *Constitutional Fragments. Societal Constitutionalism and Globalization* (OUP, 2012); G Teubner, 'Fragmented Foundations: Societal Constitutionalism Beyond the Nation State' in Dobner and Loughlin (eds), *The Twilight of Constitutionalism?* (n 7). See also the analysis in ch 2, part 2.

of law beyond the nation state have also set the foundations and scope of what would later become the 'traditional' understanding of transnational law as a self-contained 'field' of law and legal analysis. Throughout the years, transnational law has increasingly come to be associated with a set of *hybrid* regulatory standards, rules and norms enacted by *non-state* actors operating *beyond the nation state* level. These standards apply across territorial levels and societal forms of organisation; they might also interact with 'positive' legal systems and be incorporated, adjudicated and enforced at national level.[25] In this sense, transnational law is bound to interact with different legal regimes. Nonetheless, it is usually distinguished from them. Indeed, the 'traditional' framing of transnational law as a separate 'field' of legal analysis postulates a clear distinction between transnational norm-making, on the one hand, and 'positive' legal systems, treaties and agreements, on the other. Under this approach, neither national nor public international law, concluded by and binding on states, can be truly 'transnational'; any system of 'positive' law involving a degree of state participation will not qualify as 'transnational'.

While not necessarily drawing on systems theory models, the majority of legal and political accounts of transnational law and transnational regulatory governance have adhered to this notion.[26] The focus has consistently centred on societal actors, mapping their standard-setting and norm-making endeavour and locating it within an a-territorial, socially constructed level of organisation, defined as 'transnational'. Transnational legal theory, however, does not always – and need not – align to this understanding of transnational law. As the next sections purport to show, both Transnational Legal Ordering and Transnational Legal Pluralism theory have taken a different direction in their analysis of the transnational legal landscape. Similarly, this book puts forward an alternative understanding of transnational legal analysis as a methodological framework. Before turning to these theoretical constructs, however, this section will conclude the overview on legal analysis at times of globalisation by highlighting the thread and common premises in transnational legal studies. In other words, it will identify and spell out what

[25] See inter alia F Cafaggi (ed), *Enforcement of Transnational Regulation: Ensuring Compliance in a Global World* (Edward Elgar, 2012).

[26] For some examples, see Cafaggi, *Enforcement of Transnational Regulation* (n 25); JH Dalhuisen, 'Globalization and the Transnationalization of Commercial and Financial Law' (2015) 67 *Rutgers University Law Review* 23; L Cata Backer, 'Private Actors and Public Governance Beyond the State: The Multinational Corporation, the Financial Stability Board, and the Global Governance Order' (2011) 18 *Indiana Journal of Global Legal Studies* 761; KW Abbott and D Snidal, 'Strengthening International Regulation Through Transnational New Governance: Overcoming the Orchestration Deficit' (2009) 42 *Vanderbilt Journal of Transnational Law* 501; PF Kjaer, 'Transnational Normative Orders: The Constitutionalism of Intra- and Trans- Normative Law' (2013) 20 *Indiana Journal of Global Legal Studies* 783; ML Djelic and K Sahlin-Andersson (eds), *Transnational Governance. Institutional Dynamics of Regulation* (CUP, 2006); ML Djelic and S Quack, *Transnational Communities. Shaping Global Economic Governance* (CUP, 2010). For a similar perspective, albeit without reference to the terminology of 'transnational' law or regulatory governance, see also T Büthe and W Mattli, *The New Global Rulers: The Privatization of Regulation in the World Economy* (Princeton University Press, 2012).

all accounts of transnational law, as opposed to the broader debate on law and globalisation,[27] have in common.

First, transnational legal theorists employ the terminology of 'transnational' law, as opposed to 'global' law. This underscores the asymmetric nature and variable spatial reach of 'transnational' law, as opposed to any alleged forms of 'global' law applicable to the World Community. Second, all strands in transnational legal studies acknowledge the increasing disassociation of law from territoriality.[28] At the very least, this will mean that transnational legal theorists accept that regulation and norm-making might originate from socially constructed forms of organisation, rather than being anchored to specific territorial jurisdictions. However, this may entail a further analysis of how transnational norms cut across different territorial levels and are iteratively shaped and reshaped through interactions with different regulatory systems and by being applied by different sets of actors. This is described as 'recursivity'.[29] Extra-territoriality and the analysis of extra-territorial spill-overs might also be at stake.[30]

Third, transnational legal theory recognises that the nation state is no longer the only or the main site of law-making, adjudication and enforcement. Not all transnational legal scholars would accept that the nation state is not part of the transnational legal picture, or claim that it is not involved in transnational legal ordering.[31] However, all of them have left the Westphalian paradigm and 'methodological nationalism'[32] behind. As a corollary of this statement, transnational law is also acknowledged to be neither public nor private. 'Public' and 'private', 'state' and 'market' distinctions are only valid within the boundaries of the nation state.[33] Further, public and private ordering are two inter-connected poles;[34] in so far as no 'global' law, World Demos or 'public' sphere exist beyond the nation state, defining transnational law as private is unhelpful at best. From this perspective, the dichotomisation of public versus private law approaches and the entrenchment of lawyers on opposite fronts of the battlefield miss the crucial point about the social structuring of the transnational realm. Transnational law, just like 'governance', is neither public nor private; the transnational regulatory 'process' spans across the boundaries of these notions and transcends them both.

[27] In a not dissimilar perspective, see also V Heyvaert, 'The Transnationalization of Law: Rethinking Law through Transnational Environmental Regulation' (2017) 6 *Transnational Environmental Law* 205.

[28] See, eg, G Handl, J Zekoll and P Zumbansen, *Beyond Territoriality: Transnational Legal Authority in an Age of Globalization* (Martinus Nijhoff Publishers, 2012).

[29] See below, section II.

[30] See below, section IV.

[31] See below, section II.

[32] R Cotterell, 'Transnational Communities and the Concept of Law' (2008) 21 *Ratio Juris* 1; P Zumbansen, 'Law After the Welfare State: Formalism, Functionalism and the Ironic Turn of Reflexive Law' (2008) 56 *American Journal of Comparative Law* 769.

[33] For an argument that the distinction between the two gets very slippery out of the nation state boundaries, see S Cassese et al, 'The Enforcement of Transnational Private Regulation: A Fictitious Oxymoron' in Cafaggi (ed), *Enforcement of Transnational Regulation* (n 25) 331.

[34] P Zumbansen, 'Sustaining Paradox Boundaries: Perspectives on the Internal Affairs in Domestic and International Law' (2004) 15 *European Journal of International Law* 197, 211.

Finally, transnational legal studies acknowledge law's increasing pluralisation. In this sense, the rejection of legal formalism and positivism and the adoption of a legal pluralist perspective are both inherent to transnational legal theory. Equally, transnational legal scholars embrace the notion of legal hybridisation. Although they need not place hybrid standards enacted by non-state actors at the centre of their enquiry, transnational legal theorists will still accept that the boundaries between 'law' and 'non-law', 'regulation' and 'norm-making' have become increasingly blurred. In other words, they will include societal regulation and self-regulation within the scope of their enquiries.

These are the five broad premises shared by all strands of transnational legal theory. This book draws on these foundations, taking them as a starting point for its alternative construction of transnational legal analysis as a methodological framework. It is against the overall backdrop of these premises that the following sections explore Transnational Legal Ordering and Transnational Legal Pluralism theory.

II. Transnational Legal Ordering Theory and Transnational Legal Orders

The analytical journey leading to Transnational Legal Ordering ('TLO') theory started with an exploration and mapping of inter-governmental, trans-governmental and transnational dynamics of transatlantic regulatory coordination,[35] which was later complemented by an enquiry into state change and transnational law.[36] TLO theory and the conceptualisation of Transnational Legal Orders ('TLOs') draw on these insights and yet push the analysis further.

Terminologically, legal ordering is defined as 'transnational' rather than 'global' for the reasons mentioned in the first section. In the absence of a global or supranational legal framework, the term 'global' law is misleading in that legal ordering is bound to have a variable spatial reach and is subject to varying degrees of application and enforcement.[37] The 'legal' aspect of legal ordering, as under any socio-legal perspective, encompasses positive law as well as hybrid regulatory governance and norm-making. Finally, the notion of 'ordering' refers to the ability of transnational norms to alter normative orientations and shape social behaviour.[38]

[35] MA Pollack and G Shaffer, 'Transatlantic Governance in Historical and Theoretical Perspective' in MA Pollack and G Shaffer (eds), *Transatlantic Governance in the Global Economy* (Rowman and Littlefield Publishers, 2001).

[36] G Shaffer, 'Transnational Legal Ordering and State Change' in G Shaffer (ed), *Transnational Legal Ordering and State Change* (CUP, 2013).

[37] TC Halliday and G Shaffer, 'Transnational Legal Orders' in TC Halliday and G Shaffer (eds), *Transnational Legal Orders*, (CUP, 2015) 4.

[38] ibid 7 ff.

A TLO is defined as 'a collection of formalised legal norms and associated organisations and actors that authoritatively order the understanding and practice of law across national jurisdictions'.[39] The scope and boundaries of specific TLOs are identified by reference to discrete areas of regulation. TLOs, however, may or may not exist in a particular regulatory field. Further, they may be highly or only partially developed. This is a consequence of different levels of contestation in the creation, adoption and practice of transnational norms,[40] resulting in varying degrees of territorial reach and overall settlement of TLOs. The entrenchment of a TLO is defined as its 'institutionalisation'.[41] Such 'institutionalisation' is then measured against two indicators: 'normative settlement' and 'alignment'.

The former refers to the extent to which transnational norms are applied across jurisdictions and levels of societal organisation, changing normative expectations and thus structuring social behaviour.[42] The latter notion addresses the degree of normative contestation in the construction of transnational socio-legal ordering and in the processes shaping specific TLOs. 'Alignment' measures the univocal definition and specification of regulatory problems, which is related to the purposes of any prominent norm-making actors operating at transnational level and the extent to which they share a common vision on regulatory aims. Indeed, the 'struggle over the definition or specification of a problem lays the foundation for a struggle over a set of prescriptions to produce a particular outcome'.[43] This will result in a different framing of the scope of relevant TLOs. Where 'alignment' is low, 'normative settlement' will be partial at best, and a TLO will therefore have a low level of 'institutionalisation' or might not be institutionalised at all.[44]

Unlike many accounts of transnational law, TLO theory encompasses the nation state dimension and other 'positive' legal regimes, including public international law, whenever 'positive' law has been relevant to the socio-legal construction of TLOs. Indeed, the starting point of TLO theory was the search for a new perspective accommodating 'processes of local, national, international and transnational public and private law-making and practice in dynamic tension within a single analytical frame'.[45] For this reason, TLO theorists have criticised a narrow understanding of transnational law as 'non-state law, or governance by non-state actors'.[46]

[39] ibid 11.

[40] TC Halliday and G Shaffer, 'Researching Transnational Legal Orders' in Halliday and Shaffer (eds), *Transnational Legal Orders* (n 37).

[41] Halliday and Shaffer, 'Transnational Legal Orders' (n 37) 42 ff.

[42] ibid.

[43] ibid 8.

[44] For an analysis of different scenarios, see Halliday and Shaffer, 'Transnational Legal Orders' (n 37) 46 ff.

[45] ibid 3.

[46] TC Halliday and G Shaffer, 'With, Within and Beyond the Nation State: The Promise and Limits of Transnational Legal Ordering', in P Zumbansen (ed), *The Oxford Handbook of Transnational Law* (OUP, 2021). Direct citations in this section, however, refer to an earlier version of the chapter, published as a research paper; see TC Halliday and G Shaffer, 'With, Within and Beyond the Nation State: The Promise and Limits of Transnational Legal Ordering', *University of California, Irvine Legal Studies Research Paper no 2016/59*, 1.

TLOs embrace both bottom-up and top-down norm-making processes;[47] 'national law and practice remain integral to the formation and institutionalisation of legal norms' and 'are neither viewed as being bypassed by transnational legal ordering nor as being autonomous from processes of international and transnational legal norm-making and conveyance'.[48] Transnational legal ordering is thus constructed 'with, within and beyond the state'.[49] More specifically, the nation state dimension is relevant to transnational legal ordering and the development of TLOs for three reasons. First, state officials, who represent states and their interests, are among the actors involved in processes leading to transnational legal ordering.[50] In this sense, the development of TLOs reflects societal as well as state-driven dynamics. Second, transnational legal ordering can transform states in so far as the latter participate in transnational processes.[51] Third, the nation state is one of the sites where transnational norms will be recursively applied and enforced and where TLOs will become institutionalised.[52] This is where the notion of 'recursivity', ie the contested creation, modification and entrenchment of transnational legal ordering 'between different levels of social organisation through which legal norms become institutionalised',[53] comes into play. The state is directly or indirectly part of the complex 'interaction of law-making and practice across different levels of social organisation', which involves 'top-down, bottom-up, horizontal and transversal processes through which legal norms are constructed, flow, settle and unsettle'.[54] From this perspective, transnational rules, standards or norms will also have to be embedded and applied at national level for a TLO to become institutionalised.[55]

Turning to different 'positive' legal systems and public international law, these are also encompassed within the socio-legal notion of a transnational legal order. TLO theory recognises the role played by public international law in the socio-legal construction of TLOs.[56] To provide one example, it has described the emergence of the arbitral legal order as resulting from the interaction of 'international hard law (such as the New York Convention), international soft law (such as UNCITRAL model rules), national law and national and transnational arbitral practice'.[57] From this perspective, TLO theorists have criticised 'traditional' accounts of state-less transnational law, where state-centric and state-driven public international law is regarded as distinct from transnational law.

[47] Halliday and Shaffer, 'Transnational Legal Orders' (n 37) 16.
[48] ibid 20.
[49] See n 46 above.
[50] See n 46, 3 ff.
[51] ibid.
[52] ibid.
[53] Halliday and Shaffer, 'Transnational Legal Orders' (n 37) 16. See also TC Halliday, 'Recursivity in Global Norm Making: A Socio-Legal Agenda' (2009) 5 *Annual Review of Law and Social Sciences* 263.
[54] See n 46, 3.
[55] ibid 3, 4 and also 16 (acknowledging that TLOs frequently fail to become institutionalised because states become sites of resistance to transnational legal norms).
[56] ibid 9.
[57] ibid 7.

TLO theory has provided an all-encompassing framework for the analysis of different TLOs. Further, it has illuminated how the nation state, national law and other 'positive' legal systems are, in fact, constituent parts of transnational socio-legal ordering. However, TLO theory regards transnational legal ordering as a hybrid 'field', or 'quasi-field', of law and norm-making. The socio-legal foundations of the theory imply that, as already explained, transnational legal ordering will encompass any 'formalised legal norms and associated organisations and actors'.[58] Nonetheless, the analysis of a separate body of norms still lies at its heart. In this sense, TLO theory draws on an understanding of transnational law as a 'field', rather than as a 'methodology'. The underlying premise is that the sites of norm-making and actors involved in the relevant processes are changing; however, the specific objects of enquiry are TLOs, understood as developing and hybrid 'quasi-fields' of norm-making. From this perspective, the enquiry into the increasing transnationalisation of legal ordering within discrete regulatory areas may be compared to accounts of law's Europeanisation in specific regulatory sectors, or to investigations of how regulatory challenges are tackled at the level of public international law.

Whilst acknowledging the strengths of TLO theory, this book does not take this perspective. Taking the governance of agricultural biotechnologies into consideration, a circumscribed focus on the norm-making sites which have contributed to the construction of (antagonistic) forms of transnational legal ordering[59] would not be very helpful for the purposes of the present enquiry. Most importantly, it would not help deconstruct the foundations, rationales and specific implications of opposed transnational narratives and regulatory approaches; these would go undetected.

For this reason, the book turns away from an understanding of transnational law as a 'field' or 'quasi-field' and embraces a methodological approach; transnational legal analysis thus becomes a framework to deconstruct transnational narratives influencing globalisation processes. This alternative framing of 'transnational law' and 'transnational legal analysis' will be analysed in greater detail in the fourth section. The next section paves the way for this examination by exploring the theorisation of transnational law as a methodological lens under Transnational Legal Pluralism.

III. Transnational Legal Pluralism: Transnational Law as a Systems Theory Account of Law's Evolution

The foundations of Transnational Legal Pluralism theory ('TLP') rest on systems theory accounts of law's evolution at times of globalisation. Society is the backdrop

[58] See n 38 above.

[59] eg, Codex Alimentarius Commission standards, relevant international treaties and the SPS Agreement. For a more encompassing analysis of these systems against the backdrop of opposed transnational narratives on GE organisms and their uncertain risks, see chs 5 and 6.

and the context against which the analysis of TLP unfolds: drawing on Luhmann's systems theory definition of 'society as the co-existence and complex interaction (co-evolution) of different systems of societal production'[60] and on the notion of 'law as one of society's social systems',[61] TLP endeavours to investigate law as part of a society.[62]

From this perspective, the transformations of law and its 'transnationalisation' reflect the spatial re-ordering and restructuring of societal activities at times of globalisation, underlining the contingency of the association between 'society' and 'politically structured national society', 'law' and 'national law'. The development of the relationship between law and the state is framed within the overall shift 'from the [notion of the] Rule of Law through an Interventionist, Social State through to the Welfare State, before depicting a growing tension between transformations of the state into an Enabling, or Moderating State on the one hand, and new concepts of society (Risk, Knowledge, Information, Network Society) on the other'.[63] The nation state is thus identified as a mere historical and geographic emanation of a political form of societal ordering.[64]

On these grounds, TLP aims to deconstruct the changing nature of law 'in relation and response to the development of a World Society, a society understood as non-territorially confined, functionally differentiated and constituted by the co-evolution of conflicting societal rationalities'.[65] The increasing complexity and functional differentiation of the World Society are then reflected in the transformations of law. In this light, the 'transnational' legal realm does not designate a territorially demarcated level. Rather, it encompasses a de-territorialised and socially structured space of interactions, which the traditional 'national' and 'international' legal categories struggle to embrace: transnational law is both and neither,[66] as it transcends territorial and conceptual divides and cuts across forms of societal organisation.

TLP endeavours to 'bring a legal sociological perspective on law as legal pluralism together with a post-national concept of law',[67] combining a legal pluralist account of law's evolution in the globalisation era with a theorisation of transnational law as a methodology. In the first respect, it testifies that the twentieth-century legal pluralist deconstruction of national legal unity and hierarchy is

[60] P Zumbansen, 'Niklas Luhmann's Law as a Social System' (2006) 15 *Social and Legal Studies* 453, 455.
[61] ibid.
[62] Zumbansen, 'Transnational Legal Pluralism' (n 18) 168.
[63] Zumbansen, 'Law After the Welfare State' (n 32) 777.
[64] Zumbansen, 'Transnational Legal Pluralism' (n 18).
[65] ibid 147.
[66] P Zumbansen, 'Neither Public Nor Private, National Nor International: Transnational Corporate Governance From a Legal Pluralist Perspective' (2011) 38 *Journal of Law and Society* 50.
[67] P Zumbansen, 'Law and Legal Pluralism: Hybridity in Transnational Governance', *CLPE Research Paper no 42/2013*, 13.

now being shifted to the demarcation of national and transnational forms of law.[68] 'Transnational' legal pluralism is then defined as an enquiry 'into the nature of legal regulation of problems, which have long been extending beyond the confines of jurisdiction. Such regulatory challenges both inside and outside of the nation state have always been at the heart of the socio-legal orientation of the legal pluralist enquiry into the myriad contexts, forms and dynamics of norm creation'.[69]

Consequently, and turning to the second point, TLP's methodological approach implies that analysing transnational law as if it were a separate and compartmentalised legal 'field' amounts to an artificial insulation of layers of norm-production which are, instead, structurally intertwined in their dynamics. This would sever 'the forces that drive the differentiation of the legal system on the inside of the nation state from those that drive the production of law outside [of it]'.[70] Indeed, TLP is 'no longer concerned with a quest for a legal field, which could embrace and regulate the [...] border-crossing nature of hybrid regulatory interaction'.[71] Rather than as a self-standing 'field' of law, then, transnational law is understood as a *methodological lens* to deconstruct the transformations of legal institutions against the backdrop of societal differentiation and re-ordering.[72]

At the core of this enquiry lies a renewed focus on the context of norm-making at the national, international and beyond-the-state level. Under TLP, the crisis of legal analysis is understood as a mere amplification of law's fundamental problem:[73] namely, the application of legal rules of competence and authority and the implicit process wherein the problems that law seeks to tackle are dis-embedded from their societal context.[74] Law's relation to its societal context of creation and application, defined as law's 'outside', thus becomes the central object of analysis under TLP. The focus shifts away from the legal system to embrace the institutional context and societal environment in which norms are generated and applied and uncover their social construction. This lies at the core of 'methodological transnationalism'.[75] The building blocks for the deconstruction of law's institutional context, as undertaken through the transnational legal methodology,

[68] Zumbansen, 'Transnational Legal Pluralism' (n 18) 187. See also Zumbansen, 'Manifestations and Arguments: The Everyday Operation of Transnational Legal Pluralism' in Berman, *Oxford Handbook of Global Legal Pluralism* (n 13).

[69] Zumbansen, 'Transnational Legal Pluralism' (n 18) 187–188.

[70] See n 67, 5.

[71] Zumbansen, 'Transnational Legal Pluralism' (n 18) 148.

[72] ibid; n 67.

[73] Zumbansen, 'Transnational Legal Pluralism' (n 18) 166.

[74] P Zumbansen, 'Lochner Dis-Embedded: The Anxieties of Law in a Global Context' (2013) 20 *Indiana Journal of Global Legal Studies* 29.

[75] P Zumbansen, 'The Incurable Constitutional Itch: Transnational Private Regulatory Governance and the Woes of Legitimacy' in M Helfand (ed), *Negotiating State and Non-State Law. The Challenge of Global and Local Legal Pluralism* (CUP, 2015).

consist of the triad of Actors, Norms and Processes (hereafter, 'ANPs').[76] This toolbox, defined as a translation device,[77] offers 'possible translation and interaction categories to bridge different governance experiences and practices in a transnational context'.[78] In this sense, the transnational methodological lens deconstructs law's social embeddedness, structuring a parallel reading of national and transnational governance discourses[79] and reaching beyond the artificially constructed discourse on the Rule of Law.

TLP theory has the great merit of employing transnational law as a lens, casting light on its potential methodological applications. Further, through the application of the ANP toolbox and its analysis of law's 'outside', it has been used to explore the changing distribution of power and authority at times of globalisation and deconstruct the social embeddedness of law, 'relativising' and 'provincialising' the Rule of Law.[80] It has also investigated law's increasing hybridisation, unveiling new processes of regulation and self-regulation, new norms and new patterns of regulatory governance.

As anticipated since the introductory overview of this chapter, the next section puts forward an alternative understanding of transnational legal analysis as a *methodological framework*. This is indebted to TLP's focus on 'methodological transnationalism'; however, it is also clearly distinguished from TLP theory and its application of the ANP toolbox. The sociology of law and norm-making at times of global interdependencies lies at the core of TLP. This involves a close focus on who regulates, how and in whose interests; indeed, this is clearly reflected in the ANP triad. As argued elsewhere, TLP theory thus places a very strong emphasis on socio-legal questions of *agency*.[81] In a different vein, the alternative framing of transnational legal analysis as a methodological framework puts the accent on *structural* legal and regulatory questions, bypassing questions of agency.[82] At its heart lies the deconstruction of transnational narratives against the backdrop of discrete legal regimes and regulatory systems, rather than a socio-legal focus on the relevant ANPs.[83] The next section explores this notion in greater detail, illustrating the methodological framework underpinning the analysis of the book.

[76] Zumbansen, 'Lochner Dis-Embedded' (n 74); 'The Incurable Constitutional Itch' (n 75); P Zumbansen, 'Theorizing as Activity: Transnational Legal Theory in Context', in C McCrudden, U Baxi and A Paliwala (eds), *Law's Ethical, Global and Theoretical Contexts. Essays in Honour of William Twining* (CUP, 2015).

[77] Zumbansen, 'The Incurable Constitutional Itch' (n 75).

[78] P Zumbansen, 'Where the Wild Things Are: Journeys to Transnational Legal Orders, and Back' (2016) 1 *UC Irvine Journal of International, Transnational and Comparative Law* 161, 193.

[79] Zumbansen, 'Lochner Dis-Embedded' (n 74).

[80] Zumbansen, 'Where the Wild Things Are' (n 78).

[81] GC Leonelli, 'The Postmodern Normative Anxiety of Transnational Legal Studies' in P Zumbansen (ed), *The Oxford Handbook of Transnational Law* (OUP, 2021).

[82] ibid. On the significantly broader sociological debate on the notions of 'structure' and 'agency', see inter alia P Bourdieu, *Outline of A Theory of Practice* (CUP, transl. 2013), and A Giddens, *The Constitution of Society* (Polity Press, 1984).

[83] ibid.

IV. Transnational Law, Transnational Legal Narratives and Transnational Legal Analysis as a Methodological Framework

The previous sections have provided an overview of TLO and TLP theory, analysing different approaches to the conceptualisation of transnational law and transnational legal ordering. This reconstruction, together with the broader survey of different strands of law and globalisation and transnational legal studies, shows how contentious the notion of 'transnational law' still is. More than 60 years have elapsed since Jessup's Storrs Lectures;[84] nonetheless, the boundaries, scope and object of transnational legal studies are still highly controversial.

This book puts forward an alternative framing of 'transnational law' and 'transnational legal analysis', drawing on a methodological understanding of these notions. First, it does not adhere to the 'traditional' theorisation of transnational law as a hybrid field of norms and regulatory standards enacted by non-state actors operating beyond the nation state level.[85] Second, it does not analyse 'transnational law' as if it were a self-standing 'field' or 'quasi-field' of law. Finally, while drawing on TLP's methodological understanding of the notion of transnational law, it shifts the focus away from sociological questions of agency and legal context and turns to structural legal issues.[86]

For the purposes of the analysis in this book, 'transnational law' is defined as a *social reality* and a *social product* of increasing economic interdependencies and interconnections. In other words, it is the composite and highly complex *regulatory infrastructure* underpinning globalisation flows; a regulatory infrastructure which all legal categories, starting from the traditional notions of 'national' and 'international' law, fail to capture. From this perspective, 'transnational law' as a social reality is ultimately a *reflection* of law's increasing *extra-territorial impact, pluralisation* and *hybridisation.*

This transnational regulatory infrastructure is shaped and reshaped by the existence, interactions and clashes of different transnational narratives and discourses. Therefore, if we consider the field of GE organisms, the 'transnational governance' of GE organisms and their risks is the regulatory infrastructure underpinning the asymmetric globalisation of agricultural biotechnologies. This results from and reflects the coexistence of a *hegemonic* and a *counter-hegemonic narrative* on whether and how the uncertain risks posed by GE organisms should be regulated. Under the hegemonic narrative, as briefly explained in the introductory chapter, these uncertain risks must be taken in so far as no conclusive

[84] PC Jessup, *Transnational Law. Storrs Lectures in Jurisprudence at Yale Law School* (Yale University Press, 1956); P Zumbansen (ed), *The Many Lives of Transnational Law. Critical Engagement with Jessup's Bold Proposal* (CUP, 2020).

[85] For an analysis, see section I above.

[86] See section III above.

scientific evidence exists on the adverse public health and environmental effects of GE organisms; further, the costs of risk regulation are expected to outweigh the benefits of precaution in economic terms. Under the counter-hegemonic narrative, the risks associated with agricultural biotechnologies should not be taken unless GE varieties are considered safe enough for their risks to be socially acceptable. The two narratives, as already explained, are informed by broader transnational discourses on the regulation of uncertain risks and connected to the dichotomy of evidence-based and socially acceptable risk approaches.

Identifying the narratives and discourses which have shaped the transnational regulatory infrastructure, however, is only the first step. It does not tell us much, if anything at all, about their origins, rationales and implications. In the case of GE organisms, merely describing the coexistence of the two discourses does not enable us to contextualise them or assess their political, socio-economic and distributional impact. This triggers a further set of considerations. Transnational narratives do not exist in a social vacuum, nor do they appear out of thin air. Saying that they originate in the 'transnational' space is not very helpful, either; indeed, the 'transnational' legal space is recursively structured across territorial levels and societal forms of organisation. Rather, and crucially, transnational narratives are socially and politically constructed from within, across and beyond the nation state.

From this perspective, transnational legal analysis becomes a methodological framework to *deconstruct* transnational legal narratives through an examination of the regulatory sites where they originated, developed and became entrenched. If the legal narratives feeding into the transnational regulatory infrastructure originate and unfold *within*, *across* and *beyond* the nation state level, transnational legal analysis must involve an identification and an assessment of *transnationally relevant* regulatory frameworks, legal categories and case law across *national law*,[87] *positive legal systems involving state participation*[88] and *hybrid standard-setting regimes*.[89] In this sense, under 'methodological transnationalism', no segregation or compartmentalisation exists between 'transnational law' and other regulatory layers or sites of norm-making. 'Transnational law' is no more than a social product of globalisation; transnational narratives are embedded within discrete regulatory sites and can only be deconstructed through an analysis of the latter.

Further, a parallel can be drawn between the deconstruction of transnational legal narratives from within, across and beyond the nation state, on the one hand, and the dynamics driving law's transformations and increasing transnationalisation, on the other. The first part of the methodological framework, ie the deconstruction of narratives *from within* the nation state, is defined as 'extra-territoriality'. Pointing to how transnational narratives originate and are

[87] This corresponds to the 'within the nation state' branch of the methodological framework.
[88] This corresponds to the 'across the nation state' branch of the methodological framework.
[89] This corresponds to the 'beyond the nation state' branch of the methodological framework.

constructed within the nation state, and under national regulatory frameworks, means acknowledging that national law and national legal categories have an increasingly *extra-territorial* impact.[90] On these grounds, the analysis of 'extra-territoriality' reflects law's extra-territorial spill-overs at times of globalisation. Not only is the nation state an actor in transnational legal ordering or a relevant site of implementation of transnational norms.[91] National law and its extra-territorial impacts are also an integral part of the transnational picture.[92]

Turning to the second part of the methodological framework, ie the deconstruction of transnational narratives *across* the nation state level, this is no more than a reflection of legal *fragmentation*. This second dimension is defined as 'legal pluralisation'. Finally, and with regard to the third limb of the framework, assessing the construction of transnational narratives in regulatory standard-setting regimes *beyond* the nation state level entails acknowledging law's increasing *hybridisation*. Indeed, 'legal hybridisation' is the final branch.

The book employs this methodological framework to explore the hegemonic and counter-hegemonic narratives on the regulation of the uncertain risks posed by GE organisms. For this purpose, it only takes into consideration the legal systems which have been most relevant to the construction, shaping, reshaping and entrenchment of legal discourses on agricultural biotechnologies. The thread that runs through the analysis of each chapter is the deconstruction of the two narratives, as directly connected to evidence-based and socially acceptable risk approaches. Transnational legal analysis is then used as a framework to interrogate transnationally relevant regulatory frameworks and case law. This paves the way for an enquiry into the rationales, underlying value systems, goals and specific implications of the two diametrically opposed transnational narratives.

As already explained in the introduction, the first section in each substantive chapter briefly addresses four interconnected questions. The first question relates to the (hegemonic or counter-hegemonic) *narrative* which is deconstructed throughout the chapter. The second question focuses on the reasons why the legal system under analysis in the specific chapter is *transnationally relevant*. This second question asks why the legal system is analysed under the methodological framework, what the transnational impact of this system has been and how the hegemonic or counter-hegemonic narratives have been constructed, reinforced or challenged within such legal system. The third and fourth questions ask *what is the added value* of interrogating this transnationally relevant legal system. In other words, what has the examination of this legal system uncovered? How has the analysis helped deconstruct the foundations, characteristics and implications

[90] The same is true of regional/supra-national systems of law, such as EU law. For an analysis of the impact of EU regulatory action beyond the EU boundaries, see inter alia M Cremona and J Scott (eds), *EU Law Beyond EU Borders: The Extra-Territorial Reach of EU Law* (OUP, 2019).

[91] See the analysis in section II above.

[92] The same may apply to regional units and supra-national legal regimes, such as EU law; see the analysis in ch 4.

of the hegemonic or counter-hegemonic narrative on GE organisms? And how has it helped deconstruct transnational discourses on evidence-based and socially acceptable risk approaches?

Finally, deconstructing transnational narratives from within discrete legal orders also sheds light on a plurality of regulatory conflicts. Employing transnational legal analysis as a methodological framework thus leads to the identification and mapping of regulatory conflicts between national or regional legal systems, under international legal regimes, or across societal patterns of self-regulation. These conflicts reflect the coexistence and clash of opposed transnational discourses. The ensuing question is how to solve these conflicts, constructing a normative discourse on the legitimacy of transnational socio-legal ordering in the face of irreconcilable perspectives. The next sections explore this question, in advance of its application to specific legal systems in the following chapters.

Part 2. Normative Analysis: The Limits of Modern Procedural Paradigms in the Post-Modern Transnational Scenario

V. The Normative Vacuum of Transnational Legal Studies

A normative anxiety, or 'constitutional itch',[93] plagues transnational legal studies.[94] Normative questions surrounding the legitimacy of law at times of globalisation remain largely unaddressed; the normative dimension of analysis is either deliberately avoided or overlooked. The causes of this general disregard for normative stakes are twofold. First, by leaving behind the familiar 'inter-governmental' and 'trans-governmental' paradigms of analysis, 'transnational' legal theory faces the difficult task of identifying new normative yardsticks. Second, the socio-legal or sociological turn of transnational legal studies entails that little or no room is afforded to reflections on law's normative legitimacy. Rather, the focus is on the gradual and contested construction of socio-legal ordering.

Starting from the first element, an overview of the shift from 'inter-governmental' to 'trans-governmental' and then 'transnational' dynamics of legalisation casts some light on the normative conundrum of transnational legal studies.[95] The nation state lies at the heart of the 'inter-governmental' paradigm, or 'methodological nationalism'.[96] Public international law is the legal field

[93] Zumbansen, 'The Incurable Constitutional Itch' (n 75).

[94] This section and the following one draw in part on the broader analysis in Leonelli, 'The Postmodern Normative Anxiety' (n 81).

[95] For an account, see Pollack and Shaffer, 'Transatlantic Governance' (n 35).

[96] See Cotterell, 'Transnational Communities' (n 32).

associated with this perspective, while international relations is the corresponding field in political sciences. Inter-governmental processes are driven by nation state officials, who negotiate international agreements and are in a position to bind the state they are representing; their authority is derived from domestic legal rules. Public international law is thus driven by nation states, legitimised by the nation state's participation and consent, and binding on nation states. The dynamics of legal ordering in the inter-governmental landscape are clearly and neatly state-driven; for this reason, the issue of law's normative legitimacy is unproblematic. Law's legitimacy under the inter-governmental paradigm rests on the nation state. 'Input' legitimacy, grounded on representative political democracy in the nation state,[97] is the normative paradigm underpinning the internal operation of the state as well as external inter-governmental processes.

In a different vein, the methodological shift to the 'trans-governmental' lens points to the disaggregation of the nation state and the emergence of competing forms of authority. In the face of economic interconnectedness and globalisation flows, the achievement of transnational regulatory cooperation and coordination became increasingly important in order to eliminate non-tariff barriers to trade and facilitate trade liberalisation. This led to the rise of 'trans-governmental' networks of technical experts, standard-setters and regulators, working towards the harmonisation of regulatory standards. 'Soft' regulatory standard-setting regimes thus complemented 'hard' forms of public international law, based on binding legal rules and agreements. Symmetrically, allegedly neutral and objective technical expertise, or 'output' legitimacy, gradually came to replace 'input' legitimacy as a normative yardstick. Technocracy became the criterion underpinning law's normative legitimisation at the trans-governmental level and the alleged foundation of a 'new, effective and just world order'.[98]

After inter-governmental and trans-governmental legal ordering, 'trans-national' legal theory has endeavoured to take a broader perspective. As briefly explained in the first part of the chapter, transnational legal studies encompass more than mere inter-governmental or trans-governmental dynamics. By analysing different forms of socio-legal ordering against the backdrop of globalisation processes, they reflect a societal 'turn' in the analysis of law. However, this all-encompassing perspective poses a plurality of challenges for the construction of a normative discourse on law's legitimacy.

First, quite intuitively, public law-driven frameworks for the upwards 'rescaling' of nation state categories are unhelpful. As already explained, transnational

[97] For the terminology of 'input' and 'output' legitimacy, see first and foremost FW Scharpf, *Governing Europe. Effective and Democratic?* (OUP, 1999). For a similar perspective and for an analysis of the 'regulatory state' and 'non-majoritarian institutions', see G Majone (ed), *Regulating Europe* (Routledge, 1996).

[98] See AM Slaughter, *A New World Order* (Princeton University Press, 2004).

'law' or transnational 'legal ordering' are neither public nor private; they are processes.[99] Second, at a first glance, any reinstatement of the 'political' and 'democratic' element underpinning 'input' legitimacy appears to be doomed at the transnational level. 'Neither the concept of politics itself nor the institutional or procedural framework in which we would have to re-situate politics today are evident'.[100] Finally, any normative sense appears to be lost in the ever changing, socially constructed 'transnational' sphere. As increasingly complex regulatory conflicts unfold, all legal claims to validity and legitimacy are open to challenge.[101] 'A view from everywhere' thus turns out to be 'a view from nowhere'.[102]

The sociological or socio-legal 'turn' of transnational legal studies is also closely connected to the normative conundrum of transnational analysis. Taking into consideration TLP theory, its systems theory foundations hinder the construction of a normative discourse. The purpose of law as a social system is to stabilise expectations through the production of rules. The legal system instantiates its own autopoiesis by following and responding to the binary coding of 'legal' and 'illegal'.[103] Law, as an autopoietic and self-referential system, is operationally closed but cognitively open to the societal environment; in other words, it transforms societal forms of communication into norm-making processes by recoding societal discourses into the binary legal code.[104] However, it can neither determine the outcome of political or socio-economic conflicts, nor provide any overarching normative yardsticks.

The origins of 'reflexive' law, as a transposition of systems theory to legal analysis, lie in the shift from legal formalism to legal materialisation and the subsequent demise of the latter paradigm, after the crisis of the Welfare State and the turn to 'post-interventionist' law.[105] Reflexive law endeavoured to leave behind all *modern political* debates, overcoming the twentieth century understanding of law as ancillary to the 'state' or the 'markets', the 'public' or the 'private' sphere, 'redistribution' or 'freedom', 'progressive' or 'conservative' politics.[106] In this sense, it fiercely criticised legal materialisation and the underlying notion of substantive, purposive normativity, directly connected to legal interventionism in the Welfare State.[107] *Post-modern* reflexive law has reformulated all legal challenges in *sociological* terms; it has thus endeavoured to structure the procedures of autonomous societal

[99] See section I, and 33 and 34.

[100] Zumbansen, 'The Incurable Constitutional Itch' (n 75) 107–108.

[101] Leonelli, 'The Postmodern Normative Anxiety' (n 81).

[102] Zumbansen, 'The Incurable Constitutional Itch' (n 75).

[103] For an exhaustive overview, see N Luhmann, 'Operational Closure and Structural Coupling: The Differentiation of the Legal System' (1992) 13 *Cardozo Law Review* 1419; N Luhmann, *Law as A Social System* (OUP, 2004); G Teubner, 'The Two Faces of Janus: Rethinking Legal Pluralism' (1992) 13 *Cardozo Law Review*, 1443; G Teubner, *Law as An Autopoietic System* (Blackwell, 1993).

[104] Teubner, 'The Two Faces of Janus: Rethinking Legal Pluralism' (n 103).

[105] See for instance Zumbansen, 'Law After the Welfare State' (n 32).

[106] ibid.

[107] ie, it criticised the reference to and use of substantive values and political goals as criteria to underpin law's normative legitimisation. See also Leonelli, 'The Postmodern Normative Anxiety' (n 81).

systems, underpinning the development of reflection structures and reflexive processes within the autopoietic organisation of these systems.[108] By opening up to society through its own reflexive orientation, reflexive law has aimed to make post-modern law 'receptive to the full spectrum of societal rationalities'.[109] This, however, has come at a cost: normative analysis has been inevitably left behind.

Reflexive law has bypassed any form of normative enquiry into the legitimacy of law; indeed, legal re-materialisation and the re-politicisation of law beyond the nation state are regarded as perils to the expression and development of societal rationalities. In this sense, reflexive law has 'radicalised the functionalists' instrumentalisation of law as a means of social engineering by leaving the driver's seat empty'.[110] Value-neutral reflexive law cannot possibly identify any normative criteria for the solution of ubiquitous regulatory conflicts, nor are the outcomes of any regime collisions relevant.[111] Conflicts between different societal rationalities are merely understood as a force driving the autopoietic evolution and self-reproduction of the legal system.[112] The consequence is the loss of any normative angle of analysis.

The conclusions here are not dissimilar to those in the case of TLO theory and the analysis of TLOs. No clear distinction is drawn between the facticity and validity or legitimacy of law, under TLO theory.[113] Any normative aspect of analysis, in fact, is absorbed into legal realism.[114] Against this background, post-modern transnational legal studies face a post-modern normative dilemma. Despite their successful *deconstruction* of socio-legal ordering at times of globalisation, they have fallen short of *constructing* a discourse on law's normative legitimacy. They have neither identified new normative yardsticks, beyond 'input' and 'output' legitimacy, nor any normative criteria for the solution of ubiquitous regulatory conflicts.

[108] G Teubner, 'Substantive and Reflexive Elements in Modern Law' (1983) 17 *Law and Society Review*, 239, 255 and 275–277 in particular; G Teubner, 'Autopoiesis in Law and Society: A Rejoinder to Blankenburg' (1984) 18 *Law and Society Review* 291.

[109] Zumbansen, 'Law After the Welfare State' (n 32) 790.

[110] ibid.

[111] See, eg, Teubner and Fischer-Lescano, 'Regime-Collisions' (n 23).

[112] See for instance the overview in Zumbansen, 'Niklas Luhmann's Law' (n 60).

[113] On this point, see also the analysis in Leonelli, 'The Postmodern Normative Anxiety' (n 81). For a very brief engagement with normative questions under TLO theory and some suggestions surrounding the role of the nation state in this respect, see Halliday and Shaffer, 'With, Within and Beyond' (n 46) 17–18. These points are not taken into consideration in the analysis of this section, as they refer to the normative value of the nation state and how 'state institutions remain central for [...] advancing normative and instrumental aims' (18). However, this is irrelevant for the purposes of identifying transnational normative yardsticks. On the dichotomy of facticity and validity, see inter alia M Everson and C Joerges, 'Facticity as Validity: The Misplaced Revolutionary Practice of European Law' in E Christodoulidis, R Duke and M Goldoni (eds), *Research Handbook on Critical Legal Theory* (Edward Elgar, 2019); for an earlier account, see C Joerges, 'Constitutionalism and Transnational Governance: Exploring a Magic Triangle' in C Joerges, IJ Sand and G Teubner (eds), *Transnational Governance and Constitutionalism* (Hart Publishing, 2004) 351–353 and 372.

[114] Leonelli, 'The Postmodern Normative Anxiety' (n 81).

VI. Recoupling Law and Politics and Mapping Regulatory Conflicts Through Conflicts Law Theory

Conflicts Law theory offers a way forward to construct a normative enquiry into law's legitimacy at times of globalisation. The intuition underlying this theoretical construct is that politics, alone, may legitimise law and underpin long-lasting societal integration. Under Conflicts Law theory, then, reclaiming politics and democracy in the post-national constellation is the way forward to carve out a normative dimension of analysis and safeguard law's legitimacy.

Three major theoretical influences can be identified in the development of the Conflicts Law framework and the notion of Conflicts Law. The first is Habermas's discourse theory. Both Luhmann and Habermas foresaw the social dis-embedding of the economy from the nation state.[115] As already explained, Luhmann's systems theory response left politics behind through the theorisation of the legal system's autopoietic nature. In a different vein, Habermas postulated the co-originality of the public and private spheres of autonomy and defended the possibility of constructing a normative discourse on law's legitimacy beyond the nation state.[116] Habermas did not overlook the normative aspirations of law, or deny law's ability to solve political and socio-economic conflicts; nor did he relinquish the belief that an increasingly disaggregated post-national society would still be able to restructure democratic political processes, beyond the nation state paradigm of representative democracy.[117] The latter element was understood as the crucial precondition for safeguarding law's normative legitimacy. In the face of law's de-coupling from nation state-based political processes, however, the question became how to reclaim the political and democratic element in the post-national constellation. As the rationality, legitimation and motivation crisis of the Welfare State unfolded,[118] new categories had to be searched for.

In this light, Habermas's theorisation of political democracy in the post-national constellation centres on the notions of inclusion and deliberation.[119] Discursive ethics postulates a rational political deliberative process.[120] The successful construction of the deliberative process and agreement over the results of deliberation are what legitimates the final outcome, ensuring that

[115] Teubner, 'Substantive and Reflexive Elements in Modern Law' (n 108), 259 ff.; C Joerges, 'A New Type of Conflicts Law as the Legal Paradigm of the Post-National Constellation', in C Joerges and J Falke (eds), *Karl Polanyi, Globalisation and the Potential of Law in the Transnational Markets* (Hart Publishing, 2011).

[116] J Habermas, *Between Facts and Norms. Contributions to a Discourse Theory of Law and Democracy* (MIT Press, 1996), 84 ff. in particular.

[117] ibid 118 ff. and 287 ff.; J Habermas, *Legitimation Crisis* (Polity Press, 1988), 95 ff.

[118] Habermas, *Legitimation Crisis* (n 117); J Habermas, 'The New Obscurity: The Crisis of the Welfare State and the Exhaustion of Utopian Energies' in J Habermas (ed), *The New Conservatism. Cultural Criticism and the Historians' Debate* (MIT Press, 1989), 48 ff.

[119] Habermas, *Between Facts and Norms* (n 116) 118 ff., 132 ff. and 287 ff.

[120] ibid.

the relevant decision is regarded as normatively legitimate by all participants in the process.[121] Habermas's extension of the theory of discursive ethics to the rule of law culminated in the concept of legal proceduralisation.[122] From this perspective, procedural political deliberation becomes a bridge between *facts* and *norms*, law's *facticity* and its *validity* and *normative legitimacy*. On these grounds, law's normative legitimacy rests on *procedural* deliberation, and the principles underpinning law's legitimation are of a *procedural* nature.[123] This lies at the heart of the notion of legal proceduralisation, as employed under Conflicts Law theory. The Conflicts Law framework draws on a radically procedural notion of law; in the face of ubiquitous contestation, law's legitimacy is held to rest on law's own procedural ability to mediate between the different perspectives and interests at stake.[124]

Turning to the second influence of Conflicts Law, Polanyi's double movement theory comes into play.[125] Polanyi famously argued that markets are always socially embedded, advocating their analysis as 'social institutions'.[126] On these grounds, he theorised the intertwined nature of market dis-embedding movements and re-embedding counter-movements. Under Conflicts Law theory, legal analysis shall explore how the law of the post-national constellation may procedurally succeed in re-embedding the (increasingly dis-embedded) transnational markets:[127] legal proceduralisation and the deconstruction of the 'economy as a polity'[128] are both constituent parts of the Conflicts Law framework.

Conflicts Law theory has thus pursued a twofold goal: developing a procedural enquiry into law's legitimacy in the post-national constellation, and procedurally attempting to re-embed transnational markets through re-regulation. This analysis has been conducted through the identification, mapping and analysis of regulatory conflict constellations. The Conflicts Law analytical framework 'does not invoke the legacy of traditional private international law or the prevalent understanding

[121] ibid.

[122] ibid 287 ff. and 427 ff. In legal theory, see R Wiethölter, 'Proceduralization of the Category of Law' in C Joerges and D Trubek (eds), *Critical Legal Thought: An American-German Debate* (Nomos, 1985); R Wiethölter, 'Just-ifications of a Law of Society' in O Perez and G Teubner (eds), *Paradoxes and Inconsistencies in the Law* (Hart Publishing, 2006); R Wiethölter, 'Proceduralization of the Category of Law' in C Joerges, D Trubek and P Zumbansen (eds), 'Critical Legal Thought: an American-German Debate. An Introduction at the Occasion of Its Republication in the German Law Journal 25 Years Later' (2011) 12 *German Law Journal* 466.

[123] J Habermas, *Communication and the Evolution of Society* (Beacon Press, 1979) 184.

[124] See, eg, Joerges, 'A New Type of Conflicts Law' (n 115). See also Leonelli, 'The Postmodern Normative Anxiety' (n 81).

[125] K Polanyi, *The Great Transformation. The Political and Economic Origins of Our Time* (Beacon Press, 1944).

[126] C Joerges, 'Constitutionalism in Post-National Constellations: Contrasting Social Regulation in the EU and in the WTO' in C Joerges and E Petersmann (eds), *Constitutionalism, Multilevel Trade Governance and Social Regulation* (Hart Publishing, 2006), 496 ff.

[127] C Joerges and PF Kjaer (eds), *Transnational Standards of Social Protection. Contrasting European and International Governance* (ARENA/RECON, 2008).

[128] See, eg, C Joerges, B Stråth, Bo and P Wagner (eds), *The Economy as Polity: The Political Constitution of Contemporary Capitalism* (UCL Press, 2005); Joerges, 'A New Type of Conflicts Law' (n 115).

of Conflict of Laws'.[129] In other words, its application does not lead to the selection of one system of rules to the detriment of others. The third influence emerges here. Conflicts Law theory draws on Currie's legal realist account of Conflict of Laws.[130] In this sense, it acknowledges that any conflicts between legal provisions unveil conflicts between diverging policies. The choice between competing legal provisions, thus, turns out to be a political choice.[131] It is in this light that the Conflicts Law analytical framework seeks to identify a legal procedural solution agreeable to all parties, rather than a prevailing legal order or specific legal yardsticks.

Three different regulatory conflict constellations are identified under Conflicts Law theory. *Vertical* conflict constellations involve a clash between a national and an international or supra-national legal framework. The solution rests neither on the selection of rules enshrined in one of the two legal orders nor in top-down impositions. Both solutions would lead to the identification of prevailing substantive legal rules. Rather, Conflicts Law theory seeks to identify a procedural meta-norm, putting the accent on the processes which will facilitate the discursive resolution of the regulatory conflict. More specifically, in the context of vertical conflict constellations, Conflicts Law theory aims to identify a meta-norm which will *procedurally* balance *transnational integration* and *legal and value pluralism*.

Clashes between legal systems of the same level, by contrast, are at stake in *horizontal* conflict constellations. In this case, again, the focus is not on the substantive outcome, but rather on the procedures leading to decision-making. The notion of *procedural political deliberation* comes into play here; the successful solution of conflicts rests on law's procedural ability to weigh and balance technical and political considerations, mediating between different social, economic and cultural perspectives. Finally, *diagonal* conflict constellations entail a clash between legal systems and societal regulation or self-regulation. Yet again, the emphasis is on the *procedural* criteria which will enable the legal system to *re-embed* societal standards within the regulatory process.

Against this overall backdrop, and through the application of this framework, Conflicts Law theory pursues three overarching goals. These are, respectively, achieving transnational integration while preserving diversity (vertical conflicts), fostering political deliberation beyond the nation state (horizontal conflicts) and re-embedding societal governance and self-governance (diagonal conflicts). The procedural solution to these conflicts is understood as the way forward to re-politicising and re-democratising the post-national constellation, building a bridge between 'facts' and 'norms' and thus safeguarding law's normative legitimacy. The next section explores the practical applications of Conflicts Law theory at EU law and WTO law level. This, in turn, paves the way for the analysis of the framework's relevance in this book and its relevant implications.

[129] ibid 467.
[130] See inter alia B Currie, *Selected Essays on the Conflict of Laws* (Duke University Press, 1963).
[131] ibid.

VII. Applications and Limits of Conflicts Law Theory

Conflicts Law theory has two great merits. First, it has re-asserted the need for normative analysis in the post-national constellation. The framework has also carved out new normative yardsticks for the assessment of law's validity and legitimacy, beyond 'input' and 'output' legitimacy. Second, it has developed a powerful argument in favour of law's re-politicisation and re-democratisation beyond the nation state. By putting the accent on the restructuring of political processes and the notion of political deliberation, it has argued that balancing transnational integration and diversity, re-democratising the post-national constellation and building a concerted social vision through market re-regulation are the only ways forward to save law's normative legitimacy at times of globalisation. Further, these processes alone may underpin long-lasting and authentic societal integration beyond the nation state. Top-down legal homogenisation, technocracy and market dis-embedding, by contrast, are bound to eventually trigger violent societal counter-movements. The crucial relevance of the 'political' sphere and the need to re-couple law and politics thus shine through Conflicts Law theory.

Yet, the limits of legal proceduralisation surface at the application stage. The deliberative quality of political processes, the procedural accommodation of transnational integration and legal and value pluralism, and procedural market re-regulation do not exist in a vacuum. In other words, legal procedural criteria are not pre-existent; they must be generated throughout deliberative processes. On these grounds, there is no guarantee that they will be successfully identified in every political, socio-economic and cultural context.[132]

An analysis of the dynamics unfolding in the transnational EU legal space, as acknowledged by Conflicts Law theorists, sheds light on the failures of legal proceduralisation. Conflicts Law theory originated in the EU legal regime; indeed, the origins of this theory lie in 'deliberative supra-nationalism' and 'Conflicts Law Constitutionalism' in the EU.[133] These notions were developed in

[132] For an acknowledgment of this point, see Joerges, 'Constitutionalism in Post-National Constellations' (n 126) 495–496. For a similar emphasis, see Leonelli, 'The Postmodern Normative Anxiety' (n 81).

[133] For the original account of deliberative supra-nationalism, see C Joerges and J Neyer, 'Transforming Strategic Interaction Into Deliberative Problem-Solving: European Comitology in the Foodstuff Sector' (1997) 4 *Journal of European Public Policy* 609; C Joerges and J Neyer, 'From Inter-Governmental Bargaining to Deliberative Political Processes: The Constitutionalisation of Comitology' (1997) 3 *European Law Journal* 273; and C Joerges, 'Deliberative Supra-Nationalism: Two Defences' (2002) 8 *European Law Journal* 133. For an overview of the applications of Conflicts Law theory to European Union law, see inter alia Joerges, 'Constitutionalism in Post-National Constellations' (n 126) 491–527; C Joerges 'Sozialstaatlichkeit in Europe? A Conflict of Laws Approach to the Law of the EU and the Proceduralisation of Constitutionalisation' (2009) 10 *German Law Journal* 335; C Joerges, 'Unity in Diversity as Europe's Vocation and Conflicts Law as Europe's Constitutional Form' in C Joerges (ed), *After Globalisation. New Patterns of Conflict and Their Sociological and Legal Re-Constructions* (ARENA/RECON, 2011), 91 ff; and C Joerges and M Everson, 'Reconfiguring the Politics-Law Relationship in The Integration Project Through Conflicts Law Constitutionalism' (2012) 18 *European Law Journal* 644.

contraposition to three competing paradigms for understanding EU legal integration processes: ordo-liberal economic constitutionalism, functionalism and treaty constitutionalism.[134] The EU 'economic constitution' lies at the heart of the first paradigm.[135] Under functionalist models, based on a strong assertion of technocratic rule, the EU 'regulatory state' and 'non-majoritarian institutions' are entrusted with remedying market failures and maximising efficiency through the exercise of (allegedly) neutral and objective regulatory functions. From this perspective, EU institutions derive their legitimacy from their own effectiveness. 'Majoritarian' national institutions, relying on 'input' legitimacy, are in control of social, distributional and politically charged areas of governance.[136] Finally, Treaty Constitutionalism cuts across the political and legal dynamics underlying the integration-through-law agenda; however, it has failed to engage with social aspects and the EU social agenda.[137]

In a different vein, deliberative supra-nationalism and Conflicts Law Constitutionalism postulated that, in order for the EU project to succeed, EU institutions would have to foster deliberative political processes between Member States, safeguard 'unity in diversity' and complement trade liberalisation in the internal market with social re-regulation. These three elements correspond to Conflicts Law theory's overarching goals and normative criteria for the solution of vertical, horizontal and diagonal conflicts.[138] Indeed, the three conflict constellations were first identified and theorised in the analysis of EU law. Comitology was then taken into consideration as a successful way to solve horizontal conflicts,[139] the famous *Cassis de Dijon* case epitomised the successful solution of vertical conflicts,[140] and the New Approach to Harmonisation and Standards exemplified how to solve diagonal conflicts and re-embed societal regulation.[141]

Conflicts Law theory foretold that technocratic models of governance would de-couple law and politics, replacing political legitimation with mere technical agreement. This would erode the legitimacy of both EU institutions and EU law. Equally, it warned that the top-down imposition of 'one-size-fits-all' solutions, EU-wide uniformity and unconstrained trade liberalisation would gradually unravel the EU project. In this light, Conflicts Law theorists throughout the years

[134] See Joerges, 'Unity in Diversity' (n 133), and Everson and Joerges, 'Facticity as Validity' (n 113).

[135] For further details on this model, see J Hien and C Joerges (eds), *Ordoliberalism, Law and the Rule of Economics* (Hart Publishing, 2017); and Everson and Joerges, 'Facticity as Validity' (n 113).

[136] See Majone, *Regulating Europe* (n 97); for further details on the origins of the paradigm, see Everson and Joerges, 'Facticity as Validity' (n 113).

[137] For the origins of the paradigm, see JHH Weiler, 'The Community System: The Dual Character of Supranationalism' (1981) 1 *Yearbook of European Law* 257; JHH Weiler, 'The Transformation of Europe' (1991) 100 *Yale Law Journal* 2403. For further details, see Everson and Joerges, 'Facticity as Validity' (n 113).

[138] See section VI above.

[139] For the original account, see Joerges and Neyer, 'From Inter-Governmental Bargaining' (n 133).

[140] See inter alia Joerges, 'Constitutionalism in Post-National Constellations' (n 126) 501 ff.

[141] See for instance C Joerges, H Schepel and E Vos, 'The Law's Problem with the Involvement of Non-Governmental Actors in Europe's Legislative Processes: The Case of Standardisation Under the New Approach', *EUI Working Paper no 09/1999*.

have pointed to the entrenchment of EU functionalism, wherein the integration-through-law project has become an end in itself.[142] Further, they have lamented the rise of 'executive' or 'authoritarian managerialism'.[143] Finally, they have highlighted the increasing social deficit of the EU, in the face of trade liberalisation within the internal market. This has exacerbated the pre-existing conundrum of the 'EU market without a state'.[144] As Conflicts Law theory predicted, this has triggered powerful societal counter-movements, which have challenged the EU legal project. Yet, this is ultimately a reflection of law's procedural inability to solve complex regulatory, political and socio-economic conflicts. Procedural endeavours to solve EU legal conflicts, re-legitimise EU law and re-democratise transnational integration dynamics at EU level have largely failed. In this sense, the turn to 'facticity as validity'[145] is a testament to the failure of legal proceduralisation to re-legitimise law by means of procedural categories.

Similar considerations apply to the transposition of Conflicts Law theory beyond the EU legal system. Under Conflicts Law, WTO law is also interpreted as a conflict management framework within which Members attempt to solve trade-related legal conflicts arising from the extra-territorial impact of national regulations. In this light, Conflicts Law has also been transposed to WTO law. Indeed, from a Conflicts Law perspective, WTO law is the most important legal regime for the purposes of procedurally constitutionalising the post-national constellation and re-embedding the transnational markets through regulation.[146] Nonetheless, Conflicts Law theory faces similar obstacles to the ones analysed in the EU legal context when applied to the field of WTO law in an attempt to solve vertical conflict constellations.

The analysis of transnational regulatory conflicts in the highly contentious field of agricultural biotechnologies sheds light on the limits of legal proceduralisation, putting them under a magnifying glass. Against this backdrop, the next section provides a more detailed overview of the normative enquiry of the book and draws the relevant conclusions of this chapter.

[142] See in particular C Joerges, 'Three Transformations of Europe and the Search for a Way Out of Its Crisis' in C Joerges and C Glinski (eds), *The European Crisis and the Transformation of Transnational Governance: Authoritarian Managerialism Versus Democratic Governance* (Hart Publishing, 2014) 25–26 and 39; C Joerges, 'Europe's Economic Constitution in Crisis and the Emergence of a New Constitutional Constellation' (2014) 15 *German Law Journal* 985; and C Joerges, 'Integration Through Law and the Crisis of Law in Europe's Emergency' in D Chalmers, M Jachtenfuchs and C Joerges (eds), *The End of the Eurocrats' Dream. Adjusting to European Diversity* (CUP, 2016); Everson and Joerges, 'Facticity as Validity' (n 113).

[143] C Joerges and M Weimer, 'A Crisis of Executive Managerialism in the EU: No Alternative?' in G De Búrca, C Kilpatrick and J Scott (eds) *Critical Legal Perspectives on Global Governance. Liber Amicorum David M. Trubek* (Hart Publishing, 2014); Joerges and Glinski, *The European Crisis* (n 142); Everson and Joerges, 'Facticity as Validity' (n 113).

[144] For the first reference to this notion, see C Joerges, 'The Market Without a State? States Without a Market? Two Essays on the Law of the European Economy', *EUI Working Paper no 02/1996*.

[145] Everson and Joerges, 'Facticity as Validity' (n 113).

[146] See inter alia C Joerges, 'The Idea of a Three-Dimensional Conflicts Law as a Constitutional Form', *ARENA/RECON Online Working Paper no 05/2010*, 28 ff.

VIII. From Procedural Deliberative Paradigms to Substantive Deconstruction and Legal Re-Materialisation?

As explained in the first part of the chapter, the institutional strand of analysis in the book deconstructs the hegemonic and counter-hegemonic transnational narratives on the governance of GE organisms from within the regulatory sites in which they are embedded. This unveils a plurality of regulatory conflicts, which ultimately reflect the coexistence and clash of two opposed transnational discourses. The analysis identifies and maps horizontal, vertical and diagonal conflict constellations.

Chapter three explores the foundations and the implications of the hegemonic transnational narrative by undertaking an analysis of US governance of GE organisms. The enquiry also casts light on the gap between the US evidence-based model and socially acceptable risk approaches. In normative terms, the question becomes whether the clash between the hegemonic and counter-hegemonic narratives, exemplified by the transatlantic stalemate and *horizontal* regulatory conflicts over agricultural biotechnologies, is open to a legal procedural solution. The final section of the chapter develops some preliminary normative considerations by assessing whether procedural political deliberation may yield any successful results in the transatlantic deadlock. It reaches the conclusion that this is far from being the case. The analysis emphasises the unbridgeable normative gap between the US and the EU approaches; these are rooted in different regulatory premises, deploy different categories, reflect different value systems and pursue different goals. In the absence of any shared perspectives, sound scientific approaches to risk assessment and adherence to sound science, indirectly reflecting the pursuit of cost-benefit effective levels of protection, are the only grounds available for establishing cooperation, coordination and regulatory convergence. This, however, would be the form of technocratic agreement advocated by science-centred paradigms. Political deliberation, on the other hand, is bound to fail in the absence of any substantive preconditions for the construction of a normatively legitimate solution.

Chapter four turns to the EU legal regime, showing how the counter-hegemonic narrative and a socially acceptable risk approach are embedded in EU regulatory frameworks on GE organisms. However, at the regulatory implementation stage, EU institutions have largely followed an evidence-based approach. This has triggered EU-wide conflicts; EU Member States and EU civil society have throughout the years repeatedly advanced the argument that the uncertain risks posed by agricultural biotechnologies are not socially acceptable. The normative reflections of the chapter focus on the *horizontal* and *vertical* conflicts which have plagued EU regulatory governance of GE organisms. Albeit to a lesser extent, and on a smaller scale, these replicate the evidence-based versus socially acceptable risk clash inherent to the transatlantic dilemma. No suitable procedural solutions to solve persisting EU-wide conflicts have been identified; nor is the 2015 reform of cultivation of GE organisms an adequate remedy, from the perspective of political deliberative paradigms.

Chapter five illustrates how the WTO Panels and Appellate Body's interpretation and application of the SPS Agreement has considerably reinforced the hegemonic transnational narrative on the governance of uncertain risks. The chapter takes a close look at *EC – Biotech*, enquiring whether the Panel managed to carve out a procedural meta-norm to solve this *vertical* conflict and balance transnational integration with legal and value pluralism. The answer is that this is not the case. Nor have following developments, in the context of later disputes, dispelled doubts as to the balance between the two goals. Finally, chapter six maps a set of hybrid regulatory standards. Besides incorporating hegemonic and counter-hegemonic transnational discourses, some of these standards may also trigger *diagonal* conflicts. However, no procedural way to re-embed them and solve any potential conflicts is in sight.

As explained in the introductory chapter, this is the starting point for a set of broader reflections surrounding the *substantive* preconditions for *procedural* deliberation to succeed. As the unfolding of the analysis shows, these substantive preconditions are entirely lacking in the transnational controversy on GE organisms. This does not mean that procedural political deliberation will never work. Yet, a focus on the relevant substantive aspects is all the more important, given that successful procedural deliberation largely results from pre-existing shared perspectives, values and goals.

Further, this deconstruction of the substantive rationale and the implications of the respective approaches helps distinguish between genuine political deliberation and technocratic agreement, drawing a clearer line between the two notions. As already mentioned in the first chapter, the procedural focus of deliberative paradigms may otherwise end up obscuring the contested issues and values at stake. In this respect, for instance, the contribution of substantive analysis emerges from the evaluation of the attempts at transatlantic coordination and the assessment of the 2015 EU reforms on the cultivation of GE organisms.[147]

The final question to address is how to solve the conundrum of normative legitimacy at the transnational level, when procedural political deliberation fails. What happens if, in the *post-modern* transnational universe, *modern* paradigms struggle to construct normatively legitimate solutions to increasingly complex regulatory conflicts? What if the procedural margins for transnational re-democratisation and transnational re-coupling of law and politics fade? In this regard, the concluding chapter suggests that a turn back to legal materialisation might be the only way to solve the post-modern normative conundrum. A *substantive deconstruction* of the values, goals and issues at stake in transnational conflict constellations should therefore be followed by a *construction* of *substantive*, *purposive* normative arguments.[148]

[147] See chs 3 and 4, respectively.
[148] See also the analysis in Leonelli, 'The Postmodern Normative Anxiety' (n 81).

3

Extra-Territoriality: Foundations and Implications of the Transnational Hegemonic Narrative within US Governance of GE Organisms

This chapter deconstructs transnational narratives on agricultural biotechnologies and their uncertain risks *from within* the nation state; this corresponds to the first limb of transnational legal analysis as a methodological framework. As explained in chapter one, this introductory section addresses a set of preliminary questions relating to the application of the framework.

Starting from the first question, the object of analysis of this chapter is the hegemonic narrative on agricultural biotechnologies; this is connected to and informed by broader discourses on evidence-based risk governance. The second point relates to the reasons why the analysis focuses on US governance of GE organisms, and the transnational relevance of this legal system. The narrative on the economic and social benefits of agricultural biotechnologies, as opposed to the economic and social costs of precautionary regulation in this field, was originally constructed within the US. Not only were GE varieties originally developed in the US. US regulatory frameworks and policy, as the following sections illustrate, also reflect a clear pro-biotechnology stance. A rich literature has analysed the US sound scientific approach to the regulation of GE organisms, examining attempts to export this regulatory model and recourse by the US to forum-shopping techniques.[1]

All in all, the US legal system is the regulatory site where the hegemonic narrative on GE organisms and their uncertain risks originated. From this perspective, the US approach to the governance of GE organisms has had a transnational impact. US discourses on agricultural biotechnologies and regulating uncertain risks have become part of broader transnational narratives; these narratives

[1] See M Pollack and G Shaffer, *When Cooperation Fails. The International Law and Politics of Genetically Modified Foods* (OUP, 2009) 116, and D Vogel, *The Politics of Precaution. Regulating Health, Safety and Environmental Risks in Europe and the United States* (Princeton University Press, 2012). See also the analysis of *EC – Biotech* in ch 5, section VII.

have then been reshaped, reinforced or challenged across different legal systems. Notions and regulatory categories such as sound science or economic cost-benefit analysis, developed and employed in US risk governance, have gained increasing transnational relevance, well beyond the boundaries of the US jurisdiction. This reflects the logics of extra-territoriality. In an increasingly interconnected world, national or regional legal frameworks, governance approaches and regulatory categories will often have extra-territorial – transnational – application and impact; transnational discourses may then be informed by national or regional law.

What is, however, the added value of examining US regulation of agricultural biotechnologies, with a view to uncovering the foundations and implications of the hegemonic narrative? How does the analysis cast light on the rationale, overarching goals and impact of the hegemonic narrative? And how does it help deconstruct transnational discourses on evidence-based risk governance, more generally? As the following sections show, the analysis of US governance of GE organisms provides an opportunity to explore the far-reaching implications of evidence-based approaches; these dynamics are examined in practice, as unfolding in a specific regulatory field and legal system. In this sense, taking a close look at the US evidence-based system helps uncover the foundations and impacts of the dominant discourse on agricultural biotechnologies from within the regulatory site where this discourse originally developed.

The first section of the chapter provides a broad overview of US regulation of agricultural biotechnologies. This is followed by a more detailed analysis of the relevant regulatory arrangements. The fifth and the sixth sections take a step back from the technicalities of the US system and focus on sound science approaches to risk assessment, adherence to sound science and recourse to economic cost-benefit analysis. These sections show how US governance of GE organisms is informed by these notions; they look back to the regulatory arrangements analysed in the preceding sections, but evaluate them under a different light. On these grounds, the fifth and the sixth sections *use* the analysis of US governance of GE organisms to explore the hegemonic narrative, identifying and highlighting the characteristics, advantages and disadvantages of evidence-based approaches.

The US regulatory approach illuminates the connections between sound science approaches to risk assessment, adherence to sound science and cost-benefit analysis, showing that the assumption that sound science must be relied on is informed by considerations surrounding the economic cost-benefit effectiveness of risk regulation. The allocation of authority to US technical-scientific agencies, the potential impact of deregulation on the grounds of sound science and cost-benefit analysis, the dilemmas of coexistence and the consequences for US conventional or organic farming are then *used* to shed light on the hegemonic narrative on agricultural biotechnologies and transnational discourses on evidence-based risk regulation. The seventh section summarises the relevant findings, identifying the substantive implications of the narrative and the underlying vision of society's common good. Finally, the eighth section sketches out some preliminary considerations pertaining to the normative strand of enquiry. It thus briefly discusses the prospects for a solution to the long-standing transatlantic – horizontal – conflict over agricultural biotechnologies.

I. From the Origins to the 2019 Executive Order: The Product-Based Model and Further Regulatory Streamlining

Traditional selective breeding and hybridisation through the controlled pollination of plants have been used for centuries to select desirable traits in crops and to improve them.[2] By the 1950s, the application of mutagenesis technology to plant breeding had developed commercial value; by the 1970s, it had been widely accepted by plant breeders.[3] In those years Watson and Crick's discovery of the double helix structure of DNA, together with subsequent experiments connecting different pieces of DNA, heralded the advent of recombinant DNA (rDNA) mediated gene transfer, otherwise known as genetic modification.[4]

Important advances in the technology of rDNA, as applied to the genetic modification of seeds, took place throughout the 1970s. Yet, the scientific community highlighted and called attention to the uncertain public health and environmental risks associated with genetic modification techniques. A call for a public moratorium on rDNA research was then issued in 1974. This was followed by discussions at a number of conferences, notably the 1975 Asilomar Conference, with a view to addressing potential risks and identifying adequate precautions.[5]

Since these early times, US regulators and market stakeholders noted the economic advantages and opportunities associated with the further development of this technology. A set of specific rules applying to rDNA research was developed from 1976 onwards by the US National Institutes of Health's (NIH) Recombinant DNA Advisory Committee.[6] A few years later, in 1983, the US National Academy of Sciences published a report on the risk assessment of rDNA technology, and the NIH authorised the first environmental release of a GE organism.[7] In 1984, President Reagan's administration established an ad hoc committee within the

[2] For an overview of the history and development of agricultural biotechnologies, see CA Wozniak et al, 'An Introduction to Agricultural Biotechnology Regulation in the US' in CA Wozniak and A McHughen (eds), *Regulation of Agricultural Biotechnology: The United States and Canada* (Springer, 2012) 3 ff.

[3] See A McHughen and SJ Smith, 'Regulation of Genetically Modified Crops in USA and Canada: American Overview', in Wozniak and McHughen (eds), *Regulation of Agricultural Biotechnology* (n 2) 37–38.

[4] ibid 35 ff.

[5] ibid 37–38. See also the account in Vogel, *The Politics of Precaution* (n 1) 43 ff.

[6] McHughen and Smith, 'Regulation of Genetically Modified Crops' (n 3) 40.

[7] ibid.

Office of Science and Technology Policy ('OSTP'); this was entrusted with the task of outlining a framework for the governance of GE organisms. The aim was to put in place regulations which would ensure science-based assessments of GE products, without stifling any technological innovations and undermining the competitiveness of the US industry.[8] This resulted in the adoption of the 1986 OSTP's Coordinated Framework for the Regulation of Biotechnology.[9] While it was further updated in 1992 and 2017,[10] the Framework is still the cornerstone of the US regulatory apparatus for the governance of GE products.

The Framework sets a regulatory presumption that bioengineering techniques, understood as *processes*, do *not* pose any *inherent risks*. In so far as genetic engineering processes are held not to pose inherent risks, a general presumption applies that GE products, as a *class*, are *substantially equivalent* to their *conventional counterparts*. This point has been consistently reaffirmed in both the 1992 and 2017 updates to the original 1986 Framework.[11] Drawing on this regulatory presumption, the US regime follows a *product-based* model for the governance of the uncertain risks posed by GE organisms, rather than a *process-based* model. This adheres and conforms to the findings of scientific reports from the National Research Council of the US National Academy of Sciences.[12] GE products, as a category, are considered substantially equivalent to their non-genetically engineered counterparts in that 'the same parameters of biochemistry, genetics and physiology apply to all organisms regardless of origin'.[13] As a result, they are also considered to be as safe for public health and the environment as their conventional counterparts to the extent that the process of genetic engineering has not altered specific features of the relevant products. The 2017 Updated Framework explicitly states that 'it is the characteristics of the biotechnology product, the environment into which it will be introduced and the applications of the product that determine its risk (or lack thereof)'.[14] On these grounds, the 'exercise of

[8] Wozniak et al, 'An Introduction' (n 2).

[9] Executive Office of the US President, Office of Science and Technology Policy, *Coordinated Framework for the Regulation of Biotechnology*, 26 June 1986.

[10] See in particular Executive Office of the US President, Office of Science and Technology Policy, *Update to the Coordinated Framework for the Regulation of Biotechnology*, 4 January 2017.

[11] ibid 4. At the current stage, different considerations apply to the regulation of GE animals in the US. This aspect is not taken into consideration in this chapter, as it would go beyond the scope of the present analysis. See also n 12 below.

[12] For the original reports, see US National Research Council, *Introduction of Recombinant DNA-Engineered Organisms into the Environment: Key Issues* (National Academies Press, 1987); US National Research Council, *Field Testing Genetically Modified Organisms: Framework for Decisions* (National Academies Press, 1989); more recently, see US National Academies of Sciences, Engineering and Medicine, *Genetically Engineered Crops: Experiences and Prospects* (National Academies Press, 2016). For further information, see McHughen and Smith, 'Regulation of Genetically Modified Crops' (n 3) 41, citing further reports from 2000, 2002, 2004 and 2010. Again, it is worth stressing that at the current stage different considerations apply to the regulation of GE animals in the US; in this case, a *process-based* model has (so far) been followed.

[13] Wozniak et al, 'An Introduction' (n 2) 5.

[14] *Update to the Coordinated Framework for the Regulation of Biotechnology*, n 10, at 6.

agency oversight within the scope afforded by statutes should be commensurate with the risk posed by the introduction of the biotechnology product and should not turn on the fact that it was created or has been altered by a particular process or technique'.[15]

In other words, any potential risks are associated with specific GE products, their genetic traits and their characteristics; broader consideration of uncertainties regarding the effects of the use of genetic engineering processes are not taken into account. The first consequence of this is that, at a general level, a *comparative assessment* of GE varieties vis-à-vis their non-GE counterparts lies at the heart of the system. A risk assessment and ad hoc procedures will only apply where the process of genetic engineering has altered specific features of the relevant products.[16] Under process-based models, by contrast, a more thorough *risk assessment* takes place for each and every GE variety. Further, as a direct result of the product-based model, different GE products will be more or less stringently regulated and their uncertain risks more or less thoroughly assessed in light of their specific features. It is worth noting that, back in 1983, the Environmental Protection Agency advocated a process-based approach on precautionary grounds. Had this recommendation been implemented, the Agency would have had exclusive authority for the regulation of GE organisms; further, it would have been in charge of assessing the uncertain health and environmental risks posed by each GE variety.[17] By contrast, the adoption of the product-based model paved the way for a different regulatory architecture, involving a different distribution of regulatory authority between federal agencies.

The adoption of a product-based model and the presumption of substantial equivalence have had the effect of leaving GE products under the regulatory umbrella of pre-existing, general statutes applying to conventional products.[18] As summarised, genetic modification was considered neither sufficiently risky nor sufficiently novel to warrant the enactment of an ad hoc regulatory framework.[19] Ultimately, GE organisms are regulated on the grounds of their end use. This has resulted in shared, at times overlapping, and yet variable assessments and

[15] ibid, at 8.

[16] See below, the analysis in sections II, III and IV. A *risk* assessment will only take place where GE organisms have specific characteristics, ie where they cannot be considered substantially equivalent to their conventional counterparts; for instance, in the case of GE crops which could pose plant pest risks (see section II) or in the case of plant-incorporated protectants (see section III). GE crops which do not have characteristics associated with potential plant pest risks are non-regulated (see section II.A, for products going through the 'Am I Regulated?' scheme; and section II.B, for further deregulation after the 2020 reform). Equally, GE foods which have gone through a comparative assessment and which are held to be substantially equivalent to their conventional counterparts will not be the object of a risk assessment (see section IV).

[17] See Pollack and Shaffer, *When Cooperation Fails* (n 1) 45.

[18] The general statutory framework applies; however, new federal regulations have been enacted by the relevant regulatory agencies. See sections II, III and IV.

[19] Pollack and Shaffer, *When Cooperation Fails* (n 1) 67.

oversight of GE products[20] by three federal bodies: the Animal and Plant Health Inspection Service ('APHIS') within the United States Department of Agriculture ('USDA'), the Environmental Protection Agency ('EPA') and the Food and Drugs Administration ('FDA'). At a general level, the APHIS is in charge of the regulation of GE products as long as they may pose plant pest risks. The EPA's regulatory remit extends to plant-incorporated protectants and herbicide tolerant GE organisms, as the EPA is in charge of regulating pesticides and maximum residue levels of pesticides. The FDA regulates GE food and feed varieties.

In 1986, the authors of the Coordinated Framework had already envisaged potential coordination issues. Indeed, the Framework established a Biotechnology Science Coordinating Committee to facilitate coordination and communication.[21] Years later, the same issues of regulatory coordination, overlaps, information exchange and asynchronous authorisations re-surfaced. This resulted in the 2017 enactment of the Updated Framework, which sought to address these issues.[22] Particular attention was paid to food and feed varieties that have been engineered to be insect or disease-resistant, or resistant to one (or more) herbicides. These used to fall under the regulatory remit of each of the three agencies.[23]

The consequence of the adoption of a product-based model, combined with a flexible, if not streamlined, regulatory approach at agency level, has been a rather quick entrenchment of the commercial cultivation of GE varieties in the US. This has gone hand in hand with an increasing presence of GE food and feed, or food components, on the US market. The first commercially grown GE crop was the FLAVR SAVR delayed-ripening tomato variety, back in 1994.[24] By 2011, 94 per cent of soybeans, 90 per cent of cotton, 88 per cent of corn and more than 50 per cent of canola varieties were GE.[25] Since then, many more crops have been developed and grown; research on GE varieties now covers cereals, rice, fruits, vegetables and oilseeds. Further, as mentioned in the introductory chapter, a new generation of techniques have been increasingly deployed in the past few years. The latest USDA data still show a steady increase in adoption rates for GE crops.[26]

Against this backdrop, a path dependent approach to the governance of agricultural biotechnologies appears to have become entrenched in the US. This does not mean that arguments on the safety and sustainability of GE products, their

[20] See below, sections II, III and IV; some products are under the (overlapping) regulatory remit of more than one agency, other products may be the object of a streamlined procedure only. All in all, it is fair to suggest that no agency can ever have a complete and exhaustive overview of a product and its characteristics.

[21] Wozniak et al, 'An Introduction' (n 2) 4.

[22] See n 10.

[23] ibid; see part G, 39 ff., for specific case studies. However, see section II.B for the 2020 APHIS's reform.

[24] McHughen and Smith, 'Regulation of Genetically Modified' (n 3) 37.

[25] Wozniak et al, 'An Introduction' (n 2) 2.

[26] See the USDA's Economic Research Service Database at www.ers.usda.gov/ and the ISAAA database at www.isaaa.org/.

commercial and market opportunities or their benefits for farmers and consumers are unanimously accepted. Quite to the contrary, these points are still highly controversial in public debates. Environmentalists and consumer advocates have been amongst the fiercest denigrators of GE organisms. Recent data shows that, in terms of consumer preferences, demand for products certified as non-GE or organic has increased by over 400 per cent in the past years.[27] Also, the stakes are particularly high for organic farmers, whose produce is threatened by large-scale cultivation of GE varieties; this constituency has often voiced its concerns in the public debate.[28]

Rather, and in a different vein, regulatory path dependency in the US governance of agricultural biotechnologies refers to how unlikely any shift towards a more stringent approach to genetic engineering is. The 1986 Coordinated Framework and the approach of regulatory agencies have paved the way for the large-scale commercial cultivation of GE varieties, which in turn has resulted in the ubiquitous adventitious presence of GE components in seeds and crops and of GE ingredients in foods. The views and the interests of specific constituencies, notably biotech corporations, biotech companies and GE crop growers, have been protected and have prevailed over those of different constituencies. This has crystallised specific agricultural and market practices and policy orientations, as well as power dynamics.

Further, this trend has been considerably reinforced by the 2019 Executive Order on Modernizing the Regulatory Framework for Agricultural Biotechnology Products.[29] The Order advocates a science-based, timely, efficient and transparent approach to the governance of GE organisms. It maintains that recent advances in biotechnologies have 'the potential to revolutionise agriculture and thereby enhance rural prosperity and improve the quality of American lives' and that biotechnology 'can help the Nation meet its food production needs, raise the productivity of the American farmer, improve crop and animal characteristics, increase the nutritional value of crop and animal products and enhance food safety'.[30]

To this end, it mandates the Federal Government to adopt regulatory approaches which are proportionate responses to the risks posed by GE varieties, to avoid arbitrary and unjustifiable distinctions across like products developed through

[27] Advisory Committee on Biotechnology and the 21st Century Agriculture, *A Framework for Local Coexistence Discussions. A Report of the Advisory Committee on Biotechnology and the 21st Century Agriculture (AC21) to the Secretary of Agriculture*, December 8, 2016, 56.

[28] ibid. See section VI.C on the adventitious presence of GE components in seeds, crops and foods and the issue of coexistence.

[29] 84 FR 27899-27902, US President, Executive Order 13874 of 11 June 2019, *Modernizing the Regulatory Framework for Agricultural Biotechnology Products*. This followed the enactment of a 2016 national strategy for modernising regulation of GE organisms; see Executive Office of the US President, Emerging Technologies Interagency Policy Coordination Committee's Biotechnology Working Group, *National Strategy for Modernizing the Regulatory System for Biotechnology Products*, September 2016.

[30] 2019 Executive Order, section 1.

different technologies and to promote future innovations and competitiveness.[31] More specifically, the Order maintains that the Federal Government shall base all regulatory decisions on scientific and technical evidence, taking into account economic factors, and making regulatory determinations based on risks associated with the product and its intended use. On these grounds, it directs the USDA, the EPA and the FDA to 'identify relevant regulations and guidance documents within their respective jurisdiction that can be streamlined', and to 'use existing statutory authority, as appropriate, to exempt low-risk products of agricultural biotechnology from undue regulation'.[32] In a similar vein, section 6 of the Order requests all Agencies to conduct a review of their regulations and guidance that may apply to agricultural biotechnologies designed to have significant benefits, taking steps to update them and remove undue barriers.

Against the background of this introductory analysis, the next sections provide a detailed account of the regulatory remit and exercise of regulatory authority by the APHIS, the EPA and the FDA. The aim is to assess the operation and consequences of the product-based model in practice. This overview paves the way for an analysis of how an evidence-based approach is inherent to the US governance of agricultural biotechnologies. The enquiry will then focus on the relevant implications.

II. The Role of the APHIS: GE Organisms and Plant Pest Risks

A. Regulation and Regulatory Implementation before the 2020 Reform

Within the USDA, the APHIS is in charge of protecting agriculture from pests and diseases.[33] Its regulatory role in the field of GE products is laid out in title 7 (Agriculture), part 340 of the Code of Federal Regulations ('CFR'). These rules were originally enacted in 1987, under the authority of the 1912 Plant Quarantine Act and 1957 Federal Plant Pest Act: these legislative acts were later subsumed into the 2000 Plant Protection Act ('PPA').[34] Since 1987, the regulations in the CFR were amended seven times.[35] As explained in the next sub-section, major revisions

[31] ibid, section 3.

[32] ibid, section 4.

[33] See the USDA's website for further information on the APHIS's role and remit: www.usda/gov/.

[34] 7 USC, ss 7701 ff.

[35] In 1988, 1990, 1993, 1994, 1997, 2005 and 2020; the amendments included, inter al, exemptions from the requirement for permits and the creation of the notification and petition procedures. See 84 FR 26514-26541, Docket No APHIS-2018-0034, 6 June 2019, Proposed Rules, *Movement of Certain Genetically Engineered Organisms* (hereafter, '2019 APHIS Proposal') 26514.

of part 340 were adopted in May 2020. This sub-section provides a broader overview by describing the regulatory arrangements in place prior to the 2020 reform.

At a general level, in accordance with the regulatory remit of the USDA, the APHIS regulates GE products which are known or suspected to be *plant pests* or which could pose *plant pest risks*. These products are defined as 'regulated articles'. The old version of section 340.1 CFR provided a twofold definition of 'regulated articles'. First, any organism produced or altered through genetic engineering was considered a regulated article if its donor organism, recipient organism, or vector or vector agent belonged to any genera or taxa designated in section 340.2 and met the definition of a plant pest, or if it was 'an unclassified organism and/or an organism whose classification is unknown, or any product which contains such an organism'. A donor organism is the organism from which genetic material is obtained and transferred; the recipient organism is the organism receiving the genetic material, while vectors or vector agents are the organisms or objects used in the transfer.[36]

The old version of section 340.2 included a list of taxa and groups of organisms which were deemed to be or to contain plant pests. Note 4 in section 340.2 added that 'any organism belonging to any taxa contained within any listed genera or taxa is only considered to be a plant pest if the organism can directly or indirectly injure, or cause disease or damage in any plants or parts thereof, or any processed, manufactured or other products of plants'. Symmetrically, the old version of the regulations provided that 'a particular unlisted species within a listed genus would be deemed a plant pest for purposes of section 340.2, if the scientific literature refers to the organism as a cause of direct or indirect injury, disease or damage to any plants, plant parts or products of plants'.[37]

Second, 'any other organism or product altered or produced through genetic engineering which the Administrator determine[s to be] a plant pest or ha[s] reason to believe is a plant pest'[38] used to fall in the category of 'regulated articles'. The second part of the definition did not refer to any plant pest components of the GE product; rather, it focused on the GE product's ability to act as a plant pest, causing direct or indirect injury, disease or damage to other plants. Since 2011, developers have been given the chance to make enquiries about the status of GE organisms, under the 'Am I Regulated?' scheme. The APHIS conducts a preliminary review of GE varieties with a view to determining whether they should be considered regulated articles, omitting a more comprehensive analysis of potential changes in plant pest impacts, impacts on non-target organisms and propensity for increased weediness.[39] The outcome is a mere finding of regulated or non-regulated status.

[36] 7 CFR 340.1 (old version).
[37] 7 CFR 340.2, note 4 (old version).
[38] 7 CFR 340.1 (old version).
[39] See 2019 APHIS Proposal, (n 35) 26520.

Pursuant to the old version of section 340.0, no person could introduce any regulated article unless the APHIS had either been notified of the introduction in accordance with section 340.3 or had issued an ad hoc permit under section 340.4.[40] Notifications and permits were both defined as 'authorisations'. The 'introduction' of regulated articles covers movements into or through the US, inter-state movements, environmental releases and attempts thereat.[41] As of July 2018, the APHIS had issued more than 19,500 authorisations for environmental release, 14,000 authorisations for importation and around 12,000 for inter-state movement.[42]

The notification process, introduced in 1993 and applied in the vast majority of cases, provided a fast-track and streamlined procedure for the environmental release of genetically engineered products. Under the old version of section 340.3, regulated articles could be the object of a notification as long as they met six cumulative requirements.[43] Notifications had to include information about the phenotype, genetic loci, encoded proteins or functions and donor organisms for all genes and the method of transformation. They also had to provide the names and location of the original and destination facilities, the location of the field site for environmental release, the size of the introduction and the date and duration of environmental release.[44] The relevant deadlines were at least 10 days prior to the day of introduction, in case of inter-state movement, and at least 30 days in case of importation or environmental release.[45]

Further, unlike under the permit procedure, a set of broad and generic performance-based standards used to apply to any introductions under the notification procedure. These encompassed general requirements to prevent regulated articles from inadvertently mixing with non-regulated plant materials. Field test reports had to be submitted to the APHIS within six months after termination of the field tests. These had to include all resulting data, methods of observation and an analysis of any detrimental effects on plants, non-target organisms or the environment. It is worth noting that in 2005 the USDA's Office of Inspector General ('OIG') reached the conclusion that, in order to effectively minimise risks of inadvertent release during field trials under the notification procedure, the APHIS should have not relied on general performance-based standards, but should have requested specific written protocols before approving the field trial. In 2015, the same body noted that the APHIS had not yet implemented these recommendations.[46]

[40] 7 CFR 340.0 (old version). For some exemptions, see 7 CFR 340.2(b) (old version).
[41] 7 CFR 340.1 (old version).
[42] 2019 APHIS Proposal (n 35) 26515. The APHIS has denied slightly more than 1,600 requests for authorisation, the majority for lack of sufficient information; these requests have often been re-submitted at a later stage. Specific data is available on the APHIS's website, at www.aphis.usda.gov/aphis/ourfocus/biotechnology/permits-notifications-petitions/sa_permits/status-update/release-permits.
[43] 7 CFR 340.3(b) (old version).
[44] 7 CFR 340.3(d)(2) (old version).
[45] 7 CFR 340.3(d)(3) (old version).
[46] In this respect, see the information in 2019 APHIS Proposal (n 35) 26515.

Section 340.4 regulated the permit procedure. Under the old version of section 340.1, a 'permit' was defined as a 'written permit issued by the administrator for the introduction of a regulated article under conditions determined by the administrator, not to present a risk of plant pest introduction'. Any regulated articles which could not be the object of the notification procedure fell in the 'residual' category of permit applications. In this case, the applicant had to forward all relevant information at least 120 days prior to environmental release. Where the APHIS determined that the application was complete, a 120-day deadline for the APHIS to review the dossier applied.[47]

The information required under the permit procedure for the purposes of characterising the GE organism and scheduling field trials was more detailed and specific than the data requested for notification purposes.[48] After its review of the application and data, the APHIS made a decision as to the grant or denial of the permit. Where a permit was granted, a set of conditions had to be complied with.[49] Most importantly, the regulated article had to be maintained and disposed of in such a manner as to prevent the dissemination and establishment of plant pests, it had to be kept separate from other organisms and it could only be maintained in the areas and premises specified in the permit. Unlike under the notification procedure, the APHIS could attach further conditions to the permit. The agency had to be notified within 24 hours or as soon as possible in case of accidental or unauthorised release, or within five working days if the regulated article was found to have characteristics substantially different from those listed in the application.

Like under the notification procedure, a field test report had to be submitted to the APHIS within six months after the termination of the field test. This included any effects on plants, non-target organisms and the environment, and the methods of observation.[50] If a permit was denied or withdrawn, the applicant had a right to appeal the decision within 10 days.[51] Permits were usually denied in cases where technical and scientific information was missing from the applicant's dossier, or procedural requirements had not been complied with.[52]

Finally, the old version of section 340.6 provided for a petition process for the determination of non-regulated status.[53] Any person could submit a petition to seek a determination that a regulated article should no longer be regulated under part 340; this process applied to both categories of regulated articles, irrespective of whether they were the subject of the notification or permit procedure.

[47] 7 CFR 340.4(b), and (c) for limited permits (old version).
[48] 7 CFR 340.4(b) (old version).
[49] 7 CFR 340.4(f)(1) to (11) (old version).
[50] 7 CFR 340.4(f)(9) (old version).
[51] 7 CFR 340.4(g) (old version).
[52] As of March 2020, the APHIS had only denied 6 permits for inter-state movement and 16 permits for release. See the APHIS's database at www.aphis.usda.gov/aphis/ourfocus/biotechnology/permits-notifications-petitions/sa_permits/status-update/release-permits.
[53] 7 CFR 340.6 (old version). This was introduced in 1993.

The petitioner could supplement, amend, withdraw or re-submit a petition without prior approval from the APHIS.

Pursuant to section 340.6, a petitioner had to explain the factual grounds as to why the organism should no longer be regulated, including the results of field trials and data from other tests.[54] Overall, a petitioner for deregulation would aim to substantiate the argument that the GE variety was unlikely to pose greater plant pest risks than the unmodified organism from which it was derived. On these grounds, the petitioner was invited to submit data and information on the specific plant pest risks posed by the GE variety. These included any:

> plant pest characteristics, disease and pest susceptibilities, expression of the gene product, new enzymes or changes to plant metabolism, weediness of the regulated article, impact on the weediness of any other plant with which it can interbreed, agricultural or cultivation practices, effects [...] on non-target organisms, indirect plant pest effects on other agricultural products, transfer of genetic information to organisms with which it cannot interbreed, and any other information which [the APHIS] believes to be relevant to a determination.[55]

Based on all available information, the APHIS would then respond to the petitioner within 180 days and make a decision as to the approval or denial of the petition.[56] The vast majority of petitions were accepted by the APHIS; as of March 2020, the APHIS had deregulated 128 varieties. Cases of denial or withdrawal of petitions were limited to dossiers lacking important information.[57] Where a petition was approved, the formerly regulated variety was deemed not to pose any greater plant pest risks than its conventional counterpart and, as such, was no longer within the regulatory remit of the APHIS. Thus, the movement, importation, environmental release and cultivation of the deregulated GE variety was no longer subject to any regulatory conditions, and the APHIS no longer had any monitoring or oversight role.[58] The same occurred in the case of a decision to extend non-regulated status.[59] An extension of non-regulated status could be granted by the APHIS due to autonomous analysis or on request. In either case, an article was deemed not to pose potential plant pest risks on the grounds of its similarity (in terms of genetic construct) to an antecedent (deregulated) article.

To conclude, it is necessary to briefly mention the APHIS's obligations under the National Environmental Protection Act ('NEPA').[60] Pursuant to the act, federal

[54] 7 CFR 340.6(c)(1) to (5) (old version).

[55] 7 CFR 340.6(c)(4) (old version).

[56] 7 CFR 340.6(d) and (f) (old version).

[57] As of March 2020, the APHIS had approved 128 petitions; 4 were pending, 32 had been withdrawn and 1 had been found to be incomplete. For further information, see www.aphis.usda.gov/aphis/ourfocus/biotechnology/permits-notifications-petitions/petitions/petition-status.

[58] It is worth clarifying that the APHIS did not prohibit the commercialisation of GE organisms that had not been granted a determination of non-regulated status. However, before the 2020 reform, developers in practice only marketed varieties after a petition and after obtaining non-regulated status.

[59] 7 CFR 340.6(e) (old version).

[60] 42 USC, ss 4321 ff. On environmental impact statement, see in particular s 4332(2)(C). For further information, see www.aphis.usda.gov/aphis/ourfocus/biotechnology/SA_Environmental_Documents.

agencies are under an obligation to conduct an Environmental Assessment ('EA') whenever they take a decision which might have an environmental impact, and they cannot categorically exclude adverse effects. Where the EA leads to the conclusion that the activity may have a significant impact, a more detailed Environmental Impact Statement ('EIS') is required. Where this is not the case, the agency will adopt a Finding of No Significant Impact ('FONSI'). In both cases, ie under both the EA and EIS procedures, the public has an opportunity to provide comments prior to the agency's final decision.

Any in-depth analysis of the APHIS's compliance with its obligations under the NEPA would go beyond the circumscribed scope of this chapter; nonetheless, it is worth noting that the APHIS has traditionally been reluctant to conduct EISs. More specifically, the APHIS has in the past lost lawsuits relating to its decisions to authorise field trials[61] as well as lawsuits on the decision to deregulate GE crops in response to a petition.[62] These lawsuits centred on compliance with the NEPA.[63]

B. The 2020 Reform

In June 2019, in line with the 2016 national strategy for modernising regulation of GE organisms,[64] the APHIS published a proposal for revisions to its regulations on the movement of GE organisms, as enshrined in part 340 of the Code of Federal Regulations.[65] The proposal aimed to respond to advances in genetic engineering in light of the APHIS's regulatory experience, 'reducing [the] regulatory burden for developers of organisms that are unlikely to pose plant pest risks' and '[...] facilitating the development of new and novel [GE] organisms'.[66]

This document sets out the rationale and scope of the proposal. The 2019 proposal incorporates elements from two previous proposals, dating back to 2008 and 2017.[67] Most importantly, the 2017 proposal advocated revising the regulations with a view to '[analysing] plant pest and noxious weed risks of GE

[61] Field trials in Oregon (GE turfgrass), Hawaii (GE maize and sugarcane) and Washington DC (GE bentgrass) were the objects of these lawsuits; for more information, see McHughen and Smith, 'Regulation of Genetically Modified Crops' (n 3) 45.

[62] A determination of non-regulated status for a GE alfalfa and a GE sugar beet variety were the object of these lawsuits; a further lawsuit ensued from cultivation of GE crops in proximity of a National Wildlife Refuge in Delaware. For more information, see MR Grossman, 'Genetically Modified Crops and Food in the United States: The Federal Regulatory Framework, State Measures and Liability in Tort' in L Bodiguel and M Cardwell (eds), *The Regulation of GMOs. Comparative Approaches* (OUP, 2010) 304; MR Grossman, 'Genetically Modified Food and Feed and the US National Environmental Policy Act' (2007) 3 *European Food and Feed Law Review* 373; and McHughen and Smith, 'Regulation of Genetically Modified Crops' (n 3) 45–46.

[63] For relevant amendments after the 2020 APHIS's reform, see the new text in 7 CFR 372.5.

[64] See n 29.

[65] 2019 APHIS Proposal (n 35).

[66] ibid, 26514.

[67] See 73 FR 60007-60048, Docket No APHIS-2008-0023, 9 October 2008; and 82 FR 7008-7039, Docket No APHIS-2015-0057, 19 January 2017.

organisms *prior to* imposing regulatory restrictions', rather than '[regulating] *before* analysing risks' (emphasis added).[68] Under the 2017 proposal, market actors could request the APHIS to conduct an assessment and to evaluate whether a GE organism was likely to pose plant pest risks. Where this was found not to be the case, the GE variety would not have fallen within the APHIS's regulatory remit and would have been non-regulated, tout court. For GE organisms with the same traits as non-regulated GE varieties, an assessment would not have been necessary at all.

In other words, the notification and permit procedures, as followed by field trials and the possibility to request a petition, would have been replaced by a preliminary assessment and evaluation of potential plant pest risks, in the absence of field trials. Where a GE organism was found unlikely to be a plant pest, it would not have been regulated. Commentators and stakeholders expressed concerns surrounding the 2017 proposal due to the vagueness of this 'risk-based system'; the specific 'risks' triggering a finding that a GE variety ought to be regulated and the method of assessing such risks in the absence of field trials, monitoring and oversight were largely considered to be unclear.[69] This system, later incorporated into the proposal for reform adopted in May 2020, reverses the regulatory presumption that field trials must precede *deregulation*, where potential plant pest risks might exist, to embrace the opposite view that some preliminary assessment should precede any form of *regulation*.

The 2020 reform has eliminated the pre-existing definition of a regulated article. Under the old version of part 340, as already explained, a GE organism qualified as a regulated article if its donor organism, recipient organism, vector or vector agent were a plant pest *or* if the APHIS had reason to believe that the GE organism might pose plant pest risks. The new text of section 340.1 lays out two broad sets of exemptions. Under section 340.1(b), the regulations do not apply to plants that have been modified such that they contain either a single modification of a type listed in paragraphs (b)(1) to (b)(3), or additional modifications determined by the APHIS under the procedure laid out in paragraph (b)(4). Paragraphs (b)(1) to (b)(3) respectively refer to: genetic modification as a change resulting from the cellular repair of a targeted DNA break in the absence of an externally provided repair template; genetic modification as a targeted single base pair substitution; and genetic modification introducing a gene known to occur in the plant's gene pool, or making changes in a targeted sequence to correspond to a known allele of such a gene or to a known structural variation in the gene pool. Pursuant to paragraph (b)(4), the APHIS may exempt plants with additional modifications, 'based on what could be achieved through conventional breeding'. The relevant proposals for exemption may either be initiated by the APHIS or follow a request for exemption.

[68] 2019 APHIS Proposal (n 35) 26515 and 26516.
[69] As acknowledged in the 2019 APHIS Proposal (n 35) 26515.

These exemptions cover a plurality of GE organisms obtained through NBTs,[70] referred to in the document as 'plant breeding innovations'.[71] The rationale for these exemptions is that the genetic mutations obtained in these plant varieties could have been achieved through conventional plant breeding methods; indeed, the USDA's intention not to regulate products of 'plant breeding innovations' was already codified in a 2018 Statement by the Secretary of Agriculture.[72] The APHIS's proposal document of 2019 concluded that 'where genetic modifications are similar in kind to those modifications made through traditional breeding, the plant pest risks *should* also be *similar*' (emphasis added);[73] while risks might exist, they are considered manageable.[74] It is worth noting that the final version of the regulations, as adopted in May 2020, differs from the original text of the 2019 proposal. The specific categories of genetic modification listed in paragraph (b) have been amended.[75] Further, the paragraph (b)(4) procedure for the APHIS to exempt different GE varieties that do not fall within any of the listed categories was missing in the original 2019 proposal. This provision was only added in the final version.

Additionally, under the new section 340.1(c)(1) and (2), the regulations do not apply to GE plants with a plant-trait-mechanism of action combination which has previously undergone a regulatory status review, and has been classified by the APHIS as non-regulated. Further, they do not apply to GE plants with a plant-trait-mechanism of action combination which has been granted a determination of non-regulated status in response to a petition.[76] In this respect, the APHIS's premise is that 'regulatory efforts should focus on the properties of the GE organism itself rather than on the method used to produce it'.[77] In the 2019

[70] See ch 1, section I.

[71] After the reform, 'genetic engineering' is defined under s 340.3 as 'techniques that use recombinant, synthesised or amplified nucleic acids to modify or create a genome'. According to the 2019 APHIS Proposal (n 35) 26522, this encompasses the use of synthetic DNA, in vivo DNA manipulation and genome editing. It does not cover marker-assisted breeding, tissue culture and protoplast, cell or embryo fusion or chemical or radiation-based mutagenesis; however, organisms obtained through these techniques have always been excluded from the APHIS's regulatory remit, and the APHIS has never considered them to constitute genetic engineering.

[72] For the 2018 USDA Statement on Plant Breeding Innovations by Secretary Perdue, see the USDA's website, www.aphis.usda.gov/. In November 2014, the APHIS granted a petition relating to a GE variety of alfalfa obtained through RNA interference (RNAi) and a petition relating to the GE 'Innate' potato, also obtained through RNAi. In February 2015, the GE 'Arctic' apple variety, also obtained through RNAi, was granted a petition. In April 2016, the APHIS announced that a GE non-browning mushroom variety obtained through CRISPR was not a regulated article and did not fall within its regulatory remit. In the past few years, a number of GE varieties obtained through ZFN and TALENs have also been found not to be regulated articles.

[73] 2019 APHIS Proposal, 26516 and 26517.

[74] ibid, 26519.

[75] For the original proposal, see the text of s 340.1 in the 2019 APHIS Proposal.

[76] 7 CFR 340(1)(c)(1) and (2). 7 CFR 340.1(d) adds a further and rather obvious exemption: GE organisms which the APHIS determined not to be regulated articles under the 'Am I Regulated?' process retain their non-regulated status.

[77] 2019 APHIS Proposal, 26516.

proposal, the APHIS noted that the old system was based on an 'event-by-event' approach, whereby each transformation event was assessed separately where plant pest risks might exist.[78] The 2020 reform embraces a different approach. The focus has shifted to the mechanism of action ('MOA'), defined as the 'biochemical process(es) through which genetic material determines a trait'.[79] Whenever MOA combinations have already been the object of some assessment, the resulting GE organism will be exempt from regulation under part 340.

It is significant that the 2019 proposal started off by setting exemptions, rather than by providing a definition of regulated articles. Indeed, under the new system, *non-regulation* has become the rule and *regulation* and regulatory oversight the residual category, if not the exception. The proposal explained that developers of GE organisms falling under any of the two broad exempted categories would use a self-determination mechanism to certify[80] that their GE varieties are non-regulated. Under the new section 340.1(e), developers *may* request confirmation from the APHIS that the GE variety falls within one of the exemptions. In this case, however, the APHIS will not conduct a preliminary risk assessment, require any field tests or exercise any oversight.

Where a GE variety does not fall within one of the exempted categories, developers will request a regulatory status review, under section 340.4. The new regulatory status review is presented as similar to the 'Am I Regulated?' process; it is meant to be 'objective, rapid and based on transparent predetermined criteria'.[81] However, this streamlined process of preliminary assessment could have far-reaching consequences. Under section 340.4(b)(2), if the APHIS 'does not identify a *plausible pathway* by which the GE plant or its sexually compatible relatives would pose an increased plant pest risk relative to the comparator(s) in the initial review, the GE plant is *not* subject to the regulations in this part [...]' (emphasis added).[82] In other words, the APHIS will have to *prove* that a GE variety has *hazardous* (plant pest) *characteristics* and *establish* a *plausible pathway* for the *materialisation* of the relevant *risks*, in order for the GE variety to be *regulated*; the 'plausible pathway' threshold appears to set a quite high standard of proof on causality.

Non-regulated status could then be granted to GE varieties which have never before been evaluated by the APHIS on the grounds of a streamlined, fast-track assessment, and in the absence of any field trials. Indeed, the new form of review will merely focus on the basic biology of the plant prior to modification, the MOA and the resulting trait.[83] This is considered sufficient for the purposes of evaluating

[78] ibid, 26517.
[79] ibid, 26517 and 26526, explaining that a specific trait might be achieved through different MOAs.
[80] ibid, 26517.
[81] ibid, 26257.
[82] Importantly, this has changed since the enactment of the 2019 proposal; the original version referred, more generally, to 'potential plant pest risks'. See the originally proposed text in 2019 APHIS Proposal, 26538 and 26539, 340.4(b)(3)(i). The 2020 version of this provision has set a higher standard of proof for the APHIS.
[83] 2019 APHIS Proposal, 26517. See 7 CFR 340.4(b)(1).

any plant pest risks of a GE variety.[84] The 'APHIS does not intend for submitters to generate experimental data specifically for a regulatory status review'; this includes experimental assessments of any potential plant pest risks.[85] Further, reports from field test trials will no longer be necessary; this reverses the pre-2020 requirement that a petition for determination of non-regulated status must *follow* field trials conducted under either the notification or the permit procedure. The rationale for this revision is that 'in many cases [the APHIS] would have been able to evaluate the plant pest risks associated with a GE organism without field test data'.[86] On these grounds, field trials are considered unnecessary.[87]

Under section 340.4(b)(3)(i):

> if the APHIS does identify a plausible pathway by which the GE plant or its sexually compatible relatives would pose an increased plant pest risk relative to the comparator(s) in the initial review, the requestor may apply for a permit and/or request that the APHIS conduct an evaluation of the factor(s) of concern identified in the initial review to determine the likelihood and consequence of the plausible increased plant pest risk. The APHIS may request additional information as needed to evaluate the factor(s) of concern.

Reference to the 'likelihood and consequence of the plausible increased plant pest risk' points to the characterisation of the probability of occurrence of adverse effects and estimation of their severity. Field tests, however, might or might not be mandated.

The evaluation could still result in a finding that the GE variety is unlikely to pose increased plant pest risks, or that the relevant risks are negligible. If this is the case, yet again, the GE variety will be classified as non-regulated and monitoring and oversight will be beyond the APHIS's remit.[88] All in all, it is only where the APHIS identifies *substantive evidence* that the GE variety *poses* increased *plant pest risks* relative to the comparator(s) that the permit procedure will apply.[89] Where developers have requested and obtained a permit prior to the end of a regulatory status review, the conclusion in the latter procedure that the GE variety is unlikely to pose increased plant pest risks will result in the termination of the permit and a declaration of non-regulated status.

Finally, after the reform, the notification and petition processes no longer exist. The petition process is no longer necessary, as the great majority of GE organisms will either be exempt under section 340.1, or found to be non-regulated articles after the regulatory status review process; as already explained, permits will be a residual case. Equally, the notification process is unnecessary after the reform.

[84] 2019 APHIS Proposal, 26526.
[85] ibid, 26525.
[86] ibid.
[87] ibid, 26526.
[88] 7 CFR 340.4(b)(3)(iii).
[89] 7 CFR 340.4(b)(3)(iii) and 340.5.

According to the APHIS, eliminating the notification procedure will also solve the aforementioned problems highlighted by the OIG audits.[90]

Against this backdrop, the reform has considerably reduced the APHIS's regulatory role and remit. Only GE organisms with an MOA-trait combination which has never before been assessed by the APHIS and the most complex cases of modification by means of NBTs are subjected to a streamlined regulatory status review, similar to the 'Am I Regulated?' procedure. The review is likely to result in a determination of non-regulated status in the vast majority of cases, and this will occur in the absence of any field trials or monitoring. Permits, field tests and the adoption of specific risk mitigation measures only apply to a handful of regulated articles, which have been positively found to pose substantial plant pest risks during the assessment of the GE plant-trait-MOA combination. As mentioned above, regulation, authorisations and regulatory oversight have ultimately become the exception, rather than the rule.

III. The Role of the EPA: Plant-Incorporated Protectants

The EPA regulates the marketing and use of pesticides in the US. For this reason, pesticides created through biotechnology are encompassed within its regulatory remit. The legal bases for the EPA's exercise of authority are to be found in the Federal Insecticide, Fungicide and Rodenticide Act ('FIFRA')[91] and the Federal Food, Drug and Cosmetic Act ('FFDCA'), as amended by the Food Quality Production Act ('FQPA').[92] The FIFRA provides for the EPA's role in registration of pesticides. The FFDCA entrusts the EPA with the task of setting tolerances (ie maximum residue levels) or exemptions from tolerances for any allowable pesticide residues in food or feed.

Under the FIFRA, the term 'pesticide' means any substance or mixture of substances intended for preventing, destroying, repelling or mitigating any pest, and any substance or mixture of substances intended for use as a plant regulator, defoliant or desiccant.[93] The definition of 'pest' encompasses insects, rodents, nematodes, fungi and weeds, as well as other forms of terrestrial or aquatic plant or animal life and viruses, bacteria or other micro-organisms.[94] Pesticides may not be sold, distributed or used in any state unless they have been registered with the EPA. The EPA shall register a pesticide if it has, inter alia, determined that '[…] (C) it will perform its intended function without *unreasonable adverse effects* on the environment; and (D) when used in accordance with widespread and commonly

[90] See above, section II.A, and 2019 APHIS Proposal, 26528.
[91] 7 USC, ss 136 ff.
[92] 21 USC, ss 321 ff.
[93] For the complete definition, see 7 USC, s 136(u).
[94] 7 USC, s 136(t).

recognised practice it will not generally cause *unreasonable adverse effects* on the environment' (emphasis added).[95] 'Unreasonable adverse effects' are defined as:

> (1) any *unreasonable risk* to *man* or the *environment*, taking into account the economic, social and environmental costs and benefits of the use of any pesticide, or (2) a human dietary risk from residues that result from use of a pesticide in or on any food inconsistent with the standard under section 346a of title 21.[96]

The relevant standard in the FFDCA, as amended by the FQPA, is the one of a 'reasonable certainty that no harm will result from aggregate exposure to the pesticide chemical residue […]'.[97]

In accordance with the general statutory framework, the EPA also regulates pesticides created through biotechnology and their residues. The EPA thus regulates crop varieties which have been engineered through the transfer of specific genetic material in order to contain 'proteins or other chemicals that serve as a natural defence against pests […]'.[98] For instance, corn, cotton and potato varieties have been engineered to produce proteins which are toxic to some insect pest species.[99]

A plant-incorporated protectant ('PIP') is defined as 'a pesticidal substance that is intended to be produced and used in a living plant, or in the produce thereof, and the genetic material necessary for production of such a pesticidal substance. It also includes any inert ingredient contained in the plant, or produce thereof'.[100] 'Inert ingredient' means:

> any substance, such as a selectable marker, other than the active ingredient, where such a substance is used to confirm or ensure the presence of the active [pesticidal] ingredient, and includes the genetic material necessary for the production of the substance, provided that genetic material is intentionally introduced into a living plant in addition to the active [pesticidal] ingredient.[101]

Further, the EPA regulates herbicides applied to herbicide-resistant GE crops. As already explained, many crop varieties have been genetically engineered to be resistant to one or more herbicides. In these cases, the EPA has so far shared regulatory authority with the APHIS. The former regulates the pesticide (ie the applicable herbicide), while the APHIS regulates the GE crop.

The existing regulations for notification of PIPs date back to 2001. As section 174.1 CFR expressly states, the characteristics of PIPs, their biological

[95] 7 USC, s 136a(c)(5).

[96] 7 USC, s 136(bb).

[97] 21 USC, s 346a(b)(2)(A)(ii).

[98] See 'EPA's Regulation of Biotechnology for Use in Pest Management', available on the EPA's website, www.epa.gov/.

[99] ibid. Most varieties have so far been engineered through Bacillus Thuringiensis (*Bt* varieties) to be resistant to insect pests.

[100] 40 CFR 174.3.

[101] 40 CFR 174.3. This may include antibiotic resistance markers. For a list of approved inert ingredients, see 40 CFR 174.700 and 174.705.

properties and their ability to spread and multiply in the environment distinguish them from traditional pesticides and warrant the application of ad hoc procedures. All PIPs must be registered with the EPA in order to be sold, distributed and used in the US.[102] As of October 2018, the EPA had approved and registered 32 active PIP ingredients and cancelled five.[103] In line with the general pesticides framework, the EPA also required a re-assessment and re-registration for *Bt* (Bacillus Thuringiensis) varieties between 2001 to 2010.[104] The EPA grants experimental use permits for field trials of PIP GE crops covering an area of more than ten acres,[105] with a view to generating scientific data to substantiate a request for registration, and assesses submissions on a case-by-case basis. It has exempted a number of pesticidal substances produced through the breeding of sexually compatible plants[106] from all the FIFRA requirements. Three more categories of PIPs were proposed for exemption, but were denied it after receipt of public comments.

General data requirements for the purposes of PIP registration include product characterisation, information on mammalian toxicity, allergenicity potential, effects on non-target organisms, environmental fate and, where applicable, insect resistance management plans.[107] The EPA requires scientific studies and data from field trials in order to conduct its own risk assessments, which are then subjected to the Scientific Advisory Panel ('SAP') for review, and in some instances to other forms of peer review.[108] The SAP, made up of external experts, is independent from the EPA. The agency may also request that applicants conduct specific studies, for the purpose of its assessment.

Importantly, the EPA also conducts risk assessments on gene flow, ie the movement of transgeneses (PIPs) from GE crops into weeds or other crops and the hybridisation of the latter (*Bt*-enhanced varieties). This may pose environmental as well as consumer protection issues, in so far as GE crops may pass their pesticidal traits to wild plants[109] or the pesticidal substances may enter the food supply.

[102] 40 CFR part 174, subpart C.

[103] 13 active PIP ingredients were approved in corn, 9 in cotton, 5 in soybean, 3 in potato and 2 in other varieties. Cancelled active PIP ingredients were used in corn varieties. See www.epa.gov/ingredients-used-pesticide-products/current-and-previously-registered-section-3-plant-incorporated.

[104] 7 USC, s 136a(c)(2), on the EPA's potential determination that additional data are required to maintain in effect an existing registration of a pesticide, and s 136a(g) relating to the periodic review of registrations of pesticides. See also www3.epa.gov/pesticides/chem_search/reg_actions/pip/1-overview.pdf and www3.epa.gov/pesticides/chem_search/reg_actions/pip/bt-corn-terms-conditions.pdf.

[105] 40 CFR part 174, subpart U. If the field trial site is below ten acres, the APHIS used to be in charge; after the 2020 reform, it will probably no longer have oversight functions over these field trials. See 2019 APHIS Proposal (n 35).

[106] 40 CFR 174.21 and 174.25.

[107] On data requirements, see www.regulations.gov/docketBrowser?rpp=50&po=0&D=EPA-HQ-OPP-2008-0835.

[108] See 'Introduction to Biotechnology Regulation for Pesticides', available on the EPA's website, www.epa.gov/.

[109] For instance, disrupting local ecosystems by changing the makeup of local plants, crowding out related species and changing the local habitat; see 'EPA's Regulation of Biotechnology for Use in Pest Management', available on the EPA's website, www.epa.gov/.

For PIP potato and corn varieties the EPA has determined that no significant risk exists; while the assessment is more straightforward for GE potatoes, the introgression of genes into wild varieties (teosintes or tripsacum) from Zea mays is merely considered to be 'unlikely' under natural conditions. On the other hand, risks of gene transfer from *Bt* cotton to wild or feral cotton relatives exist in some areas of the US, including Hawaii and Florida. This has resulted in prohibitions on commercial sale or use in these areas.[110]

Further, the EPA assesses ecological risks to non-target organisms, measured as a function of toxicity levels and (expected) exposure. Exposure occurs primarily if non-target organisms feed on the pesticidal plants or due to exposure to pollen or cross-pollination, where a transfer of new traits to other wild varieties takes place.[111] The containment of the gene products, the degree of specificity with which the PIP targets pest species and the concentration of the active (pesticidal) ingredient in plant tissues and soil residues are all relevant to the assessment.[112] The EPA operates through a tiered system in its tests on representative non-target terrestrial and aquatic species; where adverse effects are identified in a tier I species, the EPA proceeds with tests at a higher tier level, and in particular field testing.[113] It also assesses the environmental fate of specific proteins in soil. In a 2001 report, the SAP recommended that field tests should be conducted 'in *Bt* fields in a variety of soil types and climatic conditions', with a view to determining 'the amount, concentration and persistence of biological activity of [PIP] proteins in the soil'; this is of course liable to affect the risks to non-target organisms.[114] Since then, 'experiments addressing the amounts and persistence of [d-endotoxins] in the soil have been submitted and reviewed for current registrations'.[115]

Finally, the EPA has exercised its risk management and risk mitigation functions through the enactment of insect resistance management plans ('IRM').[116] So far, these have been implemented in the commercial cultivation of *Bt* crops. When insects develop resistance to pesticides, including PIPs, increasing quantities of pesticide are needed; this has highly detrimental environmental and public health effects. The term 'IRM' describes a set of 'practices aimed at reducing the potential for insect pests to become resistant to a pesticide'.[117]

Elements and considerations as diverse as knowledge of pest biology, levels of toxins expressed in the GE crop, refuge design and deployment, field monitoring

[110] See 'Introduction to Biotechnology Regulation for Pesticides', available on the EPA's website, www.epa.gov/, 12, 13 and 14.
[111] ibid, 15 and 16.
[112] ibid, 16.
[113] ibid, 17: 'This provides the opportunity to evaluate pesticidal effects (both direct and indirect) on a much broader spectrum of non-target species under more natural exposure conditions [...]'.
[114] ibid, 23.
[115] ibid, 18.
[116] See, eg, www.regulations.gov/docket?D=EPA-HQ-OPP-2011-0922.
[117] See 'Introduction to Biotechnology Regulation for Pesticides', available on the EPA's website, www.epa.gov/, at 24.

and remedial action are at stake in the implementation of IRM systems. For instance, the EPA has determined that a 20 per cent non-*Bt* corn field refuge requirement (in the corn-belt) and a 50 per cent non-*Bt* corn field refuge requirement (in cotton-growing areas) delays insect resistance. This is because refuges, ie percentages of crop land where *Bt* varieties are not grown, provide 'for the production of insects that may randomly mate with rare resistant insects surviving the *Bt* crop', delaying the evolution of resistance.[118] The EPA requires registrant firms to submit a Compliance Action Plan ('CAP'), to coordinate its implementation and to take responsibility for it. However, the EPA maintains general oversight of the process. Purchasers of *Bt* seeds sign a grower agreement, which contractually binds them to comply with IRM programmes. Surveys, compliance monitoring programmes, on-farm visits and inspections are usually undertaken by the relevant registrant companies. Growers who do not comply with their contractual obligations may be denied the use of *Bt* seeds permanently. Remedial action plans should also be in place; where resistance has developed, remedial measures go as far as requiring growers to treat crops with pest control systems or destroy their crops, and sales and distributions of affected *Bt* crops must be discontinued.[119]

In sum, the EPA exercises more intense regulatory oversight than the APHIS. First, unlike the APHIS, it does not grant deregulated status to PIPs. Quite to the contrary, all PIPs must be registered and the EPA maintains regulatory oversight and monitoring; yearly reports on sales and distributions of PIPs must also be submitted to the EPA. Moreover, the agency conducts periodic reviews and may ask for re-registration of a PIP, requesting further scientific data and experimental tests where needed. Second, the EPA conducts its own risk assessments and often requests further scientific opinions from the SAP or external bodies. The EPA's risk assessments appear to be more comprehensive than the APHIS's assessments.[120] Finally, the EPA pursues specific risk management and risk mitigation policies, including restrictions on the sale and distribution of GE crops in areas where gene flow might occur and the establishment of IRM systems. In this sense, as the next sections explain, a distinction can be drawn between the EPA's approach to the governance of GE organisms and the one followed by the APHIS and the FDA.

IV. The Role of the FDA: GE Food

The FDA regulates the safety of human food and animal feed under the Federal Food, Drug and Cosmetic Act ('FFDCA'). Under section 402(a)(1) of the act, a food shall be deemed to be adulterated if it bears or contains any added poisonous

[118] ibid, 25.
[119] ibid, 30.
[120] See, eg, the documents available at www.epa.gov/ingredients-used-pesticide-products/current-and-previously-registered-section-3-plant-incorporated.

or deleterious substance which may render it injurious to health.[121] As noted in the 1992 Statement of Policy on Foods Derived from New Plant Varieties, the FDA 'regards any substance that is not an inherent constituent of food or whose level in food has been increased by human intervention to be added within the meaning of section 402(a)(1) of the act'.[122] Where a potentially hazardous substance has not been added, ie where it is naturally occurring in food, 'food shall not be considered adulterated [...] if the quantity of such substance in such food does not ordinarily render it injurious to health'.[123] Thus, the safety standard is more stringent for added substances than for naturally occurring ones.[124] Market actors introducing food to the market are under a statutory obligation to ensure that food complies with the above safety standards. The FDA may exercise its enforcement powers under the act.

Under section 402(a)(2)(c), a food is also deemed to be adulterated 'if it is or if it bears or contains [...] any food additive that is unsafe within the meaning [of section 409 of the FFDCA]'.[125] Under section 409(a) of the act,

> a food additive shall, with respect to any particular use or intended use of such additive, be deemed to be unsafe [...] for the purposes of [section 402(a)(2)(c)] unless [...] there is in effect, and it and its use or intended use are in conformity with, a regulation issued under this section prescribing the conditions under which such additive may be safely used.[126]

Section 409(b) provides for a petition process, whereby 'any person may, with respect to any intended use of a food additive, file with the Secretary a petition proposing the issuance of a regulation prescribing the conditions under which such additive may be safely used'.[127] This amounts to a formal pre-marketing authorisation procedure, where market petitioners must provide scientific evidence to prove to a reasonable degree of certainty that no adverse effects are associated with the intended use of the additive.[128]

Nonetheless, this formal pre-marketing review and approval process does not apply to each and every food additive. Two broad exemptions apply. The first category includes so-called 'prior-sanctioned substances'; these are substances that were determined to be safe before the adoption of the amendment. The second category encompasses substances which are generally recognised by experts as safe, either in the light of scientific evidence or on the basis of their history of use in foods. These ingredients, which are classified 'Generally Recognised As

[121] 21 USC s 342(a)(1).
[122] FDA, Statement of Policy – Foods Derived from New Plant Varieties, Final, May 1992, 13.
[123] 21 USC s 342(a)(1).
[124] Statement of Policy – Foods Derived from New Plant Varieties, (n 122) 13.
[125] 21 USC s 342(a)(2)(C)(i).
[126] 21 USC, s 348(a).
[127] 21 USC, s 348(b).
[128] Statement of Policy – Foods Derived from New Plant Varieties (n 122) 14.

Safe' ('GRAS'), do not qualify as food additives and do not require an authorising regulation.[129]

Since its 1992 Statement of Policy, the FDA has taken the view that existing statutory authority is 'fully adequate to ensure the safety of new food ingredients and foods derived from new varieties of plants, regardless of the process by which such foods and ingredients are produced'.[130] Drawing on a product-based approach, it has held that foods derived from GE organisms do not pose any different or greater safety concerns than foods developed by traditional plant breeding[131] and that 'the regulatory status of a food, irrespective of the method by which it is developed, is dependent upon the objective characteristics of the food and the intended use of the food (or its components)'.[132] On these grounds, GE organisms are regulated within the general framework of sections 402(a) and 409 of the FFDCA and the FDA's implementing regulations.

Section 402(a) is the most relevant provision; the developers of GE organisms are legally responsible for evaluating the safety of the GE food and any relevant substances, in order to comply with this section. Section 409, on the other hand, has a residual application. In 1992, the FDA noted that in the case of GE foods 'it is the transferred genetic material and the intended expression product or products that could be subject to food additive regulation, if such material or expression products are not GRAS'.[133] However, the FDA anticipated that both the transferred genetic material (nucleic acids) as well as the intended expression products (proteins, carbohydrates, fats and oils, including variations in molecular structure) would have GRAS status and would be exempt from food additive regulations. Thus, novel proteins or other novel substances 'that differ significantly in structure, function or composition from substances currently found in food'[134] were considered the only likely case where the FDA might make a finding of non-GRAS status and exercise its regulatory powers under the food additive provisions. Back in 1998, a coalition of societal stakeholders sought to challenge the FDA's application of GRAS status to GE food and feed; this could have resulted in more intense regulatory scrutiny by the FDA, which would have been under an obligation to qualify GE foods as additives and regulate them as such. However, the court dismissed the action and thus refrained from encroaching on the FDA's discretion.[135]

The system has evolved over the years through regulatory practice and the FDA's specific application of the general framework to the case of GE food and feed. In 1992, the FDA recommended that developers of GE food and feed consult

[129] See 21 USC, s 321(s) and 21 CFR 170.3 and 170.30. The general recognition of safety through scientific procedures requires the same quantity and quality of scientific evidence as is required to obtain approval of the substance as a food additive by means of the petition process.

[130] Statement of Policy – Foods Derived from New Plant Varieties (n 122) 15.

[131] ibid, 19.

[132] ibid, 4.

[133] ibid, 17.

[134] ibid.

[135] *Alliance for Bio-Integrity v Shalala*, 116 F Supp 2d 166, 177 (D DC 2000).

with the agency prior to marketing GE varieties. Although these consultations ('Biotechnology Final Consultations') are not mandatory, biotech firms and corporations have regularly taken part in them. The relevant procedures are laid out in the original 1992 Policy and 1996 Guidance to Industry, as revised in 1997.[136] In 2001, the FDA proposed a new rule on pre-market notification; this would have required all developers to submit a scientific and regulatory assessment dossier for GE food and feed varieties 120 days prior to marketing.[137] The rule was never adopted and remains at draft stage.

The 1997 FDA's Guidance on Consultation Procedures is very clear in stating that:

> during the consultation process the FDA does not conduct a comprehensive scientific review of data generated by the developer. Instead, the FDA considers [...] whether any unresolved issues exist regarding the food from the new plant variety that would necessitate legal action by the agency, [...] [e.g.] significantly increased levels of plant toxicants or anti-nutrients, reduction of important nutrients, new allergens or the presence in food of an unapproved food additive.[138]

This approach is typical of a product-based model; a thorough risk assessment and evaluation of all available scientific data, studies and information, as would be mandated under process-based models, is replaced by a more circumscribed comparative assessment. The latter focuses only on the characteristics of the GE product, as identified by the developer, vis-à-vis the ones of its conventional counterpart. A risk assessment will only ensue if specific characteristics have been identified throughout the comparative assessment.

Initial consultations are the first step in the process. These aim to facilitate the resolution of any regulatory issues, as the FDA may provide indications on the data and information to be included in the developer's safety assessment. The developer then submits a *summary* of its own safety and nutritional assessment (known as a 'Biotechnology Notification File', or 'BNF'). In this document, biotech firms should provide sufficient information to support the conclusion that the GE variety is as safe and as nutritious as its conventional counterpart,[139] comparing the attributes, materials, components and nutrients of the GE variety vis-à-vis the parental variety. According to the 1997 Guidance, this should include a description of the applications or uses of the food,[140] information on the genetic material

[136] FDA, Consultation Procedures under FDA's 1992 Statement of Policy for Foods Derived from New Plant Varieties, Final, October 1997.

[137] 66 FR 4706-4738, Docket No 00N-1396, 18 January 2001, Proposed Rules, *Premarket Notice Concerning Bioengineered Foods*. In a similar vein, draft guidance from 2010 on regulatory submissions under the Biotechnology Final Consultations and the 2015 Draft Guidance on the Use of Antibiotic Resistance Marker Genes in Transgenic Plants were never finalised.

[138] Consultation Procedures (n 136) 2.

[139] Statement of Policy – Foods Derived from New Plant Varieties (n 122) 20.

[140] Further information may be required in the case of animal feed, as feed from few plants or one plant is likely to be a significant portion of the animal diet.

and specification of the intended effects of the modification, including its expected effects on the composition and properties of the food, as well as information comparing the characteristics of the food to that of food derived from the parental variety. In such comparisons, special emphasis should be placed on the concentration and bioavailability of nutrients, the presence of toxicants (or antinutritional factors) and allergenic potential.[141] The safety and nutritional value of newly introduced proteins and the identity, composition and nutritional value of modified carbohydrates, fats and oils are also covered.[142]

At the time of writing, the FDA has conducted consultations and cleared the way for the marketing of 186 GE food and feed varieties.[143] In the great majority of cases, GE plants are used to make ingredients for food products; examples are corn starch used in soups and sauces, corn syrup used as a sweetener, corn, canola or soybean oils used for the production of breads, snacks and sauces, and sugar from sugar beet or sugar cane.[144] However, other varieties are used as animal feed or unprocessed human food. The relevant traits range from herbicide resistance (sometimes associated with altered fertility), insect resistance and virus resistance to altered ripening, altered growth properties, changes in composition or combinations of these traits.

The FDA closes biotechnology consultations with a letter; letters for each BNF are available on the FDA's public database.[145] All letters start by providing a very concise overview of the GE product's traits, the genetic engineering process employed to achieve them and its intended uses. The FDA then remarks that, based on its assessments, the biotech firm has concluded that the variety is not materially different in composition, safety or other relevant parameters from human and animal food currently on the market. Exceptions apply: notably, all cases where genetic engineering has resulted in a change to the composition of the food or feed. Where this is the case, the FDA discusses with the developer and agrees a descriptive term to be employed for additional labelling purposes, which discloses the differences with the conventional counterpart[146] (eg 'low gossypol

[141] Consultation Procedures (n 136) 3. As acknowledged since 1992, genetic engineering can have unintended or unexpected effects, starting from an 'alteration in the concentration of important nutrients, increases in the level of natural toxicants, or the transfer of allergens from one species to the another'; see Statement of Policy – Foods Derived from New Plant Varieties, 19–20. Further, 'mutations unrelated to the desired modification may be induced; undesirable traits may be introduced along with the desired traits; […] inactivation of host genes or altering control of its expression; introduced gene product or metabolic product affected by genetic change may interact with other cellular products to produce a deleterious effect'. See Statement of Policy – Foods Derived from New Plant Varieties, 9–10.

[142] Statement of Policy (n 122) 20.

[143] As of June 2020, these include soybean, cotton, canola, corn, flax, sugar beet, rice, creeping bentgrass, wheat, alfalfa, starch potato, sugarcane, tomato, squash, potato, papaya, radicchio, cantaloupe, plum, apple and pineapple varieties. A number of GE varieties obtained through NBTs are also included. The first record of voluntary consultations dates back to 27 January 1995. For more information, see www.accessdata.fda.gov/scripts/fdcc/index.cfm?set=Biocon&sort=FDA_Letter_Dt&order=DESC&startrow=1&type=basic&search=.

[144] See www.fda.gov/.

[145] ibid.

[146] See also Statement of Policy (n 122) 18.

dehulled cotton meal', consultations on the name 'golden rice', 'high oleic soybean oil' or 'laurate canola oil'). The FDA then notes that the developer has concluded that the GE variety does not raise issues that would require a pre-market review or approval by the FDA.

Developers' assessment summaries are available on the public database. All of them are very concise; indeed, developers do not need to produce scientific evidence, data or literature proving that the variety is, at the current state of knowledge, considered safe. Rather, they can limit the analysis to a general overview of the GE product, conducting a comparative analysis and describing the reasons why the variety does not substantially differ from the conventional counterpart. Assessment summaries appear to have varying levels of depth and detail. Some conduct a more thorough analysis, encompassing detailed characterisations of proteins, compositional analysis, effects of processing and cooking and results of specific studies; others do not. Finally, all letters conclude by adding that, whilst the FDA has no further questions concerning the GE food or feed, it is the developer's continuing responsibility to ensure that any foods marketed are safe, wholesome and in compliance with all applicable legal and regulatory requirements. This clause refers to market actors' responsibility under section 401(a)(1) of the FFDCA. Ultimately, responsibility rests with the developers of GE food. The Biotechnology Consultations do *not* amount to a formal *authorisation process*; *nor* does the FDA exercise any specific *post-marketing monitoring*.

Against this backdrop, what role is left for section 409 of the FFDCA and the pre-marketing approval process for food additives? According to the 1992 Policy, the FDA has determined that '[constituent] substances [of GE food and feed] should be subject to regulation under section 409 of the act in those cases when the objective characteristics of the substance raise questions of safety sufficient to warrant formal pre-market review and approval'.[147] An instance where this could occur is the case of new non-pesticidal proteins produced by new plant varieties, ie proteins that differ significantly in structure or function from those currently found in food.[148] These have been the object of ad hoc – non-binding – recommendations, dating back to 2006.[149] According to the recommendations, developers of new plant varieties should liaise with the FDA and provide an early food safety assessment of new proteins. Under the recommendations, developers should particularly focus on an assessment of the amino acid similarity between the new protein and known allergens or toxins.[150]

[147] ibid, 5.
[148] ibid, 20.
[149] FDA, Guidance for Industry: Recommendations for the Early Food Safety Evaluation of New Non-Pesticidal Proteins Produced by New Plant Varieties Intended for Food Use, Final, June 2006, 5: the notion of a new protein refers to 'any non-pesticidal protein produced in a new plant variety that is new to the plant species, or is a native protein that has been produced at a significantly elevated level, or is a native protein from a part of a plant that is not normally ingested, and will now be produced in a part of the plant that is normally ingested, and has not been the subject of a completed biotechnology consultation or a completed early food safety evaluation with the FDA'.
[150] ibid, 9.

An ad hoc database contains all response letters to New Protein Consultations ('NPCs');[151] the FDA has repeatedly drawn the conclusion that, based on the developer's evaluation, the potential presence in the food supply of low levels of new proteins will not raise food safety concerns. In its letters, the FDA has encouraged developers to participate in appropriate regulatory review processes prior to marketing foods derived from GE varieties expressing new proteins. Yet, it is unclear whether any of these new proteins have ever been the object of a *petition* and *express approval* by the FDA. At the moment, there is no evidence that this has happened. According to available data, the only food additive petition ever made and regulation ever adopted dates back to 1994 and relates to Calgene's Aminoglycoside 3'-phosphotransferase II; in two other cases, the Food Master Files for Bt10 and FLAVR SAVR resulted in a GRAS determination.[152] On these grounds, it is legitimate to infer that section 409 FFDCA is a dead letter in the assessment of GE food and feed varieties.

All in all, as this section has shown, the FDA has taken a soft approach to the governance of food and feed derived from GE plants. The bulk of the responsibility for comparative assessments, monitoring and ensuring that GE food and feed are safe is shifted onto biotech firms. Further, the FDA has, throughout the years, refrained from exercising more intense regulatory oversight through food additive approvals. This soft approach has recently been confirmed and extended by the FDA's Plant and Animal Biotechnology Innovation Action Plan.[153] In this document, which followed a 2017 request for public comments on foods derived from plants produced through NBTs, the FDA outlines its broader strategy to the assessment of innovations in both plant and animal biotechnologies. The plan mostly focuses on animals altered through genome editing NBTs.[154] However, it also proposes a degree of deregulation in future updates to the procedures for voluntary pre-market consultations with industry in the field of plant biotechnology, 'to reflect the FDA's 25 years of experience with foods derived from biotechnology plants and considering any additional issues related to genome editing of food crops'.[155] The explicit goal is to lessen administrative burdens and foster innovation. Overall, the proposed regulatory changes seem to be aligned with the ones brought forward by the APHIS.

To conclude, a few words must be spent on labelling. In the 1992 Policy, as already mentioned, the FDA took the view that foods derived from GE plants do

[151] See www.accessdata.fda.gov/scripts/fdcc/index.cfm?set=NPC.

[152] See www.fda.gov/food/consultation-programs-food-new-plant-varieties/food-master-files-food-additive-petitions.

[153] FDA, Plant and Animal Biotechnology Innovation Action Plan, 2019.

[154] ibid, 4–5. Any detailed analysis of these proposals would be beyond the circumscribed scope of analysis of this chapter. However, see the recent ruling of the US District Court for the Northern District of California on Aquadvantage salmon, the first genetically engineered commercial animal food variety approved by the FDA; *Institute for Fisheries Resources et al v FDA*, No 16-cv-01574-VC (Northern District of California 2020).

[155] ibid, 5.

not substantially differ from conventional foods. In line with this presumption, the FDA never laid out any mandatory labelling requirements for GE food and feed, as a class.[156] It only required specific labelling for GE foods with a materially different composition to conventional foods, and issued guidance for manufacturers willing to label foods as containing or not containing GE ingredients.

This changed with the enactment of the National Bioengineered Food Disclosure Standard, which established a mandatory disclosure scheme.[157] This federal act followed the adoption of a stringent 2014 Vermont law on GE product labelling, as well as a set of other state bills and proposals.[158] Explicit federal pre-emption applies, so these state laws have been superseded by the federal law.[159] The federal act reasserts that, for the purposes of the national disclosure scheme, GE foods shall be treated as being as safe as their conventional counterparts.[160] The act offers food manufacturers the option of disclosing the genetically engineered nature of foods and ingredients in the form of a text, symbol, electronic link, digital link or alternative reasonable disclosure options.[161] Consumer associations have strongly criticised the potential use of electronic and digital links, which are likely to be inaccessible, unintelligible or misleading to consumers. The act put the Agricultural Marketing Services at the USDA in charge of developing a national mandatory labelling scheme; the USDA was thus entrusted with the task of identifying the necessary requirements and procedures, and determining the relevant thresholds of GE components for foods to fall within the remit of the national standard.

All relevant information is now enshrined in the USDA's National Bioengineered Food Disclosure Standard, within the CFR.[162] Further information is available on the USDA's website.[163] The implementation date of the Standard was 1 January 2020, although this has been delayed until 1 January 2021 for small food manufacturers; the mandatory compliance date is 1 January 2022. Any detailed analysis of the new labelling rules would exceed the scope of this chapter; however, it is worth noting that the requirements laid out in the standard are not stringent. First, if an ingredient includes an inadvertent amount of a bioengineered substance, below the threshold of five per cent, the specific ingredient does not trigger mandatory disclosure.[164] Second, if the bio-engineered ingredient is used as an incidental

[156] Lack of mandatory labelling requirements was also challenged in *Alliance for Bio-Integrity v Shalala* (n 135).

[157] US Congress, National Bio-Engineered Food Disclosure Standard (Public Law 112–216) of 29 July 2016.

[158] See Vermont State Law no 120/2014 Relating to the Labelling of Food Produced with Genetic Engineering (H.112). For further information, see also www.ncsl.org/research/agriculture-and-rural-development/state-legislation-addressing-genetically-modified-organisms-report.aspx.

[159] S 295.

[160] S 293(b)(3).

[161] S 293(d).

[162] 7 CFR, part 66.

[163] For further information, see the USDA's website, www.usda.gov/.

[164] Under the Vermont State Law of 2014, the (considerably more stringent) threshold was 0.9% of the total weight of the product.

additive, it does not need to be included in the ingredient list or disclosed. Finally, small food manufacturers with annual receipts below US$2,500,000 are completely exempt from labelling obligations. Overall, the flexible approach of the Disclosure Standard reflects the regulatory presumption of substantial equivalence, as reiterated in the Bioengineered Food Disclosure Law: GE food and feed are assumed to be as safe as their conventional counterparts.

V. Sound Science Approaches and Adherence to Sound Science: Deconstructing their Implications Through an Analysis of US Governance of GE Organisms

This section focuses on sound science approaches to risk assessment and adherence to sound science. The first sub-section provides a brief overview of these regulatory notions. The second sub-section explores how a sound science approach to the governance of the uncertain risks posed by GE organisms is embedded in the US framework, with particular focus on the APHIS's and the FDA's regulatory remit and their exercise of regulatory powers. This part of the analysis explains in what sense the hegemonic narrative on GE organisms and evidence-based discourses on risk governance, which are premised on a sound science approach to risk assessment and adherence to sound science, are reflected (and in fact originated) in the US legal regime. Finally, the third sub-section uncovers the implications of sound science approaches and regulatory focus on sound science. It assesses the underlying criteria for the distribution of regulatory authority together with the broader impact of this model on the level of health and environmental protection that is pursued, using the analysis of US governance of GE organisms to explore and deconstruct the hegemonic narrative and evidence-based discourses.

A. Sound Science, Risk Assessment and Regulatory Frameworks

As anticipated in the first chapter, ideal evidence-based approaches are premised on recourse to a *sound science approach* to risk assessment and adherence to *sound science*. For the purposes of the enquiry in this book, 'sound science' is associated with positive and conclusive scientific proof of the existence of a hazard and pathway for the materialisation of a risk. Regulatory focus is on scientific proof of unsafety, as opposed to establishing whether a product is sufficiently safe for its uncertain risks to meet the intended level of protection and comply with the threshold of acceptable risk.

From this perspective, hazard-related uncertainties surrounding the existence of a direct causal link between the properties of a product or process and specific adverse effects are ultimately irrelevant. In so far as science cannot provide conclusive proof of the existence of a hazard, remaining uncertainties are regarded as 'theoretical'.[165] Equally, risk-related uncertainties pertaining to the existence of a risk and the pathway for its materialisation will be regarded as 'theoretical uncertainty'.[166] Considerations as to whether the available scientific evidence is sufficient for an adequate and reliable characterisation of uncertain risks are also largely irrelevant.[167] Yet again, sound science postulates a focus on what is known, proven and established at the current stage of technical-scientific knowledge. Further, the existence of different bodies of scientific opinion and diverging data is unproblematic; regulatory focus on sound science posits reliance on majority (sound scientific) opinion.

The notion of a sound science approach to risk assessment is more encompassing. If 'sound science' ultimately refers to conclusive scientific proof of specific hazards and risks, a 'sound science approach' to risk assessment includes specific evaluations pertaining to multiple forms of uncertainty and variability; as explained in greater detail in the first chapter, this is where 'science-policy choices' come into play.[168]

Sound science approaches to risk assessment are contraposed to prudential approaches. The gap between sound science and prudential approaches may be reflected in recourse to different models for hazard identification and for hazard characterisation, different forms of probabilistic modelling as regards the assessment of potential exposures, the application of different safety factors to address variability, and reliance on different defaults, assumptions and forms of expert judgments. Sound scientific risk assessments are also likely to be less comprehensive than prudential risk assessments; this reflects the different extent to which *stricto sensu*, hazard-related and risk-related uncertainties are addressed by risk assessors and taken into consideration as a matter of risk assessment policy. In the context of governance of GE organisms, an example is the decision to resort to comparative assessments, rather than conducting comprehensive risk assessments.

Further, a sound science approach might emerge from the specific framing of regulatory arrangements, when the threshold triggering regulatory intervention is set. An example is the presumption of substantial equivalence between GE organisms as a class and their conventional counterparts, and the reliance on a product-based model for the governance of GE organisms, as opposed to process-based models. Adherence to a product-based model draws on the lack of conclusive scientific proof that GE organisms are not as safe for public health and the environment as their conventional counterparts. The opposite applies to process-based models, which draw on a prudential approach and aim to dispel *stricto sensu* and hazard-related uncertainties as to the potential risks posed by genetic engineering processes.[169] Equally, a sound science approach and regulatory focus on sound

[165] See ch 1, section III.B. See also the analysis in ch 5, sections II, III, VII and VIII.A.
[166] See ch 1, section III.B. See also ch 5, sections IV, V and VI.
[167] See for instance ch 5, sections VI, VII and VIII.A.
[168] See ch 1, section III. See also ch 5, sections V and VIII.B (on the gap between sound scientific and prudential safety factors, assumptions, probabilistic modelling and expert judgement).
[169] See ch 4.

science may be reflected in specific regulatory or (deregulatory) arrangements. As the next sub-section explains in greater detail, a sound science approach might result in the decision to deregulate products where, on the basis of summary assessments, no positive evidence of specific adverse effects or significant adverse effects has been identified; the application of a sound science approach might also result in a decision not to regulate at all.

Finally, another feature which is often associated with a sound science approach is greater reliance on data generated by market applicants or notifiers, ie greater reliance on 'regulatory science' as opposed to 'research science'.[170] Regulatory science focuses on testing hypotheses to prove that there is no scientific evidence of significant risk, ie that a product is not unsafe. Research science, on the other hand, generally seeks to ascertain whether a product is safe. Thus,

> regulatory science usually tests hypotheses that effects do *not occur*, whereas efficacy trials and ecological research usually test hypotheses that effects will *occur*. The most rigorous tests of hypotheses for the *absence* of effects tend to be laboratory studies, while the most rigorous tests of hypotheses for the *presence* of effects tend to be field studies (emphasis added).[171]

As expressly acknowledged,

> [under regulatory science] the criterion for deciding whether further testing is required is a judgment about the best balance between the *costs* of over-testing some activities that pose low risks and the *costs* of incorrectly determining that high risk activities pose low risks (emphasis added).[172]

Against the backdrop of this introductory analysis, the next sub-section explores how and on which grounds a sound science approach to the governance of the uncertain risks posed by GE organisms is embedded in the US framework.

B. Sound Science and US Governance of GE Organisms

Sound science permeates the US framework for the governance of GE organisms. As noted throughout this chapter, and as further detailed in the above sub-section, the regulatory presumption that GE techniques do not pose any inherent risks and

[170] See S Jasanoff, *The Fifth Branch: Science Advisers as Policy-Makers* (Harvard University Press, 1990). This exposes regulators to information asymmetries. On the 'Monsanto Papers' issue and the glyphosate controversy in the US and the EU, see inter alia GC Leonelli, 'The Glyphosate Saga and the Fading Democratic Legitimacy of EU Risk Regulation' (2018) 25 *Maastricht Journal of European and Comparative Law* 582. For another example, see the 'Dicamba' controversy and court litigation, *National Family Farm Coalition and Others v Environmental Protection Agency*, No 17-70810 (9th Circuit 2020).

[171] A Raybould et al, 'Regulatory Science, Research Science and Innovation in Agricultural Biotechnology', in Wozniak and McHughen (eds), *Regulation of Agricultural Biotechnology: The United States and Canada*, (Springer, 2002) 325.

[172] ibid 322.

that GE organisms, as a class, are substantially equivalent to their conventional counterparts reflects sound scientific opinion. Indeed, references to a *science-based* approach are ubiquitous in the Coordinated Framework, federal documents and agencies' policies.

Starting from an analysis of the APHIS's regulatory remit and exercise of authority, the pre-2020 framework already drew on a sound science approach. The 'Am I Regulated?' scheme allowed for a preliminary review of GE products which had not been engineered through plant pest components to determine whether they were regulated articles, ie whether they might cause direct or indirect injury, disease or damage to plants. This preliminary review did not assess potential changes in plant pest impacts, impacts on non-target organisms or propensity for increased weediness; it was conducted on the basis of the GE product's composition alone. Yet, it could result in a finding of non-regulated status, with all the related implications.

This reflects a sound science, rather than prudential, approach. Plants may pose *direct* plant pest risks, by directly injuring other plant varieties, or *indirect* risks. In the latter case they may become reservoirs for pests or diseases, increasing the number or distribution of pests and exacerbating plant pest issues in the area; they might also harm or suppress populations of beneficial non-target organisms, for instance pollinators or predators of plant pests. Further, depending on its weediness potential, a GE crop might become a weed, increase the weediness of sexually compatible crops, or even transmit its trait to crops with which it does not interbreed.[173] The assessment of direct or indirect plant pest risks thus involves very complex evaluations, which were totally missing from the APHIS's evaluation under the 'Am I Regulated?' scheme. This shows how uncertainties as to potential adverse environmental effects have been regarded as largely irrelevant for regulatory purposes.

Similar considerations apply to the preconditions for the use of the streamlined notification procedure, before 2020. Again, assessing whether a GE variety should be considered as a weed in the area of environmental release or whether it could be toxic to non-target organisms on the mere grounds of its specific composition does not reflect a prudential approach. Under the old regulatory framework, this was exacerbated by the APHIS's use of general performance-based standards to minimise inadvertent release during field trials. The permit scheme, as explained, posed more stringent conditions. However, the framework did not contain any specific indication of the elements that should have been taken into account for the purpose of granting or denying a permit, identifying 'high risk' cases or determining the conditions to be attached to a permit. As already mentioned, US courts have in the past years found that the APHIS failed to take a sufficiently cautious approach; in their rulings, they concluded that an EIS was warranted, and that the agency should have conducted one.[174]

[173] See the acknowledgment in the 2019 APHIS Proposal (n 35) 26521–26526.
[174] See section II.

Finally, the petition process allowed petitioner firms to request a determination of non-regulated status for a previously regulated article. Where deregulation was granted, the APHIS no longer played any monitoring or oversight role; the same occurred in cases where non-regulated status was extended. This clearly reflects a sound science approach to the assessment of the uncertain risks posed by GE crops; lack of proof of unsafety justifies deregulation. It is worth noting that, back in 2008, the Government Accountability Office recommended that the APHIS put in place a system to monitor deregulated GE crops and assess their effects on the environment and on conventional or organic agriculture.[175] This recommendation was never implemented.

The 2020 reform has marked a further alignment to sound science approaches and will significantly reinforce sound science discourses in the US governance of GE organisms. As explained, the focus has shifted from making a case that a GE variety does not appear to pose plant pest risks, in order for it to be deregulated, to making a case that it will pose plant pest risks, for it to be regulated at all. This clearly reflects a sound science approach.

The APHIS has never regulated stacked events, ie combinations of deregulated articles bred together to produce a hybrid. However, it used to follow an 'event-by-event' approach, regulating each event separately on the grounds that 'the locus of insertion, which varies from one transformation event to another, even using identical DNA constructs and host plant genotypes, may give rise to different inserted gene expression patterns, gene product levels and perhaps affect other features as well'.[176] After the reform, this approach has been abandoned in favour of a MOA approach. Any GE plant-trait-MOA combinations which have previously been found unlikely to pose plant pest risks will not fall within the scope of the new regulations, ie they will automatically be non-regulated.

Equally, a significant number of GE organisms produced through NBTs will be covered by a specific exemption, reflecting the assumption that these genetic modifications could have been achieved through traditional breeding. This makes the gap between the APHIS's approach to the governance of GE crops and prudential risk assessment even broader; *stricto sensu* uncertainties and hazard-related uncertainties on potential adverse environmental effects are considered irrelevant. Under these two broad exemptions, the vast majority of GE crops will be the object of neither authorisation, nor field trials or any other forms of communication, monitoring and oversight.[177] The self-determination mechanism could also pose a

[175] See Government Accountability Office (GAO), *Genetically Engineered Crops: Agencies Are Proposing Changes to Improve Oversight, but Could Take Additional Steps to Enhance Coordination and Monitoring* (GAO-09-60, November 2008) 11, 24–34.

[176] McHughen and Smith, 'Regulation of Genetically Modified Crops' (n 3) 42.

[177] This is expected to be particularly problematic in the case of GE plants producing plant-made industrial or pharmaceutical components, and small-scale field testing of PIPs. In the former case, GE components from deregulated crop varieties which have been the object of self-certification might easily enter the food chain, in the absence of any monitoring and oversight. In the latter case, it is still unclear which agency will now be in charge for small scale field trials for PIPs – see 2019 APHIS Proposal (n 35) 26518. On the past 'StarLink' controversy, see inter alia M Lee, *EU Regulation of GMOs* (Edward Elgar, 2008), 28.

plurality of challenges, in so far as the APHIS might lose track of which GE varieties are being released and cultivated and whether they actually fall within one of the exempted categories.

Where a GE organism is not exempt from regulation and developers cannot resort to the self-determination mechanism, a regulatory status review applies. However, GE varieties which have never before been evaluated by the APHIS will be assessed through a streamlined, fast-track regulatory status review procedure; this involves neither field trials nor the production of any experimental data. The APHIS will focus on the MOA and resulting traits, assessing whether any elements indicate that the GE organism has hazardous (plant pest) characteristics and whether a risk is likely to materialise; this is, clearly, in line with a sound science approach. Where a prima facie case can be made that GE varieties do not have these characteristics or that the potential risks are unlikely or negligible, these will also be granted non-regulated status. In the opposite case, a further stage of review will ensue and a permit might be issued. The conditions or threshold of risk under which a regulatory status review might reach these conclusions are unclear and unspecified.

Against this backdrop, the APHIS's proposal for reform is heavily influenced by a sound science approach. The proposal combines a shift towards less prudential methods of assessment (such as MOA-centred assessments), blanket exemptions for broad categories of GE organisms, a further de-formalisation of relevant procedures (the new regulatory status review and the residual application of permits), and a strong emphasis on sound science. This fully reflects the sound science assumption that risks must be taken as long as the specific adverse effects of a product and the materialisation of a risk have not been positively established; the unsafety of a product should be proven before it is regulated.

Finally, a few words must be spent on the EPA and the FDA's approach. In the field of GE organisms, the EPA's exercise of regulatory authority is distinctive in that the agency follows a more prudential approach than the APHIS and the FDA. As described in the third section, the EPA conducts more encompassing risk assessments than its 'sister' agencies, requests further opinions from the independent SAP, maintains regulatory oversight of PIPs and might ask for further assessments for the purposes of re-registration.[178] The opposite applies to the FDA. As explained in detail in the fourth section, the agency would have the authority to formally approve components of GE organisms as food additives,[179] but it has refrained from doing so by resorting to the GRAS presumption. In recent years, as new proteins are developed which do not meet the substantial equivalence test and which have never before been assessed, the FDA has still chosen to conduct streamlined biotechnology

[178] However, as already mentioned, this might change in response to the directives of the 2019 Executive Order.

[179] See also 21 USC, s 348(b) and (c): 'safety' is defined as 'a reasonable certainty [...] that the substance is not harmful under the intended conditions of use'. Under s 321(u), 'safety' refers to public (human and animal) health.

consultations rather than mandating authorisations. As explained, developers' summary dossiers focus on a comparative assessment of the GE organism vis-à-vis its conventional counterpart. Developers do not conduct a thorough risk assessment and do not generate experimental or additional data; further, the analytical depth and breadth of the dossiers is variable. In this sense, the FDA clearly focuses on the absence of evidence that a GE variety is unsafe. Moreover, the recent FDA's Plant and Animal Biotechnology Innovation Action Plan proposes a further degree of deregulation for plant varieties obtained through NBTs. In this sense, the FDA's proposal is closely aligned with the 2020 APHIS reform.

A sound science approach to the assessment of GE organisms and the governance of their uncertain risks can clearly be seen as central to the US system; the partial exception is the EPA's more prudential approach to PIPs. The next sub-section endeavours to explore the implications of this approach, uncovering them by reference to the analysis of the US system.

C. Unpacking the Implications of Sound Science Approaches and Adherence to Sound Science

The analysis of US governance of GE products helps uncover the implications of sound science approaches and adherence to sound science by providing a concrete example of a specific legal system and its practical implementation, thereby moving us beyond mere abstract theory. In this sense, as explained at the beginning of this chapter, this section *uses* the analysis of US governance of GE organisms to explore the implications of the hegemonic narrative, identifying and highlighting the rationale and characteristics of evidence-based approaches. More specifically, this sub-section addresses two points.

The first point relates to questions of distribution of power and allocation of authority. The evidence-based process is linear,[180] as a sound science approach to risk assessment, adherence to sound science and reliance on cost-benefit analysis for the purposes of risk management are set along a regulatory continuum. Unsurprisingly, technical regulatory agencies are entrusted with both risk assessment and risk management.[181] These are considered value-neutral and objective functions, to be exercised by technical bodies on the grounds of their epistemic authority.

US regulation of GE organisms offers a good example, in that both functions are allocated to a set of federal agencies. In this sense, US governance of agricultural biotechnologies exemplifies a shift of authority away from the political

[180] On 'linear' and 'iterative' approaches, see E Fisher, 'Framing Risk Regulation: A Critical Reflection' (2013) 4 *European Journal of Risk Regulation* 125.

[181] Even though different offices are in charge of these functions: see for instance the EPA's website, www.epa.gov.

sphere and towards the realm of technocracy: technical experts are entrusted with the task of determining the legally relevant threshold of risk. Federal agencies can ultimately decide to what extent and how to assess the uncertain risks posed by GE varieties, whether to maintain regulatory oversight or deregulate them, and whether to enact risk mitigation measures. Legislative requirements and specifications are minimal; the entire system is characterised by de-proceduralisation.[182] Thus, the US governance of GE organisms clearly reflects a technocratic model of risk regulation.

By contrast, socially acceptable risk approaches are grounded in an iterative evaluation of scientific evidence in light of the level of protection set by regulators.[183] Risk assessment should draw on a prudential approach and take uncertainties into due consideration. OLFs may feed into the determination of how high the intended level of protection should be, and how low the corresponding threshold of acceptable risk. When scientific evidence is inconclusive and a risk may be too high to meet the intended level of protection, the precautionary principle may apply. Ultimately, the decision as to whether and to what extent the positive results of a risk assessment or persisting uncertainty are legally relevant results from an iterative evaluation of science in light of the intended level of protection and all relevant factors at stake. In accordance with the iterative nature of the process, and again unsurprisingly, risk assessment and risk management functions are usually allocated to different authorities in regulatory systems influenced by socially acceptable risk approaches; risk management and final decision-making rest with political institutions.[184]

Both models and their corresponding regulatory options come at a price. The allocation of risk management functions and final decision-making power to political authorities can obscure the overlaps between the two stages of the risk regulation process. It can also blur the lines of accountability for decision-making, as risk managers operate in a grey area at the interface between technical expertise and political evaluations. However, separation of authority goes hand in hand with a twofold (implicit) acknowledgment. First, in the face of multiple uncertainties and high levels of scientific complexity, risk assessment unavoidably incorporates 'science-policy choices'; it is not value-neutral. Second, risk management entails a political balancing operation; determining what weight should be given to persisting uncertainty, establishing the intended level of protection in a specific regulatory field and setting out the acceptable level of risk for society are considered 'eminently political' responsibilities.[185] Accordingly, final decision-making

[182] See sections II to IV above.

[183] See n 180.

[184] See ch 4 for more details.

[185] With reference to the EU legal order, see European Commission, COM(2000)1 Final, *Communication from the Commission on the Precautionary Principle*, 15, sub-section 5.2.1. In EU case law, see also Case T-13/99, *Pfizer*, 201: [Technical experts], although they have scientific legitimacy, have neither democratic legitimacy nor political responsibilities. Scientific legitimacy is not a sufficient basis for the exercise of public authority'; for further details, see ch 4.

authority lies with political risk managers. Symmetrically, technocratic models of risk governance lend themselves to a different criticism. The price which is paid for the allocation of authority solely to technical experts is a disregard for the specific implications of different approaches to risk assessment, and for the value-laden nature of the entire risk governance process.

The second point relates to the level of protection pursued and achieved. Quite intuitively, sound science approaches and adherence to sound science are potentially liable to result in less protective standards, and ultimately in less protection, than prudential approaches and a regulatory focus on persisting uncertainty. US governance of GE organisms, and particularly recent developments thereto, provide good examples in this respect. The APHIS's decision via the 2020 reform to rely on a self-determination mechanism, to conduct a streamlined regulatory review in the vast majority of cases and to eliminate field trials poses a plurality of challenges.[186] The same applies to the FDA's proposals. This begs the question *why*, in the face of scientific complexity, the presumption applies that sound science approaches *must* be adhered to and sound science *must* be relied on. Looking back to the APHIS reform, for instance, why should conclusive scientific proof of the existence of a hazard and actual materialisation of a risk be required, for the purposes of regulating uncertain risks?

The underlying premise of the evidence-based regulatory ideal is that sound science is neutral and objective; for this reason, it should inform risk regulation standards. Reductionist accounts equate a sound science approach and adherence to sound science to *scientific* method; regulatory focus on uncertainties and recourse to the precautionary principle, when uncertain risks may not meet the intended level of protection, allegedly draw on *non-scientific* (political and public opinion) considerations. Controversial cases in the field of risk regulation, as explained in the first chapter, are then analysed through the prism of the 'science' versus 'politics' dichotomy. From this perspective, the question raised above would get an easy and straightforward answer. Yet, the picture is much more complex than these accounts suggest.

At a general level, the discourse on allegedly monolithic sound science approaches and sound scientific evidence disregards scientific pluralism and scientific complexity.[187] This fails to acknowledge that, in the face of persisting uncertainty, sound science does not necessarily provide factually 'correct' answers.

[186] Risks of hybridisation and crop to crop gene flow always exist in the field of agricultural biotechnologies; see the analysis of EPA's risk management in section III, and the acknowledgment in N Ellstrand, 'Over a Decade of Crop Transgenes Out-of-Place', in Wozniak and McHughen (eds), *Regulation of Agricultural Biotechnology* (n 2).

[187] On the notion of trans-scientific issues, ie questions which cannot be unequivocally answered by science due to time and resource constraints, despite being formulated in the language of science, see V Walker, 'The Myth of Science as a "Neutral Arbiter" for Triggering Precautions' (2003) 26 *Boston College International and Comparative Law Review* 197, 198 ff, and G Majone, 'Foundations of Risk Regulation: Science, Decision-Making, Policy Learning and Institutional Reform' (2010) 1 *European Journal of Risk Regulation* 5.

It also obscures the normative frames through which science is evaluated. As explained in the first chapter, recourse to more or less prudential approaches to risk assessment will affect the *evidence base* that regulators rely upon.[188] Different approaches to risk assessment, resulting in diverging evidence, beg the question why such differences exist. Recourse to different safety factors or assumptions and reliance on more or less prudential models encapsulate different normative assumptions surrounding uncertainty and its relevance for the purposes of decision-making. Further, the varying extent to which regulators focus on sound scientific proof of the existence of specific hazards and the materialisation of specific risks, as opposed to persisting uncertainty, will have an impact on the *inferences* drawn from the available scientific evidence. This is also a consequence of different underlying normative premises.

Overall, a normative component is inherent to risk assessment policy and to the determination that persisting uncertainties are scientifically relevant. Equally, the decision that a risk can be appropriately characterised and that it is 'negligible' or 'low' is influenced by a set of normative judgments. Scientific subjectivity is difficult for lay persons to detect; yet, in contexts of scientific pluralism and complexity, normative premises always influence the framing of the relevant scientific questions, the subsequent scientific inferences and the final determinations.

If evidence-based models are neither neutral and objective, however, what is the *normative frame* informing sound science approaches and adherence to sound science? Can this normative frame shed further light on the presumption that sound science must be adhered to, and uncertain risks must be conclusively proven before regulating? These questions are addressed in greater detail in the following section, from the specific vantage point of cost-benefit analysis.

VI. Cost-Benefit Analysis: Deconstructing its Implications Through an Analysis of US Governance of GE Organisms

This section examines cost-benefit analysis. The first sub-section focuses on this regulatory toolbox, its underpinning rationale and its origins within the US regulatory system. The second sub-section shows how recourse to cost-benefit analysis is embedded in US governance of GE organisms. Finally, the third sub-section sheds light on the connections between sound science approaches, adherence to sound science and economic cost-benefit analysis, and explores the far-reaching implications of pursuing a cost-benefit effective level of protection.

[188] For an example in US risk governance, see V Walker, 'A Default-Logic Model of Fact-Finding for US Regulation of Food Safety, in M Everson and E Vos (eds), *Uncertain Risks Regulated* (Routledge, 2009) 146 ff.

A. Cost-Benefit Analysis

Recourse to economic cost-benefit analysis and the pursuit of cost-benefit effective levels of environmental and public health protection are typical of the ideal evidence-based regulatory model. Risk management necessarily involves a balancing operation, and cost-benefit analysis mandates a quantitative assessment and balancing of the economic costs and benefits of regulation. Cost-benefit analysis is premised on an application of the criterion of expected optimisation; this underpins a calculation of the probability of events and a calculation of expected utilities. Postulating under this model that all events and all consequences can be consistently compared, all uncertain events are attributed a level of probability, and all consequences are calculated in terms of expected utility. The best alternative will be the one bearing the highest expected utility; this is known as the rule of maximisation of expected utility.[189] On these grounds, as emphasised, cost-benefit analysis 'is not designed to be just one among many tools brought to bear in policy debates, [but is] a comprehensive attempt to incorporate all the relevant factors into a unified framework to produce a policy recommendation'.[190]

The origins of regulatory applications of cost-benefit analysis date back to the three US presidencies of the 1970s.[191] The application of economic cost-benefit analysis has then been entrenched as the de facto rule in the US regulatory apparatus since the years of Reagan's presidency. Executive Order 12291 of 1981 entrusted agencies with the duty to undertake a full cost-benefit analysis. Pursuant to the Order, and in accordance with the criterion of maximisation of aggregate wealth, regulation could not be enacted unless its benefits outweighed the economic costs associated with regulatory burdens.[192]

In 1993, with the enactment of Executive Order 12886, President Clinton retained cost-benefit analysis as a regulatory toolbox, while reworking some of the applicable criteria and amending the relevant administrative processes.[193] Agencies are under a duty to 'assess both the costs and the benefits of intended regulation and […] propose or adopt a regulation *only* upon a reasoned determination that the benefits of the intended regulation *justify* its costs' (emphasis added).[194] Further, when 'an agency determines that a regulation is the best available method

[189] For a detailed overview, see Majone, 'Foundations of Risk Regulation' (n 187). This paragraph draws in part on Majone's description of cost-benefit analysis.

[190] S Rose-Ackerman, 'Precaution, Proportionality and Cost-Benefit Analysis: False Analogies' (2013) 4 *European Journal of Risk Regulation* 281, 284.

[191] S Shapiro, 'The Evolution of Cost-Benefit Analysis in US Regulatory Decision-Making' in D Levi-Faur (ed), *Handbook on the Politics of Regulation* (Edward Elgar, 2011) 386.

[192] 46 FR 13193-13198, US President, Executive Order 12291 of 17 February 1981, *Federal Regulation* (US National Archives).

[193] 58 FR 51735-51835, US President, Executive Order 12866 of 30 September 1993, *Regulatory Planning and Review*. See section 4 on 'Planning Mechanism'; section 5 on 'Existing Regulations'; and Section 6 on 'Centralized Review of Regulations'.

[194] See section 1(b)(6).

of achieving the regulatory objective, it shall design its regulations in the most cost-effective manner to achieve the regulatory objective'.[195] On these grounds, the Order addresses both the *stricto sensu* economic cost-benefit effectiveness of regulatory action, and the necessity of the specific regulatory measures enacted to pursue the relevant goals.[196]

A 'regulation' is broadly defined to encompass 'an agency statement of general applicability [...] that is designed to implement, interpret or prescribe law or policy or to describe the procedure or practice requirements of an agency'.[197] 'Significant regulatory actions' by executive agencies, as defined under the Order,[198] are subject to a centralised review process conducted by the Office of Information and Regulatory Affairs ('OIRA') within the Office of Management and Budget ('OMB').[199] For any significant regulatory actions, executive agencies shall provide the OIRA with an assessment of the relevant costs and benefits. For significant regulatory actions having an annual effect on the economy of US$100 million or more, or adversely affecting a number of interests, a fully-fledged regulatory impact analysis is required.[200]

The 1993 Order marked a shift towards a softer approach to the application of cost-benefit analysis. Regulatory benefits should justify (rather than outweigh or exceed) the relevant costs, qualitative measures of costs and benefits may be included where quantification would be too complex, and distributive impacts and equity may be taken into account when choosing alternative regulatory approaches.[201] This trend was confirmed by two following Executive Orders, enacted under the Obama presidency.[202] Yet, the regulatory philosophy has ultimately remained unchanged. The rationale for the application of cost-benefit analysis is that aggregate wealth maximisation and the greatest *net* beneficial *protection* of public health and the environment should be pursed as a regulatory goal.

With the enactment in January 2017 of an Executive Order on 'Reducing Regulation and Controlling Regulatory Costs',[203] the requirement for US regulation to comply with cost-benefit analysis has then been significantly strengthened. Section 2(a) of the 2017 Executive Order maintains that 'whenever an executive department or agency [...] promulgates a new regulation, it shall identify at least

[195] Section 1(b)(5). See also 1(b)(11).

[196] eg, in the field of risk governance, the cost-benefit effectiveness of the level of public health and environmental protection pursued, as well as the necessity of the specific risk management measures selected to comply with that level of protection.

[197] Section 3(d).

[198] Section 3(f).

[199] Section 6(a)(3)(A).

[200] Section 6(a)(3)(B) and (C).

[201] Section 1(a).

[202] 76 FR 3821-3823, US President, Executive Order 13563 of 18 January 2011, *Improving Regulation and Regulatory Review*; 76 FR 41587-41588, US President, Executive Order 13579 of 11 July 2011, *Regulation and Independent Regulatory Agencies*.

[203] 82 FR 9339-9341, US President, Executive Order 13771 of 30 January 2017, *Reducing Regulation and Controlling Regulatory Costs*.

two existing regulations to be repealed'.[204] As further clarified by section 2(c), 'any new incremental costs associated with new regulations shall, to the extent permitted by law, be offset by the elimination of existing costs associated with at least two prior regulations'.[205] The benefits of any new regulatory act shall, in accordance with cost-benefit analysis, justify the relevant costs; further, the costs associated with the new act shall be compensated by the elimination of the regulatory costs connected to two pre-existing acts. In these terms, it may be assumed that regulators will only have an incentive to adopt a new regulatory act where the benefits expected of the new act are greater than (or at least equal to) the sum of the benefits flowing from two pre-existing acts, which will be repealed.[206]

In the field of risk governance, the application of cost-benefit analysis postulates a calculation of the marginal costs and benefits of regulatory interventions aimed at managing uncertain risks. A fully-fledged application of cost-benefit analysis implies that, in situations of scientific uncertainty, regulation shall *not* be enacted *unless*, or shall *only* be enacted *in so far as*, the expected public health and environmental benefits outweigh regulatory costs. Cost-benefit analysis may inform the enactment of risk governance frameworks,[207] decisions regarding product authorisations, including the determination of the legally relevant threshold of probability of occurrence of adverse effects,[208] and the adoption of specific risk management and risk mitigation measures. The extent to which US risk governance measures conform to economic cost-benefit analysis is impossible to gauge. Not only may regulatory practice vary across agencies and specific regulatory areas; also, agencies will not be bound by the tenets of cost-benefit analysis where a statute expressly provides for the application of different criteria.[209] Nonetheless, it is fair to argue that the US system of risk governance is *informed* by the pursuit of cost-benefit effective levels of environmental and public health protection.

[204] ibid, section 2(a).

[205] ibid, section 2(c).

[206] It is worth noting that the shift from the mere application of cost-benefit analysis in the context of specific regulatory acts to the consideration of the costs and benefits associated with regulating different issue areas is likely to have pervasive and long-lasting effects, triggering regulatory competition across different regulatory areas. The rule enshrined in the 2017 Order ensures that the total regulatory costs and burdens either remain unchanged, or decrease. However, given that benefits must always justify the relevant costs under cost-benefit analysis, regulators will hardly manage to preserve the same overall level of benefits, when adopting a new act. It is reasonable to assume that, in the majority of cases, more regulatory costs will be cut than regulatory benefits are obtained.

[207] See, eg, sub-section B below, analysing the 2020 APHIS's reform.

[208] See, eg, the 'unreasonable adverse effects' criterion enshrined in FIFRA, pointing to the pursuit of a cost-benefit effective level of protection in US regulation of pesticidal products; see n 89 in ch 1, and this chapter, section III. See also the open acknowledgment, in the Silver Book, that cost-benefit analysis should as far as possible be employed by the EPA to determine the legally relevant threshold of probability of adverse effects, and further recommendations in this direction; see n 91 in ch 1.

[209] See Executive Order 12866 of 30 September 1993 (n 193) section 1(a). See also C Sunstein, 'Cost-Benefit Analysis and Arbitrariness Review' (2017) 41 *Harvard Environmental Law Journal* 1, for an analysis of the limits to judicial review of compliance with the duty to conduct a formal cost-benefit analysis and adhere to its results.

According to one advocate of cost-benefit analysis, the rule of maximisation of expected utility 'does not guarantee better actual results than other decision rules'; however, 'it does guarantee consistency in decision-making'.[210] According to other supporters of this model, despite its limitations, 'quantitative cost-benefit analysis is the best available method for assessing the effects of regulation on social welfare'.[211] On these grounds, the advocates of cost-benefit analysis contend that risk regulation in the US has gradually shifted towards a more efficient and more effective policy-making and regulatory model. From this perspective, different approaches have thus been positioned along a continuum from the least to the most sophisticated: from prohibitions, the criterion of the lowest feasible risk and the elimination of significant risk to, at the end of the continuum, the entrenchment of cost-benefit analysis.[212] The next sub-section assesses how cost-benefit analysis is embedded in US governance of GE organisms.

B. Cost-Benefit Analysis and US Governance of GE Organisms

Regulatory focus on cost-benefit effectiveness was clearly identifiable in the 1986 Coordinated Framework[213] and is even clearer in the 2019 Executive Order on GE organisms. The latter expressly mentions the need to take economic factors into account when taking decisions, with the aim of streamlining regulatory procedures and removing undue trade barriers.[214] The Order aims to foster scientific and technological developments in the field by minimising regulatory burdens and economic costs for developers and by facilitating trade in GE organisms. It clearly reflects the regulatory determination that, taking as a reference point what has been positively proven and established at the current stage of technical-scientific knowledge, the economic costs ensuing from the regulation of GE organisms should not outweigh the relevant benefits. The text of the Order is permeated with a pro-biotechnology stance; for instance, it explicitly mentions that GE organisms can help increase yields, raise productivity and improve crop and animal characteristics.[215]

[210] Majone, 'Foundations of Risk Regulation' (n 187) 9.

[211] Sunstein, 'Cost-Benefit Analysis' (n 209) 7; see also C Sunstein, *The Cost-Benefit Revolution* (MIT Press, 2018). For arguments in favour of application of cost-benefit analysis, see inter alia M Adler and E Posner, 'Rethinking Cost-Benefit Analysis' (1999) 109 *Yale Law Journal* 165; M Adler and E Posner, 'Implementing Cost-Benefit Analysis when Preferences are Distorted' in M Adler and E Posner (eds) *Cost-Benefit Analysis: Legal, Economic and Philosophical Perspectives* (University of Chicago Press, 2001); C Sunstein, *Risk and Reason. Safety, Law and the Environment* (CUP, 2002); JD Graham, 'Saving Lives through Administrative Law and Economics' (2008) 157 *University of Pennsylvania Law Review* 395; R Revesz and M Livermore, *Retaking Rationality: How Cost-Benefit Analysis Can Better Protect the Environment and our Health* (OUP, 2008).

[212] Majone, 'Foundations of Risk Regulation' (n 187).

[213] See section I, above.

[214] 2019 Executive Order, sections 4 and 6.

[215] ibid, section 1.

The same focus on cost-benefit analysis and the cost-benefit effectiveness of the regulatory arrangements can clearly be traced back to the APHIS's proposal for reform of 2019. The APHIS's pre-2020 regulations already incorporated considerations surrounding economic cost-benefit effectiveness. The best example was the existence of the two-pronged 'notification' and 'permit' system; the former, streamlined procedure responded to cost-benefit analysis tenets. The APHIS's reluctance to reform the notification procedure in accordance with the OIG's audit recommendations, attaching specific conditions to field trials authorisations, was also motivated by a concern that this would not respond to economic cost-benefit effectiveness.[216] Other examples included the APHIS's practice of deregulating GE varieties in response to petitions for non-regulated status, and its reluctance to conduct EISs. However, this regulatory trend has been considerably strengthened by the 2020 reform.

The 2019 proposal for reform remarked that the opportunity costs of delayed innovation should be taken into consideration together with all relevant compliance costs of regulation.[217] The new regulations have the aim of 'reducing regulatory burdens for developers of organisms that are unlikely to pose plant pest risks'[218] and are expected to result in significant economic savings.[219] They expressly draw on the Coordinated Framework's guiding principle that 'in order to ensure that limited Federal oversight resources are applied where they will accomplish the greatest *net* beneficial *protection* of public health and the environment, oversight will be exercised *only* where the risk […] is *unreasonable* (emphasis added)'.[220] According to the 2019 proposal for reform, savings to the regulated community will result from 'a reduced need to collect field data, fewer reporting requirements and lower management costs. Costs now associated with petitions for non-regulated status would be […] eliminated where permits are no longer necessary'.[221] An analysis of cost savings scenarios follows, with a specific focus on the annual costs borne by the private sector and by the APHIS.

As this concise overview shows, the APHIS's deregulatory framework is clearly informed by and respondent to cost-benefit analysis. As the next subsection explains in greater detail, exploring all relevant consequences, the same applies to the USDA's governance of coexistence of GE, conventional, organic and identity-preserved crops. The USDA has taken a very soft approach to governance of coexistence; this has been limited to a set of non-binding recommendations for private stakeholders.[222] This regulatory choice complies with economic cost-benefit analysis; in so far as the cultivation of GE crops is expected to maximise

[216] See the express acknowledgment in 2019 APHIS Proposal (n 35) 26528.
[217] ibid, 26535.
[218] ibid, 26514.
[219] ibid, 26516.
[220] ibid., citing the 1986 Coordinated Framework as well.
[221] ibid, 26534.
[222] See *A Framework for Local Coexistence Discussions* (n 27).

aggregate wealth, the distribution of regulatory costs and benefits across societal groups is ultimately irrelevant.

Finally, and by way of conclusion, it is worth mentioning that the FDA's approach to GE food and feed is also strongly influenced by the application of cost-benefit analysis. The FDA's lack of approval or authorisation of GE food varieties, combined with the lack of any comprehensive risk assessment, reliance on developers' summary dossiers and the absence of post-marketing monitoring, exemplifies a cost-benefit effective approach; these regulatory arrangements respond to the principle of aggregate wealth maximisation. The corollary, as the next sub-section explains, is that developers maintain full responsibility for the safety of the relevant products.

C. Unpacking the Implications of Cost-Benefit Analysis

The analysis of US governance of GE products helps unpack the implications of cost-benefit analysis and its application to risk management, in practice. Crucially, it also helps unravel the connections between sound science approaches, adherence to sound science and economic cost-benefit analysis. This is the first point addressed in this sub-section.

A close focus on regulatory cost-benefit effectiveness, as shown above, emerges from the US framework for the governance of GE organisms. Hazards and risks are not conclusively established in the field of agricultural biotechnologies; alternatively, the relevant risks are deemed negligible. Overall, from an evidence-based perspective, adherence to sound science would be sufficient to justify the decision to take uncertain risks. The repeated emphasis on the economic benefits of GE organisms and the economic costs of regulation underscores how economic considerations and the pursuit of a cost-benefit effective level of protection are indirectly at stake. The twofold reference to the sound scientific basis of the regulatory arrangements and their conformity to economic cost-benefit analysis highlights the connections between the two elements, along the linear continuum of the evidence-based regulatory process: the assumption that sound science approaches *must* be adhered to and that sound science *must* be relied on is informed by considerations surrounding the economic cost-benefit effectiveness of risk regulation. When evidence-based approaches are being applied to cases where hazards and risks have been conclusively established, as illustrated in the first chapter, regulatory action will be *directly* informed by economic cost-benefit analysis. Yet, the very assumption that sound science must be relied on *indirectly* reflects the pursuit of a cost-benefit effective level of protection.[223]

[223] ie, as anticipated in the introductory chapter, the intended (enhanced or cost-benefit effective) level of protection comes into play indirectly when regulators decide what weight should be given to different forms of uncertainty, as a matter of risk assessment policy or regulatory focus.

This sheds some light on the rationale and the overarching goals of evidence-based approaches. Picking up the question which was left unanswered in section V, then, the presumption that hazards and risks must be conclusively established for uncertain risks to be regulated applies *because* this regulatory choice responds to economic cost-benefit effectiveness. Far from being neutral and objective, recourse to sound science approaches and adherence to sound science are informed by the pursuit of a cost-benefit effective level of protection. This is the non-scientific *normative frame* underlying evidence-based approaches and the assumption that uncertain risks must be taken.

The next stage consists of an analysis of the implications of evidence-based approaches. A rich literature exists on the limits of cost-benefit analysis. From an ethical perspective, these have been criticised for creating artificial values and monetising goods such as public health and environmental protection.[224] Commentators have underscored that, far from being value-neutral, the choice to balance economic costs and public health and environmental benefits reflects a normative commitment to utilitarianism and puts economic costs front and centre stage.[225] The relevant economic valuations have also been widely and repeatedly criticised for being inaccurate and implausible; particular attention has been paid to the over-estimation of economic costs, the practice of discounting future public health and environmental benefits,[226] and the specific methods applied to calculate the values of risk reduction.[227] On these grounds, the argument has been put forward that cost-benefit analysis is biased against regulation, and has inherently anti-regulatory results. Further, the complexity and lack of transparency of this method have been the object of criticism.[228] The present analysis is limited to applications of cost-benefit analysis in the field of risk regulation; more specifically, this sub-section takes into consideration three fundamental implications of recourse to cost-benefit analysis, from a risk governance perspective.

First, cost-benefit analysis aims to accomplish the greatest *net* beneficial *protection* of public health and the environment; as already explained, the benefits flowing from regulating health and environmental risks are assessed against all relevant economic costs. This results in economically based or informed *limits* for regulatory intervention. In the words of the Coordinated Framework, 'oversight will be exercised only where the risk [...] is unreasonable'.

[224] S Kelman, 'Cost-Benefit Analysis: An Ethical Critique' [1981] *AEI Journal on Government and Society Regulation* 33; F Ackerman and L Heinzerling, 'Pricing the Priceless: Cost-Benefit Analysis of Environmental Protection' (2002) 150 *University of Pennsylvania Law Review* 1553; F Ackerman and L Heinzerling, *Priceless: on Knowing the Price of Everything and the Value of Nothing* (New Press, 2004).

[225] See inter alia D Dreisen, 'Is Cost-Benefit Analysis Neutral' (2006) 77 *University of Colorado Law Review* 335.

[226] See inter alia L Heinzerling, 'Discounting Life' (1999) 108 *Yale Law Journal* 1911; Ackerman and Heinzerling, 'Pricing the Priceless' (n 224).

[227] L Heinzerling, 'The Rights of Statistical People' (2000) 24 *Harvard Environmental Law Review* 189.

[228] See inter alia Ackerman and Heinzerling, 'Pricing the Priceless' (n 224); Ackerman and Heinzerling, *Priceless* (n 224).

On these grounds, cost-benefit analysis does not enable regulators to pursue enhanced levels of public health, consumer or environmental protection. Cost-benefit analysis identifies a *baseline* threshold of safety: the probability of occurrence of adverse effects and their severity should not be such that, at the current stage of technical-scientific knowledge, not regulating would not be economically cost-benefit effective. Thus, as seen in the case of GE organisms, the relevant potential adverse effects should not be unreasonable or excessive, taking the economic benefits of the product or process at stake and the economic costs of regulation into account. This, however, might disregard society's willingness to pay a high economic cost to protect an interest that they prioritise. Under socially acceptable risk approaches, by contrast, the level of protection set in a regulatory field need not be cost-benefit effective. As mentioned in the first chapter, regulators may decide to minimise exposures to hazardous substances, no matter whether risks are deemed 'negligible' in other jurisdictions, or determine that no level of exposure to highly hazardous substances can be deemed 'safe' or 'acceptable'.

Second, through the application of cost-benefit analysis, evidence-based approaches are liable to result in lower rather than higher levels of protection, in so far as potential adverse effects may be *underestimated*. Cost-benefit analysis has been famously portrayed as a life-saver as well as a money-saver.[229] Yet, this argument is highly controversial and open to dispute. The advocates of cost-benefit analysis have argued that 'by ignoring one of the key lessons of economics and policy analysis – that decisions should be based on marginal costs and benefits – [other approaches] waste resources that could have been used to control more risks'.[230] From this perspective, cost-benefit analysis leads to a more efficient distribution of limited resources.[231] Different approaches, on the other hand, will result in less rather than more protection overall.[232] Similar arguments have been formulated by reference to behavioural economics, and developed on cognitive grounds. According to this version, precautionary approaches rely on cognitive biases and cognitive mistakes which are typical of the individual dimension.[233]

[229] For references to this terminology, see Ackerman and Heinzerling, 'Pricing the Priceless' (n 224) 1561, referring to a famous statement by JD Graham.

[230] See Majone, 'Foundations of Risk Regulation' (n 187) 13; in a similar way, see also G Majone, 'What Price Safety? The Precautionary Principle and Its Policy Implications' (2002) 40 *Journal of Common Market Studies* 89.

[231] See also 2019 APHIS Proposal (n 35) 26516.

[232] Majone, 'Foundations of Risk Regulation' (n 187) 13.

[233] These encompass loss aversion, entailing disregard of the potential benefits associated with the decision to take a risk; the myth of a benevolent nature; availability heuristics, focusing on the cognitive distinction between lay people and experts; probability neglect; system neglect, including the potential misallocation of resources which could be more efficiently allocated to reduce other risks; and trade-off neglect. See C Sunstein, *Risk and Reason. Safety, Law and the Environment* (CUP, 2002); C Sunstein, 'Beyond the Precautionary Principle' (2003) 151 *University of Pennsylvania Law Review* 1003; C Sunstein, *Laws of Fear. Beyond the Precautionary Principle* (CUP, 2005); C Sunstein, 'Precautions Against What? Perceptions, Heuristics and Culture' in JB Wiener et al (eds), *The Reality of Precaution. Comparing Risk Regulation in the United States and Europe* (Routledge, 2011). Particular emphasis has been placed on the notions of trade-off neglect and risk-risk trade-offs. Under these

These analyses raise some important points. By moving out of the realm of quantitative cost-benefit assessment, and by giving expression to public perception of risk, socially acceptable risk approaches are of course liable to misallocate resources which could be used to target more or more salient risks.[234] Nonetheless, the argument on the life-saving role of cost-benefit analysis is still fraught with controversy and should come with several caveats.

To begin with, under the linear continuum of evidence-based approaches, cost-benefit analysis is meant to be applied by taking into account what has been positively and conclusively established in sound scientific risk assessments. In the face of scientific complexity and multiple uncertainties, however, the entire calculation of regulatory costs and benefits by reference to this evidence base is liable to underestimate uncertain risks. The determination that the economic costs of regulation outweigh its benefits and the conclusion that regulation is unwarranted might then have detrimental public health and environmental effects. For example, this might occur with the APHIS's decision to rely on self-determinations, deregulate organisms obtained through NBTs and eliminate field trials. Under socially acceptable risk approaches, by contrast, regulators may focus on persisting uncertainty and resort to the precautionary principle, whenever uncertain risks might not comply with the intended level of protection in a specific regulatory field.

Further, non-discernible or non-fatal adverse effects and specific impacts on vulnerable constituencies will hardly be caught and taken into due consideration when cost-benefit analysis is applied. While probabilities may be low, however, adverse effects may still materialise in specific cases or under some exposure scenarios. All in all, in so far as the greatest *net* beneficial *protection* of public health and the environment is pursued, an evaluation of these effects is bound to be marginal in cost-benefit assessments. This, however, can hardly result in a high level of protection.

accounts, recourse to the precautionary principle is alleged to expand risks in other fields; for instance, a precautionary approach to GE organisms will increase the risks of food insecurity, or a precautionary approach to the governance of specific pesticidal products may result in the use of more hazardous pesticides. While the points on trade-off neglect and risk-risk trade-offs are important, these accounts fail to demonstrate that socially acceptable risk approaches are bound to increase the overall level of risk, or increase risks in other areas. The reason is that these accounts neglect the consideration of qualitative factors and the development of a long-term vision for sustainable approaches across different sectors which are typical of socially acceptable risk approaches. By way of example, a precautionary approach to GE organisms will not increase the risks of food insecurity if food sovereignty (as opposed to market-driven food security) approaches are followed; indeed, from this perspective, GE organisms have not played any meaningful role in the fight against food insecurity. See below, the analysis in the second part of ch 6. To provide another example, the ban of a pesticidal product will not result in use of more hazardous pesticides if the substitution principle is being applied, a long-term vision for sustainable models of agriculture is under development and relevant regulation is implemented. For a criticism of Sunstein's approach and of 'fear of democracy' in risk governance, see S Kahan, DM Slovic et al, 'Fear of Democracy: A Cultural Evaluation of Sunstein on Risk' (2006) 119 *Harvard Law Review* 1071. Interestingly, see the connections between the critique of Sunstein's 'fear of democracy' in risk governance and Sunstein's later work on nudges and libertarian paternalism; RH Thaler and C Sunstein, *Nudge. Improving Decisions about Health, Wealth and Happiness* (Yale University Press, 2008); C Sunstein, *Choosing Not to Choose. Understanding the Value of Choice* (OUP, 2015).

[234] Majone, 'Foundations of Risk Regulation' (n 187) 14.

Further problems arise in cases where economic stakes are very high; in these cases, recourse to cost-benefit analysis may result in the selection of a higher threshold of probability of occurrence of adverse effects than the results of risk assessment might have otherwise warranted in different regulatory contexts. As expressly acknowledged in the Silver Book, by taking into account costs and other non-risk factors,

> regulatory decisions [will not be] necessarily congruent with risk assessment. That is, concern about, for example, economic consequences or societal impacts may outweigh public health or environmental concerns in such a way as to make a regulatory decision [...] less protective [...].[235]

In areas where economic impacts or expected economic advantages are high, the application of cost-benefit analysis can then result in less protective standards.

These problematic aspects are further exacerbated by issues relating to the techniques employed to conduct cost-benefit analyses. As already mentioned, the over-estimation of the economic costs of regulation, the practice of discounting future public health and environmental benefits, and the specific methods applied to calculate the values of risk reduction have come under the spotlight and have been the object of in-depth analysis.

To draw a summary, the application of cost-benefit analysis at the risk management stage may only result in more rather than less protection in so far as uncertain risks have not been underestimated due to adherence to sound science, a close focus on the relevant economic stakes, and the specific techniques employed for the purposes of cost-benefit calculus. Further, it will only result in more protection in so far as it may be assumed that more salient risks will be identified by regulators and will (in turn) not be underestimated. Overall, it is legitimate to conclude that the application of cost-benefit analysis is liable to underestimate risks and result in lower levels of protection.

Finally, turning to the third and conclusive consideration on the implications of cost-benefit analysis, recourse to (selective) *quantitative* cost-benefit calculus does not allow for the evaluation of *qualitative* OLFs. These, on the other hand, may be taken into account under socially acceptable risk approaches. Under evidence-based models, OLFs are considered immaterial to the risk regulation process and irrelevant to the determination that a risk is acceptable. OLFs are considered the domain of 'politicised' approaches.[236] Yet, it is worth underscoring that economic cost-benefit effectiveness is nothing more than a specific OLF at stake in the risk regulation process. Neither cost-benefit effectiveness and aggregate wealth maximisation nor public opinion, sustainability or distributional concerns are

[235] Silver Book (n 51) ch 1; for a practical example in US risk regulation, see P Pascual, W Wagner and E Fisher, 'Making Method Visible: Improving the Quality of Science-Based Regulation' (2013) 2 *Michigan Journal of Environmental and Administrative Law* 467–468.

[236] In the field of agricultural biotechnologies, see inter al Pollack and Shaffer, *When Cooperation Fails* (n 1).

'objective' and 'neutral' matters of 'pure' science. From this perspective, there is no intrinsic or substantive difference between (quantitative) economic OLFs and other (qualitative) OLFs; both are non-scientific in nature.

The dichotomy between a focus on the economic opportunities of GE organisms, on the one hand, and broader debates on their sustainability and specific advantages and disadvantages, on the other, permeates the entire transnational controversy on agricultural biotechnologies. As explained since the introductory chapter, questions surrounding the environmental sustainability of GE organisms, their ability to increase crop yields at times of climate change or the extent to which they can tackle transnational food insecurity are highly disputed.

Economic cost-benefit analysis puts the regulatory burdens borne by market actors and the economic costs associated with regulation front and centre stage. Enacting cost-benefit effective risk regulation measures responds to the overarching goals of aggregate wealth maximisation; it yields considerable economic benefits to developers, firms and corporations, relieving them of the economic costs associated with higher levels of protection or precautionary risk regulation and thus facilitating technological-scientific developments and innovations. The opposite applies to socially acceptable risk approaches, which are liable to stifle innovation.

Nonetheless, evidence-based approaches do not allow for consideration of different questions, so long as risk regulation measures comply with economic cost-benefit analysis. This has a range of implications. A prominent example in the field of agricultural biotechnologies is the one of coexistence. This raises issues pertaining to the distribution of regulatory costs and benefits across different constituencies.[237]

Distributional stakes and the distributional impact of regulation are not central concerns of cost-benefit analysis. This does not mean that they are not assessed. In the US legal order, for instance, Executive Orders 12866 and 13563 list 'distributive impacts' and 'equity' among the factors to be evaluated.[238] However, it means that a fully-fledged application of cost-benefit analysis postulates the selection and adoption of the regulatory approach which will maximise aggregate wealth in quantitative terms. On these grounds, a qualitative analysis of the constituencies that will bear the costs or reap the benefits associated with risk regulation and any connected risk management measures is ultimately bound to be marginal for the purposes of final decision-making.

The entrenchment of the cultivation of GE crops in the US has gone hand in hand with the increasing adventitious presence of GE components in seeds and crops.[239] This is of particular economic and socio-economic concern for organic

[237] See ch 4 for an analysis of coexistence issues and how the relevant OLFs feed into the setting of the intended level of protection, under socially acceptable risk approaches.

[238] Executive Order 12866 (n 193), section 1(a) and 1(b)(5); and n 202, section 1(b) and (c). See also 2019 APHIS Proposal (n 35) 26534, referencing the Regulatory Flexibility Act and yet emphasising that where regulation is necessary, regulatory approaches that maximise *net* benefits should be selected.

[239] ibid for further detailed information and data.

farmers and growers of identity-preserved crops;[240] these societal groups may suffer economic losses as a result of contamination, and might not be able to sell their produce on the market.[241] The APHIS's 2019 proposal for reform also acknowledges that 'as acreage of any given GE crop increases and as a greater variety of crops are modified [...], the potential for more instances of [cross-pollination, commingling and] unintended presence of a GE organism increases'.[242] For this reason, the adoption of effective coexistence policies is all the more important to organic farmers and growers of identity-preserved crops. However, as anticipated in the previous sub-section, the USDA has taken a very soft approach to the coexistence of GE, conventional, organic and identity-preserved crops.[243] This regulatory choice complies with the overarching tenets of economic cost-benefit analysis. Nonetheless, it has caused several problems.

As a consequence of the USDA's soft approach, organic farmers and growers of identity-preserved crops have often had to bear the regulatory 'compliance' costs and practical burdens associated with the enactment of coexistence measures. Further, these measures are difficult to implement; this adds an additional layer of complexity. Due to these difficulties, the viability and profitability of non-GE alternative agricultural models has been indirectly threatened by the entrenchment of agricultural biotechnologies. In turn, this has a range of implications for consumer choice, in so far as non-GE or organic produce becomes more expensive on the marketplace.[244]

Against this backdrop, the USDA's cost-benefit effective approach to coexistence has ultimately shifted the economic costs and burdens associated with regulation away from GE crop growers and re-allocated them to organic farmers. This has triggered social conflicts as well as court litigation.[245] In a similar vein, the FDA's cost-benefit effective choice not to authorise GE food and feed is liable to shift externalities and economic costs onto consumers, if a GE product is found to be unsafe. The only remedy would be litigation; in this sense, the choice of 'downstream' litigation remedies in lieu of an 'upwards' authorisation process shifts costs away from the private sector and regulatory agencies and re-allocates them to the broader consumer 'constituency'. Yet again, OLFs such as high food quality or the

[240] For further information, see *A Framework for Local Coexistence Discussions* (n 27).
[241] ibid.
[242] 2019 APHIS Proposal (n 35) 26535.
[243] See *A Framework for Local Coexistence Discussions* (n 27).
[244] ibid.
[245] American scholars have often engaged in analyses of coexistence, assessing potential remedies under tort law. See inter alia Grossman, 'Genetically Modified Crops' (n 62); AB Endres, 'GMO: Genetically Modified Organism or Gigantic Monetary Obligation? The Liability Schemes for GMO Damage in the United States and the European Union' (1999) 22 *Loyola LA International and Comparative Law Review* 453; and AB Endres, 'Coexistence Strategies, the Common Law of Biotechnology and Economic Liability Risks' (2008) 13 *Drake Journal of Agricultural Law* 115. For an analysis of coexistence in EU law, see Lee, *EU Regulation of GMOs* (n 177); and M Lee, 'The Governance of Coexistence Between GMOs and Other Forms of Agriculture: A Purely Economic Issue?' (2008) 20 *Journal of Environmental Law* 193.

protection of specific groups and vulnerable constituencies do not register on the radar of evidence-based approaches.

This concludes the overview of the implications of economic cost-benefit analysis, conducted by means of an analysis of US governance of GE organisms. The next section ties the strings of the institutional analysis of the chapter, drawing all relevant conclusions.

VII. Conclusions of the Institutional Analysis. Deconstructing the Hegemonic Narrative and Evidence-Based Discourses from Within the Nation State: The Centrality of Individual Rights

As explained at the beginning of this chapter, the US legal system is the regulatory site where the hegemonic narrative on GE organisms and their uncertain risks originated. US discourses on agricultural biotechnologies and evidence-based risk regulation have become part of broader transnational narratives. Notions and regulatory categories such as sound science or cost-benefit analysis, developed and employed in US risk governance, have gained increasing transnational relevance, well beyond the boundaries of the US jurisdiction. On these grounds, this chapter has interrogated the US legal system as a transnationally relevant site of norm-making, using the analysis of US governance of GE organisms to explore and deconstruct the hegemonic narrative and transnational discourses on evidence-based risk governance.

The fifth and sixth sections have focused on sound science approaches to risk assessment, adherence to sound science and recourse to cost-benefit analysis. The enquiry into US governance of GE organisms has helped unravel the connections between these notions. Far from being neutral and objective, as the analysis has shown, the assumption that sound science approaches must be followed and sound science must be adhered to is informed by considerations surrounding the economic cost-benefit effectiveness of risk regulation. The chapter has then unpacked the specific implications, advantages and disadvantages of evidence-based approaches, showing what the pursuit of a cost-benefit effective level of protection entails in practice.

The analysis of evidence-based risk governance in the US shows that the transnational hegemonic narrative on the costs of precautionary regulation and the benefits of agricultural biotechnologies, according to which the uncertain risks posed by GE organisms must be taken, is socially and politically constructed. This also sheds light on the gap between the hegemonic and counter-hegemonic narratives, and between evidence-based and socially acceptable risk discourses. The different approaches produce specific regulatory outputs, pursue specific goals and reflect specific value systems.

The maximisation of aggregate wealth and the pursuit of the greatest *net* beneficial *protection* of public health and the environment, as explained in the sixth section, lie at the heart of evidence-based discourses. In the case of GE organisms, the costs to market-led scientific and economic development are understood as outweighing the public health, environmental and social benefits of more stringent regulatory approaches. Ultimately, society's common good is associated with market-driven scientific and technological development and the exercise of individual trade rights. The assumption is that this *economic dividend*, ie the maximisation of aggregate wealth, will result in *positive spill-overs* and benefit the rest of society.[246]

Socially acceptable risk approaches, on the other hand, enable regulators to take into consideration more than sound science and cost-benefit analysis. The assumption that market-driven technological innovations benefit society is not accepted in cases where regulators wish to prioritise enhanced levels of protection and consideration of specific OLFs at stake. In the case of agricultural biotechnologies, as the next chapter illustrates, reliance on socially acceptable risk approaches has so far largely resulted in the determination that the uncertain risks posed by GE products are not worth taking. Overall, the possibility (if not the attempt) to strike a different balance between individual market freedoms and collective stakes underlies socially acceptable risk approaches. Under these models, regulation should ultimately benefit individuals as part of a community and in their capacity as citizens and consumers.

Against this overall backdrop, the hegemonic and counter-hegemonic narratives and evidence-based and socially acceptable risk approaches to the governance of GE organisms reflect different underlying visions of *society's common good* and a different *balance* between *individual* freedoms and *collective* interests.[247] On these grounds, and taking the gap between the approaches into due consideration, can science or political deliberation help to solve transnational regulatory conflicts? Can a normatively legitimate legal discourse be constructed to reconcile the two paradigms? This is the final point that the chapter addresses.

VIII. Preliminary Normative Reflections: When (Sound) Science and Procedural Deliberation Fail

This final section sketches out some preliminary considerations pertaining to the normative strand of enquiry. It briefly discusses the prospects for a solution to the transatlantic conflict over agricultural biotechnologies; under the Conflicts Law theoretical framework, this qualifies as a horizontal regulatory conflict.

[246] In this respect, see also the analysis in the second part of ch 6.

[247] See also S Jasanoff (ed), *States of Knowledge: the Co-Production of Science and Social Order* (Routledge, 2004); S Jasanoff, *Designs on Nature. Science and Democracy in Europe and the United States* (Princeton University Press, 2005).

As already clarified, evidence-based and socially acceptable risk approaches are ideal types. No legal system perfectly aligns to either of the two models; the gap between the APHIS's and the FDA's regulations, on the one hand, and the EPA's more cautious approach to PIPs, on the other, provides a practical example in the context of the US system. Further, as the next chapter demonstrates, regulatory frameworks informed by a socially acceptable risk approach may still be implemented in an evidence-based manner. Yet, in the specific case of the governance of GE organisms, the gap between the two ideal types emerges quite clearly.

This chapter has extensively shown what results from adherence to evidence-based approaches, conducting the analysis by means of an enquiry into the US system. Socially acceptable risk perspectives, examined throughout the next chapter on the EU regulation of GE organisms, largely result in the opposite findings. Against this background, the paradigmatic transatlantic clash on GE organisms can be used to test the prospects of science and deliberative practices to identify normatively legitimate solutions and solve transnational regulatory conflicts. In other words, it provides a first opportunity to assess the ability and the limits of both science and procedural political deliberation to generate agreement in the face of persisting scientific uncertainty and political and social controversy. For this reason, this final section anticipates some information relating to the EU regulatory system. This is necessary in order to sketch out the relevant normative reflections. Normative considerations surrounding the gap between evidence-based and socially acceptable risk approaches in the field of agricultural biotechnologies will then be developed in greater depth and detail in the following chapter.[248]

The origins of the transatlantic conflict date back to the 1990s. In 1996, EU Member States' opposition to biotechnologies reached its highest level pending the authorisation of Bt-176 maize.[249] After authorisation of this variety by the European Commission, notwithstanding opposition by 14 out of 15 Member States in comitology, the Environmental Council of Ministers resorted to a de facto moratorium on new authorisations in 1999, pending the enactment of a new regulatory framework. National bans on GE varieties authorised at EU level followed suit. The moratorium lasted until 2004; in 2003, as explained in chapter five, the US, Canada and Argentina filed a complaint to the WTO.[250]

In 2000, the European Commission issued a Communication on the Precautionary Principle,[251] the cornerstone of the forthcoming legislation. In the following years, the relevant legislative acts were enacted. The post-moratorium EU regulatory framework draws on a *process-based* model, involving all-encompassing, *prudential* risk assessments of single GE varieties (including stacked events).

[248] By analysing the gap between the EU institutions' approach to governance of GE organisms, and the different perspective of a majority of EU Member States and EU civil society; see ch 4.
[249] For a detailed reconstruction of the dynamics of conflict, see Vogel, *The Politics of Precaution* (n 1).
[250] See the analysis of relevant facts and legal questions in ch 5, section VII.
[251] European Commission, COM(2000)1 Final, (n 185) section 5.

Authorisations for environmental release and marketing (including cultivation) of GE products and for the marketing of GE food and feed are time-limited; post-marketing monitoring and traceability obligations are in place, and GE varieties cannot be deregulated. Further, the authorisation procedure expressly allows for the application of the *precautionary principle* and the consideration of *OLFs*.[252]

Far from solving the controversy, however, this regulatory framework has triggered the enactment of a plurality of national safeguard measures; this aspect is analysed in detail in chapter four. In 2015, the regime was reformed again to allow Member States the possibility to opt-out from the cultivation of GE crops. At the time of writing, only one GE crop variety is authorised for commercial cultivation. This adamant resistance to the entrenchment of GE crops reflects a focus on their uncertain environmental risks, concerns about the governance of coexistence, strong views on the impact that agricultural biotechnologies can have on alternative agricultural models, and persisting doubts as to the environmental sustainability of GE varieties and their socio-economic advantages.[253] The authorisation of GE food varieties has also been highly controversial.

A rich literature exists on the transatlantic stalemate, which has been held to epitomise 'when cooperation fails'.[254] The causes of the conflict,[255] the

[252] See ch 4, for a detailed analysis.

[253] See *ch 4*.

[254] Pollack and Shaffer, *When Cooperation Fails* (n 1).

[255] In this respect, different commentators in different disciplinary areas have emphasised different sets of factors. According to some accounts, cultural and societal factors have played a crucial role in shaping public perception of risk and consumer aversion to GE organisms; see for instance M Echols, 'Food Safety Regulation in the European Union and the United States: Different Cultures, Different Laws' (1998) 4 *Columbia Journal of European Law* 525; G Skogstad, 'Internationalization, Democracy and Food Safety Measures: the (Il)Legitimacy of Consumer Preferences?' (2001) 7 *Global Governance* 293; G Skogstad, 'Contested Accountability Claims and GMO Regulation in the European Union' (2011) 49 *Journal of Common Market Studies* 895. If US consumers have historically been sceptical about the safety of natural foods and traditional processes of production, public opposition in the EU has recurrently targeted the safety of techniques such as genetic engineering, nanotechnology or animal cloning. Vogel's explanatory framework has focused on the role and reciprocal interaction of different variables, including the political orientation and policy preference of government officials, the regulatory criteria applied to risk assessment and risk management, and public opinion; see Vogel, *The Politics of Precaution* (n 1) 12 ff. Vogel has also emphasised the impact of food safety scares and policy failures in the EU throughout the 1990s, starting from the BSE (Bovine Spongiform Encephalopathy, commonly known as 'mad cow') disease food scandal; see, eg, C Ansell and D Vogel, 'The Contested Governance of European Food Safety Regulation' in C Ansell and D Vogel (eds), *What's the Beef? The Contested Governance of European Safety* (MIT Press, 2006). Further, Vogel has set the conflict on agricultural biotechnologies against the background of his theorisation of a transatlantic shift in precaution, whereby the US and the EU have been defined as 'ships passing in the night'. According to Vogel's analysis, precautionary risk regulation simultaneously retrenched and entrenched across the two sides of the Atlantic in the early Nineties; the governance of GE organisms is considered a paradigmatic example of this 'regulatory flip-flop'. See Vogel, *The Politics of Precaution* (n 1). Wiener et al have challenged this framing; see for instance Wiener et al, *The Reality of Precaution* (233). Finally, in their study of the transatlantic conflict, Pollack and Shaffer have argued that polarisation has neither been caused by cultural factors nor by institutional design. Rather, they have claimed that the transatlantic deadlock has been caused by the ability of interest groups to capitalise on pre-existing cultural and institutional differences. See Pollack and Shaffer, *When Cooperation Fails* (n 1) 22 ff.

forum-shopping techniques employed by the US and EU[256] and the many attempts to achieve coordination and regulatory convergence[257] have been extensively analysed throughout the years. Pollack and Shaffer have provided a comprehensive account of transatlantic attempts to achieve regulatory coordination and convergence in the field. Their analysis includes failed attempts through bilateral and multilateral inter-governmental negotiations, within trans-governmental networks of technical experts and regulators, and in transnational fora.[258] The latest attempt at transatlantic coordination in food safety, consumer protection and environmental matters was made under the umbrella of the negotiations for the Transatlantic Trade and Investment Partnership ('TTIP'). With respect to GE organisms, the US advocated ad hoc clauses on agricultural biotechnologies and an acceptance of low-level presence of unauthorised GE components in crops or food by the EU. Like previous attempts, these negotiations largely failed.[259]

Pollack and Shaffer have argued that the transatlantic debate on technical-scientific matters of risk assessment has been characterised by 'deliberation'. According to this representation, on the other hand, no deliberation has taken place in the 'politicised' field of risk management.[260] On these grounds, they have taken the view that political disagreement over risk management issues has prevented the development of a trans-governmental New World Order to technocratically manage food safety concerns. The blame has been largely put on the EU's allegedly arbitrary, 'politicised' and protectionist precautionary approach to agricultural biotechnologies.[261] Under this framing, 'technocratic deliberation' offers the only possible solution to the conflict. Trans-governmental networks of technocrats 'provide the setting for [...] transnational deliberative democracy',[262] and a trade-off exists between politics and successful deliberation.[263]

[256] For an analysis of the relationship between the SPS Agreement and Cartagena Protocol on Biosafety to the Convention on Biological Safety, see inter alia N Krisch, *Beyond Constitutionalism. The Pluralist Structure of Postnational Law* (OUP, 2010). On forum-shopping techniques, see Pollack and Shaffer, *When Cooperation Fails* (n 1) 235 ff. See also M Pollack and G Shaffer, 'The Challenge of Reconciling Regulatory Differences: Food Safety and GMOs in the Transatlantic Relationship' in M Pollack and G Shaffer (eds), *Transatlantic Governance in the Global Economy* (Rowman and Littlefield Publishers, 2001) 167 ff.

[257] Pollack and Shaffer, *When Cooperation Fails* (n 1) 85–112 and 113–175.

[258] ibid.

[259] For a detailed overview on relevant arrangements from a pro-TTIP perspective, see inter alia A Alemanno, 'The Regulatory Cooperation Chapter of the TTIP: Institutional Structure and Democratic Consequences' (2015) 18 *Journal of International Economic Law* 625; A Alemanno and JB Wiener, 'The Future of International Regulatory Cooperation: TTIP as a Learning Process Toward a Global Policy Laboratory' (2016) 78 *Law and Contemporary Problems* 101.

[260] Pollack and Shaffer, *When Cooperation Fails* (n 1) 102–112; 113–115; and 166 ff.

[261] ibid 62 ff.

[262] ibid 16.

[263] ibid 108–112.

This account is clearly influenced by modern, science-centred paradigms. The analysis in this section sets aside the terminology of 'technocratic deliberation',[264] and replaces it with the notion of agreement through science. The relevant question then becomes whether science can help generate agreement and identify normatively legitimate solutions in complex regulatory cases. As noted since the introductory chapter, reference to scientific matters *may* help build consensus in cases where uncertainties are very low, agreement very solid and scientific evidence is undisputed. Where these preconditions are missing, however, the picture becomes increasingly complex and normative frames are bound to play a greater role: in the face of scientific pluralism and high levels of complexity, the boundaries between 'facts' and 'values' fade. Where the advantages associated with a product or process are disputed, the determination that a risk is acceptable will be even more controversial, regardless of whether such risk is deemed 'negligible' in specific contexts or jurisdictions.

This chapter has emphasised that a normative component is inherent to the regulation of uncertain risks. As argued since the introductory chapter, the determination of the threshold of legally relevant adverse effects is never a mere scientific matter. Where different normative frames are applied, as in the case of agricultural biotechnologies, the gap between sound science vis-à-vis prudential approaches to risk assessment, and adherence to sound science vis-à-vis regulatory focus on uncertainties, will be reflected in the relevant evidence base and inferences. As coexisting product and process-based models of governing GE organisms illustrate, and as the next chapter further explores, the very framing of the relevant scientific questions can be irreconcilable where science is analysed through different normative lenses.[265] Against this backdrop, and as science-centred accounts indirectly testify, *agreement through science* refers to regulatory convergence by means of adherence to *sound science*.[266]

This perfectly reflects the hegemonic transnational narrative on agricultural biotechnologies, and the underlying tenets of evidence-based approaches. Yet, this form of regulatory coordination results in the choice of one specific approach, and normative frame, over another. As this chapter has illustrated, sound science is not 'pure' science. Science cannot provide a single 'correct' answer in the field of risk regulation: different approaches reflect different value systems and pursue different goals. In so far as the normative component of the risk regulation process remains unaddressed, then, adherence to sound science cannot provide

[264] As explained since the first chapter, the Habermasian notion of deliberation refers to rational communicative processes surrounding scientific as well as normative (political, socio-economic and cultural) factors. For this reason, this section uses the different terminology of 'agreement through science'.

[265] See in particular ch 4, section V.

[266] In cases where hazards have been conclusively proven and risks have been characterised, on the other hand, science-centred accounts usually assume that the cost-benefit effective baseline of protection identified by reference to sound science is a neutral, objective and universal benchmark. Under this framing, regulatory systems pursuing enhanced levels of protection are alleged to focus on 'hazards' rather than on 'risks'; see ch 1 and n 105 therein.

a universally agreeable and normatively legitimate solution to complex regulatory conflicts. To the contrary, reliance on sound science (and cost-benefit effectiveness considerations) will always be open to challenge by stakeholders who focus on persisting scientific uncertainty (and different factors).

The ensuing and final question, then, is whether the horizontal transatlantic conflict could be solved through political deliberation. Procedural deliberative paradigms, as already explained, acknowledge the need to address normative factors, with a view to procedurally identifying a normatively legitimate solution. Rational communicative processes and deliberative practices should set the ground for the identification of agreeable solutions; genuine agreement, in turn, ensures that the final solution will be regarded as normatively legitimate by all actors. The long history of failed attempts at transatlantic regulatory coordination testify to considerable difficulties in identifying a mutually agreeable and thus normatively legitimate solution. The parties have hardly missed any opportunities to engage in negotiations at different levels and within different fora. However, this has not produced significant improvements.

This chapter's analysis of the US regulatory system through the lens of evidence-based approaches shows that the failure of procedural deliberation at the transatlantic level is ultimately unsurprising. As briefly explained, and as further illustrated in the following chapter, the US and EU frameworks for governance of GE organisms are informed by diametrically opposite approaches. The balances struck between the values and interests at stake in this field are different; this is reflected in different governance arrangements, different regulatory categories and different goals. The *substantive* gap between the two governance approaches is far too broad for deliberative *procedural* practices to generate consensus among relevant actors. Universally acceptable regulatory solutions cannot be identified; overall, no connection exists between the underlying normative premises, which influence the scientific framing of the relevant questions, the ensuing scientific inferences and the final determinations.

As explained in the introductory chapter, this does not imply that procedural deliberative attempts to reconcile different perspectives are irrelevant for the purpose of identifying normatively legitimate solutions. However, it means that procedural deliberation is bound to fail in the absence of specific substantive preconditions: most importantly, common values and goals. If the gap between different approaches is unbridgeable, as it is in the transatlantic regulation of agricultural biotechnologies, the failure of political deliberation will be the mere procedural reflection of irreconcilable substantive perspectives. Where societal complexity and irreconcilable normative frames come into play, rational communicative processes and deliberative practices are insufficient to generate true agreement and identify truly legitimate solutions. Following this analytical thread, the next chapter sheds further light on the unbridgeable gap between evidence-based and socially acceptable risk approaches. The analysis is conducted by focusing on EU regulatory frameworks and EU regulatory implementation.

4

Across Extra-Territoriality and Legal Pluralisation: EU Regulation of GE Organisms. The Counter-Hegemonic Narrative and the Question of Regulatory Implementation

The counter-hegemonic narrative is under analysis in this chapter. With regard to the reasons why the EU legal system is interrogated as a transnationally relevant legal regime, EU governance of GE organisms has a twofold relevance: the enquiry cuts across the two dimensions of extra-territoriality and legal pluralisation. In the first respect, EU regulation of GE organisms has been central to the construction of the counter-hegemonic narrative on agricultural biotechnologies and has had a powerful impact on transnational discourses. Just like in the case of US governance of GE organisms, the EU regulatory approach and EU regulatory categories have transnational relevance and have become a constituent part of transnational counter-hegemonic discourses, resonating well beyond the boundaries of the EU.[1] From this perspective, the analysis deconstructs the transnational counter-hegemonic narrative *from within* the EU regional legal system.

In the second respect (legal pluralisation), the EU legal regime is analysed as a supra-national system in its own right. EU governance of GE organisms impacts on EU Member States' governance of GE crops and GE food and feed. This adds a further layer of analysis, as the EU and EU Member States have repeatedly clashed over the implementation of the regulatory framework. On these grounds, the chapter also deconstructs the counter-hegemonic narrative *across* the nation state (EU Member State) level.

This brings us to the last questions on methodology. What does the analysis uncover, and how does it help deconstruct the counter-hegemonic narrative on agricultural biotechnologies? How does the enquiry shed light on socially

[1] In a similar perspective, emphasising the role played by the EU and its attempts to export its regulatory approach, see M Pollack and G Shaffer, *When Cooperation Fails. The International Law and Politics of Genetically Modified Foods* (OUP, 2009) 116. From a legal pluralist perspective, see also the analysis in N Krisch, *Beyond Constitutionalism. The Pluralist Structure of Postnational Law* (OUP, 2010).

acceptable risk discourses? To begin with, the analysis shows how a socially acceptable risk approach is embedded in EU *regulation* of GE organisms.[2] The EU regulatory framework is characterised by a prudential approach to risk assessment, an emphasis on different forms of uncertainty, the pursuit of enhanced levels of protection and reference to the precautionary principle and OLFs. While the EU regulatory framework reflects socially acceptable risk models, however, *regulatory implementation* at EU level has ultimately drawn on evidence-based approaches. For the purposes of the present analysis, this has led to a regulatory asymmetry. On the one hand, the EU's regulatory approach to agricultural biotechnologies has powerfully shaped the counter-hegemonic narrative on GE organisms and fed into transnational discourses on socially acceptable risk. On the other hand, the evidence-based implementation of the framework at EU level has caused controversy within and between EU Member States.

The analysis points to the gap between the EU institutions' adherence to an evidence-based model, in the implementation of the relevant regulatory arrangements, and the socially acceptable risk perspective taken and advocated by a majority of EU Member States and the greater part of EU civil society. EU institutions, notably the Commission at risk management level, have ultimately failed to do justice to national and societal views that the intended level of protection must be very high in the field of agricultural biotechnologies, and the threshold of socially acceptable risk correspondingly low. It is overall unsurprising that OLFs have never been *expressly* taken into account.[3] Yet, taking the specificities of EU risk governance into due consideration, it is surprising that OLFs have never *implicitly* fed into a determination that, in the face of persisting uncertainty and in so far as more sustainable alternatives are available, the risks posed by agricultural biotechnologies are not socially acceptable at EU level. By conforming to an evidence-based approach, EU institutions have then failed to identify a politically and socially acceptable threshold of risk. This has resulted in persisting deadlock and horizontal and vertical regulatory conflicts.

Better than the examination of the EU regulatory framework, then, the analysis of EU-wide controversies at the regulatory implementation stage sheds light on the rationale of socially acceptable risk approaches, their characteristics, the relevant regulatory categories and their broader political and socio-economic implications. The analysis of the EU governance of GE organisms and EU case law in this field thus illustrates the broader vision underlying socially acceptable risk discourses, just like the previous chapter has endeavoured to do in respect of evidence-based risk regulation. In other words, the chapter shows what adherence to socially acceptable risk approaches entails in practice.

[2] As well as in the EU system of risk regulation, at a more general level. See below, sections II and III.

[3] As suggested by Lee, it is already so difficult for a regulatory focus on uncertainty to compete with adherence to sound science that directly pointing to OLFs may be no more than a self-defeating argument; 'when factors beyond risk do enter the regulatory process, they generally provide a process to allow dangers'. See M Lee, 'Beyond Safety? The Broadening Scope of Risk Regulation' (2009) 62 *Current Legal Problems* 280–281.

The intractability of the conflict at EU level also exemplifies the unbridgeable gap between evidence-based and socially acceptable risk approaches in the field of GE organisms. The analysis picks up the preliminary normative reflections of chapter three and develops them in greater depth and detail. Yet again, the normative strand of enquiry points to the limits of science and procedural deliberation to facilitate consensus in controversial cases. The analysis illustrates the gap between more or less prudential approaches to risk assessment and a regulatory focus on sound scientific proof of hazards and risks, as opposed to persisting uncertainties. These result in differences in the relevant evidence base and in the inferences drawn.

In turn, different approaches to risk assessment and the different extent to which uncertainties are taken into account reflect the pursuit of different levels of protection, and are informed by different positions as regards recourse to the precautionary principle and consideration of OLFs. In other words, the normative frames through which science is being evaluated and the consequent threshold of acceptable risk are radically different. As the analysis shows, the very framing of the relevant scientific questions can be irreconcilable where diametrically opposed approaches to risk governance are being followed. On these grounds, science fails to generate genuine agreement where normative premises and perspectives diverge. As explained since the introductory chapter, in the face of scientific uncertainty and complexity, technical expertise cannot provide a single 'correct' and agreeable answer.

Turning to procedural political deliberation, again, the analysis of this chapter shows how this is also bound to fail due to the gap between evidence-based and socially acceptable risk approaches in this field. This is a gap that procedural arrangements or cooperative efforts cannot possibly bridge. The *substantive* (normative) preconditions to *procedurally* reconstruct genuine forms of agreement, ie shared values, perspectives and goals, are missing in this regulatory area. Consequently, horizontal and vertical conflicts are bound to remain unsolved.

The first section sets the stage for the analysis, providing an overview of the procedural arrangements enshrined in the 2001 Directive on the deliberate release of GE organisms and the 2003 Regulation on GE food and feed. The second and third sections illustrate how a prudential approach to risk assessment, a focus on scientific uncertainty and a socially acceptable risk approach to risk management are embedded in both legislative instruments; the analysis is set against the broader backdrop of the EU institutional architecture of risk governance.

The fourth, fifth and sixth sections focus on the implementation of the regulatory framework at risk assessment and risk management level. In so doing, they contrapose the EU institutions' evidence-based perspective to the claims of civil society and Member States. The gap between the two models is explored through an analysis of relevant case law. The deconstruction of clashing substantive approaches, with all relevant implications, has a twofold value: it illuminates the features of socially acceptable risk models, and shows the inadequacy of both science and procedural deliberation to solve the relevant conflicts. The eighth and ninth sections then analyse the 2015 EU reform of the cultivation of GE crops. The analysis shows how, from a socially acceptable risk perspective, this is an unsatisfactory compromise. The final section draws together all relevant conclusions from the chapter.

I. The pre-2015 Regulatory Framework: The 2001 Deliberate Release Directive and the 2003 Food and Feed Regulation

Directive 2001/18/EC (hereafter, 'the Directive') regulates the deliberate release into the environment of GE organisms and applies to GE organisms 'as [products] or in products'.[4] Regulation (EC) No 1829/2003 (hereafter, 'the Regulation') regulates GE organisms falling in the category of GE '[human] food or [animal] feed'.[5] Both the Directive and the Regulation use the terminology of 'GMOs', rather than 'GE organisms'. However, as the next paragraphs explain, the scope of application has now been broadened to encompass organisms obtained through NBTs, beyond transgenesis ('traditional' genetic modification through recombinant DNA).

Article 2(5) of the Regulation ('Definitions') references the definition of a 'GMO' in Article 2(2) of the Directive and relevant exemptions in Annex I B of the same legislative act. Under Article 2(2) of the Directive, a GMO is defined as 'an organism, with the exception of human beings, in which the genetic material has been altered in a way that does not occur naturally […]'. Part 1 of Annex I A of the Directive provides a non-exhaustive list[6] of techniques of genetic modification, including

[4] Directive 2001/18/EC of the European Parliament and of the Council of 12 March 2001 on the Deliberate Release into the Environment of Genetically Modified Organisms and Repealing Council Directive 90/220/EEC, [2001] OJ L106/1, Art 1. See below, sections VIII and IX, on the 2015 reform. See also the amendments in Directive 2008/27/EC of the European Parliament and of the Council of 11 March 2008 amending Directive 2001/18/EC on the Deliberate Release into the Environment of Genetically Modified Organisms, as Regards the Implementing Powers conferred on the Commission, [2008] OJ L81/45. Arts 6, 13, 25 and 28 of the Directive have been recently amended by Regulation (EU) 2019/1381 of the European Parliament and of the Council of 20 June 2019 on the Transparency and Sustainability of the EU Risk Assessment in the Food Chain and Amending Regulations (EC) No 1829/2003, (EC) No 1831/2003, (EC) No 2065/2003, (EC) No 1935/2004, (EC) No 1331/2008, (EC) No 1107/2009, (EU) 2015/2283 and Directive 2001/18/EC, [2019] OJ L231/1. The amendments aim to enhance the publicity and transparency of the risk assessment process.

[5] Regulation (EC) No 1829/2003 of the European Parliament and of the Council of 22 September 2003 on Genetically Modified Foods, [2003] OJ L268/1, Art 3(1). Arts 5(3), 6(7), 10(1), 11(2), 17(3), 18(7), 22(1), 23(2), 29(1) and (2) and 30 of the Regulation have been recently amended by Regulation 1381/2019 (n 4). The amendments aim to enhance the publicity and transparency of the risk assessment process.

[6] See the text of Annex I A ('inter alia'), and Art 2(2)(a) of the Directive.

'recombinant nucleic acid techniques involving the formation of new combinations of genetic material by the insertion of nucleic acid molecules [...] into a host organism in which they do not naturally occur' (traditional transgenesis), 'techniques involving the direct introduction into an organism of heritable material' and 'cell fusion of hybridisation techniques'. Part 2 of Annex I A expressly excludes three techniques, which are not considered to result in genetic modification. Further, under Article 3(1), the Directive shall not apply to organisms obtained through the techniques of genetic modification listed in Annex I B. Pursuant to Annex I B, these include mutagenesis and the fusion of plant cells of organisms which can exchange genetic material through traditional breeding methods.

NBTs, whether involving genome editing or not,[7] are not mentioned in either of the Annexes. This triggers questions surrounding the status of organisms obtained through these techniques: more specifically, whether they qualify as 'GMOs' and whether they fall within the scope of application of the regulatory framework. These matters were raised in Case C-528/16 *Confédération Paysanne*,[8] where the French Conseil d'État referred four questions to the European Court of Justice ('ECJ') for a preliminary ruling on a case involving herbicide-tolerant rape varieties obtained through new mutagenesis techniques. By its first question, the referring court asked whether organisms obtained through new mutagenesis techniques qualify as 'GMOs' within the meaning of Article 2(2).[9] Article 3(1) provides that the Directive shall not apply to organisms obtained through the techniques of *genetic modification* listed in Annex I B; this Annex includes mutagenesis. As confirmed by the ECJ,[10] new mutagenesis techniques do qualify as genetic modification techniques.

More importantly, in the second part of its first question, the referring court enquired whether Articles 2(2) and 3(1), read in conjunction with the express mutagenesis exemption of Annex I B, should be interpreted as meaning that the scope of application of the Directive excludes '*all* organisms and seeds obtained by mutagenesis, or *only* organisms obtained by [...] mutagenesis methods [...] existing before those measures were adopted' (emphasis added).[11] This question addressed the crucial point of the case: the applicability of the regulatory framework to organisms obtained through new techniques of genetic engineering, unknown at the time the framework was enacted. The ECJ answered this question by interpreting the relevant provisions in light of the precautionary principle.[12] Taking a dynamic and evolutionary perspective,[13] and having due regard to the

[7] See ch 1, section I.
[8] Case C-528/16, *Confédération Paysanne and Others v Premier Ministre and Ministre de l'Agriculture, de l'Agroalimentaire et de la Forêt*, EU:C:2018:583.
[9] Case C-528/16, *Confédération Paysanne*, 25.
[10] ibid 27–38.
[11] ibid 25.
[12] ibid 52.
[13] ibid 41–54.

text of Recital (17) of the Directive,[14] it ruled that the mutagenesis exemption of Article 3(1) and Annex I B

> must be interpreted as meaning that *only* organisms obtained by means of techniques/methods of mutagenesis which have *conventionally been used* in a number of applications and have *a long safety record* are excluded from the scope of that Directive (emphasis added).[15]

After the ECJ's decision in this case, organisms obtained through new mutagenesis techniques are subject to all obligations arising from the Directive. On these grounds, and by direct analogy, any organisms obtained through NBTs now qualify as 'GMOs' and fall within the scope of application of the 2001–2003 regulatory framework. As the ECJ broadened the Directive's scope of application in the specific case of mutagenesis, narrowly interpreting an express regulatory exemption, the same would certainly occur with GE organisms obtained through different NBTs.[16] Against this backdrop, in the EU legal system, 'GE organisms' have ultimately come to be defined as 'GMOs'. However, as already explained, the former category is in fact broader than the latter. For this reason, this chapter will continue to use the more accurate terminology of 'GE organisms'.

As briefly mentioned in chapter three, EU governance of GE organisms draws on a process-based model. As such, the presumption that genetic engineering

[14] See the text of Recital (17) to the Directive: 'This Directive should not apply to organisms obtained through certain techniques of genetic modification which have conventionally been used in a number of applications and have a long safety record'.

[15] Case C-528/16, *Confédération Paysanne*, 51 and 54. For a more detailed analysis of the case, see GC Leonelli, 'Judicial Review of Compliance with the Precautionary Principle from *Paraquat* to *Blaise*: Quantitative Thresholds, Risk Assessment and the Gap between Regulation and Regulatory Implementation' (2021) 22 *German Law Journal* 184.

[16] In that these techniques have not been conventionally used and do not have a long safety record. It is worth adding that before the ECJ delivered its ruling in *Confédération Paysanne* the Commission had requested three opinions on synthetic biology from the Scientific Committee on Health and Environmental Risks, the Scientific Committee on Emerging and Newly Identified Health Risks and the Scientific Committee on Consumer Safety; see SCHER, SCENIHR and SCCS, *Opinion on Synthetic Biology I, Definition* (2014); SCHER, SCENIHR and SCCS, *Opinion on Synthetic Biology II, Risk Assessment Methodologies and Safety Aspects* (2015); SCHER, SCENIHR and SCCS, *Opinion on Synthetic Biology III, Risks to the Environment and Biodiversity Related to Synthetic Biology and Research Priorities in the Field of Synthetic Biology* (2015). In 2017, the Commission's Scientific Advice Mechanism published an explanatory note covering all NBTs; see European Scientific Advice Mechanism, High Level Group of Scientific Advisors, *New Techniques in Agricultural Biotechnology* (2017). In March 2019, after the ruling in *Confédération Paysanne* and on a request from the Commission, an ad hoc study on the detection of food and feed obtained by means of new mutagenesis techniques was finalised; see European Network of GMO Laboratories, *Detection of Food and Feed Plant Products Obtained by New Mutagenesis Techniques* (2019). Further information on the implementation of the ECJ's ruling is available at https://ec.europa.eu/food/plant/gmo/modern_biotech_en and https://ec.europa.eu/food/plant/gmo/post_authorisation/detection_methods_en. In November 2019, the Council requested the Commission to provide a study on NBTs. See Council Decision EU 2019/1904 of 8 November 2019 Requesting the Commission to Submit a Study in Light of the Court of Justice's Judgment in Case C-528/16 Regarding the Status of Novel Genomic Techniques under Union Law and a Proposal, if Appropriate in View of the Outcomes of the Study, [2019] OJ L293/103. The study has not been finalised yet. As of June 2020, no organism obtained through NBTs involving genome editing is authorised for placing on the market in the EU; nor are any applications for authorisation pending.

techniques do not pose inherent risks and the presumption of substantial equivalence do not apply. Each and every GE variety, including stacked events, goes through a mandatory authorisation process. This includes a thorough and all-encompassing risk assessment,[17] followed by authorisation by political risk managers. GE varieties are not deregulated after approval. Authorisations cannot exceed 10 years, and renewals of authorisation must be sought after the expiry of the original authorisation.[18] In the majority of cases, post-marketing monitoring will also apply.[19] Further, stringent traceability and labelling obligations are in place.[20]

The Directive applies to applications for the environmental release of GE organisms for research or experimental purposes, applications for the dissemination and cultivation of GE crops, and applications to place GE products other than food and feed on the market.[21] Part B of the Directive deals with deliberate release for any purpose other than placing on the market, whereas Part C (Articles 12 to 24) regulates authorisations to place GE organisms 'as or in products' on the market.

Where GE organisms are being released in the environment for experimental purposes, the applicant shall submit a notification to the competent authority of the Member State[22] where the environmental release will take place. The notification must include a technical dossier, information relating to the conditions of release and potential receiving environment, information on the interactions of the GE variety with the environment, a monitoring plan and an environmental risk assessment. The competent national authority will then indicate whether it is satisfied that the proposed release meets the requirements of the Directive. The notifier may only proceed with the release after receiving written consent by the national authority, and shall comply with the specific conditions set by the authority.[23]

[17] See section II for a detailed overview.

[18] See Recitals (48) and (49) and Arts 13(2)(d), 15(4) and 17(6) of the Directive, as well as Arts 7(5) and 19(5) of the Regulation.

[19] Post-market monitoring is compulsory under the Directive: see Recitals (20), (43) and (44) and Arts 5(1)(c) and 20(1). See also Annexes III A and VII to the Directive. In the case of GE food or feed, on the other hand, post-market monitoring will apply if deemed appropriate: see Recital (35) and Arts 5(3)(k), 17(3)(k) and 23(2)(b) of the Regulation.

[20] On traceability, see Recitals (41) and (42) and Art 4(6) of the Directive, as well as Recitals (23) and (29) and Art 2(2) of the Regulation. On labelling, see Recitals (33), (40), Arts 13(2)(f), 19(3)(e), 21, 26 and Annex IV of the Directive, as well as Recitals (16) to (24), Recital (29) and Arts 1(c), 5(3)(f), 5(3)(g), 6(5)(d), 12, 13 and 14(1) of the Regulation. For a detailed overview on traceability and labelling obligations, including the specific and stringent EU thresholds for labelling, see Regulation (EC) No 1830/2003 of the European Parliament and of the Council of 22 September 2003 Concerning the Traceability and Labelling of Genetically Modified Organisms and the Traceability of Food and Feed Products Produced from Genetically Modified Organisms and Amending Directive 2001/18/EC, [2003] OJ L268. See also Case C-442/09, *Bablok and Others*, EU:C:2011:541.

[21] For all relevant definitions, see Art 2(3) and (4) of the Directive.

[22] See Art 4(4) of the Directive.

[23] See Art 6.

Notifications for placing GE varieties on the market must also be submitted to the national competent authority of the Member State where they will take place.[24] Such notifications must include a technical dossier on the GE variety, a full environmental risk assessment, conditions for placing the product on the market, a proposed period of consent (not to exceed 10 years), a plan for monitoring, proposals for labelling and packaging and a summary of the dossier.[25]

Annex II of the Directive lays out the principles for environmental risk assessment, and Annexes III and IV list the general information required for the purposes of the notifications. A case-by-case, full environmental risk assessment must be conducted. As explained in further detail in the next section, risk assessment shall take into account any direct, indirect, immediate, delayed, cumulative and long-term effects associated with the GE product, including the interaction of the GE variety with the relevant ecosystems and with other GE varieties.[26]

Although the competent national authorities are in charge of assessing the dossier and environmental risk assessment, the procedure widely engages other Member States and EU institutions. Pursuant to Article 13, upon receipt of a notification for placing a GE variety on the market, the competent national authorities shall forward the relevant documents to the Commission, which shall then forward them to the regulatory authorities in the other Member States.[27] The competent national authority will then draft an assessment report, drawing its conclusions as to whether the GE variety should be authorised. The assessment report will also be circulated. Annex VI includes guidelines for drafting the assessment report.[28]

Articles 15 ('Standard Procedure') and 18 ('Procedure in Case of Objections') provide for the next steps in the process. National authorities and the Commission may request further information, make comments or present reasoned objections to the authorisation. All comments and objections will be circulated. If there are no objections, or if any outstanding issues are resolved, the competent national authority which originally received the application will give its consent in writing, informing the Commission and the Member States.[29]

If an objection is raised and maintained or if the original assessment report concludes that the GE variety should not be authorised, the Commission may request that the applicant provide further data and shall seek an opinion from the European Food Safety Authority (hereafter, the 'EFSA').[30] The EFSA GMO Panel

[24] See Art 13(1); however, see below in this section for the 'one door one key' procedure under the 2003 Regulation.

[25] See Art 13(2), (3) and (4).

[26] See Annex II to the Directive.

[27] Art 13(1).

[28] See Art 14.

[29] Art 15(3) and (4).

[30] See Art 18. The original version of Arts 18 and 28 of the Directive refers to the relevant 'Scientific Committee(s)': however, after the enactment of Regulation No 178/2002, the EFSA's Panel on GMOs (GMO Panel) has replaced all committees. For more information on the EFSA, see Regulation (EC) 178/2002 of the European Parliament and of the Council of 28 January 2002 Laying Down the General Principles and Requirements of Food Law, Establishing the European Food Safety Authority and

will then conduct its assessment of the GE variety. Since the enactment of the Directive, objections have been recurrently raised against authorisations; for this reason, the procedure has consistently been escalated to the EU level, involving the EFSA. Moreover, it is worth underlining that the practical relevance of the Directive's regulatory arrangements has diminished considerably throughout the years. There are two main reasons for this. First, in the face of persisting EU-wide controversy over the commercial cultivation of GE organisms, the number of applications for the authorisation of GE crop varieties has dramatically decreased. At the time of writing, only one GE crop is authorised for cultivation in the EU.[31] Second, the majority of applications for the authorisation of GE crops have been filed under the 2003 Regulation, in accordance with the 'one door one key' approach[32] detailed below.

The 2003 Regulation applies to authorisations of GE varieties for food use,[33] food containing or consisting of GE varieties[34] and food produced from or containing ingredients produced from GE varieties.[35] Articles 15 and 16 of the Regulation extend the same definitions to the category of GE feed. The Regulation draws on a more centralised process than the Directive. Member States only act as 'postmen'.[36] Upon receipt of an application, national authorities must forward the technical dossier and all relevant documents to the EFSA. The EFSA should engage with national scientific authorities[37] and with its own Advisory Forum, made up of Member States' experts; however, it will be fully in charge of risk assessment.

Where an overlap exists between the scope of application of the 2001 Directive and the 2003 Regulation, ie where an authorisation is being sought for a GE crop intended for use as human food or animal feed, the applicant may opt for the 'one door one key' approach. The applicant can thus file a single application under the 2003 Regulation: in this case, the environmental risk assessment prescribed under the Directive will be incorporated into the Regulation's authorisation process. The 2003 Regulation respectively provides that the EFSA *may* 'ask the appropriate food

Laying Down Procedures in Matters of Food Safety, [2002] OJ L31/1, the General Food Law (hereafter, 'GFL'). The GFL has been recently amended by Regulation 1381/2019 (n 4).

[31] For more information, see the EU database at www.webgate.ec.europa.eu/dyna/gm_register/index_en.cfm. As of June 2020, there are 13 cotton varieties, 33 maize varieties, 5 oilseed rape varieties, 21 soybean varieties and 1 sugar beet variety authorised for use as food or feed or any other use except cultivation; in some cases, specific authorisation for a variety include additional stacked events. The (MON810) maize variety is currently the only variety authorised for cultivation; the renewal of the authorisation is ongoing as of June 2020.

[32] For use of this terminology, see N De Sadeleer, 'Marketing and Cultivation of GMOs in the EU. An Uncertain Balance Between Centripetal and Centrifugal Forces' (2015) 6 *European Journal of Risk Regulation* 532, 534.

[33] See the 2003 Regulation, Art 3(1)(a) and 4(4). On the requirements for applications, see also Commission Implementing Regulation (EU) No 503/2013 of 3 April 2013 on Applications for Authorisation of Genetically Modified Food and Feed in Accordance with Regulation (EC) No 1829/2003, [2013] OJ L157/1.

[34] ibid, Art 3(1)(b) and 4(4).

[35] ibid, Art 3(1)(c) and 4(4).

[36] De Sadeleer, 'Marketing and Cultivation' (n 32) 538.

[37] See for instance Art 5(2)(b).

assessment body of a Member State to carry out a safety assessment'[38] and that it *shall* 'ask a national competent authority to carry out the environmental risk assessment'.[39] The requirement that a national authority shall conduct the environmental risk assessment aims to rebalance the centralised process underlying the Regulation. The possibility for an applicant to resort to the Regulation procedures may otherwise contradict the different rationales of the two legislative acts.

Once the EFSA Panel has delivered its opinion, the decision enters the risk management stage. The Commission shall enact a draft decision and submit it to comitology.[40] The comitology system involves committees of Member State representatives acting as a check and balance on the Commission, when the latter is exercising its delegated or implementing powers.[41] Under comitology rules, the draft proposal is first submitted to the Committee of National Representatives, which must reach a decision by qualified majority. Where this proves impossible, the Commission's draft proposal may be submitted to the Appeal Committee, also made up of representatives from the Member States.[42] Where the Appeal Committee, in turn, cannot reach a decision by qualified majority, the ball is back in the Commission's court. The Commission may then decide to approve the draft decision single-handedly, withdraw it, or submit a revised draft proposal.[43]

This concludes the preliminary, general overview of the regulatory framework. The next sections analyse the 2001 Directive and 2003 Regulation against the backdrop of the notions of prudential risk assessment, scientific uncertainty, precaution and OLFs. The analysis illustrates how the EU regulatory framework reflects a socially acceptable risk approach to the governance of GE organisms.

II. The EU Regulatory Framework and Socially Acceptable Risk Approaches: Prudential Risk Assessment and Uncertainties

The 2001 Directive and the 2003 Regulation reflect a *prudential* approach to risk assessment and a clear focus on *scientific uncertainty*. Recital (4) of the Directive underlines that the environmental release of GE organisms may have irreversible effects. Recitals (5) and (6) mandate that any uncertain risks should be assessed to protect human health and the environment. Recital (19) provides that a

[38] Art 6(3)(b).

[39] Art 6(3)(c).

[40] See the references in Arts 7(1), 7(3), 19(1), 19(3) and 35 of the Regulation.

[41] See the procedures laid out in Regulation (EU) No 182/2011 of the European Parliament and of the Council of 16 February 2011 Laying Down the Rules and General Principles Concerning Mechanisms for Control by Member States of the Commission's Exercise of Implementing Powers, [2011] OJ L55/13.

[42] Art 5(4), Reg 182/2011.

[43] Art 6(3), Reg 182/2011.

case-by-case environmental risk assessment should always be carried out prior to release, taking due account of any potential cumulative and long-term effects associated with interaction with the environment.[44] Importantly, Recital (21) calls on Member States and the Commission to 'ensure that systematic and independent research on the potential risks involved in the deliberate release or the placing on the market of [GE organisms] is conducted'. This aims to rebalance the information asymmetry between developers of GE organisms, who are in charge of submitting relevant technical-scientific data, and regulators.[45]

Under Article 4(2), any person shall, before submitting a notification for environmental release for field trials or for placing a GE variety on the market, carry out an environmental risk assessment.[46] Annex II to the Directive provides a detailed overview of the objectives, general principles and methodology for environmental risk assessment.[47] Intended, unintended, direct, indirect, immediate, delayed as well as cumulative long-term effects should be taken into consideration.[48]

Reference to the precautionary principle, to be understood in this context as reference to a prudential risk assessment, is made in part B of Annex II ('General Principles'). Other principles mentioned therein include a comparison of the characteristics of the GE variety with the characteristics of the conventional counterpart (comparative assessment, focusing on substantial equivalence), transparency, and a case-by-case risk assessment, taking into consideration factors such as the intended scale of release or use, the potential receiving environment and the interactions between them.[49] The final determination of the level of risk posed by a GE variety should result from an evaluation of the probability of each adverse effect combined with the magnitude of the consequences.

The first step in the process consists of the identification of the characteristics which may cause adverse effects.[50] Potential adverse effects may include toxic or allergenic effects, effects on the dynamics and genetic diversity of populations of species in the receiving environment (leading to a potential decline in biodiversity), altered susceptibility to pathogens, the creation of new reservoirs or vectors, the development of antibiotic resistance and effects on biogeochemical cycles. All in all, the main potential adverse effects are the likelihood that the GE variety

[44] See also the text of Art 4(3) of the Directive.

[45] In this respect, see also the general reform of the EFSA and transparency and publicity of risk assessment, including data formats, in Reg 1381/2019 (n 4). See n 4 for the specific amendments to the Directive.

[46] See also Recital (22).

[47] As complemented by specific EFSA's protocols. See the amendments provided for in Commission Directive (EU) 2018/350 of 8 March 2018 amending Directive 2001/18/EC of the European Parliament and of the Council as Regards the Environmental Risk Assessment of Genetically Modified Organisms, [2018] OJ L67/30.

[48] See Annex II, Principles for the Environmental Risk Assessment, section C, as modified by Directive (EU) 2018/350.

[49] Annex II, part B.

[50] Annex II, part C, section C.3.

will become persistent and invasive in natural habitats, the potential for crop to crop gene transfer and hybridisation, and any effects on target and non-target organisms.[51]

The following steps in the process involve an evaluation of the likelihood of adverse effects and the potential consequences of each adverse effect. In accordance with a prudential approach, the Annex provides that 'potential adverse effects shall not be discounted on the basis that they are unlikely to occur';[52] for the purposes of hazard characterisation, risk assessors should assume that potential adverse effects will occur.[53] Further, and crucially, the Annex underscores that both the probability of adverse effects and the magnitude of the potential consequences of each adverse effect are influenced by the *environment* of release and the *manner* or *scale* of release.[54] At the end of this process, the authority will estimate the relevant risks and define a risk management strategy. Risk management measures should be taken into account when assessing the relevant margins of risk.[55]

On these grounds, the environmental risk assessment prescribed under the 2001 Directive is clearly informed by a prudential approach. Not only does it draw on a process-based model, but it also mandates a cautious approach to the evaluation of any direct or indirect potential adverse effects and their probabilities.[56] A prudential focus on all forms of uncertainty, as categorised since the first chapter, is directly advocated for the purposes of risk assessment. Further, the criteria laid out for the environmental risk assessment and notification under Annex III A emphasise the crucial relevance of factors such as geographical location, the climatic and geological characteristics of the areas, the ecosystems where the GE variety will be disseminated,[57] the scale of release, and risk mitigation measures, for the purpose of assessing risk in practice.[58] This reflects an attempt to conduct thorough, all-encompassing risk assessments.

The authorisation process engages different scientific authorities, including national agencies, the Commission and the EFSA. After a GE variety is authorised, stringent post-marketing monitoring obligations apply. The requirements for monitoring plans are enshrined in Annex VII, according to which monitoring should 'confirm that any assumption regarding the occurrence and impact of potential adverse effects of the [GE variety] are correct […] or identify the occurrence of adverse effects'.[59] Also, as already mentioned, authorisations are time-limited; renewals of authorisations will take the results of monitoring into account.

[51] See also ch 3.
[52] Annex II, part C, section C.3, point 1.
[53] ibid, point 2.
[54] ibid, points 2 and 3.
[55] ibid, points 5 and 6.
[56] The same criteria shall apply to the assessment report drafted by national competent authorities; see Annex VI.
[57] On the diversity of European ecosystems, see also Art 31(7)(a).
[58] See Annex III A, at III(A), (B) and (C), and Annex IV A(5).
[59] Annex VII A. See also Recitals (20), (43) and (44), and Art 5(1)(c).

Similar considerations apply to the 2003 Regulation. Recital (2) provides that a high level of protection of human life and health should be ensured. Crucially, Recital (6) specifies that 'whilst substantial equivalence is a key step in the procedure for assessment of the safety of [GE foods], it is not a safety assessment in itself'. This is a direct acknowledgment that the 2003 Regulation has fully embraced a process-based model.

Recital (9) references the principles introduced in the 2001 Directive and Regulation (EC) No 178/2002 (the 'General Food Law', GFL).[60] Thus, it provides that GE foods should only be authorised after a 'scientific evaluation of the highest possible standard, to be undertaken under the responsibility of the EFSA, of any risks which they present for human and animal health'. Under Article 4(1), GE food or feed must not have adverse effects on human health, animal health or the environment, mislead the consumer or differ from the food which it is intended to replace to such an extent that its normal consumption would be nutritionally disadvantageous for the consumer. The EFSA's assessment of GE varieties and following opinion are regulated under Article 6. Article 5(3)(e) expressly encourages applicants to provide 'independent peer-reviewed studies [...] and any other material which is available to demonstrate that the food complies with the criteria referred to in Article 4(1)'.[61] Authorisations are limited to 10 years.[62] Unlike in the case of the Directive, however, post-marketing monitoring is not mandatory. Rather, monitoring and reporting obligations will apply where appropriate and on the basis of the risk assessment.[63]

This overview has shown that a prudential approach to risk assessment is embedded in the EU governance of GE organisms, as regulated under the 2001 Directive and the 2003 Regulation. This also reflects the focus on scientific uncertainty which is typical of socially acceptable risk discourses. The same commitment to prudential risk assessments is enshrined in the EU risk regulation system, at a more general level. This is best or most clearly exemplified by the text of the 2000 Communication from the Commission on the Precautionary Principle.[64]

The Communication stipulates that a prudential approach is 'part of risk assessment policy which is determined before any risk assessment takes place [...]; it is therefore an integral part of the scientific opinion delivered by the risk evaluators'.[65] As the Communication expressly acknowledges, the limits of scientific knowledge

[60] See n 30.

[61] See also how Arts 5(3) and 6(7) of the 2003 Regulation have been amended by Art 2 of Regulation 1381/2019 (n 4), in regards of data format and publicity obligations.

[62] See Art 7(5).

[63] See Recital (35), Arts 5(3)(k) and 17(3)(k). Where applications are submitted under the one door one key procedure, monitoring for environmental effects is always in place; see Arts 5(5)(b) and 17(5)(b).

[64] European Commission, COM(2000)1 Final, *Communication from the Commission on the Precautionary Principle*, 12, section 5.

[65] bid. The Communication draws a distinction between the notions of 'prudential' risk assessment and 'precautionary' risk management, noting that the confusion between the two stems from the fact that scientific uncertainty is the factor which may trigger recourse to the precautionary principle.

may affect each of the four constituent stages of risk assessment: hazard identification, hazard characterisation, appraisal of exposure and risk characterisation. At a general level, the Communication maintains, scientific uncertainty may result from 'five characteristics of the scientific method: the variable chosen, the measurements made, the samples drawn, the models used and the causal relationship employed'.[66] Uncertainty may also stem from controversies on existing data, a lack of relevant data or an inability to collect reliable data.[67]

Under a prudential approach, risk assessors shall take a very cautious perspective when identifying and characterising potential hazards, assessing the probability of occurrence of adverse effects as resulting from exposure to a hazard, and evaluating the magnitude of the potential consequences. They shall also conduct as comprehensive an assessment as technically possible, analysing persistent, reversible and delayed effects. Finally, they should provide information on the reliability of the relevant assessments and, importantly, cast light on persisting uncertainty.[68] As the Communication concludes, 'risk managers should be fully aware of […] uncertainty factors when they adopt measures based on the scientific opinion delivered by the evaluators'.[69] Indirect confirmation of the need for risk assessors to adhere to a prudential approach can be found in ubiquitous references, in the EU Treaties and EU regulatory frameworks, to the overarching goal of a high level of public health and environmental protection.[70]

Against this overall backdrop, we can conclude that risk assessment of GE organisms should conform to a prudential approach. This approach is embedded in the 2001–2003 regulatory arrangements; it is also inherent to the EU system of risk governance, on a broader scale. This reflects adherence to the socially acceptable risk regulatory ideal. The first section has explained that the EFSA has de facto become the central reference point for the risk assessment of GE varieties. Under the GFL, as referenced in the 2003 Regulation, the EFSA is in charge of risk assessment and risk communication[71] within the limits of its remit. More specifically, it 'shall provide scientific advice and scientific and technical support for the [Union's] legislation and policies in all fields which have a direct or indirect impact on food and feed safety' and shall supply independent information on any relevant scientific matters.[72] The fifth section of this chapter enquires as to what extent the EFSA has adhered to a prudential approach in the field of agricultural biotechnologies.

[66] ibid, 13, sub-section 5.1.3.
[67] ibid.
[68] ibid, 13, sub-section 5.1.2.
[69] ibid, 14, sub-section 5.1.3.
[70] See below, section III. The intended (cost-benefit effective or enhanced) level of protection, as explained in ch 1, is the normative frame coming into play when a prudential or sound science approach to risk assessment is adhered to and when regulators focus on sound science or scientific uncertainty and insufficiency.
[71] See Arts 3(11), 3(13) and 6(2) of the GFL, as amended by Regulation 1381/2019, for relevant EU definitions; see also the new Art 8(a), (b) and (c) of the GFL.
[72] See Art 22(2) of the GFL. Generally, see Arts 22 and 23 of the GFL.

III. The EU Regulatory Framework and Socially Acceptable Risk Approaches: The Notion of Intended Level of Protection, The Precautionary Principle and OLFs

The 2001–2003 framework expressly stipulates that the precautionary principle and any relevant OLFs at stake should be taken into due consideration for the purposes of risk management. The precautionary principle, as this section explains, may apply. OLFs may also feed into the determination of the intended level of protection and threshold of acceptable risk. This reflects the possibility to pursue enhanced levels of protection and take non-economic factors into account, when making the final decision as to whether uncertain risks are worth taking. In accordance with the socially acceptable risk regulatory ideal, the level of protection pursued by regulators is not bound to be cost-benefit effective.

Recital (8) of the Directive clearly states that 'the precautionary principle has been taken into account in the drafting of this Directive and must be taken into account when implementing it'. Equally, Article 1(1) maintains that the Directive's objective is to approximate laws and protect human health and the environment, in accordance with the precautionary principle. Article 4(1) reiterates that:

> Member States shall, in accordance with the precautionary principle, ensure that all appropriate measures are taken to avoid adverse effects on human health and the environment which might arise from the deliberate release or the placing on the market of [GE organisms].

OLFs are also expressly mentioned. Recital (9) provides that Member States may take into account ethical aspects when GE organisms are released or placed on the market, while according to Recitals (57) and (58) European or national committees may be consulted on ethical issues associated with biotechnology; Article 29 provides for the relevant consultation procedures.[73] Finally, Recital (62) and Article 31(7)(d) deal with the range of socio-economic OLFs involved in the regulatory governance of GE organisms. Both mention that the Commission's reports on GE organisms should contain a separate chapter addressing 'the socio-economic advantages and disadvantages of each category of [GE organisms], which will take due account of the interests of farmers and consumers'. This enshrines a commitment to take into consideration qualitative factors, as well as the distributional implications of risk regulation.

The 2003 Regulation takes a similar approach, allowing for consideration of both OLFs and the precautionary principle. The objective of the 2003 Regulation, under Article 1(a), is to provide the basis to pursue a high level of protection of

[73] See also Art 31(8) of the Directive.

human life and health, animal health and welfare, the environment and consumer interests, whilst ensuring the effective functioning of the internal market. Therefore, as noted above, Article 4(1) provides that GE food must not '(a) have adverse effects on human health, animal health and the environment; (b) mislead the consumer; (c) differ from the food which it is intended to replace to such an extent that its normal consumption would be nutritionally disadvantageous for the consumer'.

The text of Recital (32) is identical to Recital (19) of the GFL; the latter Regulation is referenced in various parts of the 2003 Regulation, with important implications.[74] According to Recital (32) of the 2003 Regulation:

> it is recognised that, in some cases, scientific risk assessment alone cannot provide all the information on which a risk management decision should be based, and that *other legitimate factors* relevant to the matter under consideration may be taken into account (emphasis added).

Article 7(1) of the 2003 Regulation clearly states that, when exercising its risk management functions and submitting a draft proposal to comitology, the Commission shall take into account

> the opinion [of the EFSA], any relevant provisions of [EU] law and *other legitimate factors* relevant to the matter under consideration.[75] Where the draft decision is not in accordance with the opinion of the Authority, the Commission shall provide an explanation for the difference (emphasis added).

Unlike OLFs, the precautionary principle is not expressly referenced in the 2003 Regulation. However, as mentioned above, 'any relevant provisions of [EU] law' shall be taken into account. The GFL is referenced throughout the 2003 Regulation;[76] the 2001 Directive is also referenced in various parts.[77] Recital (9) of the 2003 Regulation, in particular, maintains that the authorisation procedure of GE food and feed shall include the principles laid out in the 2001 Directive and the GFL. Most importantly, these encompass the precautionary principle.

The GFL provides a legislative definition of the principle. Under Article 7(1), where

> following an assessment of available information the possibility of harmful effects on health is identified but scientific uncertainty persists, provisional risk management measures necessary to ensure the high level of health protection chosen in the [Union] may be adopted […].[78]

[74] Besides the new references to the GFL added by Reg 1381/2019, see Recital (9) and (43) and Art 1, 2, 6, 10, 18, 22, 34 and 35 of the 2003 Regulation.

[75] See also (42) on ethical issues.

[76] See n 74.

[77] The 2001 Directive is referenced in Recitals (7), (9), (23), (26), (29), (33) and (35) and Arts 2, 5, 6, 7, 17, 18, 19, 20, 29, 43 and 45 of the 2003 Regulation.

[78] See Art 7(2) of the GFL for reference to specific conditions in the application of the precautionary principle.

According to Recital (21) of the GFL,

> in those specific circumstances where a risk to life or health exists but scientific uncertainty persists, the precautionary principle provides a mechanism for determining risk management measures or other actions in order to ensure the high level of health protection chosen in the [Union].[79]

Further, Article 6(3) GFL stipulates that

> risk management shall take into account the *results of risk assessment*, and in particular [...] [the EFSA's opinions], *other factors legitimate* to the matter under consideration and the *precautionary principle* where the conditions laid down in Article 7(1) are [met] (emphasis added).

Both the 2001 Directive and the 2003 Regulation thus allow for consideration of any relevant OLFs at stake and the precautionary principle; a socially acceptable risk approach to risk management shines through the regulatory framework. The same commitment to enable risk managers to identify an EU-wide threshold of socially acceptable risk underlies the entire EU risk regulation system.[80]

Undeniably, two different souls coexist in EU risk regulation.[81] The first draws on the assumption that risk regulation should be evidence-based;[82] particular emphasis is laid on adherence to the positive results of risk assessments, a focus on sound science, and consideration of impact assessment (where applicable).[83] The limits of science in the face of complexity and ubiquitous uncertainties, the overarching tenets of the precautionary principle and the need to take OLFs into due consideration are embedded in the second soul, which is usually defined as 'precautionary'.[84] Clearly, the two transpose conflicting transnational discourses within the EU legal system.

The gap between the two souls has surfaced recurrently, in the implementation of EU regulatory frameworks[85] and in judicial review of EU acts.[86] This has

[79] See also Recital (20) of the GFL.

[80] For an in depth overview of the relevance of scientific uncertainty and the precautionary principle in EU risk regulation, see the analysis in Leonelli, 'Judicial Review of Compliance with the Precautionary Principle' (n 15) and GC Leonelli 'Acknowledging the Centrality of the Precautionary Principle in Judicial Review of EU Risk Regulation: Why It Matters' (2020) 57 *CML Rev* 1773.

[81] A Alemanno, Annotation of Case C-77/09, *Gowan Comércio Internacional e Servicos Lda* v. *Ministero della Salute*, EU:C:2010:803, (2011) 48 *CML Rev* 1329; see also A Alemanno, 'Risk Versus Hazard and The Two Souls of EU Risk Regulation: A Reply to Ragnar Lofstedt' (2011) 2 *European Journal of Risk Regulation*, 169.

[82] ibid.

[83] Impact assessment may be defined as a nuanced and much broader EU version of cost-benefit analysis. For a concise overview of its application to EU risk regulation, see M Weimer, *Risk Regulation in the Internal Market. Lessons from Agricultural Biotechnology* (OUP, 2019), 74 to 78.

[84] Alemanno, n 81.

[85] Notably, in the field of agricultural biotechnologies and in the controversial case of glyphosate's re-approval. With regard to the former, see inter alia GC Leonelli, 'The Perfect Storm: GMO Governance and the EU Technocratic Turn' in M Peeters and M Eliantonio (eds), *Research handbook on EU Environmental Law* (Edward Elgar, 2020). On glyphosate, see inter alia GC Leonelli, 'The Glyphosate Saga and the Fading Democratic Legitimacy of EU Risk Regulation' (2018) 25 *Maastricht Journal of European and Comparative Law* 582.

[86] See the in depth analysis in Leonelli, 'Acknowledging the Centrality of the Precautionary Principle' (n 80).

resulted in some 'variable geometry' in the field of EU risk governance. Further, the socially acceptable risk soul has been the object of repeated challenges throughout the years. Criticisms have targeted the lack of adherence to sound scientific standards in risk assessment, regulatory measures departing from the positive results of risk assessments,[87] and the procedural standard of review employed by the EU Courts in challenges involving acts which are deemed too restrictive.[88]

Nonetheless, it is worth underlining that a socially acceptable risk approach is inherent to the *institutional architecture* of EU governance and encoded in the DNA of EU risk regulation. First, the pursuit of a high level of protection and the precautionary principle are enshrined in the Treaties.[89] Equally, all legislative frameworks in the field of EU risk governance make express reference to the precautionary principle[90] and OLFs.[91] Neither adherence to sound science nor impact assessment have a comparable status within the EU legal system. Second, risk management rests with political decision-makers; this aspect is discussed in some further detail at the end of this section. If the results of risk assessment and economic (cost-benefit effectiveness) evaluations were *all* that risk managers ought to take into consideration, risk management functions would have been allocated to technical regulatory agencies, as occurs in legal systems drawing on evidence-based approaches.[92]

Yet again, the EU socially acceptable risk approach to risk management is best or most clearly exemplified by the contents of the 2001 Communication on the

[87] See inter alia A Alemanno, 'The Fabulous Destiny of Bisphenol A (BPA)' (2010) 1 *European Journal of Risk Regulation* 397; A Alemanno, 'The Science, Law and Politics of Neonicotinoids and Bees. A New Test Case for the Precautionary Principle' (2013) 4 *European Journal of Risk Regulation* 191.

[88] See inter alia Alemanno, n 81; AM Janssen and M Van Asselt, 'The precautionary principle in Court. An analysis of post-*Pfizer* case law' in M Van Asselt, E Versluis and E Vos (eds), *Balancing between Trade and Risk. Integrating Legal and Social Science Perspectives* (Routledge, 2013), 197; AM Janssen and N Rosenstock, 'Handling uncertain risks: An inconsistent application of standards?' (2016) 7 *European Journal of Risk Regulation* 144. For the opposite perspective, see Leonelli, 'Acknowledging the Centrality of the Precautionary Principle' (n 80).

[89] References to the principle that a high level of public health and environmental protection shall be ensured are ubiquitous in EU legislation as well as in the Treaties, starting from Art 114(3) and 191(2) of the Treaty on the Functioning of the European Union ('TFEU'); see the Consolidated Version of the Treaty on the Functioning of the European Union, [2012] OJ C326. See also the *Communication from the Commission* (n 64) 8. In the Treaties, the precautionary principle is enshrined in Art 191(2) TFEU.

[90] In legislative acts, besides the already mentioned provisions in the 2001 Deliberate Release Directive and 2003 GM Food and Feed Regulation, see inter alia Recital (21) and Arts 6(3) and 7(1) of the GFL; Recital (8) and Arts 1(4) and 13(2) of the PPP Regulation, cited in n 103 in ch 1; and Recitals (9) and (69) and Arts 1(3) of the REACH Regulation, cited in n 107 in ch 1. See below in this section for an overview of the *Communication from the Commission on the Precautionary Principle*.

[91] In legislative acts, besides the already mentioned provisions in the 2001 Deliberate Release Directive and 2003 GM Food and Feed Regulation, see inter alia Recital (19) and Arts 3(12), 5(1), 6(3) and 7(2) of the GFL; and Art 13(2) of the PPP Regulation. The comparative assessment procedure under the PPP Regulation, the substitution principle and the socio-economic procedure under the REACH Regulation, as already mentioned at n 107 and 109 in ch 1, reflect the relevance of specific OLFs under EU regulation. See below in this section for an overview of OLFs under the *Communication from the Commission on the Precautionary Principle*.

[92] See Leonelli, 'The Glyphosate Saga' (n 85).

Precautionary Principle. The Communication expressly states that the economic impact of risk governance, notably the evaluation of regulatory cost-benefit effectiveness, is only one among many factors to be taken into consideration for the purposes of risk management.[93] Impact assessment is meant to support decision-making, but need not inform the final regulatory output.[94] As the Communication clarifies, in the face of persisting scientific uncertainty, a society may be willing to pay a high economic price to protect (public health and environmental) interests to which it attaches priority.[95] While precautionary regulatory measures might not be cost-benefit effective, they will still comply with the intended level of protection.[96] In this sense, a tension between individual trade and market access rights and collective stakes underlies the precautionary principle and the notions of intended, enhanced or precautionary levels of protection.[97]

Further, where relevant and applicable, political risk managers should take OLFs into due consideration. These may include public opinion,[98] the availability and efficacy of alternative risk mitigation measures,[99] the socio-economic implications[100] and distributional impacts of different regulatory measures,[101] an analysis of any advantages and disadvantages associated with the relevant product or process, the overarching tenets of the substitution principle, and a long-term vision for the development of sustainable approaches in specific regulatory fields. At a general level, as already explained, taking OLFs into account calls for a qualitative analysis of the implications of risk regulation.

[93] *Communication from the Commission* (n 64) 18, sub-section 6.3.4.

[94] See inter alia Case C-343/09, *Afton Chemical*, EU:C:2010:419, 30. For recent developments as regards the interpretation of EU risk managers' obligation to conduct an impact assessment, see Case T-584/13, *BASF Agro and Others* v *Commission*, EU:T:2018:279. While the Better Regulation agenda did strengthen evidence-based discourses at EU level, considerations surrounding the economic cost-benefit effectiveness of risk regulation have never had the same status and role that they have in the US regulatory system. Further, the European Green Deal agenda has brought forward a different emphasis on sustainability and OLFs, which is hardly reconcilable with economic cost-benefit effectiveness.

[95] *Communication from the Commission* (n 64) 19, sub-section 6.3.4.

[96] On the notion of 'intended level of protection' or 'appropriate level of protection', see inter alia *Communication from the Commission* (n 64) 1, point 3, at 3, point 6, at 7, section 1, at 8, sections 2 and 3, at 12, section 5, and at 16, section 6.2.

[97] ibid, 7, section 1, making reference to 'the dilemma of balancing the freedom and rights of individuals, industry and organisations with the need to reduce the risk of adverse effects to the environment, human, animal or plant health'. For the acknowledgment that 'the protection of public health should undoubtedly be given greater weight than economic considerations' see 19, sub-section 6.3.4. Further, the Communication expressly stipulates that 'the measures envisaged must produce an *overall advantage* as regards *reducing risks to an acceptable level*'; the overall public health and environmental advantage is therefore *not* framed as a *net advantage*. See 18, sub-section 6.3.4.

[98] *Communication from the Commission* (n 64) 19, sub-section 6.3.4, referencing 'acceptability to the public'.

[99] ibid, referencing the 'efficacy of alternative [risk management/regulatory] options'.

[100] ibid, referencing 'the socio-economic impact of the various [risk management/regulatory] options'.

[101] eg, see ch 3, section VII, or the below sections on governance of coexistence and the distributional implications of different regulatory approaches. For a direct reference to OLFs, see also the afore mentioned Recital (19) of the GFL. For particular emphasis on OLFs and the role that they (should) play under EU risk regulation, see M Lee, *EU Environmental Law, Governance and Decision-Making* (Hart Publishing, 2014), 84 ff.

Unsurprisingly, the Communication also provides a definition of the precautionary principle; this is more accurate and more encompassing than the one in the GFL. According to this version, the precautionary principle is relevant 'in the event of a potential risk, even if this risk cannot be fully *demonstrated* or *quantified* or its *effects determined* because of the insufficiency and inconclusive nature of the scientific data' (emphasis added)'.[102] Clearly, this definition encompasses within its formulation all forms of uncertainty, as categorised and illustrated in the first chapter.

> Absence of scientific proof of the existence of a cause-effect relationship, a quantifiable dose/response relationship or a quantitative evaluation of the probability of the emergence of adverse effects following exposure should not be used to justify inaction.[103]

Minority scientific opinion may also be relied on.[104] On these grounds, whether

> to invoke the precautionary principle is a decision exercised where scientific information is *insufficient, inconclusive, or uncertain* and where there are indications that the possible effects on the environment or human, animal or plant health may be potentially dangerous and *inconsistent* with the *chosen level of protection* (emphasis added).[105]

As explained in the second section, the Communication advocates a prudential approach to risk assessment. However, and crucially, it also acknowledges the limits of technical risk assessment, as a process; indeed, it provides a list of scenarios where uncertainties and scientific complexity can affect the reliability or accuracy of the results of risk assessment. These are the cases where the precautionary principle may apply, with a view to enacting measures in compliance with the EU intended level of protection. Where the relevant risk assessment conforms to a prudential approach, EU risk managers will draw on the relevant findings; they may then decide not to authorise a product or process, or to enact stringent risk management measures. By contrast, where a risk assessment is deemed insufficiently prudential, EU risk managers may disregard its results and refer to alternative evidence. Equally, EU risk managers may draw different inferences from the results of relevant risk assessments. They may then reach the conclusion that uncertainty should be further dispelled before a risk can be socially accepted, or enact stringent risk management measures. Indeed, under the EU legal system, risk assessment is only meant to inform the technical knowledge of political risk managers.[106]

The decision to have recourse to the precautionary principle, the determination of the threshold of socially acceptable risk and the identification of the intended level of protection are expressly defined in the Communication as

[102] *Communication from the Commission* (n 64) 13, section 5.1.
[103] ibid, 16, section 6.2.
[104] ibid.
[105] ibid, 7, section 1; at 9, section 3; and at 12, section 5. On the general principles for the application of the precautionary principle, see 17 ff., section 6.3.
[106] See the analysis in Leonelli, 'Acknowledging the Centrality of the Precautionary Principle' (n 80).

'eminently political responsibilities'.[107] Risk managers, rather than technical risk assessors, are entrusted with these tasks.[108] Ultimately, risk managers should decide whether 'safe is safe enough'.[109] This indirectly acknowledges that *normative evaluations* are inherent to the characterisation of a risk and to the determination that it is acceptable. The attempt to reconcile functional and political-democratic legitimacy, as spelled out in the cornerstone *Pfizer* case,[110] underlies the entire EU risk regulation architecture; however, the dominance of political-democratic legitimacy shines through the EU model of risk regulation.[111] This builds on the implicit recognition that science will not always provide factually 'correct' answers and that different approaches to risk assessment, different inferences and different regulatory responses are all informed by different normative frames. For this reason, where uncertain risks might not meet the intended level of protection, final decision-making power shall rest with political risk managers.

On these grounds, and as this section has endeavoured to show, a socially acceptable risk approach to risk management is embedded in the 2001–2003 regulatory framework on GE organisms. At a more general level, as the second part of this section has explained, the EU system of risk governance is informed by the socially acceptable risk regulatory ideal. Against this overall backdrop, how have political risk managers exercised their functions in the field of agricultural biotechnologies, and to what approach have they adhered? Most importantly, have they succeeded in identifying a *socially* and *politically agreeable* EU threshold of acceptable risk? These are some of the questions that the next sections aim to address.

IV. Regulatory Implementation: From Socially Acceptable Risk to Evidence-Based Approaches

A rich literature exists on the implementation of the 2001–2003 framework in the EU.[112] Academic commentators have mostly focused on the procedural

[107] *Communication from the Commission* (n 64) 15, sub-section 5.2.1, and 21, section 7.

[108] See COM(1997)176 Final, *Commission Communication on the General Principles of Food Legislation in the European Union*; COM(1997)183 Final, *Commission Communication on Consumer Health and Food Safety*; and COM(1999)719 final, *White Paper on Food Safety*.

[109] See Lee, 'Beyond Safety?' (n 3) 244, stressing that 'there is no value-free way of resolving the acceptability of risk'.

[110] See, eg, Case T-13/99, *Pfizer*, 149.

[111] ibid 201.

[112] See inter alia M Lee, *EU Regulation of GMOs* (Edward Elgar, 2008), 39 ff and 80 ff; M Lee, 'The Governance of Coexistence Between GMOs and Other Forms of Agriculture: A Purely Economic Issue?' (2008) 20 *Journal of Environmental Law* 193; M Geelhoed, 'Divided in Diversity: Reforming the EU's GMO Regime' (2016) 18 *Cambridge Yearbook of European Legal Studies*, 20; P Dąbrowska Klosinska, 'EU Governance of GMOs: Political Struggles and Experimentalist Solutions?' in CF Sabel and J Zeitlin (eds) *Experimentalist Governance in the European Union* (OUP, 2010); Weimer, *Risk Regulation in the Internal Market* (n 83); M Weimer and G Pisani, 'Expertise and Justification. The Contested Legitimation of the EU Risk Administration' in M Weimer and A de Ruijter (eds), *Regulating*

arrangements enshrined in the Directive and Regulation and relevant procedural aspects. The regulatory framework has been defined as a model of experimentalist governance,[113] multi-level governance,[114] decentralised administrative cooperation[115] and deliberative governance.[116] These accounts emphasise that the involvement of different territorial levels, agencies, institutions and stakeholders aimed to enhance the legitimacy of EU regulation in the field of agricultural biotechnologies, facilitating cooperation, coordination, sharing of information and discussion in relation to any relevant matters at stake in the risk governance of GE organisms. At the heart of the framework lies the attempt to foster procedural deliberation and build consensus, as well as the acknowledgment that authoritative decision-making by the EFSA and the Commission would not lead to legitimate governance.[117] This model was thus meant to embed the EFSA and the Commission in a transnational network of cooperating actors, safeguarding against top-down decision-making at EU level.[118]

As proved by the troubled implementation of the framework and as extensively documented throughout the years, the procedural arrangements enshrined in the Directive and the Regulation have not paved the way for political deliberation and have not managed to solve the underlying horizontal and vertical conflicts. Procedural strands of analysis have emphasised the Commission's failure to follow a deliberative approach[119] and the coexistence of mutually constitutive and mutually reinforcing trends of scientification and politicisation.[120] From this perspective, the entrenchment of different stakeholders in radical positions has undermined procedural deliberation, limiting any prospect of generating consensus and identifying agreeable solutions on the governance of GE organisms.

The following sections provide a different account of the conflict on agricultural biotechnologies, exploring it through the lens of evidence-based and socially acceptable risk approaches. The enquiry has a twofold relevance. First, the

Risks in the European Union. The Co-Production of Expert and Executive Power (Hart Publishing 2017); M Weimer, 'Risk Regulation and Deliberation in EU Administrative Governance – GMO Regulation and Its Reform' (2015) 21 *European Law Journal* 622; M Weimer, 'Risk Regulation, GMOs and the Challenges to Deliberation in EU Governance: Politicisation and Scientification as Co-Producing Trends', in C Joerges and C Glinski (eds), *The European Crisis and the Transformation of Transnational Governance: Authoritarian Managerialism Versus Democratic Governance* (Hart Publishing, 2014); S Poli, 'The Member States' Long and Winding Road to Partial Regulatory Autonomy in Cultivating Genetically Modified Crops in the EU' (2013) 4 *European Journal of Risk Regulation* 143.

[113] Dąbrowska-Klosinska, 'EU Governance of GMOs' (n 112), 181 ff. in particular.

[114] M Lee, 'Multi-Level Governance of GMOs in the EU. Ambiguity and Hierarchy', in L Bodiguel and M Cardwell (eds), *The Regulation of GMOs. Comparative Approaches* (OUP, 2010).

[115] Weimer, 'Risk Regulation and Deliberation in EU Administrative Governance' (n 112) 627.

[116] ibid; see also Weimer, *Risk Regulation in the Internal Market* (n 83).

[117] Dąbrowska-Klosinska, 'EU Governance of GMOs' (n 112) 191–193 and 211–212.

[118] Weimer, 'Risk Regulation and Deliberation in EU Administrative Governance' (n 112) 627.

[119] ibid.

[120] Weimer, *Risk Regulation in the Internal Market* (n 83); Weimer and Pisani, 'Expertise and Justification. The Contested Legitimation of the EU Risk Administration' (n 112); M Weimer, 'Risk Regulation and Deliberation in EU Administrative Governance' (n 112).

analysis of EU-wide controversies at the regulatory implementation stage sheds light on the rationale of socially acceptable risk approaches, their characteristics, the relevant regulatory categories and their broader political and socio-economic impact. As already mentioned, the clash between the EU and EU Member States as regards regulatory implementation matters in this field illustrates the overarching goals and broader vision underlying socially acceptable risk discourses. From this perspective, the analysis helps to deconstruct the implications of the counter-hegemonic narrative and of socially acceptable risk discourses. This aspect is picked up again in the preliminary conclusions of the seventh section.

Second, the examination of EU-wide regulatory conflicts aims to illustrate that procedural deliberation does not exist in a political and social vacuum. Most importantly, the success of deliberation rests on a pre-existing background of shared values, goals and perspectives. Where these substantive elements are lacking, procedural political deliberation is bound to fail. An analysis through the lens of the two ideal regulatory types shows that these preconditions do not exist in the specific case of agricultural biotechnologies. On the one hand, GE organisms are far too sensitive in environmental, public health and socio-economic terms for a majority of EU Member States and for civil society to accept their entrenchment in the EU. A plurality of EU Member States and societal stakeholders have consistently claimed that the uncertain risks posed by GE organisms are neither socially acceptable nor worth taking, when persisting scientific uncertainty, the intended EU level of protection, the overarching tenets of the precautionary principle and all relevant OLFs are taken into consideration.

On the other hand, the field of agricultural biotechnologies is far too sensitive in international trade terms for EU institutions not to adhere to evidence-based risk regulation in the implementation of the regulatory framework.[121] The relevance of *stricto sensu* uncertainties and hazard-related uncertainties in this regulatory field, where science is ultimately unable to establish specific adverse effects, adds a further layer of complexity. Most importantly, unlike in other instances,[122] the Commission has consistently refused to depart from the positive results of risk assessments and has refrained from taking the precautionary principle and OLFs into consideration. In so doing, it has failed to do justice to national and civil society's claims that, in the field of agricultural biotechnologies, the intended level of protection must be very high and the threshold of acceptable risk very low. Ultimately, the Commission has failed to identify an *agreeable* EU threshold of *socially acceptable risk*.

As argued in chapter three, the gap between evidence-based and socially acceptable risk approaches can hardly be bridged in the field of agricultural biotechnologies; uncertainty persists, the public health and environmental values at stake

[121] See also ch 3, section VIII, and ch 5, section VII.

[122] See ch 5, section VIII, for an overview of the different stance on the administration of hormones as growth promoters, despite disputes being brought under the SPS Agreement.

are highly important and the relevant OLFs are objects of intense controversy. As the analysis of the following sections show, shared substantive perspectives, values and goals cannot quite be identified where the relevant actors are drawing on the two diametrically opposed regulatory models.

Nor can science, by any means, generate genuine agreement. In the face of scientific complexity and scientific pluralism, different approaches to risk assessment, different interpretations of the 'same' or 'different' science and different scientific inferences drawn from the relevant risk assessments or alternative studies come into play. As the next section clearly shows, the very framings of the relevant scientific questions can be irreconcilable. All in all, science can neither provide a single 'valid' answer, nor succeed in facilitating agreement in controversial cases. Different normative premises will result in references to different scientific evidence, a different interpretation of available data, and different conclusions. Governance of GE organisms is, without doubt, one of these controversial cases.

Against this overall backdrop, the following sections conduct an analysis of EU risk assessment and risk management of GE organisms. The analysis emphasises the gap between the EU institutions' approach, on the one hand, and societal and Member State perspectives, on the other.

V. The Substantive Gap between the EFSA's Approach and More Prudential Perspectives: *TestBioTech*

As illustrated in the second section, the 2001 Directive and 2003 Regulation mandate a prudential approach to technical-scientific risk assessment of GE crops and GE food or feed. A socially acceptable risk approach is thus reflected in the regulatory framework. This section shows that the EFSA's assessments have not been prudential enough to do justice to societal views that, in this regulatory field, the level of protection must be very high and the threshold of acceptable risk correspondingly low. From this perspective, the agency has failed to implement the regulatory framework in a sufficiently prudential manner.

Commentators have recurrently focused on the procedural governance arrangements underlying the framework. The EFSA has been criticised throughout the years for its insufficient engagement with national scientific authorities and for its unwillingness to consider different scientific opinions and different data.[123] Other commentators minimise this aspect. For instance, it has been argued that the EFSA is not required to compose diverging risk assessments, even though it shall seek to harmonise risk assessment procedures through its scientific guidelines.[124] Others have claimed that diverging risk assessments and diverging

[123] See inter alia Geelhoed, 'Divided in Diversity' (n 112); Lee, 'Multi-Level Governance' (n 114) 111 ff.

[124] For this view, see A Alemanno, 'The European Food Safety Authority at Five' (2008) 3 *European Food and Feed Law Review* 2, 24.

scientific opinions are the result of consideration of non-scientific elements at Member State level.[125] From a different perspective, other scholars have pointed to the shift from the cooperative model of networked multi-level governance envisaged in the Directive and the Regulation to what has been defined as the EFSA's 'insertion of epistemic authority'.[126]

Research has confirmed that the GMO panel at the EFSA was in the past quite disinclined to consider diverging risk assessments undertaken by national scientific authorities.[127] Thus, the EFSA's practice at risk assessment level did not live up to the high expectations raised by the framework's experimentalist model of governance. Not only is this difficult to reconcile with the 2001–2003 framework, but also with the EFSA's relationship with national scientific authorities under the GFL.[128] Pursuant to Recital (44) and Article 22(7) and (8) therein, the EFSA shall cooperate closely with national scientific authorities and exchange information with a view to minimising the potential for diverging scientific opinions. It should also engage constructively with the members of its Advisory Forum, which is made up of Member States' experts working for national scientific bodies. Under Article 30, the EFSA 'shall exercise vigilance in order to identify at an early stage any potential source of divergence between its scientific opinions and the scientific opinions issued by other bodies carrying out similar tasks';[129] where it identifies a potential source of divergence, it shall contact the body in question to share information and identify potentially contentious scientific issues.[130] Where substantive divergences have been identified in the assessments of the EFSA and national scientific authorities, the EFSA and the national authority 'shall be obliged to cooperate with a view to either resolving the divergence or preparing a joint document clarifying the contentious scientific issues and identifying the relevant uncertainties in the data [...]'.[131]

As noted, the Commission soon realised the importance of deliberative communication between the EFSA and national authorities. Throughout the years, it has repeatedly encouraged the EFSA to consult national authorities, act as a moderator to build EU-wide consensus and address any contentious issues

[125] Poli, 'The Member States'' (n 112) 147 ff.; S Poli, 'Scientific Advice in the GMO Area' in A Alemanno and S Gabbi (eds) *Foundations of EU Food Law and Policy. Ten Years of the European Food Safety Authority* (Routledge, 2014), 127 and 133.

[126] Weimer, 'Risk Regulation, GMOs and the Challenges to Deliberation in EU Governance' (n 112) 302–306; and Weimer, 'Risk Regulation and Deliberation in EU Administrative Governance' (n 112) 628 ff.

[127] See M Van Asselt and E Vos, 'Wrestling with Uncertain Risks: EU Regulation of GMOs and the Uncertainty Paradox' (2008) 11 *Journal of Risk Research* 281; Weimer and Pisani, 'Expertise and Justification' (n 112).

[128] Further, the role of Member States within the EFSA has been further strengthened by the recent 2019 amendments to the GFL; see Regulation 1381/ 2019 (n 4) Art 1.

[129] Art 30(1) GFL.

[130] Art 30(2) GFL.

[131] Art 30(4) GFL.

raised at national level in its final opinions.[132] Some authors have underlined that the EFSA has made progress throughout the years; this evolution has been defined as a gradual shift from the EFSA's former 'control' model to an increasingly 'deliberative' one.[133] The opinions delivered on the *Herculex* maize 1507 and the EH92-527-1 *Amflora* potato varieties show some development in this respect; the EFSA has more thoroughly engaged with diverging national risk assessments and provided a more explicit and detailed account of the relevant margins of uncertainty.[134] Moreover, and for the first time since the creation of the EFSA, two scientists from the Biological Hazard Panel disagreed with the final majority opinion, raising objections to the risk assessment of EH92-527-1 *Amflora* potato.[135]

Analysing conflicts over risk assessment against the background of the two 'control' and 'deliberative' paradigms points to procedural aspects, ie the EFSA's increasing *procedural* engagement with national authorities and its reliance on deliberative *procedural* practices. However, disagreements over the EFSA's *substantive* conclusions persist and are far from being solved.[136] Ultimately, deliberative inter-institutional practices have failed to generate agreement 'through science' at EU level. If we consider the peculiarities of the case of GE organisms, this is overall unsurprising. As reiterated in the second section, uncertainties can emerge from each and every stage of the risk assessment process. Notably, in the case of agricultural biotechnologies, uncertainties surrounding the existence of a hazard or the actual materialisation of a risk may come into play. In the face of scientific complexity, uncertainty can also emerge from diverging results in different studies, either because they employ different models or because they draw on different measurements and data.

Crucially, the scope of risk assessment will be differently framed in light of different normative premises and perspectives. Pursuing a very high level of protection in a specific regulatory field and advocating a very low threshold of acceptable risk will involve specific 'science-policy choices'.[137] It will also entail very thorough assessments, with a view to generating additional data and dispelling uncertainty. This is not likely to occur where a prudential approach is not being followed. Thus, the evidence base is bound to vary when different approaches to risk assessment are

[132] Dąbrowska Klosinska, 'EU Governance of GMOs' (n 112) 209. See also Weimer, 'Risk Regulation, GMOs and the Challenges to Deliberation in EU Governance' (n 112).

[133] See Weimer and Pisani, 'Expertise and Justification' (n 112); see also M Weimer and G Pisani, 'The EU Adventures of 'Herculex'. Report on the EU Authorization of the Genetically Modified Maize 1507' (2014) 5 *European Journal of Risk Regulation* 208, 209 ff.

[134] Weimer, 'Risk Regulation, GMOs and the Challenges to Deliberation in EU Governance' (n 112) 304 ff.; and Weimer, 'Risk Regulation and Deliberation in EU Administrative Governance' (n 112) 629; Weimer and Pisani, 'Expertise and Justification' (n 112) and 'The EU Adventures of 'Herculex'' (n 133).

[135] Weimer and Pisani, 'Expertise and Justification' (n 112). See also Weimer, *Risk Regulation in the Internal Market* (n 83) 129.

[136] See Leonelli, 'The Perfect Storm' (n 85). For a similar focus on the substance and nature of the EFSA's opinions, see Geelhoed, 'Divided in Diversity' (n 112).

[137] See ch 1, section III.

being adhered to. Equally, normative perspectives will impact on the (more or less cautious) evaluation and interpretation of available data and the relationship between the scientific evidence and the relevant conclusions, ie the inferences drawn.[138] This dimension emerges very clearly in the regulatory conundrum on GE organisms.

This section thus offers an alternative reconstruction of the conflict, focusing on the substantive gap between the EFSA's approach and the approach advocated by different stakeholders. As a preliminary consideration, it is worth noting that the EFSA has been recurrently criticised for its excessive reliance on the applicants' dossiers and for failing to take into due account alternative data and peer-reviewed scientific literature.[139] Research has also documented how, in the case of environmental risk assessment of GE crops, the EFSA's approach has been characterised by an evaluation of risks in an artificial 'vacuum'.[140] The agency has then been criticised for failing to take into due consideration the scale of release of GE crops, the potential receiving environment and the interactions between them, as well as the climatic, geographical and geological characteristics of the areas and the specific ecosystems where a GE variety will be disseminated.[141] At a more general level, the EFSA's opinions have been challenged for being insufficiently prudential.[142] The gap between the EFSA's approach and the more prudential approach advocated by national authorities and societal stakeholders is perfectly exemplified by the *TestBioTech* cases. The rest of this sub-section conducts an analysis of Case T-177/13, to illustrate this point.[143]

In Case T-177/13, three NGOs resorted to Article 12 of the Aarhus Regulation to seek the annulment of a Decision of the Commission, whereby the latter had rejected their request for an internal review of a 2012 Commission Implementing Decision authorising the placing on the market of a GE soybean variety.[144] The applicants put forward four pleas in law in support of their action, lamenting an alleged absence of substantial equivalence between the GE soybean and its conventional counterpart, an alleged failure to assess synergistic/combinatorial effects and toxicity, and an alleged absence of exhaustive immunological assessments. The points raised by the applicants can be divided into two broader sets of complaints. Under the former set of complaints, the applicants challenged the EFSA for failing to interpret the relevant data or scientific literature in a sufficiently prudential way, taking scientific uncertainty into due account. Under the latter, the applicants

[138] Which might as well relate to the question whether the available evidence is sufficient or sufficiently reliable to determine that uncertain risks meet the intended level of protection; see ch 1, section III.

[139] See inter alia Geelhoed, 'Divided in Diversity' (n 112), and Van Asselt and Vos, 'Wrestling with Uncertain Risks' (n 127).

[140] For further information see Van Asselt and Vos, 'Wrestling with Uncertain Risks' (n 127), 288 ff.

[141] See, eg, Geelhoed, 'Divided in Diversity' (n 112), and Lee, *EU Regulation of GMOs* (n 112).

[142] See GC Leonelli, 'GMO Authorisations and The Aarhus Regulation: Paving the Way for Precautionary GMO Governance?' (2019) 26 *Maastricht Journal of European and Comparative Law* 505.

[143] Case T-177/13 *TestBioTech and Others* v. *Commission* EU:T:2016:736. For an in depth analysis, see Leonelli, 'GMO Authorisations' (n 142). See also Leonelli, 'The Perfect Storm' (n 85).

[144] For more details, see Leonelli, 'GMO Authorisations' (n 142).

lamented that the EFSA had failed to conduct a thorough and comprehensive risk assessment and failed to dispel persisting uncertainty.

Examples of the first group of complaints include the applicants' claim that the EFSA failed to take account of the high number of statistical differences between the composition of the GE soybean and its conventional counterpart, having relied on data obtained using a large number of different reference substances;[145] the applicants' argument that the EFSA incurred an error of assessment in drawing the conclusion that data from field trials did not show any biologically relevant phenotypic and agronomic changes;[146] and the applicants' point that the Agency ignored abundant scientific literature on uncertainty surrounding the synergistic or combinatorial effects of new proteins.[147] Further, the applicants lamented that the EFSA had not taken into due consideration scientific literature on potential safety concerns raised by specific interactions between proteins,[148] or the existence of evidence showing that Bt toxins have adverse effects on the health of mammals.[149] All these complaints involved diverging interpretations of data or scientific studies. The EFSA's response to the Commission consistently refers to the irrelevance of these studies or data for the purposes of the final opinion,[150] the unlikeliness of the relevant safety concerns, or the applicants' failure to provide any new scientific information that might change the EFSA's conclusions.[151] This sheds light on the unbridgeable gap between the EFSA's and the applicants' understanding of how the relevant data should be interpreted, in so far as the latter clearly took a more prudential perspective.

The second group includes complaints surrounding the EFSA's failure to conduct specific risk assessments, with a view to dispelling uncertainty and establishing that the GE variety is safe enough for its risks to be socially acceptable. Through this set of complaints, the applicants clearly implied that the EFSA's assessment had not been comprehensive enough. For instance, the applicants lamented that the EFSA did not require Monsanto to include the parents (single events in a stacked event) in field trials as comparators,[152] and that it had failed to request the applicant to investigate the effect of specific biotic and abiotic stressors on the GE variety;[153] they also added that

> scientific research indicating that [herbicide] spraying may have unintended effects on plants cannot simply be dismissed on the ground that it relates to cultivations other than soybean, and findings made about other cultivations provide scientifically relevant data.[154]

[145] Case T-177/13 *TestBioTech*, para 127.
[146] Paras 153-155.
[147] Paras 194 and 198.
[148] Paras 203 ff.
[149] Paras 245 and 246.
[150] Para 155.
[151] Paras 203 and 246.
[152] Para 123.
[153] Para 159.
[154] Para 165.

Under their second plea, the applicants remarked that the EFSA had failed to require appropriate field trials, which would allow for a sufficient assessment of the expression of new proteins in different environmental conditions,[155] and to examine the effects of the GE variety on the reproductive system, together with the potential transfer of biologically active compounds of the modified soybean through consumption.[156] Taking an unequivocal evidence-based perspective, the Commission noted that the study relied on by the applicant 'did not include any new scientific evidence showing effects impacting on safety'.[157] Further, the applicants pointed to the EFSA's failure to conduct an exhaustive immunological assessment[158] and allergenicity assessment, on the grounds that interactions causing allergenicity were 'unlikely'.[159]

Perhaps more worryingly, the EFSA's finding that further *risk assessments* were not warranted was at times explicitly based on the results of *comparative assessments* between the GE variety and its conventional counterpart. This is hard to reconcile with the logics of process-based models; as the 2003 Regulation reads, 'whilst substantial equivalence is a key step in the procedure for assessment of the safety of [GE foods], it is not a safety assessment in itself'.[160] By the first part of their third plea, the applicants lamented that the EFSA had failed to thoroughly and appropriately investigate specific characteristics that could reveal unintended effects; the EFSA had found that such risk assessment was not warranted in light of the results of the comparative analysis.[161] Similarly, the applicants claimed that the EFSA had used its preliminary finding of substantial equivalence to avoid an exhaustive toxicity assessment,[162] an assessment of the impact of processing the GE variety[163] and an assessment of the potential effects of spraying the GE soybean with glyphosate and maintenance pesticides.[164] These complaints illustrate a silent and problematic shift towards comparative assessment, as opposed to the notion of risk assessment enshrined in the 2001 Directive and 2003 Regulation.

Against this backdrop, the gap between the EFSA's approach and the scientific perspectives of different stakeholders emerges very clearly from *TestBioTech*. The EFSA's risk assessments are not perceived as being comprehensive and prudential enough, in substantive terms, to persuade stakeholders that scientific uncertainty has either been dispelled, or taken into due consideration, in the Agency's final findings. Therefore, the EFSA's assessments have not been prudential enough to do justice to societal views that, in this regulatory field, the level of protection must be very high and the threshold of acceptable risk correspondingly low.

[155] Para 211.
[156] Para 236.
[157] Para 240.
[158] Para 260.
[159] Para 271.
[160] See above, section II, as well as ch 3.
[161] Paras 138, 139 and 150.
[162] Paras 184 ff.
[163] Paras 221 and 222.
[164] Para 227.

VI. The Substantive Gap in Risk Management: The Commission's Alignment with Evidence-Based Risk Governance versus Socially Acceptable Risk Approaches

As widely documented throughout the years, comitology has been plagued by dissent in the field of GE organisms. Controversies at committee level have consistently affected the possibility of building a qualified majority in favour or against the Commission's draft proposals for the authorisation of GE varieties. This has prevented the development of legitimate supra-national decision-making,[165] frustrating Member States' attempts to play any meaningful role in the governance of GE organisms. Decision-making has in fact been monopolised by the Commission, which has been the only force behind authorisations in the post-moratoria phase.[166] Under the 'new' comitology rules, after a failure to achieve a qualified majority in comitology, the Commission is entitled to withdraw its proposal or submit a new draft Regulation.[167] However, the Commission has consistently refrained from exercising this power, single-handedly opting for authorisation. This has triggered a plurality of national bans and restrictions on GE organisms, with Member States alternatively resorting to Article 114 TFEU, the safeguard measures enshrined in the 2001 Directive and the 2003 Regulation, or the enactment of specific national measures on coexistence.[168]

Further, as highlighted by commentators over years of research, the Commission has consistently aligned with the positive results of the EFSA's opinions, submitting draft proposals in favour of authorisation.[169] Indeed, it has been famously described as a 'blind driver taking directions from the passenger in the back seat'.[170] On these grounds, as emphasised by procedural accounts of the conflict, political deliberation has certainly failed to solve horizontal conflicts in the risk management of GE organisms.[171] First, deadlock in comitology has undermined deliberative cooperation.[172] Thus, the procedural dynamics of comitology in this field have not fulfilled the promise of re-democratisation by means of deliberative practices. Second, as argued by one author, the Commission's approach to risk

[165] Dąbrowska-Klosinska, 'EU Governance of GMOs' (n 112) 194.
[166] For special emphasis on this point, see Geelhoed, 'Divided in Diversity' (n 112).
[167] See above, the overview in section I.
[168] See below, the next sub-sections.
[169] According to Weimer and Pisani, the only instance where the Commission sought to depart from the EFSA's positive opinion was in the authorisation of the *Herculex* variety; see Weimer and Pisani, 'Expertise and Justification' (n 112) and 'The EU Adventures of 'Herculex' (n 133), and Weimer, *Risk Regulation in the Internal Market* (n 83) 130. The initial proposal was modified at a later stage.
[170] E Vos, 'Responding to Catastrophe: Towards a New Architecture for EU Food Safety Regulation?" in CF Sabel and J Zeitlin (eds) *Experimentalist Governance in the European Union* (OUP, 2010) 174.
[171] Weimer, *Risk Regulation in the Internal Market* (n 83).
[172] ibid.

management has incrementally shifted from a 'deliberative' to a 'control' model.[173] Despite its attempts to mediate, request further opinions from the EFSA and delay authorisations, the Commission has ultimately ended up rubberstamping the EFSA's opinions.[174]

An analysis through the lens of evidence-based and socially acceptable risk approaches offers a different account. Under this alternative framing, the entrenchment of the 'control' model is a *procedural* reflection of the Commission's *substantive* adherence to an evidence-based approach. This different form of analysis casts light on the gap between the position of societal constituencies and a majority of EU Member States, on the one hand, and the Commission's failure to identify an agreeable threshold of socially acceptable risk, on the other.

As explained since the introductory chapter, socially acceptable risk approaches do not mandate any specific regulatory outcome. The identification of the threshold of acceptable risk results from an iterative evaluation of uncertain risks in light of the values at stake, the intended level of protection, the overarching tenets of the precautionary principle and any relevant OLFs. For this reason, adherence to a socially acceptable risk approach by no means implies pursuit of zero risk or the lowest possible threshold of risk. High risks might be considered worth taking, with all factors taken into account, whereas lower risks might be deemed unacceptable. Rather, the two distinctive features of a socially acceptable risk approach are consideration of *more than* sound science and economic cost-benefit effectiveness, and consensus regarding an acceptable threshold of risk.

The controversy over EU risk management and the authorisation of GE organisms is a perfect, paradigmatic example of the clash between evidence-based and socially acceptable risk approaches. The Commission has consistently adhered to an evidence-based approach to risk management.[175] All it has ever taken into consideration in its proposals for the authorisation of GE varieties are risk assessments and their positive results, ie sound science. The Commission has never exercised its broad administrative discretion[176] to depart from the results of risk assessments. It has never relied on uncertainties emerging from different stages of the risk assessment process or from different studies and data. Nor has it ever found that, in the face of persisting uncertainty, the available evidence was insufficient to determine that the relevant risks would meet the intended level of protection. Equally, it has never found that uncertainties should be further dispelled.[177] On these grounds, it has never resorted to the precautionary principle.

[173] ibid and Weimer and Pisani, 'Expertise and Justification' (n 112).

[174] ibid.

[175] Leonelli, 'The Perfect Storm' (n 85). On the Commission's 'technocratic' perception and understanding of its own mandate, see first and foremost Lee, *EU Environmental Law* (n 101) 54 ff; see also Weimer, *Risk Regulation in the Internal Market* (n 83).

[176] For a comprehensive overview, see Leonelli, 'Acknowledging the Centrality of the Precautionary Principle' (n 80).

[177] See Leonelli, 'GMO Authorisations' (n 142).

Nor has it ever taken the highly disputed OLFs at stake in this field into consideration. Most importantly, as anticipated in the introductory section, OLFs have never *implicitly* fed into the determination that the intended level of protection must be very high in this field, and the threshold of socially acceptable risk correspondingly low.[178] This would have entailed a close focus on uncertainty, which is hard to reconcile with the Commission's consistent choice throughout the years to propose the authorisation of GE varieties.

All in all, in this very sensitive field,[179] the Commission has felt under close scrutiny. It has never ventured to suggest that the uncertain risks posed by GE organisms might not comply with the EU's intended level of protection and might not be worth taking. This clearly reflects the dominant transnational narrative on evidence-based risk governance. By contrast, a plurality of Member States and societal stakeholders across the EU have clearly followed a socially acceptable risk approach. In the case of GE food and feed, these actors have taken into consideration persisting uncertainty, enhanced public health and consumer protection, the overarching tenets of the precautionary principle and any potential advantages or disadvantages associated with GE products, in so far as more sustainable alternatives are available to consumers and farmers. On these grounds, as testified by deadlock in comitology[180] and Member State and EU-wide resistance to GE foods, these actors have reached the conclusion that the uncertain risks posed by GE organisms are neither socially acceptable nor worth taking.

This is even clearer in relation to the cultivation of GE crops, which have been far more controversial than the authorisation of GE food and feed. OLFs play a prominent, almost unique role in this case. By feeding into the balancing process, OLFs make the threshold of socially acceptable risk even lower for the regulation of cultivating GE crops. This explains why this regulatory area has been the object of higher levels of dispute.

First, cultivation of GE organisms triggers issues surrounding uncertain adverse environmental effects on ecosystems and biodiversity, either because of the possibility of gene flow and hybridisation or because of potential impacts on target or non-target organisms. These are environmental risk matters, potentially involving the application of the precautionary principle. The environmental sustainability of GE crops, particularly in the case of herbicide or multi-herbicide resistant crops, also comes into play.

[178] As noted since the first chapter, OLFs are not scientific in nature; however, the same is true of considerations surrounding the economic cost-benefit effectiveness of risk regulation. All in all, (non-scientific) OLFs play the same role under socially acceptable risk approaches that (non-scientific) cost-benefit analysis plays under evidence-based approaches; they both feed into the determination of the intended level of protection and threshold of acceptable risk. See the overview in ch 1, section III, and the analysis in ch 3, section VI. For particular emphasis on the Commission's failure to take OLFs into due account, see Lee, *EU Regulation of GMOs* (n 122).

[179] See n 121 above.

[180] It is undeniable that no qualified majority has ever formed; however, a majority of Member States throughout the years has consistently voted against authorisations.

Second, the availability and efficacy of coexistence measures affects potential levels of contamination and adventitious presence of the GE components in seeds, crops and food. As shown in chapter three, the combination of the widespread cultivation of GE crops and a soft approach to coexistence has resulted in the ubiquitous adventitious presence of GE components in the US food supply chain. Where coexistence measures are unavailable or ineffective and the uncertain risks posed by GE foods are generally perceived as socially unacceptable, coexistence is often framed as a public health and consumer protection issue. In this sense, under socially acceptable risk approaches, socio-economic, public health and consumer protection issues are intertwined in the governance of coexistence.[181]

Third, limited effectiveness of coexistence measures and ubiquitous adventitious presence of GE components clearly have an impact on consumer choice and can threaten conventional and organic agriculture. Fourth, and as illustrated by the analysis of US law, coexistence and all associated regulatory burdens and economic costs come with specific distributional implications. This aspect adds a further layer of complexity.

Uncertainty, the pursuit of *enhanced levels of protection*, *precaution* and the *OLFs* associated with regulating the uncertain risks posed by GE organisms are inextricably linked under iterative socially acceptable risk approaches, just like adherence to sound science and the pursuit of a cost-benefit effective level of protection are set along a linear regulatory continuum under evidence-based models. The higher the level of intended protection and the more relevant the OLFs at stake, the more averse society will be to uncertain risks. This is the backdrop against which the GE organisms dilemma has unfolded.

In the face of persisting EU-wide controversy over agricultural biotechnologies, there can be little doubt as to the Commission's failure to live up to the overarching tenets of socially acceptable risk approaches. The Commission's mere focus on sound science and on the international trade implications of the governance of GE organisms is irreconcilable with the socially acceptable risk paradigm. The Commission has then, unsurprisingly, failed to make a convincing case that the uncertain risks posed by GE organisms are worth taking.

Besides undermining the political and democratic legitimacy of EU risk regulation in this field,[182] this has triggered vertical conflicts between the EU and Member State levels. The resulting legal challenges, which have not yielded any satisfactory solutions under the rationale of the Conflicts Law framework, are analysed in the following sub-sections. Each case, in a different way, sheds some light on the socially acceptable risk perspective taken by many EU Member States. In this sense, they testify to the gap between EU adherence to evidence-based paradigms and the Member States' consistent focus on enhanced protection, precaution and OLFs.

[181] See also below, sub-section B.
[182] See Leonelli, 'The Perfect Storm' (n 85).

A. The First Group of Cases: The Centrality of the Precautionary Principle

The first group of cases involves national measures enacted on precautionary grounds or challenges on the grounds of the precautionary principle. These cases show national or societal concerns surrounding persisting uncertainty in the field of GE organisms and doubts as to the precautionary nature of EU authorisation decisions, to which Member States have responded by enacting national measures and/or invoking the precautionary principle.[183]

In Case C-06/99, *Greenpeace*,[184] a request for a preliminary ruling was made in the context of an appeal brought by this NGO, which sought the annulment of a French decree including a GE maize variety in the official list of plant species and varieties grown in France. The decree followed a positive risk assessment by the competent French authorities under Council Directive 90/220, ie the predecessor of the 2001 Directive, and Decision 97/98, whereby the Commission had authorised the placing on the market of this GE variety. Greenpeace lamented that the scientific opinion of the French authority had been delivered on the basis of an incomplete assessment,[185] and invoked the precautionary principle.[186] The questions of the referring court surrounded the interpretation of the relevant EU law provisions.[187] The aim was to ascertain whether the national authorities which had forwarded a positive opinion retained discretion not to give their consent in writing and not to allow the GE product to be placed on the market, on precautionary grounds. The NGO supported such an interpretation of the Directive, on the grounds that national authorities should be able to enact precautionary measures.

Unsurprisingly, upon an analysis of the relevant provisions, the ECJ reached the conclusion that the 1990 Directive placed the Member State concerned under an obligation to give its consent.[188] More specifically, the ECJ stressed that authorisations followed

> a procedure during which the national authorities have adopted a favourable opinion on the basis of the [assessment provided for under the 1990 Directive] and have thus had the opportunity fully to exercise their own powers to assess the [relevant public health and environmental] risks.[189]

[183] The analysis in this section does not include Case C-236/01, *Monsanto Agricoltura Italia and Others*, EU:C:2003:431. For the purposes of the present analysis, this case is of limited importance. Most importantly, legal and regulatory questions – rather than adherence to evidence-based models or socially acceptable risk approaches at the implementation level – were prominent. For an analysis, see Leonelli, 'Judicial Review of Compliance with the Precautionary Principle' (n 15).

[184] Case C-6/99, *Greenpeace France and Others*, EU:C:2000:148.

[185] Para 20.

[186] Para 40.

[187] Para 23.

[188] Paras 28 to 30; this finding drew on a textual interpretation of the relevant provisions, and on the acknowledgment that this regulatory field had been the object of harmonisation at EU level.

[189] Para 39.

With specific regard to the precautionary principle, the ECJ noted that observance of the principle was reflected in the regulatory arrangements of the Directive.[190] On these grounds, it found that national authorities did not retain the discretionary power to enact any post-authorisation precautionary measures. However, if they had

> new information which [led them] to consider that the product […] may constitute a risk to human health and the environment, [they would] not be obliged to give [their] consent, provided that [they] immediately inform the Commission and the other Member States about the new information

and resort to the ad hoc procedures laid out in the Directive.[191]

This case testifies to early controversies about the risk assessment of GE organisms and the role of the precautionary principle in final decision-making. Regulatory implementation issues and compliance with the overarching tenets of the precautionary principle were at stake in this case: it is against this specific backdrop that the national court referred its questions on the margins of national discretion in the enactment of post-authorisation precautionary measures.

Controversies over the boundaries and nature of precautionary risk management have not been solved by the enactment of the 2001–2003 framework. In Joined Cases C-58 to C-68/10, *Monsanto France*,[192] the referring court raised a number of questions regarding the 2001 Directive, the 2003 Regulation and Articles 53 and 54 of the GFL. The first question sought to clarify the correct legal basis for a French measure suspending cultivation of GE MON810 maize (notified as an 'existing product' under Article 20 of the 2003 Regulation) until after renewal of its authorisation.[193] The French measure had clearly been adopted on precautionary grounds.

The safeguard clauses of Article 23 of the 2001 Directive and Article 34 of the 2003 Regulation differ. Under the former, a Member State may provisionally restrict or prohibit the use and/or sale of a GE variety as a result of *new* or *additional* information made available *since the date of consent* and affecting the environmental risk assessment, or as a result of a *reassessment of existing information* on the basis of *new* or *additional* scientific knowledge. The Member State must have detailed grounds for considering that the GE variety constitutes a *risk* to human health or the environment, and shall follow an ad hoc procedure.[194] The clause of the 2003 Regulation stipulates that 'where it is *evident* that authorised [GE varieties] are likely to constitute a *serious risk* to human health, animal health

[190] Paras 40 to 46.

[191] Para 47. At para 57, the ECJ ruled that if the opinion of a national authority were flawed due to specific irregularities, a question on the validity of the final EU act should be referred to the ECJ.

[192] Joined Cases C-58/10 to C-68/10, *Monsanto and Others*, EU:C:2011:553.

[193] See paras 31 to 34; the French authorities had notified the measure under Art 34 of the 2003 Regulation and Art 53 and 54 of the GFL.

[194] See Art 23(1) of the 2001 Directive.

or the environment [...] measures shall be taken under the procedures provided for in Articles 53 and 54 of the [GFL]'.[195] The threshold is clearly higher under the 2003 Regulation. Further, Articles 53 and 54 of the GFL require the Commission – as opposed to Member States – to take action. The ECJ found that, in this case, the (more restrictive) procedure of Article 34 of the Regulation should apply.[196]

Crucially, by its third question, the referring court directly attempted to expand the *preconditions* for the application of Article 34. The national court enquired

> what degree of requirement, taking into account in particular the precautionary principle, is imposed, respectively, by [Article 23 of the Directive and Article 34 of the Regulation] in terms of identifying the risk, evaluating its probability and assessing the nature of its effects.

The referring court aimed to obtain a broad interpretation of the safeguard clauses in light of the precautionary principle, with a view to relaxing the stringent criteria for their application. This question suggests a specific construction of the nature of national bans and restrictions. From this perspective, and as consistently argued by Member States, these are precautionary national risk management measures enacted due to the EU institutions' failure to take the precautionary principle into account in the context of authorisation. In other words, they are enacted to comply with the national threshold of socially acceptable risk and to pursue enhanced levels of protection. The ECJ adhered to a textual interpretation of the requirements of Article 34, confirming the narrow boundaries of the safeguard clause.[197]

Finally, the issue of the interpretation of the Article 34 safeguard clause resurfaced in a fairly recent decision: Case C-111/16, *Fidenato*.[198] In this case, yet again, the referring court raised its questions in the context of proceedings involving a national ban on the cultivation of GE MON810 maize. The Italian Government had requested the Commission to enact emergency measures under the procedure laid out in Article 34 of the 2003 Regulation and Articles 53 and 54 GFL. In the meantime, the government adopted interim measures under Article 54 GFL. The Commission requested an opinion to the EFSA; the latter found that Italy had not provided any new scientific evidence justifying recourse to the emergency measures. However, the Commission then failed to submit to comitology a draft decision for the extension, amendment or abrogation of the national interim measures that Italy had in place, as it was supposed to do in accordance with Article 54 GFL. In this case the ECJ found that, in so far as EU institutions fail to comply with the procedure of Article 54 GFL, Member States may maintain or renew interim emergency measures.[199] The impact of this part of the ruling is hard to gauge, given that the Commission will usually act in accordance with the Article 54 procedure.[200]

[195] See Art 34 of the 2003 Regulation.
[196] Para 63.
[197] Para 81.
[198] Case C-111/16, *Fidenato and Others*, EU:C:2017:676. See also C-107/16, *Fidenato*, EU:C:2017:900.
[199] Para 42.
[200] See also sections VIII and IX below, regarding the 2015 reform of cultivation of GE crops.

More significantly, the ECJ was again faced with the question of whether 'considerations relating to the precautionary principle which go beyond the parameters of serious and evident risk to human or animal health or the environment [...] justify the adoption of interim emergency measures [under Article 34]'.[201] Drawing on the Advocate General's Opinion, which emphasised the different rationale, logics and textual provisions of Article 34 of the 2003 Regulation and Article 7 GFL,[202] the ECJ reached the legally tenable and unsurprising conclusion that the precautionary principle could not expand the scope of Article 34.[203] Still, this case testifies to persisting disagreements over precautionary risk management and authorisations of GE organisms.

As the analysis in this sub-section has shown, national courts have attempted to obtain a broader interpretation of the safeguard clauses in light of the precautionary principle. In so doing, they have indirectly pointed to the fact that national bans and restrictions are enacted (and commonly perceived as) *precautionary* national risk management measures, which Member States adopt to comply with the national intended level of protection and national threshold of socially acceptable risk.[204]

B. *Upper Austria*: Fleshing Out the Rationale of Socially Acceptable Risk Approaches

Better than any other case, *Upper Austria*[205] testifies to the adherence of Member States to a socially acceptable risk approach. In this case, the Republic of Austria notified the Commission of a draft law of the Upper Austria province prohibiting the cultivation of GE crops. By this notification, Austria sought a derogation from the 2001 Directive on the grounds of (what is now) Article 114(5) TFEU. This Article provides for the enactment of national measures after the adoption of an EU harmonisation measure. Measures derogating from a harmonisation measure must be based on *new scientific evidence* relating to the protection of the *environment or the working environment* on the grounds of a problem *specific* to that Member State and which has arisen *after* the adoption of the harmonisation measure. The Commission rejected the request for a derogation on the grounds that the

[201] Para 22.

[202] Opinion of Advocate General Bobek in Case C-111/16, *Fidenato and Others*, EU:C:2017:676, paras 49 to 78.

[203] Paras 46, 48 and 54. See also para 52.

[204] For actions for annulment brought against authorisations of GE varieties, see Cases T-478/10 to T-502/10, *Département du Gers v Commission*, EU:T:2011:151 (dismissed as inadmissible); and T-240/10, *Hungary v Commission*, EU:T:2013:645 (act annulled on procedural grounds).

[205] See Case T-366/03, *Land Oberösterreich and Austria v Commission*, EU:T:2005:347; and Joined Cases C-439/05 and C-454/05, *Land Oberösterreich and Austria* v. *Commission*, EU:C:2007:510 (hereafter, '*Upper Austria*').

requirements enshrined in Article 114(5) TFEU were not satisfied. Austria and Upper Austria sought the annulment of the Commission's Decision.

The arguments of Austria and Upper Austria are legally flawed in many respects, if due regard is had to the conditions stipulated by Article 114 TFEU. Nonetheless, they are highly relevant from a risk governance perspective. More specifically, they perfectly exemplify the iterative setting of the intended level of protection and threshold of acceptable risk which lies at the heart of socially acceptable risk approaches.

Starting from the requirement that *new scientific evidence* relating to the protection of the *environment* should be adduced, Austria and Upper Austria relied on a report on GE organism-free areas. The Commission requested the EFSA to issue an opinion under Articles 29(1) and 22(5)(c) of the GFL. The EFSA found that the report did not contain any new scientific evidence which would justify the derogation measures. As reconstructed in the Opinion of the Advocate General, the evidence mostly consisted of a review of existing scientific knowledge on crop to crop gene flow and crop to wild relative gene flow, with the consequent possibility of hybridisation.[206]

The evidence could neither establish a causal link between hybridisation and specific adverse effects (ie prove any hazards connected to potential hybridisation), nor evaluate or quantify the relevant risks. Further, the scientific evidence failed to identify any unusual or unique ecosystems in Upper Austria which would have required a separate environmental risk assessment or would have warranted the enactment of derogation measures on the grounds of specific environmental risks.[207] The scientific disagreements between Austria and Upper Austria, on the one side, and the EU institutions, on the other, clearly boiled down to a diverging interpretation of pre-existing scientific evidence. In the face of persisting uncertainties, Austria and Upper Austria took a precautionary perspective and found that the uncertain environmental risks posed by the cultivation of GE organisms did not comply with the national intended level of protection. Indeed, Austria expressly invoked the precautionary principle in its notification to the Commission.[208] In this respect, the case shows that Austria and Upper Austria interpreted the available evidence in light of the precautionary principle; the controversy centred on normative evaluations, against a background of uncertainty.

Turning to the requirement that the derogating measures must be adopted on the grounds of a problem *specific* to the Member State, it would have been reasonable to expect that Austria and Upper Austria would point to factors such as the scale of release of GE crops, the receiving environment, interactions between these

[206] See Opinion of Advocate General Sharpston in Joined Cases C-439/05 and C-454/05, *Upper Austria*, EU:C:2007:285.

[207] ibid para 23.

[208] See Case T-366/03, *Upper Austria*, para 56 as well as paras 70 to 72 (fourth plea in law).

two elements or the climatic, geographical and geological characteristics of the areas and the specific ecosystems where GE varieties would be disseminated.[209] These elements would have established a connection between the rationale for the enactment of the derogating measure, ie a problem specific to the Member State, and the relevant scientific evidence relating to the protection of the environment and underpinning the derogating measure.[210] In a completely different vein, Austria and Upper Austria referred to the specific farming structure in the province, emphasising the prevalence of small-scale farms and the substantial proportion of organic farming.[211] On these grounds, they placed coexistence issues at the centre of their arguments relating to a 'specific' problem. In other words, they pointed to the limited availability and efficacy of coexistence measures in Upper Austria, due to its specific farming structure.

This testifies to a legal asymmetry in Austria and Upper Austria's grounds for derogating from the 2001 Directive. As shown in chapter three, coexistence is far from being a mere economic issue. Indeed, it has important distributional implications. The limited availability or efficacy of coexistence measures is liable to result in the adventitious presence of GE components in seeds and crops and GE ingredients in foods. This (disproportionately) impacts conventional and organic farming, potentially threatening the viability of these agricultural models, and has consumer choice implications.[212] On these grounds, coexistence has a prominent socio-economic dimension. By contrast, it is much more difficult to frame coexistence measures as *stricto sensu* risk management measures, in so far as public health or environmental risks (as opposed to contamination and adventitious presence issues) are taken into consideration.

It might be that Austria and Upper Austria implicitly started from the premise that, from a precautionary perspective, the uncertain public health risks posed by the adventitious presence of GE components in food and feed are not acceptable. From this viewpoint, the limited availability and efficacy of coexistence issues would have a precautionary public health protection aspect. However, this is unrelated to the question of gene flow, hybridisation and environmental risks, as referred to in the scientific evidence adduced. The next question is whether Austria and Upper Austria sought to advance the argument that coexistence measures have an environmental protection dimension; in other words, whether they attempted to frame the limited availability and efficacy of coexistence measures as an issue exacerbating the *environmental risks* of gene flow and hybridisation

[209] See the overview in section II, above.

[210] See Case T-366/03, *Upper Austria*, para 64: 'it was for the Republic of Austria to demonstrate, on the basis of new scientific evidence, that the level of environmental protection afforded by [the 2001 Directive] was not acceptable having regard to a problem specific to that Member State which arose after the adoption [of the Directive]'.

[211] Opinion of Advocate General Sharpston in Joined Cases C-439/05 and C-454/05, *Upper Austria*, para 21.

[212] See ch 3, section VI.

in Upper Austria. This argument is difficult yet not totally impossible to make.[213] Indeed, in its opinion, the EFSA noted that 'no evidence was presented in the report to show that coexistence is an environmental or human health risk issue',[214] rather than an agricultural or socio-economic question.

It is hard to gauge what the intentions of Austria and Upper Austria were in framing their legal arguments. The Commission, on its part, has always drawn a distinction between socio-economic matters of contamination and coexistence measures, to be regulated at Member State level,[215] and issues surrounding public health and environmental risks, harmonised under the 2001–2003 framework. Overall, from a legal standpoint, it is fair to conclude that Austria's request for a derogation failed to meet the requirements of Article 114(5) TFEU. The asymmetry between the evidence adduced and the specific problem identified[216] is visible. Further, Austria and Upper Austria failed to provide 'new' scientific evidence,[217] in that their scientific disagreements centred on a precautionary evaluation of existing evidence.[218] Nor did they establish that the specific problem at issue had arisen after the adoption of the harmonisation measure, as stipulated in Article 114(5) TFEU.[219] On these grounds, it is unsurprising that the Court of First Instance and the ECJ dismissed the action for annulment.

For the purposes of the present analysis, however, the position of Austria and Upper Austria is a perfect example of a socially acceptable risk approach. Their reconstruction of the relevant issues at stake was irreconcilable with the preconditions of Article 114(5) TFEU; however, a socially acceptable risk approach to

[213] See for instance Advisory Committee on Biotechnology and the 21st Century Agriculture, *A Framework for Local Coexistence Discussions. A Report of the Advisory Committee on Biotechnology and the 21st Century Agriculture (AC21) to the Secretary of Agriculture*, December 8, 2016 19, on isolation methods; coexistence measures may under some circumstances limit the release and spread of GE organisms in the *broader environment*, thus mitigating environmental risks.

[214] Opinion of Advocate General Sharpston in Joined Cases C-439/05 and C-454/05, *Upper Austria*, para 23.

[215] See Art 26a of the 2001 Directive. For an overview of governance of coexistence in the EU and the relevant Commission's Recommendations in this field, see first and foremost Lee, *EU Regulation of GMOs* (n 122); and Lee, 'The Governance' (n 112). See also the Opinion of Advocate General Sharpston in Joined Cases C-439/05 and C-454/05, *Upper Austria*, paras 18 and 19, and sub-section C below.

[216] As explained above, Austria and Upper Austria did not quite attempt to frame coexistence as an environmental issue – rather, they focused on the adventitious presence of GE components and the impact on small-scale conventional and organic farming. In this light, the Advocate General found at para 114 of her Opinion that the '[scientific] evidence on which Austria relied related to the protection of the environment, [whereas its] concerns could not be regarded as relating specifically to the protection of the environment'. See also the ECJ's Judgment, paras 61 and 63.

[217] On this point, see paras 122, 124 and 125 of the Opinion. According to the Advocate General, a re-assessment of existing evidence leading to new conclusions could amount to 'new' scientific evidence; however, Austria and Upper Austria had failed to show how this applied to the circumstances of the case. See also para 134 of the Opinion: 'no amount of precaution can actually render that evidence or that situation new'.

[218] See paras 71, 73 and 145 of the Opinion; at para 145 the Advocate General noted that 'it is not for this or any other court to determine proper national or [EU] environmental policy. And the concerns in question are not in themselves directly relevant to the legal issues raised in this case [...]'.

[219] Opinion, paras 128 to 131.

the governance of the uncertain risks posed by the cultivation of GE organisms shines through the 'overlaps' between matters of environmental risk, as evaluated in light of the precautionary principle, and consideration of socio-economic OLFs, including the availability, efficacy and implications of coexistence. OLFs were by no means immaterial to Upper Austria's determination of the intended level of protection and setting of the threshold of acceptable risk. In its precautionary evaluation of persisting uncertainty in the environmental risks posed by the cultivation of GE organisms, Upper Austria took into account the implications of coexistence in a context of small-scale conventional and organic farming. While these OLFs are not linked to the determination that environmental risks *exist*, they are linked to the finding that such uncertain risks are – or are not – *socially acceptable*.

C. The Final Group of Cases: OLFs, Coexistence and Precaution

This last sub-section includes cases where Member States sought to prohibit or restrict trade in or cultivation of GE organisms by relying on OLFs. These cases do not exactly centre on matters of precautionary public health or environmental protection; however, an iterative evaluation of uncertain risks in accordance with a socially acceptable risk approach is inherent to the national measures. In Case C-165/08, *Commission* v *Poland*, for instance, the defendant relied on the precautionary principle at the early stages of the infringement procedure; however, when the case was brought to the ECJ, Poland structured its defence differently, focusing on OLFs. Matters of environmental risk and coexistence issues are also intertwined in the other cases under analysis. Regardless of the specific legal issues at stake in these cases, it is difficult to demarcate the boundaries between national controversies over the uncertain risks posed by GE organisms, and national controversies surrounding the relevant OLFs at stake.

In *Commission* v *Poland*,[220] the ECJ found in favour of the Commission in an action against Poland for failure to fulfil obligations under EU law. The ECJ held that, by prohibiting the free circulation of GE seed varieties and the inclusion of GE organism varieties in the national catalogue of varieties, Poland had failed to fulfil its obligations under Articles 22 and 23 of the 2001 Directive and Articles 4(4) and 16 of the 2002 Directive on the Common Catalogue of Varieties of Agricultural Plant Species.[221]

Throughout the pre-litigation procedure, Poland relied on the precautionary principle and the pervasiveness of the potential environmental risks posed by the cultivation of GE organisms; it also referred to coexistence issues.[222] In addition

[220] Case C-165/08, *Commission v Poland*, EU:C:2009:473.

[221] Council Directive 2002/53/EC of 13 June 2002 on the Common Catalogue of Varieties of Agricultural Plant Species, [2002] OJ L193.

[222] Case C-165/08, *Commission v Poland*, para 18.

to this, it stressed public opinion in opposition to GE organisms, remarking that in 2006 all Polish administrative regions unanimously adopted a resolution stating that their territories should be GE organism-free; it also emphasised the need to respect ethical principles.[223] In its defence in front of the ECJ, on the other hand, Poland only focused on the point of respect for ethical principles. More specifically, it argued that ethical considerations play no part in the context of the 2001 Deliberate Release Directive and the 2002 Directive on the Common Catalogue of Agricultural Plant Species. On these grounds, Poland claimed that EU harmonisation in the field of GE organisms is not exhaustive (in respect of ethical principles). Under this framing, Poland would have been allowed to resort to Article 36 TFEU and invoke public morality.[224]

The Commission challenged this position, arguing that the authorisation and marketing of GE varieties had undergone exhaustive harmonisation. The ECJ did not analyse this point. Rather, it held that Poland had failed to establish that the national prohibition was enacted on ethical and religious grounds.[225] Indeed, it found that 'public morality is not really being invoked as a separate justification, but as an aspect of the justification relating to the protection of human health and the environment, which is precisely the concern of Directive 2001/18'.[226] The ECJ's findings thus confirm that public controversies surrounding the *uncertain risks* posed by GE organisms and their acceptability were at stake in this case.[227]

In Case C-36/11, *Pioneer Hi Bred Italia*,[228] an Italian court requested a preliminary ruling on the interpretation of Article 26a of the 2001 Directive, on coexistence. Pursuant to Article 26a ('Measures to avoid unintended presence of GMOs in other products'),[229] Member States may take appropriate measures to avoid the adventitious presence of GE components. The Commission shall adopt general guidelines on coexistence. In the national proceedings, Pioneer Hi Bred challenged the national authorities' decision that it would not be able to assess the company's application for authorisation to cultivate (MON810) maize varieties. The reason adduced by the authorities was that coexistence rules had not yet been adopted at regional level.

First, the applicant disputed the requirement for a national authorisation for the cultivation of GE organisms, since GE varieties had already gone through the EU authorisation procedure and had already been listed in the common catalogue. While the relevant national provisions, to be further implemented by regional rules, mostly focused on coexistence matters, they also mentioned the requirement that the relevant GE organisms 'would not cause biological damage

[223] Paras 19 to 21.
[224] See the text of Art 36 TFEU.
[225] Paras 52 ff.
[226] Para 55.
[227] See also paras 61 to 63.
[228] Case C-36/11, *Pioneer Hi Bred Italia*, EU:C:2012:534.
[229] See sections VIII and IX below, for relevant changes after the enactment of the 2015 reform.

to the immediate environment, having regard to specific agroecological, environmental and pedoclimatic factors'.[230] Yet again, concerns on environmental *and* socio-economic matters were intertwined in national regulations.[231] Second, the applicant disputed the national authorities' interpretation of Article 26a, according to which the cultivation of GE organisms could not be authorised pending the adoption of regional coexistence rules. The national court referred a question surrounding the interpretation of Article 26a.

The ECJ found that, under Article 19(5) of the 2003 GM Food and Feed Regulation, authorisations of GE varieties are valid throughout the Union. Further, as clarified in Article 16(1) of the 2002 Directive on the common catalogue of agricultural plant species, seeds of varieties accepted for inclusion in the catalogue shall not be subject to any marketing restrictions.[232] In this light, the ECJ ruled that a Member State is not entitled to make the cultivation of GE organisms conditional upon a national authorisation based on public health and environmental considerations.[233] Turning to the issue of Article 26a and coexistence measures, the ECJ found that this Article could not entitle a Member State to prohibit in a general manner the cultivation of GE organisms on its territory pending the adoption of coexistence measures. Otherwise, Member States would be able to prohibit cultivation of GE organisms indefinitely by simply refraining from enacting any regulations on coexistence.[234]

The same issue re-surfaced in Case C-542/12, *Fidenato*.[235] In this case the ECJ further specified that a Member State is not entitled to make the cultivation of GE organisms conditional upon a (general) national authorisation process,[236] as the latter cannot be understood as an expression of the power to take appropriate measures to avoid the adventitious presence of GE components conferred upon Member States by Article 26a.

These cases demonstrate strong national concerns surrounding the authorisation of GE varieties; these concerns are best exemplified by the 'supplementary' national authorisation process set in place by Italy for the purposes of cultivation of GE crops. While these cases mostly focused on OLFs, environmental and public health risks were always in the background.[237] Yet again, the boundaries between *scientific uncertainty*, *precaution* and *OLFs* are blurred. Member States adhered to a socially acceptable risk approach.

[230] Case C-36/11, *Pioneer Hi Bred Italia*, para 30.

[231] Notably, these included national concerns that the EFSA's risk assessments did not do justice to national ecosystems and environmental diversity; see above, section V.

[232] Paras 63 and 64.

[233] Para 69. See also paras 70 and 71.

[234] Paras 72 to 75.

[235] Case C-542/12, *Fidenato*, EU:C:2013:298.

[236] In its previous answer in *Pioneer Hi Bred Italia*, the ECJ had only mentioned public health or environmental risk aspects – in this case, on the other hand, it clarified that national authorisation procedures may not apply even in cases where they only aim to cover and regulate coexistence.

[237] Almost as clearly as in *Upper Austria*, environmental risk and coexistence issues overlapped and were intertwined in these cases.

VII. Interim Conclusions: The Counter-Hegemonic Narrative, Socially Acceptable Risk Approaches and the Failure of Science and Procedural Deliberation

This section sketches out some interim conclusions, prior to the analysis of the 2015 reform on the cultivation of GE crops and the conclusions of the chapter. The previous sections have shown that a socially acceptable risk approach, encompassing a prudential approach to risk assessment, regulatory focus on multiple forms of uncertainty and consideration of the precautionary principle and relevant OLFs, is embedded in the EU framework for the governance of GE organisms. As anticipated in the previous chapters and in the introduction to this chapter, the counter-hegemonic narrative surrounding the regulation of GE organisms and their uncertain risks has been constructed within the EU legal regime.

The fifth and sixth sections have analysed EU-wide conflicts over the regulatory governance of agricultural biotechnologies through the lens of evidence-based and socially acceptable risk approaches. While set against the broader background of regulatory implementation matters, the enquiry has been conducted by focusing on relevant case law. In so doing, the analysis has shown the gap between EU institutions' adherence to evidence-based paradigms and Member States' and societal stakeholders' reliance on a socially acceptable risk approach. As anticipated, this overview is relevant in two ways.

First, the analysis has explored the rationale, characteristics, goals and broader implications of socially acceptable risk approaches. The iterative determination of the intended level of protection and threshold of socially acceptable risk, typical of socially acceptable risk approaches, is perfectly illustrated by the position of EU Member States and societal stakeholders in the cases analysed in the fifth and sixth sections. In turn, the analysis of the socially acceptable risk model of risk governance helps to deconstruct the specific features and implications of the counter-hegemonic narrative on GE organisms, in practice rather than in theoretical terms.

The analysis has uncovered the connections between prudential approaches to risk assessment, regulatory focus on persisting uncertainty, recourse to the precautionary principle and consideration of all relevant OLFs. The pursuit of a higher than cost-benefit effective level of protection and consideration of OLFs come into play *indirectly*, as the normative lens through which scientific questions are evaluated and the normative frame underlying the identification of the threshold of acceptable risk.[238] On these grounds, in the field of agricultural biotechnologies, reference to persisting uncertainties, recourse to the precautionary principle and evaluation of OLFs strike a specific balance between economic considerations

[238] Rather than *directly*, as occurs in cases where hazards and risks have been conclusively proven. See ch 1, section III.

and trade rights and collective interests. Notably, qualitative OLFs such as public opinion, the availability of more sustainable alternatives to GE organisms, consideration of the latter's advantages and disadvantages and all relevant distributional stakes play a prominent role. This outlines a vision of societal interests and common good which is remarkably different from the one underlying linear evidence-based approaches, analysed in chapter three.

Second, the analysis has encompassed horizontal and vertical conflicts in the EU. This enquiry has shown that the EFSA's risk assessments are generally perceived as insufficiently prudential. Societal stakeholders and Member States have lamented that persisting uncertainties are neither taken into due consideration in the agency's final findings, nor adequately dispelled. In this sense, the EFSA's risk assessments have failed to do justice to EU-wide calls for a very high level of protection and a correspondingly low threshold of acceptable risk. The clash between evidence-based and socially acceptable risk approaches to regulatory implementation is even more apparent at risk-management level. National prohibitions and restrictions testify that a plurality of Member States deem the uncertain risks posed by GE organisms to be socially unacceptable. In reaching this finding, Member States have expressly taken into consideration persisting uncertainties, the overarching tenets of the precautionary principle and the relevant OLFs at stake.

This form of analysis, as already mentioned in the fourth section, sheds some light on the limited ability of science and procedural political deliberation to generate genuine agreement and foster consensus. In the absence of very low levels of uncertainty, science and technical expertise can hardly contribute to the identification of any agreeable solutions. Even less can they point to a single 'correct' and universally acceptable answer. The scientific controversies at the heart of *TestBioTech* show this very clearly. Scientific agreement is hard to build if uncertainties persist. This becomes significantly harder where science is evaluated through different normative lenses. Not only may scientific inferences and conclusions vary. The very framings of the relevant scientific questions can also be irreconcilable, and the relevant evidence base may vary.

Similar considerations apply to procedural political deliberation. As anticipated in the fourth section, procedural deliberation is doomed in the absence of substantive preconditions: most importantly, shared normative perspectives, values and goals. Where such preconditions are lacking, as the long-standing EU deadlock on GE organisms proves, horizontal and vertical conflicts are destined to remain unsolved. Horizontal conflicts, as defined under Conflicts Law theory, will not be solved through procedural arrangements and reliance on deliberative practices. In a similar vein, it is hard to envisage any procedural meta-norm to solve increasingly complex vertical conflicts.

Against this overall background, the next section provides an overview of the 2015 EU reform of the cultivation of GE organisms. These final sections are part of the analysis of the dynamics of legal pluralisation. In other words, the enquiry is circumscribed to the EU legal system as a supra-national regime, in its own right.

The analysis endeavours to show that, while providing a compromise solution, the 2015 Directive has in fact undermined the socially acceptable risk discourse at EU level. Nor can it be understood as a successful political deliberative solution to the conundrum of agricultural biotechnologies.

VIII. Final Remarks on Legal Pluralisation (I): The 2015 Reform on the Cultivation of GE Crops

The authorisation process for GE crops has been particularly tormented since the enactment of the 2001 Directive: Directive 2015/412[239] lingered for years in the form of a proposal.[240] In 2008, for the first time, a group of Member States requested the Commission to amend the 2001 Directive so that Member States would be allowed to prohibit or restrict the cultivation of GE crops. In June 2009, the so called 'Group of 13' reformulated the request for national derogations on the grounds of the principles of subsidiarity and flexibility.[241] In 2010 came the tabling of the proposal,[242] which would provide Member States with the power to restrict or prohibit the cultivation of GE crops on grounds other than the protection of human health and the environment. However, a majority of Member States refused this proposal as an unsatisfactory compromise, which could not do justice to national concerns surrounding the *uncertain risks* posed by agricultural biotechnologies and their *acceptability*. In 2012, under the Danish presidency, the Environmental Council failed to reach a majority on the proposal.[243]

It was only in 2014 that the proposal was developed. On 3 December 2014, an informal agreement was reached by the European Parliament and the Council. The Directive was then adopted on 11 March 2015.[244] Directive 2015/412 has amended Directive 2001/18/EC by adding Articles 26b and 26c to the latter; the reform provides Member States with more discretion to restrict or prohibit the commercial cultivation of GE crops on their territory.[245] By contrast, the

[239] Directive (EU) 2015/412 of the European Parliament and of the Council of 11 March 2015 amending Directive 2001/18/EC as regards the Possibility for Member States to Restrict or Prohibit the Cultivation of Genetically Modified Organisms (GMOs) in their Territory, [2015] OJ L68.

[240] For some comments on the original proposal, see Poli, 'The Member States'' (n 112) 148 ff.; M Weimer, 'What Price Flexibility? The Recent Commission Proposal to Allow for National Opt-Outs on GMO Cultivation Under the Deliberate Release Directive and the Comitology Reform Post-Lisbon' (2010) 1 *European Journal of Risk Regulation* 345.

[241] See Council of the European Union, *Council Document no 11226/2/09 REV 2 of 24 June 2009.*

[242] COM(2010) 375 Final, *Proposal for a Regulation of the European Parliament and of the Council Amending Directive 2001/18/EC as Regards the Possibility for the Member States to Restrict or Prohibit the Cultivation of GMOs in their Territory.*

[243] Council of the European Union, *Council Document no 7153/12 of 2 March 2012*; Council of the European Union, *Council Document no 10883/1/12 of 6 June 2012.*

[244] As noted in De Sadeleer, 'Marketing and Cultivation' (n 32) 545.

[245] As of June 2020, 17 Member States and 1 region (Wallonia) have requested and obtained a restriction of geographical scope of GMO applications and authorisations; for more information, see www.ec.europa.eu/food/plant/gmo/authorisation/cultivation/geographical_scope_en. Pursuant to Art 26a

Commission's proposal to add a further article to this end (Article 34a) to the 2003 GM Food and Feed Regulation[246] was rejected by the European Parliament on 28 October 2015.

Article 26b, as added by the 2015 Directive, provides for national adjustments to the territorial scope of the cultivation of GE organisms[247] and for the enactment by Member States of measures restricting or prohibiting the cultivation in all or part of their territory of a GE organism or a group of GE organisms defined by crop or trait.[248] The two sets of measures have been defined, with good reasons, as the outcome of a 'somewhat convoluted compromise'.[249] As clarified,[250] the measures adopted under Article 26b shall not affect the free circulation of authorised GE organisms as, or in, products. They may only apply to the environmental release or commercial cultivation of GE crops.

The first part of Article 26b deals with the ex-ante adjustment of the territorial scope of cultivation of GE crops. This process shall take place before the EU authorisation is issued. Pending the process of authorisation or renewal of authorisation of a GE crop, a Member State may communicate to the Commission a request for the adjustment of the geographical scope of the authorisation, excluding all or part of its territory from cultivation.[251] The deadline for such communication is 45 days after the date of circulation of the risk assessment report.[252] Notably, no justifications are needed in the case of a request for territorial adjustment.

The Commission shall then make the Member State's demand public and present it to the applicant and to the other Member States. Accordingly, within 30 days of the Commission's presentation, a biotech firm applicant may decide to adjust the geographical scope of its application in accordance with the Member State's request, even though it is not compelled to do so. If the applicant accepts, the adjustment of the geographical scope of the application will be implemented in the written consent.[253] This means that the authorisation or renewal of authorisation

of the 2015 Directive, measures shall be taken as from April 2017 with the aim of avoiding possible cross-border contamination into neighbouring Member States in which the cultivation of a GE variety is prohibited; Art 26c, on the other hand, deals with the relevant transitional measures.

[246] ie, empowering Member States to restrict or prohibit the marketing of GE food and feed within their territory by invoking a set of compelling grounds. See COM(2015) 177 Final, *Proposal for a Regulation of the European Parliament and of the Council Amending Regulation (EC) no 1829/2003 as regards the Possibility for the Member States to Restrict or Prohibit the Use of Genetically Modified Food and Feed on their Territory*; and COM(2015) 176, *Reviewing the Decision-Making Process on genetically modified organisms (GMOs)*.

[247] See Art 26b(1), (2), (5) and (6).

[248] Art 26b(3) and (4).

[249] De Sadeleer, 'Marketing and Cultivation' (n 32) 546.

[250] Art 26b(8).

[251] Art 26b(1).

[252] The assessment report referred to is the one provided for under Art 14(2) of the 2001 Directive; or (under the one-door-one-key procedure) the one provided for under Arts 6(6) and 18(6) of the 2003 Regulation.

[253] The consent referred to is the one provided for under Art 19 of the 2001 Directive; or under Arts 7 and 19 of the 2003 Regulation.

of the GE variety will be adjusted to comply with the Member State's request, and the cultivation of the GE crop will be restricted or prohibited therein.

The second case is the one of national opt-outs, as provided for under paragraphs 3 and 4 of Article 26b. Where a biotech firm applicant refuses a request for territorial adjustment, or where no such request has been notified, Member States are still entitled to opt-out from the cultivation of an authorised GE variety and adopt measures restricting or prohibiting its cultivation in all or part of their territory. This opt-out clause, however, is subject to several conditions.

First, although the opt-outs may entail total bans[254] and may cover the entire Member State's territory,[255] they shall apply to a GE organism or a group of GE organisms defined by crop or trait.[256] In other words, Member States cannot enforce a blanket ban on the cultivation of any GE crops.[257] Second, a standstill clause applies, so that Member States shall refrain from adopting and implementing the measures for a 75-day period after communication of the draft opt-out measures to the Commission. The Commission may then release its comments on the draft opt-outs.

Third, and most importantly, a set of conditions are laid out for the enactment of the opt-out measures.[258] The opt-outs must be compliant with EU law, reasoned, proportionate, non-discriminatory and justified on the basis of one or more compelling grounds. These compelling grounds encompass: (a) environmental policy objectives; (b) town and country planning; (c) land use; (d) socio-economic impacts; (e) avoidance of presence of GE components in other products, without prejudice to Article 26a; (f) agricultural policy objectives; and (g) public policy. The list is not a closed one.[259] The grounds may be invoked individually or in combination, with the only exception of ground (g), which cannot be used individually.[260]

Pursuant to Article 26(b)(3), the compelling grounds may be differently invoked:

> depending on the particular circumstances of the Member State, region or area in which those measures will apply, but shall, *in no case, conflict* with the *environmental risk assessment* carried out pursuant to [the 2001] Directive or to Regulation (EC) No 1829/2003 (emphasis added).[261]

The next section analyses the rationale of the reform and its impact on the socially acceptable risk discourse in EU risk regulation.

[254] Rather than mere restrictions.
[255] Rather than part of it.
[256] Art 26b(3).
[257] As noted by De Sadeleer, 'Marketing and Cultivation' (n 32) 546.
[258] Art 26b(3).
[259] Art 26b(3) states that 'such measures are in addition based on compelling grounds such as those related to [...]'.
[260] Art 26b(3).
[261] ibid.

IX. Final Remarks on Legal Pluralisation (II): The 2015 Reform from a Socially Acceptable Risk Perspective. Procedural Compromises and a Twofold Substantive Defeat

The 2015 reform has striven to address the *procedural* issues arising from regulatory implementation of the 2001–2003 framework. From a socially acceptable risk perspective, however, it has overlooked the *substantive* dimension of the problem and the true nature of *normative disagreements* as to whether the uncertain risks posed by agricultural biotechnologies are socially acceptable. The changes introduced by the 2015 reform must be differently evaluated in respect of their impact at the Member State level and their broader implications for EU risk regulation, respectively.

Starting from the Member State level, the 2015 reform makes explicit reference to the principle of subsidiarity, as enshrined in Article 5(3) TEU.[262] Recital (6) of the Directive maintains that the cultivation of GE crops can be more thoroughly addressed at national level. The reason, the Recital adds, is that this is an issue with strong national, regional and local dimensions, encompassing land use, local agriculture and biodiversity protection. On these grounds, pursuant to the Preamble, more flexibility is needed in the regulation of the cultivation of GE organisms, in accordance with the tenets of vertical subsidiarity.[263]

The Directive's focus on the principles of vertical subsidiarity and flexibility, however, is intertwined with a specific framing and interpretation of the causes leading to national disagreements over the cultivation of GE organisms. Recital (7) makes direct reference to Member States' reliance on the safeguard clauses of the 2001 Directive, 2003 Regulation and Article 114(5) and (6) TFEU, and their expression of 'concerns which do not only relate to issues associated with the safety of GMOs for health or the environment'.[264] This statement suggests that, in the regulatory context of the 2015 Directive, national bans and restrictions enacted throughout the years are largely understood to reflect disagreements over the relevant OLFs at stake, rather than *uncertain risks* and their *acceptability*.

The emphasis of the Directive is visibly placed on this specific framing of the controversy. National safeguard measures are not understood as risk management measures, enacted to comply with the national intended level of protection and national threshold of socially acceptable risk. Rather, they are understood as a set of measures addressing national concerns over *mere* socio-economic OLFs; the latter are considered *immaterial* to the determination that the risks posed by GE crops are acceptable and worth taking, in the face of persisting scientific uncertainty.

[262] Art 5(3), Consolidated Version of the Treaty on European Union, [2012] OJ C 326.
[263] Recital (6), Dir 2015/412.
[264] Recital (7).

In other words, the assumption underlying the Directive is that national bans and restrictions were motivated by concerns which are ultimately *unrelated* or *irrelevant* to the regulation of uncertain public health and environmental risks. Clearly, evidence-based discourses underlie the reform. More specifically, EU legislators have failed to acknowledge that national bans and restrictions enacted prior to the reform reflected the pursuit of enhanced levels of protection. These measures relied on prudential risk assessments, a focus on persisting uncertainties and the determination of a very low threshold of socially acceptable risk, taking scientific uncertainty, the precautionary principle and all relevant OLFs into consideration. At their heart lay an evaluation of *uncertain risks* and their *acceptability*, as understood under socially acceptable risk approaches; not a mere consideration of OLFs.

In accordance with these premises, the 2015 Directive has repatriated the evaluation of a range of OLFs to the national level. The *risk* regulation stage, ie the authorisation procedure for GE crops, is still fully harmonised, with risk assessment and risk management functions staying with the competent EU authorities under the 2001–2003 framework.[265] As Article 26(b)(3) maintains, national opt-outs by reference to one or more compelling grounds shall in no case conflict with the environmental risk assessment conducted under the 2001 Directive or 2003 Regulation. Thus, national opt-outs can neither pursue higher levels of environmental protection, nor be grounded on precautionary evaluations or the finding that specific uncertain risks posed by GE crops are not acceptable. All that Member States can do is invoke OLFs; this, however, cannot do justice to national claims that the uncertain risks posed by agricultural biotechnologies are not socially acceptable.[266] In fact, an indirect acknowledgment that issues of environmental protection *and* socio-economic factors were intertwined in national decisions to enact restrictive measures emerges from compelling ground (a), on environmental policy objectives.[267] This can hardly be considered to be an OLF. Clearly, the boundaries between environmental *risk* and environmental and

[265] As also remarked by De Sadeleer, 'Marketing and Cultivation' (n 32); and S Poli, 'The Reform of EU Legislation on GMOs: A Journey to an Unknown Destination?' (2015) 6 *European Journal of Risk Regulation* 559.

[266] For an account of the increasing separation of 'facts' and 'values' in EU governance of GE organisms after the 2015 reform, see M Lee, 'GMOs in the Internal Market: New Legislation on National Flexibility' (2016) 79 *Modern Law Review* 317. For the argument that the Achilles' heel of the reform lies in the impossibility for Member States to invoke considerations on environmental risk, in so far as the opt-outs cannot conflict with the EU environmental risk assessment, see Geelhoed, 'Divided in Diversity' (n 112); elaborating on *Commission v Poland*, Geelhoed also argued that the problem could be further aggrieved by the evidentiary burden of proving that OLFs, rather than matters of environmental protection, are at stake.

[267] The indirect acknowledgment by the EU legislator that socio-economic factors *as well as* the pursuit of precautionary levels of environmental protection were intertwined in national measures arguably finds reflection in two further aspects of the reform. First, the deadline for the request of a territorial adjustment is linked to circulation of the environmental risk assessment. This suggests that questions of environmental protection and environmental risk are at stake. Second, the possibility for Member States to enact total bans is quite hard to reconcile with (and justify on the basis of) a mere focus on OLFs on the Member States' part.

biodiversity *protection*, on the one hand, and environmental *policy* objectives, on the other, are blurred.[268]

Therefore, if analysed through the lens of a socially acceptable risk approach, the 2015 reform may be defined as a lowest common denominator compromise. Indeed, it is worth stressing again that national disagreements as to the adequacy of the 2015 Directive's arrangements persisted for years and delayed its enactment. Also, a corresponding proposal for reform to the 2003 GM Food and Feed Regulation was voted down and abandoned. The 2015 Directive allows Member States more flexibility to prohibit or restrict the cultivation of GE organisms; however, as explained in the previous paragraphs, it does so at a cost. This solution fails to capture the true nature of EU-wide controversies.

Had EU institutions been willing to politically solve the conundrum of GE organisms, they would have simply acknowledged and accepted that the uncertain risks posed by agricultural biotechnologies are not regarded as socially acceptable by a majority of EU Member States and the larger part of EU civil society.[269] This would have required a shift away from the evidence-based approach followed in previous years. However, clearly EU institutions had no intention of pursuing this course of action. From this perspective, the 2015 reform can hardly be understood as a procedural deliberative response to the deadlock. Nor does it truly solve the political issues underlying the horizontal and vertical conflicts which unfolded throughout the years.[270] Member States remain 'divided in diversity',[271] while EU institutions go their own way. The differences remain irreconcilable, and the gap between evidence-based and socially acceptable risk approaches remains unbridgeable.

The final consideration relates to the impact of the 2015 reform at EU level. As explained in this section, the Directive has repatriated to the national level the evaluation of mere OLFs. As convincingly argued, it is not a case of proper de-harmonisation.[272] On these grounds, as a matter of law, nothing would seem to prevent EU institutions from taking OLFs into account throughout the authorisation process. However, the provisions of the Directive certainly imply that Member States have a key role to play in so far as the evaluation of OLFs is at stake. From a regulatory governance perspective, this suggests that after the reform EU institutions will be even less likely to take OLFs into account in their decisions

[268] In a similar perspective, see also Weimer, 'Risk Regulation and Deliberation in EU Administrative Governance' (n 112) 633.

[269] Leonelli, 'The Perfect Storm' (n 85). In a similar vein, see Lee, *EU Environmental Law* (n 101) 236.

[270] For a more optimistic interpretation of the 2015 reform, see Weimer, 'What Price Flexibility?' (n 240); and Weimer, 'Risk Regulation and Deliberation in EU Administrative Governance' (n 112).

[271] Geelhoed, 'Divided in Diversity' (n 112); in a similar perspective, see also Lee, 'GMOs in the Internal Market' (n 266).

[272] See De Sadeleer, 'Marketing and Cultivation' (n 32) 548 ff.; and Poli, 'The Reform of EU Legislation' (n 265) 566, defining the 2015 repatriation of OLFs to the Member State level as 'an optional de-activation of a [former] EU competence'.

on authorisation. From being merely *disregarded*, OLFs could then turn out to be straightforwardly *dis-embedded* from the risk regulation process.[273]

At a general level, the compartmentalisation of risk regulation and OLFs undermines socially acceptable risk approaches. Under this reconstruction, the 2015 reform has marked the end of an EU-wide socially acceptable risk approach to the governance of the uncertain risks posed by the cultivation of GE crops. In other words, it has dismantled the more or less expressly acknowledged regulatory premises of EU risk governance: that regulators may take qualitative OLFs into consideration when setting the intended level of protection and the threshold of socially acceptable risk, and that the decision to draw on prudential risk assessments and focus on persisting uncertainties is informed by the pursuit of enhanced levels of protection, the overarching tenets of the precautionary principle and consideration of OLFs.

As argued since the first chapter of the book, the determination of the legally relevant threshold of adverse effects is never a matter of 'pure' science, and normative frames are always at stake in regulation of uncertain risks. Neither evidence-based nor socially acceptable risk approaches are neutral or objective. The reform's emphasis on qualitative OLFs as *non-scientific* factors thus neglects that economic cost-benefit analysis evaluations and the pursuit of a cost-benefit effective level of protection, which indirectly inform sound science approaches to risk assessment and the assumption that sound science must be adhered to, are equally *non-scientific*.

Undoubtedly, as anticipated since the first chapter, the controversy on GE organisms is particular in many respects. Uncertainty surrounds both hazards and risks. Controversies over OLFs play a prominent role; moreover, international trade considerations have clearly and powerfully come into play. However, EU institutions have stood their ground in the past under very similar circumstances, in respect of the transnational controversy on hormones residues in meat.[274] In the case of agricultural biotechnologies, by contrast, they have ultimately failed to defend socially acceptable risk approaches.

X. Conclusions: Findings of the Institutional and Normative Strands of Enquiry

This chapter has deconstructed the counter-hegemonic narrative on GE organisms and transnational discourses on socially acceptable risk through an analysis of the EU legal system.

[273] Leonelli, 'The Perfect Storm' (n 85). In a similar perspective, taking into consideration the proposal for reform (prior to the enactment of the 2015 Directive), see Lee, *EU Environmental Law* (n 101) 243.

[274] See the analysis in ch 5; the controversy on use of hormones is also characterised by the existence of hazard-related uncertainties, the prominence of OLFs (ie the availability of more sustainable options for livestock farming and the perceived lack of any socio-economic advantages associated with the decision to run uncertain risks), and trade disputes.

The first, second and third sections have examined the EU regulatory framework, showing that the transnational counter-hegemonic narrative on risk governance and a socially acceptable risk approach are embedded therein. As anticipated since the introductory section, the counter-hegemonic narrative on the risks posed by agricultural biotechnologies has in fact been constructed from within the EU legal order. The analysis has then focused on the relevant regulatory categories, including the notions of prudential risk assessment, uncertainty, precaution and OLFs.

The following sections have turned to the question of regulatory implementation. By deconstructing the position of Member States and societal stakeholders, as emerging from relevant case law, the analysis has shed light on the features and implications of socially acceptable risk approaches. Further, the enquiry into the substantive gap between the evidence-based approach of EU institutions and the diametrically opposed position of other actors within the EU has testified to the inability of both science and procedural political deliberation to generate genuine agreement and solve conflicts. Finally, the last sections have provided an overview and critical account of the 2015 reforms on the cultivation of GE organisms.

As the entire chapter has shown, the EU system for regulatory governance of GE organisms has failed to provide normatively legitimate responses to the deadlock. Neither the implementation of the original regulatory framework nor the drafting of the 2015 reform have lived up to the tenets of the Conflicts Law framework. Procedural deliberation has failed to re-couple law and politics, and thus to resolve horizontal conflicts. Nor have vertical conflicts been satisfactorily resolved, in normative and political terms. As this chapter has endeavoured to illustrate, this is a *procedural* reflection of the *substantive* gap between evidence-based and socially acceptable risk approaches in the field of agricultural biotechnologies. In the absence of substantive preconditions, procedural deliberative practices are bound to yield no positive results; they will be insufficient to facilitate genuine political agreement and will therefore fail to identify normatively legitimate solutions.

5

Legal Pluralisation: The SPS Agreement, GE Organisms and the Impossible Quest for Scientific Objectivity. From Sound Science to Transnational Regulatory Convergence and Trade Liberalisation

Much has been written throughout the years on the WTO Agreement on the Application of Sanitary and Phytosanitary Measures ('SPS Agreement'), the interpretation of its provisions by the WTO Panels and Appellate Body ('AB'), and the applicable standard of review.[1] This chapter undertakes a different form of analysis, by directly focusing on the relevant scientific and risk regulation aspects. It conducts a close examination of the Panels' and AB's Reports against the backdrop of the notion of sound science, as opposed to relevant hazard-related, risk-related and methodological uncertainties. By deconstructing the factual and legal background of the disputes, with particular focus on *EC – Biotech*,[2] the chapter shows how the hegemonic evidence-based narrative is reflected in the WTO dispute settlement practice interpreting and applying the SPS Agreement.

The second preliminary point to address, in the context of the application of the methodological framework, relates to the transnational relevance of the SPS Agreement and the reasons why it is being interrogated for the purposes of the present analysis. The enquiry points to the far-reaching impact that *EC – Biotech* has had on the transnational debate on GE organisms. It shows how the Panel Report in *EC – Biotech* has undermined socially acceptable risk discourses on

[1] See inter alia J Scott, *The WTO Agreement on Sanitary and Phytosanitary Measures. A Commentary* (OUP, 2007); L Gruszczynski, *Regulating Health and Environmental Risks under WTO Law: A Critical Analysis of the SPS Agreement* (OUP, 2010); J Peel, *Science and Risk Regulation in International Law* (CUP, 2010); C Button, *The Power to Protect. Trade, Health and Uncertainty in the WTO* (Hart Publishing, 2004); T Epps, *International Trade and Health Protection. A Critical Assessment of the WTO's SPS Agreement* (Edward Elgar, 2008).

[2] *EC – Measures Affecting the Approval and Marketing of Biotech Products*, Panel Report (adopted 21 November 2006) WT/DS291, WT/DS292, WT/DS293 (*EC – Biotech*).

the governance of agricultural biotechnologies, pushing EU institutions towards adherence to evidence-based approaches in the implementation of EU regulatory frameworks.[3]

At a more general level, the chapter also illustrates how the interpretation and application of the SPS Agreement has considerably reinforced hegemonic discourses on sound science and evidence-based risk governance at the transnational level.[4] As the chapter shows, the WTO Panels and AB's interpretation places several constraints on the Members' ability to: (i) focus on persisting uncertainties which emerge from positive risk assessments;[5] (ii) adhere to prudential approaches to risk assessment;[6] or (iii) determine that the available scientific evidence is insufficient for the purposes of an adequate risk assessment.[7] Further, some disputes have cast doubts on the Members' right to determine their own appropriate level of protection, in situations where a risk has been scientifically established.[8]

Finally, turning to the third and fourth preliminary questions, how does the analysis uncover the foundations and overarching goals of the hegemonic narrative on GE organisms and their uncertain risks? How does it help deconstruct transnational discourses on evidence-based risk governance and sound science, more generally? What is the added value of analysing disputes brought under the SPS Agreement? This chapter sheds further light on the rationale and implications of evidence-based approaches, by unravelling the connections between *sound science approaches* to risk assessment, adherence to *sound science*, *transnational regulatory convergence* and *trade liberalisation*. An analysis of the SPS Agreement under the methodological category of 'legal pluralisation' is thus necessary to deconstruct the hegemonic narrative on GE organisms, specifically, and risk regulation, at a broader level. The remaining part of this introductory section provides a brief summary of the chapter's findings on these points.

The SPS Agreement recognises the Members' right to set their own Appropriate Level of Protection ('ALOP') and enact SPS measures conforming to it. Specific 'science-based' obligations[9] are enshrined in Articles 2.2, 5.1 and 5.7, and must be

[3] See the references in ch 4, sections IV and VI.

[4] The 'new' generation of trade and investment agreements still references the SPS Agreement provisions; on these grounds, the Agreement and its interpretation keep on having a significant impact at transnational level.

[5] See the scientific and factual background in *EC – Hormones* (sections II and III), *Australia – Salmon* (section IV), *EC – Biotech* (section VII) and all references therein.

[6] See the scientific and factual background in *Japan – Apples 21.5* (section VI), *US/Canada – Continued Suspension* (section VIII. A, in respect of the one hormone which was permanently banned), *Australia – Apples* (section VIII.B) and all references therein.

[7] See the scientific and factual background in *Japan – Agricultural Products II* (section V), *Japan – Apples* (section VI), *EC – Biotech* (section VII), *US/Canada – Continued Suspension* (section VIII.A, in respect of the five hormones which were provisionally banned), the latest disputes (section VIII.C) and all references therein.

[8] See the scientific and factual background in *Australia – Salmon 21.5* (section VI), *Japan – Agricultural Products II* (section V), *US/Canada – Continued Suspension* (section VIII.A, in respect of the one hormone which was permanently banned) and all references therein.

[9] For use of this terminology, see also Scott, *The WTO Agreement* (n 1).

complied with by the Members. Under Annex A(4) on risk assessment, Members are under a duty to produce scientific evidence regarding the likelihood of entry, establishment and spread of a pest or disease, or the potential for adverse effects on human or animal health arising from the presence of additives, contaminants, toxins or disease-causing organisms in food, beverages or feedstuffs.[10]

Ever since *EC – Hormones*, the AB has sought to identify a standard of review within the spectrum from deference to de novo review.[11] The former postulates a procedural scrutiny of Members' compliance with the obligation to conduct a risk assessment and scientifically substantiate their SPS measures. The margins of Members' discretion are broad, as in this case Members need only demonstrate that they have drawn reasonable and non-arbitrary inferences from the available scientific evidence, including the existence of persisting uncertainties. This allows Members to take different forms of scientific uncertainty into consideration when deciding whether uncertain risks meet the ALOP and whether precautionary measures are warranted.

De novo review, on the other hand, enables the dispute settlement organs to undertake a substantive examination of the relevant risk assessments. As the chapter demonstrates, this can entail a *lato sensu* (broad) de novo review of whether Members have positively proved the relevant hazards and risks,[12] or *stricto sensu* (narrow) de novo review of the soundness and 'quality' of the risk assessment establishing hazards and risks.[13] Under de novo review, proving that hazards and risks exist and that the relevant risk assessment is 'sound' is the twofold precondition for a Member to have recourse to its ALOP and enact protective measures.

In *EC – Hormones*, the AB embraced a third option: 'objective fact-finding'.[14] Yet, in the face of scientific complexity and ubiquitous uncertainties, the search for truly objective scientific criteria to underpin this standard of review has proved impossible. As the Reports clearly show, the choice is dichotomous. The dispute settlement organs have thus pursued the substantive, de novo review path. Indeed, as the chapter shows, the precondition for a Member to invoke its ALOP and rely on it when enacting SPS measures is positive, sound scientific proof of the relevant hazards and risks. The WTO Panels and AB have interpreted the Agreement's science-based obligations in such a way that hazard-related uncertainties[15] and risk-related uncertainties pertaining to risk pathways, exposures and probabilities[16] are ultimately deemed scientifically irrelevant.

[10] See below, section I.

[11] See below, section III.

[12] *EC – Hormones* (sections II and III), *Australia – Salmon* (section IV), *Japan – Agricultural Products II* (section V), *Japan – Apples* (section VI), *EC – Biotech* (section VII) and *US/Canada – Continued Suspension* (section VIII.A, in respect of the five hormones which were provisionally banned).

[13] See the disputes referenced in n 6.

[14] See below, section III.

[15] *EC – Hormones* (sections II and III), *EC – Biotech* (section VII) and *US/Canada – Continued Suspension* (section VIII.A, in respect of the five hormones which were provisionally banned).

[16] *Australia – Salmon* (section IV), *Japan – Agricultural Products II* (section V), *Japan – Apples* (section VI), *US/Canada – Continued Suspension* (section VIII, A, in respect of the one hormone which was permanently banned) and the latest disputes (section VIII.C).

In the majority of disputes brought under the Agreement, the dispute settlement organs have conducted a *lato sensu* de novo review and focused on the Members' ability to provide positive proof of hazards, risk pathways and risks, regardless of persisting uncertainties or data gaps. In these cases, they have found that Articles 5.1 and 2.2 had been violated, in that: (i) SPS measures were not maintained with sufficient scientific evidence; (ii) Members had not conducted a risk assessment within the meaning of the SPS Agreement;[17] or (iii) the relevant SPS measures were not based on such a risk assessment.[18] This focus on sound science has been complemented by a very narrow, restrictive interpretation of the notion of 'scientific insufficiency', as provided for under Article 5.7 of the Agreement.[19]

In a minority of cases, the dispute settlement organs have directly or indirectly taken issue with methodological uncertainties and prudential risk assessments, such as where Members have drawn on experimental data or over-estimated risks, with a view to addressing persisting uncertainties. In these instances, they have conducted *stricto sensu* de novo review; they have thus evaluated the quality and 'soundness' of the evidence which Members had adduced to prove hazards and risks.[20]

The hegemonic, evidence-based narrative on sound science approaches to risk assessment and adherence to sound science is thus reflected in the interpretation of the Agreement. Sound science and its underlying normative components[21] play a crucial role in the context of the Agreement's application; the opposite is true for scientific uncertainty, inconclusiveness and insufficiency. Whether by reference to the text of the Agreement, the precautionary principle or international treaties, the respondent Members' attempts to broaden the interpretation of the science-based obligations have been to no avail. In a similar vein, the AB's acknowledgment that minority opinion may be legitimately relied upon,[22] the finding that SPS measures need not 'conform to' the results of risk assessment[23] and the recognition that a

[17] See the AB Report in *Australia – Salmon* (section IV), the AB Report in *Japan – Agricultural Products II* (section V), the Panel and AB Reports in *Japan – Apples* (section VI), the Panel Report in *US/Canada – Continued Suspension* (section VIII.A, in respect of the one hormone which was permanently banned) and the Panel and AB Reports in *Australia – Apples* (section VIII.B).

[18] See the Panel and AB Reports in *EC – Hormones* (sections II and III), the Panel Reports in *Australia – Salmon* and *Australia – Salmon 21.5* (section IV), the indirect suggestion in the Panel Report in *Japan – Agricultural Products II* (para 8.63), and *EC – Biotech* (section VII).

[19] See the disputes referenced in n 7.

[20] See the disputes referenced in n 6.

[21] ie, the pursuit of a cost-benefit effective level of protection. This only comes into play *indirectly* in the disputes under analysis in this chapter, which mostly relate to cases where hazards and risks have not been conclusively established; see ch 1, section III for more details. Further, at least on its face, the SPS Agreement gives Members freedom in setting their own ALOP. The level of protection need not be cost-benefit effective; Members are entitled to pursue enhanced levels of protection, after proving the existence of a hazard and risk. However, see below the analysis of *Australia – Salmon 21.5*, *Japan – Agricultural Products II* and *US/Canada – Continued Suspension* (in respect of the one hormone which was permanently banned). In these disputes, the dispute settlement organs' review ended up encroaching on the Member's ALOP.

[22] See the analysis of the AB Report in *EC – Hormones*, section III.

[23] See the analysis of the AB Report in *US/Canada – Continued Suspension*, section VIII.A.

Member's ALOP will impact on the scope and methodology of risk assessment[24] do not appear to have had very significant implications, in practical terms. The AB's reformulation of the applicable standard of review, as developed in *US/Canada – Continued Suspension*, was soon revisited in *Australia – Apples*, and the AB's partial broadening of the notion of 'scientific insufficiency' in *US/Canada – Continued Suspension* has never been put to the test.

As demonstrated in the previous chapters, reliance on sound science approaches and adherence to sound science are far from neutral or objective. The approach of the dispute settlement organs draws on the mere acknowledgment that, in the face of ubiquitous uncertainties and scientific pluralism, a deferential reasonableness review would afford Members the opportunity to defend virtually *any* SPS measure. This would be irreconcilable with the rationale and overarching goal of WTO law, ie trade liberalisation. In other words, it would undermine any attempt at transnational regulatory convergence in SPS regulation.[25] This casts further light on the implications of the evidence-based narrative on GE organisms, and risk governance more generally. Not only do evidence-based approaches, as illustrated in the third chapter, pursue aggregate wealth maximisation and facilitate the exercise of individual trade rights. As this chapter shows, they are also linked to transnational regulatory convergence and trade liberalisation. This is the *double* economic dividend referred to in the introductory chapter.

Finally, the normative considerations of this chapter are developed against the backdrop of *EC – Biotech*. The analysis underscores the failure to identify a universally agreeable procedural meta-norm to reconcile transnational integration and legal and value pluralism. On one side of the spectrum, we find de novo review and reference to sound science. This, for the reasons explained since the third chapter,[26] cannot possibly provide a normatively legitimate and universally agreeable criterion for the resolution of complex regulatory conflicts. On the other side, deference. This, however, is irreconcilable with the overarching goals of the SPS Agreement. Behind the two, and against a backdrop of transnational diversity in the governance of uncertain risks, lies the impossibility to identify any *objective*, *self-standing* procedural criteria to generate agreement in the face of scientific uncertainty and complexity. On these grounds, the normative reflections on the vertical conflict in *EC – Biotech* point to the failure of legal proceduralisation in a context of irreducible societal diversity.

The first section of this chapter provides a very concise overview of the relevant SPS Agreement provisions. Sections two to six then deconstruct the WTO Panels and the AB's approach to scientific uncertainties and sound science, starting from *EC – Hormones*. This provides the background for the following analysis of *EC – Biotech*. The seventh section takes a closer look at this dispute, developing all

[24] ibid.

[25] For similar suggestions (set against a different analytical backdrop), see Button, *The Power to Protect* (n 1) 45, and Gruszczynski, *Regulating Health* (n 1) 188.

[26] See ch 3, sections VI, VII and IX.

relevant considerations. The following section focuses on *US/Canada – Continued Suspension*, *Australia – Apples* and the most recent Reports. This part of the analysis highlights that, in practical terms, little has changed since *EC – Biotech*. Against this overall background, the last section underlines how the interpretation of the Agreement has considerably reinforced evidence-based discourses at transnational level and draws all relevant conclusions on the deconstruction of the hegemonic narrative.

I. The SPS Agreement: Relevant Provisions

As the Preamble expressly acknowledges, the SPS Agreement was born out of the desire to establish a 'multilateral framework of rules and disciplines to guide the development, adoption and enforcement of [SPS] measures in order to minimise their negative effects on trade'. This was complemented by the recognition that Members should not be prevented from adopting or enforcing measures necessary to protect human, animal or plant life or health, as long as they are compatible with the provisions of the Agreement and the desire to improve the SPS situation in all Members.[27]

Pursuant to Article 1.1, the SPS Agreement applies to 'all sanitary and phytosanitary measures which may, directly or indirectly, affect international trade'. Annex A(1) provides a fourfold definition of SPS measures. The first category encompasses measures applied to protect animal or plant life or health within the territory of a Member from risks arising from the entry, establishment or spread of pests, diseases or disease-carrying organisms. The second includes measures protecting human or animal life or health within the territory of a Member from risks arising from additives, contaminants, toxins or disease-causing organisms in foods, beverages or feedstuffs. The third refers to measures applied to protect human life or health within the territory of a Member from risks arising from diseases carried by animals, plants or products thereof, and/or from the entry, establishment or spread of pests. Finally, the last category encompasses measures applied to prevent or limit other damage within the territory of the Member from the entry, establishment or spread of pests. SPS measures include any relevant laws, decrees, regulations, requirements and procedures; a non-exhaustive list of examples is provided for in Annex A(1).

Under Article 3.1, with a view to harmonising SPS measures on as wide a basis as possible, Members shall base their SPS measures on existing international standards, guidelines or recommendations, except as provided for in the

[27] See Recitals (1), (2) and (4). For an overview of the origins of the Agreement and its turn to 'science', beyond the GATT's focus on discrimination, see G Marceau and JP Trachtman, 'A Map of the World Trade Organization Law of Domestic Regulation of Goods: The Technical Barriers to Trade Agreement, the Sanitary and Phytosanitary Measures Agreement, and the General Agreement on Tariffs and Trade' (2014) 48 *Journal of World Trade* 351.

Agreement and in Article 3.3 in particular. SPS measures conforming to international standards, guidelines or recommendations are deemed necessary to protect human, animal or plant life or health and presumed to be consistent with the SPS Agreement and the GATT.[28] The relevant international standard-setting organisations are the Codex Alimentarius Commission, the International Office of Epizootics ('OIE') and the organisations operating within the framework of the International Plant Protection Convention; these are referenced in the Preamble, Article 3.4 and Annex A(3).[29] The Preamble recognises the important contribution of international standards, guidelines or recommendations to further the use of harmonised SPS measures and thus minimise negative effects on trade. However, it also mentions that Members are not required to change their ALOP. The latter is defined in Annex A(5) as 'the level of protection deemed appropriate by the Member establishing an [SPS] measure to protect human, animal or plant life or health'.[30]

According to Article 5.4, when determining their ALOP, Members should take into account the objective of minimising negative trade effects.[31] Pursuant to Article 3.3, Members may introduce or maintain SPS measures which result in a higher level of SPS protection than would be achieved by measures based on the relevant international standards, guidelines or recommendations. The AB has acknowledged that this is an autonomous right of Members, rather than an exception to Article 3.1.[32] According to the rather convoluted text of Article 3.3, Members can do so if there is a scientific justification, or as a consequence of the level of SPS protection which a Member determines to be appropriate in accordance with paragraphs 1 through 8 of Article 5. As a footnote clarifies, a scientific justification exists if, after an examination of available scientific information, a Member determines that the relevant international standards, guidelines or recommendations are not sufficient to achieve its ALOP. In any case, Article 3.3 provides that all measures which result in a level of protection different from that which would be achieved by international standards, guidelines or recommendations should not be inconsistent with any other provisions of the Agreement.

This is where the science-based obligations of the Agreement come into play. Pursuant to Article 2.1, Members have the right to take SPS measures that are

[28] On the difference between measures 'based on' or 'conforming to' international standards, see *EC – Hormones*, AB Report (adopted 13 February 1998) WT/DS26/AB/R and WT/DS48/1B/R, paras 160 ff. See also *India – Agricultural Products*, Panel Report (adopted 19 June 2015) WT/DS430/R, paras 7.192 ff.

[29] See also Annex A(3)(d) to the Agreement, for fields not covered by any of the three international organisations.

[30] A footnote clarifies that in other jurisdictions this is also referred to as 'acceptable level of risk'. On the difference between setting the ALOP, and enacting SPS measures to meet the ALOP, see *Australia – Salmon*, AB Report (adopted 6 November 1998) WT/DS18/AB/R, para 203.

[31] This is not tantamount to a legal obligation: see *EC – Hormones*, Panel Report (adopted 13 February 1998) WT/DS26/R/USA, para 8.166. For the purposes of the analysis of the following sections, reference is made to the Panel Report in DS26 (rather than DS48).

[32] *EC – Hormones* (AB), paras 104 and 172.

necessary for the protection of human, animal or plant life or health, provided that such measures are not inconsistent with the provisions of the Agreement. Under Article 2.2, Members shall ensure that any SPS measure is applied only to the extent necessary to protect human, animal or plant life or health, is based on scientific principles and is not maintained without sufficient scientific evidence, except as provided for in paragraph 7 of Article 5. The third requirement is of particular relevance, as the next sections show.

Article 5.1, cross-referenced in Article 3.3, stipulates that Members shall ensure that their SPS measures are based on an assessment, as appropriate to the circumstances, of the risks to human, animal or plant life or health, taking into account risk assessment techniques developed by the relevant international organisations. Annex A(4) draws a further distinction. An assessment of the risks posed by pests or diseases shall evaluate the likelihood of entry, establishment or spread of a pest or disease within the territory of an importing Member according to the SPS measures which might be applied, as well as the associated potential biological and economic consequences. An assessment of the risks posed by additives, contaminants, toxins or disease-causing organisms in food, beverages or feedstuffs shall evaluate the potential for adverse effects on human or animal health arising from their presence therein. Article 5.2 provides for a set of further elements that Members should take into account in their risk assessment. When assessing risks to animal or plant life or health and determining the SPS measures to be applied to achieve their ALOP, Members shall also take into account a list of relevant economic factors.[33]

The Article 5.1 requirement to base SPS measures on a risk assessment has been interpreted and elucidated in almost every dispute brought under the SPS Agreement. The same applies to Article 5.7, as cross-referenced in Article 3.3 and, expressly, in the context of Article 2.2. Pursuant to Article 5.7,

> in cases where relevant scientific evidence is insufficient, a Member may provisionally adopt [SPS] measures on the basis of available pertinent information, including that from the relevant international organisations as well as from [SPS] measures applied by other Members. In such circumstances, Members shall seek to obtain the additional information necessary for a more objective assessment of risk and review the [SPS] measure accordingly within a reasonable period of time.

Since *Japan – Agricultural Products II*,[34] this provision has been broken down into four specific requirements. First, the relevant scientific evidence must be 'insufficient'. Second, the relevant provisional measures must be based on available pertinent information. Third, the Member must seek the additional information necessary for a more objective assessment of risk. Fourth, the provisional measure must be reviewed within a reasonable period of time.

[33] For a more in-depth analysis, see Scott, *The WTO Agreement* (n 1) 102 and 103.
[34] See the analysis in section IV.

Finally, Article 8 (Control, Inspection and Approval Procedures) stipulates that Members shall observe the provisions of Annex C in the operation of control, inspection and approval procedures. According to Annex C(1)(a), first clause, Members shall ensure that such procedures are undertaken and completed without undue delay. As the seventh section illustrates, these provisions came into play in *EC – Biotech*. For the circumscribed purposes of the analysis in this chapter, this concludes the broad overview of the relevant SPS Agreement provisions. As the brief summary of this section has shown, the text of the SPS Agreement does not quite embrace an evidence-based approach to governance of uncertain risks. The next sections turn to an analysis of the interpretation and application of the relevant provisions, starting from *EC – Hormones*. This paves the way for the more detailed examination of *EC – Biotech*, conducted in the seventh section.

II. The Origins: *EC – Hormones* and Hazard-Related Uncertainties

In April 1996, the US requested the establishment of a Panel. It claimed that a number of EC Directives[35] were inconsistent with, inter alia, Articles 2, 3 and 5 of the SPS Agreement. Canada followed suit and submitted an analogous request. Pursuant to the EC Directives, the administration to farm animals of three naturally occurring hormones (oestradiol-17β, progesterone and testosterone) was prohibited for growth promotion purposes. As a result, the placing on the market or slaughtering of farm animals to which these substances had been administered, as well as the placing on the market of meat or meat products from such animals, was prohibited; a specific exception was the use of these natural hormones for therapeutic and zootechnical purposes, if administered by a veterinarian. The administration of three synthetic (artificially produced) hormones (trenbolone, zeranol and melengestrol acetate, 'MGA') was prohibited for any purpose.

In the US, the six hormones are approved for growth promotion purposes. In 1995, the Codex adopted a set of standards relating to residues of five of the six hormones (with the exception of MGA) in cattle or in meat and meat products of bovine origin. For trenbolone and zeranol, these standards took the form of Maximum Residue Limits ('MRLs'), calculated by reference to Acceptable Daily Intakes ('ADIs') and taking into consideration good practice in the use of veterinary drugs.[36] For the three naturally occurring hormones, on the other hand, the Codex found that setting MRLs would be unnecessary, as the residues were alleged not to pose any hazard to human health.[37] The US challenged the EC's departure

[35] This chapter refers to the 'EC' rather than the 'EU', where the disputes under analysis pre-date 2009. For a more detailed overview of the factual background of this dispute, see *EC – Hormones* (Panel), (n 31), paras2.5 ff.

[36] *EC – Hormones* (Panel), para 2.17 ff.

[37] Paras 2.21 and 2.22.

from the Codex standards and prohibitions, contending that the SPS measures were neither maintained with sufficient scientific evidence nor based on a risk assessment.

Hazard-related uncertainties were at stake in this dispute; none of the scientific studies produced by the EC could prove the existence of a causal link between residues of hormones in meat, on the one hand, and specific adverse effects on public health.[38] However, the EC's inferences were not scientifically unsubstantiated. First, the EC pointed to persisting uncertainties surrounding the mode of action of hormone residues.[39] It underlined that the Codex's scientific extrapolation that carcinogenic effects would only flow from the hormonal activity of the residues was questionable:[40] the Codex's ADIs and MRLs were established on the basis of a hormonal no-effect level, assuming that if the residues did not exert an hormonal effect they would not have any carcinogenic effects.[41] The EC's evidence could neither confirm nor exclude carcinogenicity via alternative pathways; as mentioned above, no conclusive scientific proof of hazards was available. Nonetheless, the EC claimed that it was

> entitled to follow a cautious approach and side with [...] [scientists] who placed more attention on the carcinogenic risks arising from the possible genotoxic action of these hormones, irrespective of the dose in which they were administered to animals for growth promotion [and the consequent hormonal effects].[42]

Second, the EC stressed that the scientific evidence did not address the potential interaction of residues with other substances, multiplier effects in worst case scenarios,[43] and multiple exposures in case of combinations of hormones.[44] Third, the EC's focus on persisting uncertainty was complemented by an iterative evaluation of the relevant OLFs at stake, typical of the determination of the intended level of protection and threshold of acceptable risk under socially acceptable risk approaches. One report produced by the EC stressed that positive scientific conclusions regarding the use of hormones rested upon good veterinary practice and conditions of use which would hardly be attained in reality, and that 'proven necessity and socio-economic desirability should be the criteria of acceptability for use [...] [of growth promoters]'.[45]

The first elements referenced above point to the efficacy of relevant risk management measures, as impacting on the risks posed in practice and under real life conditions. Indeed, some evidence on the problems linked to the administration of hormones and difficulties in detection and control was adduced by the EC.[46]

[38] Paras 8.119–8.128.
[39] Para 4.126.
[40] Paras 4.129 ff; see in particular paras 4.135 and 4.143–4.144.
[41] Para 2.22.
[42] Para 4.142.
[43] Para 4.36.
[44] Para 4.126.
[45] Para 2.31.
[46] See paras 4.126 ff as well as paras 4.37–4.39.

Just as importantly, reference to socio-economic desirability highlights a focus on the availability of more sustainable livestock farming practices. In accordance with socially acceptable risk discourses, the specific advantages, disadvantages and distributional implications connected to the authorisation of potentially hazardous products feed into the setting of the intended level of protection and the determination that the uncertain risks that the products may pose are worth taking.[47]

The EC did not resort to Article 5.7; rather, it claimed that the measures were definitive and scientifically substantiated by a risk assessment which highlighted persisting uncertainties.[48] On these grounds, it advocated a broad interpretation of Articles 2.2 and 5.1, in light of the precautionary principle, which the EC expressly invoked in its submissions on Articles 2.2, 3.3 and 5.1.[49] In accordance with the traditional EC/EU understanding of precautionary risk management, the EC drew a direct connection between persisting uncertainty, as emerging from a risk assessment, *and* the ALOP. Under this specific interpretation, just like under EC/EU risk regulation, the Member would have a discretionary power to take precautionary SPS measures whenever scientific evidence is *inconclusive, insufficient or imprecise* and uncertain risks may *not meet the* ALOP.[50] Symmetrically, and again just like in the EC/EU legal system, the acknowledgment of the Members' broad discretion in the evaluation of scientific evidence vis-à-vis their ALOP would go hand in hand with a deferential, standard of review.[51]

The US, on its part, took a diametrically opposite perspective. Crucially, it maintained that the *precondition* for the ALOP to form the basis for Members' regulatory action is scientific proof of a specific hazard and risk.[52] Upon arguing that the ALOP is 'a level of protection *from a risk*' (emphasis added),[53] it held that the EC had failed to prove any hazards and risks.[54] On these grounds, it contended that the EC's SPS measures were in breach of Article 2.2 and were not based on a risk assessment, as mandated by Article 5.1.

The Panel's findings largely reflect the US (evidence-based) interpretation of the Agreement. Upon noting that international (ie Codex) standards existed for five out of the six hormones at issue[55] and that the EC measures were not based on such standards,[56] the Panel turned to an examination of compliance with Article 5.

[47] See, eg, para 4.202.
[48] Para 4.239.
[49] See, eg, paras 3.6, 4.27, 4.48, 4.103, 4.108, 4.156, 4.175 and 4.202 ff.
[50] See, eg, paras 4.43 and 4.90.
[51] In judicial review of EU risk regulation, the EU Courts have consistently held that EU institutions enjoy a broad administrative discretion in areas involving complex technical-scientific evaluations. Consequently, a manifest error of assessment is all that can invalidate EU risk regulation measures. For an in-depth analysis, see GC Leonelli, 'Acknowledging the Centrality of the Precautionary Principle in Judicial Review of EU Risk Regulation: Why It Matters' (2020) 57 *CML Rev* 1773.
[52] *EC – Hormones* (Panel), para 4.87.
[53] Para 4.122.
[54] Para 4.155.
[55] Paras 8.56 ff.
[56] Paras 8.71 ff. The Panel's interpretation of SPS measures 'based on' international standards was reversed by the AB; see n 28.

It noted that, pursuant to Article 5.1, SPS measures need to be based on a risk assessment; the obligation to base SPS measures on a risk assessment was defined as 'a specific application of the basic obligations contained in Article 2.2'.[57] Throughout its analysis, the Panel identified two distinct aspects: the enquiry into the *existence* of a risk assessment within the meaning of Article 5.1 and Annex A(4), and the question whether the specific SPS measures are *based on* the relevant risk assessment. Further, the Panel found that a Member's decision to enact SPS measures relates to the determination and application of the ALOP 'against the risks to human, animal or plant life or health which have been assessed in accordance with Articles 5.1 to 5.3'.[58]

Starting from the enquiry into the existence of a risk assessment,[59] the Panel (merely) assumed that the evidence adduced by the EC qualified as a risk assessment.[60] Turning to the requirement that the SPS measures shall be based on a risk assessment,[61] the Panel engaged in a threefold examination. First, it identified the scientific conclusions reached in each of the studies. Second, it identified the scientific conclusions reflected in the EC SPS measures. Finally, it determined 'whether the scientific conclusions reflected in the EC measures [could] be considered as being in conformity with any of those reached in the studies [...]'.[62]

As illustrated above, none of the studies referenced by the EC could establish a causal link between hormone residues in meat, on the one hand, and specific adverse effects on health, on the other. Drawing on an evidence-based approach and focusing on the lack of conclusive scientific proof of any adverse effects, the Panel found that 'no scientific evidence is available which concludes that an *identifiable risk* arises from the use of any of the hormones at issue' (emphasis added).[63] On these grounds, the Panel ruled that the scientific conclusions reflected in the EC bans did not conform to any of the scientific conclusions of the relevant evidence.[64]

The EC had also invoked the precautionary principle to support its argument that the bans were based on a risk assessment. The Panel refrained from any explicit finding on the principle's relevance and status under customary international law. However, after assuming that the principle could be used as a customary rule of interpretation of public international law, it did not hesitate to state that it would 'not override the explicit wording of Articles 5.1 and 5.2 [...], in particular since the precautionary principle has been incorporated and given a specific meaning in Article 5.7 of the SPS Agreement'.[65]

[57] Para 8.93.
[58] Para 8.95.
[59] Paras 8.108 ff.
[60] Para 8.111.
[61] Paras 8.112 ff.
[62] Para 8.117.
[63] Para 8.134.
[64] Para 8.137. See also paras 8.139 ff.
[65] Para 8.157.

Therefore, after finding that no risk assessment had been carried out for the synthetic hormone MGA, the Panel concluded that the EC measures were also inconsistent with Article 2.2, insofar as they violated the more specific rights and obligations of Articles 3 and 5 of the SPS Agreement.[66] This concluded the Panel's Report, which lay the foundations for the evidence-based interpretation of Articles 5.1 and 2.2. As this section has shown, sound scientific proof of hazards and risks is a necessary precondition for Members to resort to their ALOP and use it to defend their protective measures. Persisting uncertainties and considerations as to whether uncertain risks meet the ALOP will be irrelevant where 'there is no scientific evidence of an identifiable risk'.[67]

III. The Appellate Body's Report in *EC – Hormones*: Ascertainable Risk and Theoretical Uncertainty

For the purposes of the present analysis, the AB's Report in *EC – Hormones* is relevant in so far as it confirmed the Panel's interpretative approach, while providing some further clarifications on the applicable standard of review. In its appeal against the Panel's Report, the EC developed a set of interconnected arguments relating to the Panel's alleged errors of law. Overall, the EC claimed that the Panel had erred in paying no deference to the EC's higher ALOP, no deference to the EC's specific inferences from the available risk assessments and subsequent exercise of risk management, and no deference to the EC's recourse to the precautionary principle.[68]

With respect to the applicable standard of review, the EC drew a distinction between two different approaches: de novo review and deference.[69] It argued that the Panel had conducted a form of de novo review, determining whether the EC's evaluations were factually correct and substituting its own assessment of the uncertain risks posed by hormone residues for that of the EC. Yet, as already mentioned, the Panel's approach in this dispute should rather be understood as a *lato sensu* de novo review of scientific proof of the existence of specific hazards and risks. Against this approach, the EC contraposed a deferential reasonableness review. It thus claimed that the Panel should have limited itself to checking compliance with the procedural obligations enshrined in the Agreement and assessing whether the inferences and conclusions drawn by the EC were scientifically plausible and reasonable, having regard to the available evidence.[70]

Turning to the claims concerning the EC's higher ALOP and recourse to the precautionary principle, the EC developed two different arguments. It submitted

[66] Para 8.271.
[67] Para 8.161.
[68] *EC – Hormones* (AB), (n 28), para 13.
[69] Para 15.
[70] Para 14.

that the first scenario envisaged under Article 3.3 ('Members may introduce or maintain [SPS] measures which result in a higher level of [SPS] protection than would be achieved by measures based on the relevant international standards, guidelines or recommendations, if there is a scientific justification') does not require a Member to base its measures on a risk assessment, as per Article 5.1.[71] Further, it argued that the precautionary principle, as a rule of customary public international law or general principle of law, should be used to interpret Article 5.[72] On these grounds, the EC challenged the Panel's interpretation of Article 5.1 in several respects. First, it submitted that the Panel had erred in finding that Members should adhere to the *positive results* of a risk assessment and may not focus on the *margins of uncertainty* highlighted therein.[73] In this regard, the EC emphasised that the requirement that SPS measures be 'based on' a risk assessment does not imply that they should conform to their specific results. From this perspective, SPS measures should be *informed* by scientific evidence, but need not *correspond* to the results of a risk assessment. Further, the EC also stressed that Members may adhere to majority or minority scientific opinion.[74]

The AB sought to nuance the Panel's interpretation of the science-based obligations; however, it did not quite deviate from the Panel's overall approach. Starting from the issue of the standard of scrutiny, the AB noted that the SPS Agreement provides no indications on the applicable standard of review.[75] It then found that neither de novo review nor full deference should apply. Rather, the Panels should engage in 'objective fact-finding', in accordance with Article 11 of the Dispute Settlement Understanding ('DSU').[76] The AB did not flesh out the meaning of 'objective fact-finding', or make reference to any (allegedly) objective scientific criteria. In so far as conclusive scientific proof of the existence of a hazard and risk lies at the heart of this test, as can be evinced from the rest of the AB's Report, the AB did not address the question of why sound scientific proof should be considered as 'objective', in the face of scientific complexity and ubiquitous uncertainties. Nor did the AB provide any guidance on 'objective fact-finding' in cases where scientific proof is provided but experimental data or prudential methods have been employed. Indeed, as the next sections show, these are the cases where the

[71] Para 23.

[72] Para 16.

[73] Under EU risk regulation, as already explained, EU risk managers may disregard the positive results of a risk assessment where uncertainties persist and a risk may not comply with the intended level of protection; see ch 4, sections II and III.

[74] Para 27. The EC also took issue with the Panel's distinction between risk assessment and risk management, reversed by the AB at paras 181 ff, and the Panel's interpretation of the notion of 'potential' for adverse effects in Annex A(4). At paras 182 to 184 of its Report, the AB found that 'by referring to *probability* rather than *possibility* the Panel introduced a quantitative dimension to risk' (emphasis added). However, as explained in the next section, the distinction between the notions of 'potential' and 'likelihood' is still far from clear.

[75] Para 114.

[76] Paras 116–117; see Annex II of the WTO Agreement, *Understanding on Rules and Procedures Governing the Settlement of Disputes*.

Panels conducted *stricto sensu* de novo reviews and considered that the Members' risk assessments were not 'sound'.

Second, the AB rejected the EC's interpretative construction of the first scenario in Article 3.3[77] as well as the attempt to broaden the scope of Article 5.1 by reference to the precautionary principle. Just like the Panel, the AB refrained from taking a clear position on the precautionary principle's status under public international law. After stressing that the precautionary principle has not been codified in the SPS Agreement,[78] the AB found that it is nonetheless reflected in Article 5.7. As the next sections show, this statement is debatable if due regard is had to the dispute settlement organs' narrow interpretation of this Article; Article 5.7 appears closer in its scope to a safeguard or emergency clause. Further, the AB found that the precautionary principle is also reflected in the sixth paragraph of the Preamble and Article 3.3 on the Members' right to set their own ALOP. Without doubt, these provisions are more closely aligned to the rationale of precautionary risk management: the pursuit of enhanced levels of protection. Finally, it acknowledged that when determining whether sufficient evidence exists to warrant the maintenance of an SPS measure a Panel should 'bear in mind that responsible, representative governments commonly act from perspectives of prudence and precaution where risks are irreversible'.[79] Yet, it still concluded that the precautionary principle cannot override the provisions of Articles 5.1 and 5.2.[80]

On these grounds, moving on to the interpretation of Article 5.1, the AB ultimately endorsed and confirmed the Panel's *lato sensu* de novo review of the existence of scientific proof of a specific hazard and risk. The AB started by stressing that Articles 2.2 and 5.1 should always be read together; the former informs the latter, and 'the elements that define the basic obligation set out in Article 2.2 impart meaning to Article 5.1'.[81] It then focused on the Panel's terminology of 'scientifically identified' or 'scientifically identifiable risk', which the Panel had contraposed to the 'uncertainty that theoretically always remains since science can never provide absolute certainty that a given [product] will not ever have adverse [health] effects'.[82] The AB concurred with the Panel that 'theoretical uncertainty is not the kind of risk which, under Article 5.1, is to be assessed'; it thus confirmed that an *ascertainable* (ie *positively established*) *risk* should be the object of a risk assessment and ensuing SPS measures.[83] Despite the clarification that a risk need not have a certain magnitude or meet a certain threshold for an SPS measure to comply with Article 5.1,[84] the AB ultimately failed to remove the main obstacle

[77] Para 173.
[78] Para 124.
[79] Para 124.
[80] Para 125.
[81] Para 180.
[82] Para 186.
[83] ibid.
[84] ibid.

to precautionary risk management: the overarching premise that a Member shall provide conclusive scientific proof of hazards and risks *prior to* invoking its own ALOP.

Turning to the requirement that SPS measures be based on a risk assessment, the AB elaborated further on the relationship between Articles 2.2 and 5.1. It maintained that the requirement that a measure be based on a risk assessment implies that 'the results of the risk assessment must sufficiently warrant – that is to say, reasonably support – the SPS measure at stake. The requirement [...] is a substantive requirement that there be a rational relationship between the measure and the risk assessment'.[85] The AB added that a risk assessment need not come to a monolithic conclusion, which must perfectly coincide with the conclusion in the SPS measure. In this sense, 'Article 5.1 does not require that the risk assessment must necessarily embody only the view of a majority of the scientific community'.[86] Rather, diverging minority scientific opinions may be legitimately relied upon by responsible and representative governments, acting in good faith.[87]

This clarification regarding minority opinion has broadened the Members' margins of discretion in compliance with Article 5.1; nonetheless, it is worth stressing that the burden of proof is very high on the regulating Members. Minority or divergent scientific opinion cannot be relied upon in so far as it merely points to persisting *uncertainties*; rather, such scientific opinions need to positively establish and conclusively prove the relevant *hazards and risks*. Further, as cases of *stricto sensu* de novo review show, the AB's clarification on minority opinion appears to have had limited relevance at the practical dispute settlement stage.

Ultimately, the AB confirmed the Panel's findings on the EC's breach of Article 5.1 and 2.2. This concludes the overview of the first dispute brought under the SPS Agreement. As the next sections show, the dispute settlement organs have since then built on *lato sensu* de novo review and expanded it.

IV. *Australia – Salmon* and Risk-Related Uncertainties

The dispute at the heart of *Australia – Salmon* developed against a different factual background and involved risk-related uncertainties. In March 1997, Canada requested the establishment of a Panel and challenged Australia's prohibition on the importation of fresh, chilled or frozen salmon on the grounds of (inter alia) Articles 2, 3 and 5 of the SPS Agreement. Australia identified 24 exotic disease agents of concern for aquatic animal health, potentially associated with the importation of Canadian salmon.[88] The final 1996 Australian Salmon Import

[85] Para 193. See also para 189, on the 'objective relationship' between the relevant risk assessment and the SPS measure.

[86] Para 194.

[87] ibid.

[88] *Australia – Salmon*, Panel Report (adopted 6 November 1998) WT/DS18/R, paras 2.11 ff.

Risk Analysis stressed that while the probability of establishment and spread of the pathogens was low, any diseases would be ineradicable and would have major environmental and socio-economic impacts. On these grounds, it recommended a ban on uncooked salmonid products from Canada and the US.[89]

In its submissions, Australia highlighted that multiple uncertainties persisted as to the presence of the pathogens in salmon, their tissue distribution, the effectiveness of inspections, the impact of processing on the infection, the transmission of the diseases and, overall, the specific *pathways* for the establishment and spread of the diseases.[90] In the face of extensive data gaps, scientific information on aquatic animal diseases was ultimately considered insufficient to dispel uncertainty.[91] While Australia could not provide conclusive scientific proof of the pathways for the spread of aquatic animal diseases via products for human consumption, it claimed that this possibility could not be discounted.[92] More specifically, it argued that 'sufficient scientific evidence [for the purposes of maintaining an SPS measure does] not require a demonstration of conclusive scientific evidence'.[93] In the face of significant gaps in scientific research, the evidence available was deemed insufficient to determine that Australia's ALOP would be met if chilled or frozen salmon were permitted entry.

Canada, on the other hand, claimed that the Salmon Import Risk Analysis did not meet the requirements of a risk assessment within the meaning of Article 5.1 and Annex A(4). It argued that it did not evaluate the likelihood of entry, spread and establishment of diseases, did not examine the risks on a disease-by-disease basis, and did not evaluate the risk on the basis of specific risk mitigation measures.[94] In particular, Canada stressed that the Salmon Import Risk Analysis did not focus on the probability ('likelihood') of the relevant risks, but on the mere theoretical possibility that they might occur.[95] While acknowledging that probability may be expressed in quantitative as well as qualitative terms,[96] Canada argued that Australia had failed to assess the probability that any specific pathways would be completed and that any risks would materialise. Even if the Salmon Import Risk Analysis were found to meet the requirements of a risk assessment, Canada maintained that the SPS measure was not based on it, as no rational relationship could be identified between the heat treatment requirement in the SPS measure and the scientific evidence adduced.[97]

Starting from the interpretation of the definition in the first part of Annex A(4), the Panel distinguished three components of the risk assessment process: the

[89] Para 2.30.
[90] Para 4.37.
[91] Para 4.43.
[92] See paras 4.44 ff.
[93] Para 4.77; see also para 4.80.
[94] Para 4.129.
[95] Para 4.137.
[96] Para 4.140.
[97] See paras 4.142 and 8.63.

identification of the disease (ie hazard) and relevant potential consequences, the evaluation of the general likelihood of entry, establishment and spread of the disease (ie risk) and associated consequences, and consideration of the specific likelihood under the SPS measures which might be applied.[98] Drawing on the AB's findings in *EC – Hormones* relating to the difference between 'potential for adverse effects' and 'likelihood of entry, establishment or spread', the Panel found that 'likelihood' is synonymous to probability and implies 'a higher degree or threshold of potentiality or possibility'.[99]

On these grounds, it found that a risk assessment within the meaning of the SPS Agreement and in the circumstances of the dispute should evaluate the likelihood or probability, expressed either qualitatively or quantitatively, of the introduction of the diseases and relevant consequences.[100] Yet again drawing on the AB's Report in *EC – Hormones*, the Panel also remarked that 'this requirement on how a risk assessment should evaluate risk does not at all imply that a risk assessment […] needs to demonstrate a certain magnitude or threshold level or degree of risk (expressed either quantitatively or qualitatively)'.[101] As rightly pointed out, the acknowledgement that a risk assessment focusing on the likelihood/probability of spread of a pest or disease need not demonstrate a minimum risk triggers some doubts as to the meaningfulness of any distinction between the notion of 'potential' for adverse effects and 'likelihood' of risk. The difference between the two is far from clear.[102]

The Panel merely assumed, without making a finding, that the Salmon Import Risk Analysis met the requirements of a risk assessment.[103] However, it still found that the SPS measure was not based on the relevant risk assessment in so far as it applied to salmon products other than adult ocean-caught Pacific salmon, and to the extent that it imposed heat treatment requirements.[104] In the latter respect, the Panel found that no rational scientific basis could be identified in the risk assessment to support the heat treatment requirement. Scientific data on whether or not heat treatment can inactivate the pathogens was expressly acknowledged to be insufficient, so that a rational relationship between the specific measure and the risk assessment could not be identified.[105] On these grounds, and building on its previous finding that a violation of the more specific obligations in Article 5.1 implies a violation of the more general provisions of Article 2.2, the Panel found that Australia had also acted inconsistently with the latter.[106]

[98] Para 8.72.
[99] Para 8.77, citing *EC – Hormones* (AB), para 184. See n 74.
[100] Para 8.80. See also *Australia – Salmon* (AB), para 124.
[101] Para 8.80. See also *Australia – Salmon* (AB), para 124.
[102] On this point see Scott, *The WTO Agreement* (n 1) 94.
[103] Para 8.93.
[104] Para 8.101.
[105] See paras 8.98 ff. At paras 115 ff of its Report, the AB reversed the Panel's findings in that the SPS measure was found not to consist in a heat treatment requirement, but rather in a prohibition of importation of fresh chilled or frozen salmon.
[106] Paras 8.52 and 8.99. See also *Australia – Salmon* (AB), para 138.

The AB pursued a different course of action. It found that the Salmon Import Risk Analysis neither qualitatively nor quantitatively evaluated the likelihood of entry, establishment and spread of the diseases,[107] nor considered the specific likelihood in accordance with the SPS measures which might be applied.[108] On these grounds, it reached the conclusion that the document did not meet the requirements of a risk assessment. By implication, it also found that the SPS measures were not based on a risk assessment.[109]

In its examination of whether the Salmon Import Risk Analysis had assessed the likelihood of entry, establishment and spread of the diseases, the AB reiterated that the 'risk evaluated in a risk assessment must be an ascertainable risk'.[110] Correspondingly, 'the existence of unknown and uncertain elements does not justify a departure from the requirements of Articles 5.1, 5.2 and 5.3, read together with paragraph 4 of Annex A [...]'.[111] The AB ultimately confirmed that hazards *as well as* risks need to be conclusively established; in the latter case, conclusive proof of the relevant pathways must be provided. In this sense, the AB confirmed that *risk-related* uncertainties surrounding the materialisation of a risk, just like hazard-related uncertainties, will be deemed irrelevant for the purposes of conducting a risk assessment within the meaning of the Agreement. 'A Member [can] determine its own [ALOP] to be zero risk';[112] however, conclusive proof of all relevant hazards and risks, including specific risk pathways, must be produced to resort to this possibility.

In July 1999, in the aftermath of the initial dispute, Canada requested the establishment of a Panel under Article 21.5 of the DSU. It questioned the compatibility with the Agreement of the new Australian SPS measures. Australia had conducted a new risk assessment: this evaluated the probability of entry, establishment and spread of aquatic diseases by identifying a main pathway (dispersal of wastes from commercial processing) and susceptible hosts. For seven specific diseases, the risk assessment concluded that the evisceration measures recommended by international standards would not meet Australia's ALOP, as the risks posed if eviscerated salmon were processed and waste produced would be too high.[113] In these cases, salmon would then have to be imported in consumer-ready form.[114]

Canada took issue with the prudential methodology employed in the risk assessment, which endeavoured to incorporate risk-related uncertainties through recourse to prudential scientific judgement and prudential probabilistic modelling.

[107] *Australia – Salmon* (AB), paras 119–131.

[108] Paras 132–134.

[109] Para 136. See also the clarification in paras 124 and 128; the AB found that 'some' evaluation of probability is not tantamount to 'an' evaluation (ie a proper evaluation) of probability, under the SPS Agreement.

[110] Para 125.

[111] Para 130.

[112] Para 125.

[113] *Australia – Salmon 21.5*, Panel Report (adopted 20 March 2000) WT/DS18/RW, paras 4.137 ff.

[114] Paras 2.11 ff.

For this reason, it argued that the SPS measure was not based on a risk assessment.[115] The Panel refrained from conducting a *stricto sensu* de novo review of the quality or soundness of the Australian risk assessment, and found that the Australian risk assessment complied with Article 5.1 and Annex A(4). Nonetheless, it still found that the SPS measure was *not based* on a risk assessment. More specifically, it could not identify a rational relationship between the available evidence, and the conclusion that salmon should only be imported in consumer-ready form. According to the Panel, the risk assessment referred to the presence of pathogens in the viscera, head, gills and skin of salmon. This suggested that evisceration together with the removal of head and gills and thorough washing would significantly reduce all risks.[116] On these grounds, the Panel questioned the scientific substantiation of the consumer-ready requirement. Ultimately, it found that the Australian precautionary SPS requirement, which had been enacted to manage an ascertained risk and comply with Australia's high ALOP, was scientifically unsubstantiated, as no evidence demonstrated a causal link between the consumer-ready requirement and risk reduction. As the next section illustrates, something very similar occurred in *Japan – Agricultural Products II*.

V. *Japan – Agricultural Products II* and the Scientific Substantiation of Measures Enacted to Comply with the ALOP

In October 1997, the US requested the establishment of a Panel. At the centre of the dispute was Japan's prohibition on the importation of any variety of agricultural product on which codling moth could occur until the variety had been separately tested with respect to the efficacy of treatment with methyl bromide.[117] Japan had established that codling moth was a pest of quarantine significance and had adduced pathways and probabilities for the entry, establishment and spread of the pest, together with evidence on the relevant consequences. The US, however, still challenged the compatibility of the measures on varietal testing with (inter alia) Articles 2.2, 5.1 and 5.2 of the Agreement. According to the US, Japan had not established that there was a risk of introduction of codling moth on a variety-by-variety basis *in the absence of* Japan's varietal testing requirements.[118] More specifically, the US challenged the measures in so far as there was no scientific proof that it would be necessary to test each variety. In other words, Japan had allegedly not provided any scientific evidence that the efficacy of methyl bromide

[115] Paras 4.98 ff.
[116] Paras 7.72 ff.
[117] *Japan – Agricultural Products II*, Panel Report (adopted 19 March 1999) WT/DS76/R, para 4.1.
[118] Para 4.58.

treatment changed for different varieties:[119] according to the US, there were no scientific studies supporting the theory that the specific agricultural variety of a product affected the efficacy of treatment.[120]

This dispute developed in a scenario involving a scientifically established risk. The essence of Japan's varietal testing requirement was a demonstration that methyl bromide treatment was effective on a variety, with a view to avoiding the materialisation of a previously established risk. In this sense, Japan's measure aimed at establishing the safety of imported products, vis-à-vis an ascertained (non-theoretical) risk. Clearly, this was a risk management measure enacted to comply with Japan's ALOP. In theory, in so far as a risk pathway and risk had been established, Japan should have been free to pursue a high ALOP and adopt any relevant risk management measures.[121] Nonetheless, like in *Australia – Salmon 21.5*, the issue at the heart of the controversy was the scientific substantiation of the very risk management measures enacted to comply with the ALOP.

This adds a further layer of complexity. Challenges relating to the scientific substantiation of specific SPS measures directly shift the focus from the safety of a product to its unsafety. The US took issue with its duty to prove that the products were *safe*, in so far as they could be connected to the entry, establishment and spread of a pest. In other words, it claimed that Japan had failed to scientifically demonstrate that the varietal testing measure was necessary, by positively establishing that the efficacy of treatment changed for each variety and that the agricultural products would be *unsafe* if untested. Yet again, this perfectly reflects the logics of the evidence-based transnational narrative. The dichotomy between uncertainty and sound scientific proof resurfaces.

Japan claimed that it had produced scientific evidence on the variable efficacy of methyl bromide treatment in different agricultural varieties,[122] thus fulfilling its obligations under Articles 2.2 and 5.1. Alternatively, it argued that the measure was based on Article 5.7, due to insufficient evidence of the efficacy of the treatment.[123] Unlike in the previous disputes, the Panel started its examination from Article 2.2. The Panel found that:

> for a phytosanitary measure to be maintained without sufficient scientific evidence, there needs to be a lack of an objective or rational relationship between, on the one hand, the phytosanitary measure at stake [...] and, on the other hand, the scientific evidence submitted before the Panel [...].[124]

[119] Para 4.59.
[120] Para 4.1 ff.
[121] ie, in so far as no alternative SPS measures exist which are less trade restrictive, taking into consideration technical and economic feasibility, and achieve the same ALOP: see the text of Art 5.6 of the Agreement.
[122] Paras 4.60 and 8.19 ff.
[123] Paras 4.187 ff.
[124] Para 8.29. See also *Japan – Agricultural Products II*, AB Report (adopted 19 March 1999) WT/DS76/AB/R, paras 73–77, where the AB found that Arts 5.1, 3.3 and 5.7 provide 'context' to the concept of sufficiency enshrined in Art 2.2.

The existence of an objective or rational relationship must be determined on a case-by-case basis, and in accordance with the specific circumstances of the case.[125]

The appointed experts found that Japan's evidence did not prove that the differences in efficacy of the treatment were connected to varietal differences, rather than other factors.[126] On these grounds, the Panel held that Japan had failed to establish the existence of a causal link between the differences in the efficacy of treatment in tests, on the one hand, and the difference in the agricultural varieties which were the object of the treatment, on the other.[127] It thus concluded that the varietal testing requirements were inconsistent with Article 2.1.[128] In this light, it found that it did not need to examine the alleged breach of Article 5.1.[129] Turning to Article 5.7, the Panel broke down the provision in four separate but cumulative requirements,[130] and started from an analysis of the third and fourth. It found that Japan had failed to seek information on a causal link between the divergences in treatment efficacy and varietal differences, which were necessary for a more objective assessment of the relevant risk,[131] and failed to review the varietal testing requirements within a reasonable time.[132] It thus concluded that the conditions of Article 5.7 had not been met.[133]

The Panel Report points to the failure by Japan to scientifically substantiate its risk management measures; from this perspective, the standard of review would be a *lato sensu* de novo review of positive scientific proof. Insofar as Japan had provided some data on the variable efficacy of the treatment, however, the standard of scrutiny borders a *stricto sensu* de novo review of the soundness and quality of the evidence produced by the respondent Party. Yet, there is something more to this dispute.

Like in *Australia – Salmon 21.5*, the relevant risk (probability of entry, establishment and spread of a pest) had been scientifically established. The object of the dispute was the scientific substantiation of the risk management measures selected to comply with the ALOP. On the one hand, it is undoubtedly true that Annex A(4) refers to the likelihood of entry, establishment and spread of a pest or disease *according to the SPS measures* which might be applied. In this sense, as suggested by the US, the evidence adduced by Japan could not positively establish that there was a risk of introduction of codling moth in the absence of the varietal testing requirements. On the other hand, however, these cases blur the boundaries between *lato sensu* de novo review of scientific proof of specific hazards and risks,

[125] See, eg, *Japan – Agricultural Products II*, AB Report, para 84.

[126] See paras 8.35 ff.

[127] Para 8.42.

[128] Paras 8.61–8.62.

[129] Para 8.63.

[130] See above, section I.

[131] See also *Japan – Agricultural Products II*, AB Report, para 92 for more details; importantly, the information must be 'germane' to conducting the risk assessment.

[132] See also *Japan – Agricultural Products II*, AB Report, para 92 for more details; this must be determined on a case-by-case basis, depending upon the specific circumstances and the difficulty of obtaining the relevant information.

[133] Paras 8.54 ff.

and an indirect encroachment on the Members' alleged freedom to set their own ALOP and select the SPS measures which will meet it.[134] This suggests that the Members' ability to resort to their ALOP and enact protective SPS measures in cases where hazards and risks have been established might also be undermined by the WTO Panels' review, insofar as recourse to specific SPS measures is deemed scientifically unsubstantiated.

The AB upheld the Panel's findings and added some further clarifications on the requirements of Article 5.7. Most importantly, it found that 'Article 5.7 of the SPS Agreement, to which Article 2.2 explicitly refers, is part of the context of the latter provision and should be considered in the interpretation of the obligation not to maintain an SPS measure without sufficient scientific evidence'.[135] It thus stipulated that 'Article 5.7 operates as a qualified exemption from the obligation under Article 2.2 not to maintain SPS measures without sufficient scientific evidence',[136] rather than an exception, and that 'an overly broad and flexible interpretation of that obligation would render Article 5.7 meaningless'.[137] Article 5.7 was the object of further analysis in *Japan – Apples*, to which the next section turns.

VI. *Japan – Apples*: Article 5.7 as a 'Safeguard' Clause, Compliance Proceedings and Stricto Sensu De Novo Review

In May 2002, the US requested the establishment of a Panel. At the centre of the dispute were a range of phytosanitary requirements for the importation of apples, imposed by Japan to prevent the introduction of fire blight.[138] Like *Australia – Salmon*, this dispute involved risk-related uncertainties. In the face of data gaps and scientific inconclusiveness, the evidence was insufficient for Japan to positively establish a pathway for the entry, establishment and spread of fire blight. The US claimed that there was no scientific evidence that imported mature and symptomless apples could transmit fire blight and serve as a pathway for entry; in other words, there was no proof that the chain of transmission and pathway would ever be completed.[139] Japan, on the other hand, pointed to persisting uncertainties as to whether mature and symptomless apples could still be contaminated and spread fire blight,[140] noting that the disease had spread in four jurisdictions without the relevant pathway ever being identified.[141] It also invoked studies on three potential

[134] See the clarification in n 121.
[135] *Japan – Agricultural Products II*, AB Report (n 124), para 80.
[136] ibid.
[137] ibid.
[138] For more details see *Japan – Apples*, Panel Report (adopted 10 December 2003) WT/DS245/R, para 2.19.
[139] Paras 4.53 and 4.82.
[140] Para 4.50.
[141] Para 4.68.

pathways, which it had taken into account.[142] Japan claimed that, in the face of uncertainty, Members should be entitled to rely on both direct (ie conclusive) and indirect (ie inconclusive) scientific evidence and data. Otherwise, Members would only be able to protect themselves against known and established dissemination pathways.[143]

The Panel started its examination with Article 2.2. It found that the measures were inconsistent with this Article, confirming the approach of the previous disputes and thus focusing on the existence of positive proof of a pathway. Indeed, it highlighted that 'sufficient' scientific evidence 'relates to a risk and is supposed to *confirm* the *existence of a given risk*' (emphasis added).[144] The Panel found that mature symptomless apples were unlikely to be infected, in so far as there was no sufficient scientific evidence to prove that they might harbour endophytic or epiphytic bacteria. Even where infected apples were exported by mistake, the pathway for establishment and spread would never be completed; again, there was no scientific evidence proving that the bacteria would survive in contaminated cargos and that a vector could permit contamination.[145] On these grounds, the Panel found that there was no rational and objective relationship between the available scientific evidence and the measures, that the measures had been maintained without sufficient scientific evidence, and that, for this reason, they were also disproportionate.[146]

This was later confirmed by the AB.[147] The AB found that the Panel had undertaken an objective assessment of the relevant facts and exercised its discretion in

[142] Paras 4.85 ff.

[143] Para 4.56. See paras 8.99 to 8.105 for the Panel's finding that 'indirect' or 'circumstantial' scientific evidence will be accepted, but will have a different probative value.

[144] Para 8.104.

[145] Paras 8.128–8.168.

[146] See paras 8.181 and 8.198, on the 'disproportionate' nature of measures. See also para 8.102, where the Panel found that the 'rational and objective relationship' requirement would not be satisfied if only patent insufficiency were to be considered as insufficiency. Commentators have often focused on the Panel's reference to (*stricto sensu*) proportionality in this dispute. According to some analyses, in *Japan – Apples* the Panel found that the risk of establishment and spread of fire blight was negligible. From this perspective, the Panel scrutinised Japan's ALOP and found that the phytosanitary measures enacted to comply with it were disproportionate (in *stricto sensu* terms). See for instance J Pauwelyn, 'Does the WTO Stand for Deference to or Interference with National Health Authorities When Applying the SPS Agreement?' in T Cottier and P Mavroidis (eds), *The Role of the Judge in International Trade Regulation: Experience and Lessons for the WTO* (University of Michigan Press, 2003); Button, *The Power to Protect* (n 1) 48 ff; Gruszczynski, *Regulating Health* (n 1) 110 and 111; Peel, *Science and Risk Regulation* (n 1) 227. The analysis in this section is premised on a different reconstruction. The Panel found that Japan had failed to conclusively prove the existence of a risk, in so far as the relevant pathway for the entry, establishment and spread of fire blight could not be positively established; see above in this section and n 144 in particular. Thus, it conducted a *lato sensu* de novo review. The Panel's reference to the 'disproportionate' nature of the measures is overall unsurprising; precautionary measures enacted on the basis of a prudential risk assessment and a focus on persisting uncertainty are bound to be disproportionate in *stricto sensu* terms, ie non-cost-benefit effective. As explained since ch 1, recourse to prudential approaches to risk assessment and a focus on uncertainty reflect the pursuit of enhanced (rather than cost-benefit effective) levels of protection.

[147] *Japan – Apples*, AB Report (adopted 10 December 2003) WT/DS245/AB/R, paras 143 ff.

the evaluation of the available scientific evidence.[148] More specifically, in respect of the challenges raised by Japan under Article 11 DSU and relating to the Panel's fact-finding and duty to make an objective assessment of the facts, the AB cited *EC – Hormones* and reiterated that the 'determination of the credibility and weight properly to be ascribed to [...] a given piece of evidence is part and parcel of the fact finding process and is, in principle, left to the discretion of a Panel as the trier of facts'.[149] As ruled in *Australia – Salmon*, Panels are 'not required to accord to factual evidence of the Parties the same meaning and weight as do the Parties'.[150]

With regard to Article 5.1, the Panel found that Japan's assessment was limited to an analysis of theoretical possibilities of pathways being completed, without an evaluation of the relevant probability of entry, establishment and spread of the disease.[151] In other words, as already explained, no positive scientific proof of the existence of a pathway could be identified. Further, it found that the assessment failed to evaluate the relevant risks vis-à-vis specific measures.[152] On these grounds, it concluded that Japan had failed to conduct a risk assessment within the meaning of the SPS Agreement, and that the relevant measures were not based on a risk assessment.[153] These findings were upheld by the AB.[154]

However, the most relevant clarifications in this dispute regard the interpretation of Article 5.7. The Panel took as a starting point its previous finding, under Article 2.2, that the situation addressed by Japan's measure was one where 'a wealth of information' was available.[155] It further noted that Article 5.7 refers to the notion of 'relevant scientific evidence'; this was interpreted as encompassing information supporting the Member's position, as well as any other views on the relevant risks.[156] On these grounds, it found that the 'fact that this information may not all support [the Member's] opinion is [...] not pertinent in the context of [the] first requirement of Article 5.7'.[157] In other words, whether Members 'subjectively' regard the available scientific evidence as inconclusive and insufficient for the purposes of conducting a thorough risk assessment is irrelevant. What matters, the Panel suggested, is rather whether scientific evidence is 'objectively' sufficient to conduct a sound scientific risk assessment in that situation, persisting uncertainties notwithstanding. The Panel stated that 'Article 5.7 was obviously designed to be invoked in situations where *little*, or *no*, *reliable evidence* was *available* on the subject matter at issue' (emphasis added).[158] Having found that a large quantity

[148] Paras 162 ff.
[149] Para 221, citing *EC – Hormones* (AB), para 133.
[150] Para 221, citing *Australia – Salmon* (AB), para 267.
[151] *Japan – Apples* (Panel), paras 8.228 ff.
[152] Para 8.290.
[153] Para 8.291.
[154] *Japan – Apples* (AB), paras 189 ff.
[155] *Japan – Apples* (Panel), para 8.216.
[156] ibid.
[157] ibid.
[158] Para 8.219.

of evidence was available on fire blight spread, regardless of persisting uncertainties, it concluded that the first requirement stipulated under Article 5.7 had not been met.

Clearly, the Panel embraced a very narrow interpretation of the notion of scientific insufficiency. Under this reconstruction, Article 5.7 is a *safeguard clause* put in place to enable Members to take measures in emergency situations or in cases where no reliable scientific evidence is available and it is impossible to conduct a sound scientific risk assessment. Scientific inconclusiveness or a Member's determination that the evidence is insufficient to conduct a comprehensive risk assessment, as required for the enactment of risk management measures *meeting the ALOP*, fall outside the remit of this overly restrictive interpretation of Article 5.7. From this perspective, Article 5.7 does not allow Members to take scientific uncertainty into consideration and is hardly an expression of the precautionary principle at all. Rather, this interpretation of 'scientific insufficiency' and references to the allegedly 'objective' determination that evidence is 'sufficient' perfectly reflect the evidence-based narrative.

Japan challenged this interpretation. Importantly, it drew a distinction between 'unresolved uncertainty' and 'new uncertainty'. According to Japan, the former refers to persisting uncertainty that science has not yet dispelled, while the latter regards new risks and situations where little or no reliable evidence is available.[159] By arguing that both forms of uncertainty should be covered by Article 5.7, Japan advocated a broader interpretation of the Article. This would have allowed Members to resort to the precautionary principle, in the absence of conclusive scientific proof of hazards or risks.

Overall, the AB confirmed the narrow interpretation of the Panel. First, it established a direct link between the obligation to perform a risk assessment under Article 5.1 and the first requirement of Article 5.7. Relying on a textual interpretation of the relevant Articles of the SPS Agreement,[160] it found that scientific evidence 'will be insufficient within the meaning of Article 5.7 if the body of available scientific evidence does not allow, in quantitative or qualitative terms, the performance of an adequate assessment of risks as required under Article 5.1 and as defined in Annex A to the SPS Agreement'.[161]

Second, turning to Japan's argument on new and unresolved uncertainties, the AB clarified that 'the application of Article 5.7 is triggered not by the existence of scientific uncertainty, but rather by the insufficiency of scientific evidence'.[162] The two concepts, the AB stressed, are not interchangeable. The AB further noted that 'insufficiency' encompasses a qualitative dimension. Thus, scientific evidence will not only be 'insufficient' to conduct a risk assessment where it is too limited

[159] *Japan – Apples* (AB), para 33.
[160] Paras 169 ff.
[161] Para 179.
[162] Para 184.

in quantitative terms, but also where 'a lot of scientific research has been carried out [...] without yielding reliable evidence'.[163] Clearly, qualitative insufficiency and references to the inability to conduct a 'reliable' risk assessment blur the boundaries between uncertainty and insufficiency.[164] As the next sections show, this issue was further analysed in *EC – Biotech* and in *US/Canada – Continued Suspension*.

All in all, the AB aligned with the Panel's narrow construction of Article 5.7 and rejected Japan's interpretation of the Article through the prism of uncertainty. In the aftermath of this dispute, the US brought compliance proceedings under Article 21.5. The Panel Report in *Japan – Apples 21.5* marked a further step in the direction of evidence-based approaches; this can be defined as the first unequivocal case of *stricto sensu* de novo review of the scientific evidence relied upon by a Member. Japan produced a range of new experimental studies. These related to the possible infection of apple fruits through the pedicel (stalk), supporting the assertion that mature and symptomless apples could harbour endophytic bacteria which would survive storage, as well as the possible completion of the pathway for establishment and spread of the disease.[165] The new experimental evidence adduced by Japan supported the finding that the pathway would be completed through discarded infected apples. Flies would act as vectors and pear fruits as host plants, as the timing of apple imports and pear growth coincided.[166]

Had the Panel engaged in a *lato sensu* de novo review, focusing on the Member's duty to provide scientific proof of the existence of a hazard and risk, it would have found that Japan's studies amounted to sufficient scientific evidence. However, in this dispute, the Panel opted for a *stricto sensu* de novo review. More specifically, it elaborated on the original Panel's finding that 'sufficient' scientific evidence must demonstrate the *existence* of a risk.[167] Building on this position, it found that it should also 'consider the *extent* of the relationship between the *scientific evidence* and the *risk* which this evidence is claimed to establish' (emphasis added);[168] in other words, the extent to which the scientific evidence could provide conclusive proof of the relevant risk. This implies a *stricto sensu* de novo review of the soundness and quality of the studies produced by Japan.

Drawing on the opinions of the appointed experts, the Panel found that the experimental evidence provided by Japan was not solid enough to prove that mature and symptomless apples could be infected through the pedicel, and that the pathway could be completed. The Panel thus concluded that the relevant scientific evidence was not sufficient for the maintenance of the measures and that there

[163] Para 185, citing *Japan – Apples* (Panel), para 7.9. See also *Japan – Apples* (AB), para 185, arguing that Art 5.7 could apply in cases where much scientific research has been carried out, but all available evidence is unreliable. For a more in depth analysis, see below sections VII and VII.A.
[164] On this point, see also Scott, *The WTO Agreement* (n 1).
[165] *Japan – Apples 21.5*, Panel Report (adopted 20 July 2005) WT/DS245/RW, paras 8.41–8.47.
[166] Paras 8.47 ff.
[167] See n 144.
[168] Para 8.45.

was no rational relationship between the evidence and the Japanese measures.[169] Relying on these findings, it also found that the scientific evidence did not support the conclusions of Japan's risk assessment. On these grounds, the assessment could not qualify as a risk assessment within the meaning of the SPS Agreement, and the measures were not based on a risk assessment.[170]

This has brought the evidence-based interpretation and application of the Agreement to a new level. It is worth noting that the Panel should arguably have considered the Japanese studies as part of 'minority opinion'. As the AB stipulated since *EC – Hormones*, Members may rely on minority opinion when enacting SPS measures. The Panel was quick to dismiss this objection. It found that the evidence could not 'be assimilated to minority opinion' and did not 'objectively support what Japan would like to demonstrate [...]'.[171] Yet, it provided neither a clear explanation of the reasons why the Japanese studies did not amount to minority opinion nor any reasons for finding a lack of objectivity, other than by reference to the appointed experts' opinion. Overall, the Report in *Japan – Apples 21.5* confirmed Japan's initial assertion that Members are only entitled to protect themselves against well-known and established dissemination pathways. Conclusive proof of unsafety will be required for the enactment of SPS measures.

VII. *EC – Biotech*: Hazard-Related Uncertainties, Socially Acceptable Risk and the Cartagena Protocol. Sound Science as a Meta-Norm?

The following sub-sections conduct an examination of *EC – Biotech*.[172] The analysis focuses on the gap between the complaining Parties' and the EC's arguments in the dispute, underscoring the EC's reliance on a socially acceptable risk approach to the governance of agricultural biotechnologies. Further, the analysis points to the continued focus of the dispute settlement organs on positive proof of the relevant hazards and risks, along the lines of previous Reports. From this perspective, *EC – Biotech* has reinforced the *lato sensu* de novo standard of review applied in previous disputes, while confirming a narrow interpretation of Article 5.7 and providing some further clarifications on this provision.

The first sub-section deals with the overall background of the dispute, the complainant Parties' submissions relating to the EC general moratorium and

[169] Paras 8.71 ff.

[170] See paras 8.140–8.148.

[171] Para 8.146.

[172] The analysis is limited to the aspects which are most relevant to the present enquiry into the transnational evidence-based narrative, how it is reflected in the interpretation and application of the SPS Agreement, and all relevant implications. For a detailed overview, see inter alia R Howse and H Horn, 'European Communities – Measures Affecting the Approval and Marketing of Biotech Products' (2009) 8 *World Trade Review* 49.

product-specific moratoria, and the Panel's decision in this respect. The second sub-section takes a closer look at the EC's arguments on the precautionary principle and the role of the Cartagena Protocol. The third sub-section focuses on the Panel's decision on the EC Member States' national bans.

Finally, the fourth sub-section draws together the strands of the analysis, highlighting the far-reaching impact of this dispute on the implementation of the EU framework for the governance of GE organisms. Further, this final sub-section underscores the failure by the WTO Panels and AB to identify a viable procedural meta-norm, within the meaning of Conflicts Law theory, to legitimately solve the dispute by balancing transnational integration and legal and value pluralism. In the absence of any self-standing objective scientific criteria, the analysis points to the slippery slope of *lato* (or *stricto*) *sensu* de novo review, versus deferential review of reasonableness. All in all, review of positive proof of hazards and risks and review of the soundness and quality of relevant evidence are the only available yardsticks to solve the relevant disputes *while fostering trade liberalisation*; in other words, this (twofold) standard of review indirectly pushes towards adherence to evidence-based approaches and transnational regulatory convergence. Taking the linkage between evidence-based risk regulation, regulatory convergence and trade liberalisation into due consideration, the prospects for the WTO system to legitimately solve vertical conflicts on SPS measures are bleak. Yet again, legal proceduralisation is bound to fail.

A. The EC's General Moratorium and Product-Specific Moratoria

In August 2003, after three months of consultations, the US, Canada and Argentina requested the establishment of a Panel. The dispute regarded two distinct matters: the application or implementation of the EC's regime for approval of biotech products, and a set of measures enacted by six EC Member States prohibiting the importation, marketing and sale of biotech varieties which had been previously approved at EC level.[173] All relevant varieties were obtained by recombinant DNA (rDNA) technology ('traditional' GMOs). The applicable regulatory framework consisted at the time of Regulation 258/97, Directive 90/220 and the 'new' Deliberate Release Directive (2001/18).[174] Starting from the EC level, the complaining Parties identified and challenged two specific EC 'measures': the general suspension by the EC of the approval procedure for biotech products, ie a general 'across-the-board' moratorium, and the failure by the EC to consider

[173] See *EC – Biotech*, paras 2.1 and 3.2, for the specific and slightly different requests of the three complaining Parties.

[174] See above, ch 4. The old Scientific Committee system and the old comitology rules applied at the time.

applications for the approval of a number of specific biotech products, ie a set of 'product-specific' moratoria.[175]

Throughout several rounds of written and oral submissions, the Parties put forward a considerable number of points and arguments. The complaining Parties contended that the EC had applied a de facto general moratorium on the approval of biotech products, in the period running from October 1998 to August 2003. They relied on the Declaration by five Member States at the June 1999 Council Meeting of Environment Ministers as well as following documents and statements by EC officials, confirming the existence of a de facto moratorium pending reform of the EC system for the governance of GE organisms. Indeed, this dispute is set against a complex factual background; in the wake of the 1990s' food safety scares and in the face of widespread political and societal controversy on agricultural biotechnologies, the EC was in fact in the process of amending its 'old' regulatory framework.[176]

Under the complaining Parties' construction, the de facto moratorium qualified as an SPS measure. The US claimed that in so far as the legislative framework for the approval of biotech products fell within the definition of an SPS measure, the moratorium did too, despite not being formalised or embodied in a single document.[177] According to Canada, the moratorium was tantamount to a marketing ban. In so far as a marketing ban qualifies as a measure, Canada argued that the general moratorium should also be considered as a 'measure' within the meaning of the SPS Agreement.[178] The complaining Parties thus alleged that the moratorium was inconsistent with a number of Articles of the SPS Agreement, starting with Articles 2.2 and 5.1.

Turning to the product-specific moratoria, the complaining Parties pointed to the EC's failure to consider a number of pending applications for the approval of specific biotech products. A majority of these applications were notified under the 1990 or 2001 Directives, while a few other requests were submitted under the 1997 Regulation. Some of the varieties had already been the object of a favourable risk assessment at Member State level, or both at Member State level and within the relevant EC Scientific Committee; however, the procedure did not advance due

[175] *EC – Biotech*, paras, see in particular para 4.50 (submissions of the US) and 4.80 (submissions of Canada).

[176] See inter alia paras 4.48, 4.132 and 4.143–4.145 (submissions of the US), 4.84 (submissions of Canada). See also para 4.144: 'at a Council Meeting of EC Environment Ministers in June 1999, the Environment Ministers of Denmark, Greece, France, Italy and Luxembourg issued a Declaration stating that in exercising the powers vested in them regarding the growing and placing on the market of genetically modified organisms … they will take steps to have any new authorizations for growing and placing on the market suspended'. See also para 4.397 (submissions of the US) and 4.591 and 4.1157 (submissions of Canada) for references to the reform of the 1990 Directive and the 'interim approach' followed by the EC in the meantime. On the question of traceability and labelling and the need to adopt new regulations, see paras 4.551 and 4.552 (submissions of the US), as well as 7.1271 and 7.1513.

[177] Paras 4.155 ff (submissions of the US).

[178] Paras 4.204 and 4.423–4.427 (submissions of Canada).

to failure to achieve a qualified majority in comitology. Risk assessments for other varieties had been delayed.

The Parties' analysis of the application of the SPS Agreement to the product-specific moratoria was developed along lines similar to the analysis of the general moratorium.[179] Thus, the product-specific moratoria were also considered as 'measures' within the meaning of the SPS Agreement. All in all, the complaining Parties lamented that the approval procedure had been stalled even though the relevant risk assessments had failed to identify any specific *hazards* and *risks* associated with GE varieties. Under their reconstruction, the EC's further requests for information under the approval procedure were not supported by scientific evidence; rather, they required a '*probatio diabolica*' of absence of risk.[180] Yet again, the complaining Parties challenged the consistency of the product-specific moratoria with a number of Articles of the Agreement, including Articles 2.2 and 5.1.

The EC, in its defence, categorically denied the existence of a de facto moratorium.[181] Rather, it argued that EC institutions had engaged in a thorough evaluation of the 'potential benefits and risks'[182] of each GE variety under the applicable regulatory framework and in accordance with a precautionary approach.[183] For the purposes of the present analysis, two aspects deserve particular attention.

The first aspect relates to the EC's constant emphasis on the uncertain risks posed by GE organisms, the choice to pursue a prudential approach to risk assessment and to adopt a precautionary model of risk management, and the political and socio-economic stakes associated with authorisation of GE varieties. Starting from scientific uncertainty, the EC made repeated reference to hazard-related uncertainties surrounding crop to crop gene flow and hybridisation, effects on non-target organisms, allergenicity and toxicity (including the question of interactions between herbicide-resistant GE crops and herbicides), and development of antibiotic resistance.[184] The same, undisputed EC focus on persisting uncertainty emerges from the following Panel's analysis of the EC evaluation of specific applications (the 'product-specific moratoria'). In other words, the EC contended that the delays in the approval of individual GE varieties had been caused by the need to conduct prudential, thorough and all-encompassing risk assessments, requesting additional evidence whenever needed and taking persisting uncertainties into due consideration. Turning to the precautionary principle, the EC called into question 'scientific and regulatory debates at the international level [...], including the process that led to the conclusion of the Cartagena Protocol'.[185] This point will be the object of more detailed analysis in the next sub-section.

[179] See, eg, paras 4.184 ff (submissions of the US) and para 4.222 (submissions of Canada).
[180] See, eg, paras 4.839 ff (submissions of the US).
[181] See paras 4.331, 4.334, 4.353, 4.369.
[182] Para 4.331.
[183] Paras 4.331 and 4.334.
[184] eg paras 4.335 ff, 4.500 ff and 4.1094.
[185] Para 4.332. In various parts of the submissions, the EC supported its own position by reference to the Protocol.

Further, the EC stressed the socio-political complexity of the case, referencing political (Member State) and societal controversies over GE organisms and their advantages and disadvantages, the potential socio-economic disruption caused by contamination of conventional or organic crops, the debate on coexistence and a range of other OLFs. These included issues relating to the environmental sustainability of GE organisms, increased herbicide resistance as a result of the cultivation of herbicide-resistant GE crops, and increased pest resistance.[186]

In so doing, the EC ultimately acknowledged that EC-wide disagreements on the authorisation of GE varieties were the expression of a *socially acceptable risk* approach to the evaluation of their uncertain risks. Precautionary evaluations as well as a range of OLFs fed into the determination of the intended level of protection and threshold of socially acceptable risk; as a result, the actors involved in the authorisation process opted for a very cautious approach, suggesting that the uncertain risks of GE organisms would neither be socially acceptable nor worth taking until uncertainty had been dispelled and their sufficient safety had been established in so far as technically possible. In the face of scientific complexity and taking the precautionary principle and all OLFs into due consideration, the uncertain risks posed by GE organisms were perceived as too high to meet the intended level of protection in the field, regardless of the absence of any positive scientific proof of hazards and risks. Clearly, this approach is irreconcilable with the complaining Parties' evidence-based perspective as well as *lato sensu* de novo review of the existence of 'ascertainable risk'. Yet, it is worth noting that in this dispute the EC went so far as to expressly invoke its own ALOP, societal values, OLFs and sustainability issues.[187] It even stressed that, under EU risk regulation, positive scientific opinions on a risk assessment do not bind the risk manager.[188]

The second aspect deserving particular attention relates to the applicability of specific Articles of the SPS Agreement to the facts of the case. Drawing on its categorical denial of a de facto moratorium and its arguments on prudential risk assessment and precautionary risk management, the EC claimed that only Article 8 and Annex C of the Agreement were applicable to the facts of the dispute. More specifically, it underlined that the alleged failure to deal with certain product applications could only be challenged as the application of an SPS measure, but not as an SPS measure itself.[189] Building on this premise, it argued that there had not been any 'undue delays' within the meaning of Annex C point 1(a). The EC stressed that, far from being unjustifiable, the delays resulted from legitimate requests for additional information which would be necessary for the purposes of a prudential risk assessment and to comply with precautionary standards of risk management.[190]

[186] Paras 4.332 and 4.339.
[187] See in particular paras 4.500 ff.
[188] Paras 4.744 ff.
[189] Paras 4.360 and 4.361.
[190] Paras 4.362–4.365. See also para 4.783.

Any detailed analysis of the Panel's findings in this complex dispute would go beyond the narrow scope of this chapter. For the purposes of the present enquiry, it will suffice to provide a broad overview of the Panel's Report, while focusing on the findings which are more closely related to governance of GE organisms and the EC's approach. The Panel started by examining whether the EC approval procedures qualified as SPS measures within the meaning of Annex A(1) of the SPS Agreement. Upon a detailed analysis of the legislative instruments vis-à-vis Annex A(1)(a) to (d), it found that this was the case.[191] After a thorough reconstruction of the factual background of the dispute and relevant actions or omissions of the Commission and Member States, the Panel then found that a general de facto moratorium on approvals had been in effect between June 1999 and August 2003.[192]

Turning to an examination of the moratorium's inconsistency with Article 5.1, however, the Panel noted that the EC's

> decision to apply a general moratorium on approvals should be characterised as a procedural decision to delay final substantive approval decisions. The decision was procedural in nature insofar as it was a decision relating to the application, or operation, of the existing EC approval procedures.[193]

For this reason, it concluded that the general moratorium did not provide for 'requirements or procedures' within the meaning of Annex A(1) and could not qualify as an SPS measure.[194] On these grounds, the Panel found that the EC had not acted inconsistently with any of the obligations in the Agreement, by applying a general de facto moratorium. The exception was Article 8 and Annex C(1)(a) first clause.

The Panel's interpretation of the phrase 'undue delay' in this dispute is relevant in that it fits within the broader evidence-based interpretation of the Agreement. According to the Panel's reconstruction, 'undue delay' refers to '(a period of) time lost by inaction or inability to proceed' which is 'unjustifiable' and 'goes beyond what is warranted'.[195] The relevant determinations, the Panel added, must be made on a case-by-case basis and take account of facts and circumstances.[196] Delays caused by measures which are not based on scientific evidence, the Panel continued, may in some cases be 'undue'.[197]

[191] See the conclusions at para 7.432. The EC argued that the measures at stake in this dispute pursued multiple objectives and, as such, did not fall under the scope of the SPS Agreement in certain, specific respects; for this reason, they should have been reviewed separately under more than one Agreement (see paras 4.356 ff, 4.519 ff and 4.748 ff). For an analysis of this aspect of the dispute, see inter alia J Peel, 'A GMO By Any Other Name … Might Be an SPS Risk! Implications of Expanding the Scope of the WTO SPS Agreement' (2007) 17 *European Journal of International Law* 1009.

[192] Paras 7.1272 and 7.1285.

[193] Para 7.1739.

[194] Para 7.1383.

[195] Para 7.1495.

[196] Para 7.1497.

[197] Para 7.1500.

The Panel found that Members applying approval procedures must be allowed to 'take the time that is reasonably needed to determine with adequate confidence whether their relevant SPS requirements are fulfilled [...]', including assessing any new or additional information.[198] It thus contended that no tension exists between Annex C(1)(a), first clause, and a prudent and precautionary approach.[199] Unsurprisingly, however, the Panel found that:

> evolving science, scientific complexity and uncertainty and limited available scientific information and data are not [...] grounds for delaying substantive approval decisions, and [...] the SPS Agreement does not envisage that Members in such cases defer making substantive SPS decisions.[200]

Where scientific evidence is sufficient to perform a risk assessment, the Panel noted, Members must base their measures on a risk assessment. Where the evidence is insufficient, they should resort to Article 5.7.[201]

On these grounds, it ultimately rejected the EC's contention that the delays in the approval procedures were justified by the need to conduct comprehensive risk assessments and dispel persisting uncertainty. After finding that the general de facto moratorium had led to undue delays in the completion of at least one approval procedure for a biotech product, it concluded that the EC had failed to observe the provisions of Annex C(1)(a), first clause, and had therefore also acted inconsistently with Article 8 of the Agreement.[202] Due regard must be had to the specificities of this dispute, including the political declarations by a number of Member States that they would obstruct any new authorisations pending reform of the EC regime on GE organisms. Yet, the Panel's interpretation confirms that persisting hazard-related and risk-related uncertainties, together with the attempt to dispel them in so far as technically possible, have no role to play in the context of Annex C.

Similar considerations apply to the Panel's analysis of the product-specific measures.[203] In this instance, for the same reasons set out in the examination of the general moratorium, the Panel once again found that the EC had not acted inconsistently with any of the obligations in the Agreement; the exception was Article 8 and Annex C(1)(a) first clause. In only three out of 27 cases did the Panel find that the time taken by the relevant institutions had not been unjustifiably long. For the remaining GE varieties, the Panel concluded that the EC's failure to consider the application had resulted in undue delays in the completion of the approval procedure. Yet again, due regard must be had to the specifics of this dispute. In this sense, it is difficult to discern the impact on the Panel's review of

[198] Para 7.1498.
[199] Para 7.1522.
[200] Para 7.1526.
[201] Para 7.1525.
[202] Paras 7.1568 and 7.1569.
[203] Paras 7.1628 ff.

the political peculiarities of the case, as opposed to matters of risk regulation and uncertainty. However, it is worth stressing that at least some of the applications were particularly controversial in scientific terms.[204]

B. Conflicting Narratives, Conflicting Goals: The Case of the Cartagena Protocol. Interpreting the SPS Agreement in Light of the Precautionary Principle?

In *EC – Biotech*, as already occurred in *EC – Hormones*, *Japan – Agricultural Products II* and *Japan – Apples*, the respondent Party sought to broaden the scope of the science-based obligations through recourse to the precautionary principle. Under EU risk regulation, as already explained in chapter four, the precautionary principle comes into play when scientific evidence is imprecise, inconclusive or insufficient and uncertain risks might not meet the intended level of protection. Similar constructions of the precautionary principle were more or less explicitly submitted by Australia and Japan in disputes under the SPS Agreement: the bottom line is the connection between persisting scientific uncertainty, on the one hand, and consideration of a Member's ALOP, on the other. As already seen, this is irreconcilable with the interpretation by the dispute settlement organs of Articles 5.1 and 2.2. Nor is it reconcilable with their restrictive interpretation of Article 5.7.

Like in *EC – Hormones*, in *EC – Biotech* the EC invoked the precautionary principle as a general principle of public international law. Unlike in previous disputes, however, it also invoked the principle in the broader context of, and as codified within, two public international law treaties: the 1992 Convention on Biological Diversity and the 2000 Cartagena Protocol on Biosafety to the Convention on Biological Diversity.[205] The Preamble of the former Convention provides a baseline and rather restrictive definition of the principle, stipulating that 'where there is a threat of *significant* reduction or loss of biological diversity, *lack of full scientific certainty* should not be used as a reason for postponing measures to avoid or minimise such a threat' (emphasis added).[206] The latter Protocol's provisions more closely relate to the governance of GE organisms; further, while cross-referencing the very ambiguous definition in Principle 15 of the Rio Declaration,[207] the Protocol provides a 'stronger' and more specific application of the precautionary principle at the practical regulatory implementation level.

[204] See, eg, paras 7.2247 ff, on EC-92, where the Panel found that delays were unjustified.

[205] See the Convention on Biological Diversity of 5 June 1992 (1760 *U.N.T.S.* 69), and the Cartagena Protocol on Biosafety to the Convention on Biological Diversity: Text and Annexes (Montreal, Secretariat of the Convention on Biological Diversity, 2000).

[206] Convention on Biological Diversity, Recital (9).

[207] Cartagena Protocol, Recital (4) and Art 1. See the analysis below in this section.

The Cartagena Protocol, now complemented by the 2011 Nagoya – Kuala Lumpur Supplementary Protocol,[208] aims to ensure an adequate level of protection in the transboundary transfer, handling and use of living modified organisms ('LMOs')[209] that may have adverse effects on the conservation of biological diversity, also taking into account risks to human health.[210] To this end, it has established an Advance Informed Agreement ('AIA') for the importation of LMOs intended for release into the environment, together with relevant procedures and information requirements.[211] Much has been written throughout the years on this Protocol.[212] From a *stricto sensu* risk regulation perspective, and for the purposes of the present analysis, it is important to stress the reasons why the EC invoked the Protocol.

The Protocol's Decision Procedures for the transboundary movement of LMOs and LMOs intended for use as food or feed or for processing provide that:

> lack of scientific certainty due to insufficient relevant scientific information and knowledge regarding the extent of the potential adverse effects of [an LMO] on the conservation and sustainable use of biological diversity […] shall not prevent [a] Party from taking a decision, as appropriate, with regard to the import of the [LMO] […] in order to avoid or minimise such potential adverse effects.[213]

Article 12 provides for review of decisions 'at any time in light of new scientific information on potential adverse effects'; further, Article 26 explicitly addresses socio-economic considerations (OLFs).

Finally, and perhaps most importantly, Annex III (Risk Assessment) stipulates that 'lack of scientific knowledge or scientific consensus should not necessarily be interpreted as indicating a particular level of risk, an absence of risk, or an acceptable risk'. This provision reflects a 'strong' version of the precautionary principle, close to the understanding invoked by respondent Parties in disputes under the SPS Agreement. Pursuant to this Annex, 'risk assessment should be carried out on a case-by-case basis. The required information may vary in nature and level of detail from case to case, depending on the [LMO] concerned, its intended use and the likely potential receiving environment'. On these grounds, 'the process of risk assessment may […] give rise to a need for further information about specific subjects, which may be identified and requested during the assessment process'. Further, '[…] *uncertainty* regarding the level of risk […] may be

[208] See the Nagoya – Kuala Lumpur Supplementary Protocol on Liability and Redress to the Cartagena Protocol on Biosafety of 2010, available at www.treaties.un.org/pages/.

[209] Cartagena Protocol, Art 3(g).

[210] ibid, Arts 1, 2(2) and 4.

[211] ibid, Arts 7–12.

[212] See inter alia the analysis in N Krisch, *Beyond Constitutionalism. The Pluralist Structure of Postnational Law* (OUP, 2010); C Bail, R Falkner and H Marquard (eds), *The Cartagena Protocol on Biosafety. Reconciling Trade in Biotechnology with Environment and Development?* (Earthscan, 2002); M Pollack and G Shaffer, *When Cooperation Fails. The International Law and Politics of Genetically Modified Foods* (OUP, 2009) 116; Peel, *Science and Risk Regulation* (n 1) 297 ff.

[213] Cartagena Protocol, Arts 10(6) and 11(8).

addressed by requesting *further information* on the specific issues of concern [...]' (emphasis added).

As this concise overview shows, the Protocol embodies a prudential approach to the risk assessment of LMOs and a precautionary perspective on management of the risks associated with their transboundary movement. This explains why the EC claimed that the Protocol 'would assist the Panel in the process of interpreting WTO rules [...]'.[214] The EC highlighted that the international community 'has agreed that special rules are needed to address [GE organisms] [...] and that, in the face of scientific uncertainty, states' actions should be based on precaution'; indeed, the Cartagena Protocol is 'based on the understanding that the inherent characteristics of [GE organisms] require them to be subject to rigorous scrutiny so as to ensure that they do not cause harm to the environment or human health or cause socio-economic disruptions'.[215] Clearly, employing the Protocol to interpret the relevant provisions of the SPS Agreement supported the EC's contention that it had merely engaged in a thorough evaluation of the risks of each GE variety under the applicable regulatory framework, without any undue delays or further breaches of the SPS Agreement.[216]

The Panel examined the EC's point relating to the interpretation and application of the SPS Agreement by reference to relevant rules of international law.[217] The complaining Parties disputed the possibility of employing the Convention and Protocol as interpretative elements. More specifically, they claimed that they were neither relevant to the interpretation of any particular provision of WTO law nor applicable to the relations between the Parties of the dispute.[218] The Panel noted that, pursuant to Article 3.2 of the DSU, the WTO Agreements shall be interpreted 'in accordance with customary rules of interpretation of public international law', as reflected in Article 31 of the Vienna Convention on the Law of Treaties.[219] The two Conventions invoked by the EU fell under Article 31(3)(c) of the Vienna Convention (other relevant rules of international law applicable in the relations between the Parties to be taken into account in the interpretation of a treaty, together with the 'context'). However, the Panel underlined that Article 31(3)(c) makes express reference to rules 'applicable in the relations between the Parties'.

After an analysis on Article 2.1(g) of the Vienna Convention,[220] it went on to enquire whether the Convention on Biological Diversity and the Cartagena Protocol were applicable in the relations between the WTO Members in the dispute. It found that this was not the case. The US had not ratified the Convention on Biological Diversity, while Canada and Argentina had not ratified the Cartagena

[214] Para 4.358, referencing the AB's findings in *US – Shrimp*, AB Report (adopted 6 November 1998), WT/DS58/AB/R.
[215] Para 4.332.
[216] Paras 4.331 and 4.334.
[217] Paras 7.49 ff.
[218] Paras 7.57 ff (submissions of the US) and 7.61 (submissions of Canada).
[219] Paras 7.65 ff. See Vienna Convention on the Law of Treaties of 23 May 1969 (1155 *U.N.T.S.* 331).
[220] Para 7.68.

Protocol (which the US had not even signed).[221] On these grounds, it found that neither of the Conventions could be taken into consideration for the purposes of interpreting the WTO Agreements in the dispute.

This spared the Panel from the unattainable objective of reconciling the Cartagena Protocol's focus on scientific uncertainty, precaution and OLFs and the traditional, evidence-based interpretation of the SPS Agreement. Squaring the circle and interpreting the SPS Agreement in light of the Protocol would have been impossible; the gap between the Protocol's reference to prudential risk assessments and precaution[222] and the requirement of 'sound' scientific proof of hazards and risks under the SPS Agreement is too broad. The two reflect diametrically opposed discourses on the regulation of uncertain risks, and an irreconcilable framing of the relevant scientific questions. As much as the interpretation of the SPS Agreement reflects and contributes to the hegemonic evidence-based narrative, the Protocol is an expression of counter-hegemonic socially acceptable risk approaches.

In respect of the EC's arguments on the precautionary principle as a general principle of international law, the Panel acknowledged that Article 31(3)(c) of the Vienna Convention is sufficiently broad to encompass customary international law and recognised general principles of international law.[223] The question to address, then, surrounded the nature of the precautionary principle as a general principle of international law. The EC contended that the principle had 'become a fully-fledged and general principle of international law',[224] incorporated into five different environmental conventions: the 1982 World Charter for Nature,[225] the 1992 Rio Declaration,[226] the 1992 United Nations Framework Convention on Climate Change,[227] and the already mentioned Convention on Biological Diversity and Cartagena Protocol. It also noted that the precautionary principle finds expression in Articles 3.3 and 5.7 of the SPS Agreement.[228] The complaining Parties disputed this position, claiming that the precautionary principle is neither a customary rule of international law nor a general principle. Rather, they contended that it is an approach to risk governance that lacks a single agreed-upon formulation under public international law. In any case, drawing on *EC – Hormones*, they maintained that it could not override the textual provisions of the SPS Agreement.[229]

At the outset, it is worth mentioning that there is some merit in the complaining Parties' argument on the lack of a single agreed formulation of the principle within

[221] Paras 7.74 and 7.75. See also paras 7.94 and 7.95, on the relevance of Cartagena Protocol to dispute.
[222] See Annex III to the Cartagena Protocol, in particular.
[223] Para 7.67.
[224] See paras 4.523 and 7.78.
[225] UN General Assembly, World Charter for Nature, 28 October 1982, A/RES/37/7.
[226] 1992 Rio Declaration on Environment and Development, 14 June 1992, A/CONF.151/26 (vol I), 31 ILM 874 (1992).
[227] UN General Assembly, United Nations Framework Convention on Climate Change, 20 January 1994, A/RES/48/189.
[228] Para 4.523.
[229] Paras 4.539 ff and 7.80–7.82.

the field of public international law.[230] As demonstrated in this chapter, Article 3.3 of the SPS Agreement only amounts to a partial recognition of the principle, ie the freedom of Members to set a high ALOP (enhanced levels of protection) *after* providing conclusive scientific proof of hazards and risks. Additionally, the narrow interpretation of Article 5.7 as a safeguard clause, as further examined in the next sub-section, is hardly compatible with the logics of the precautionary principle.

Turning to the five international conventions mentioned by the EC, we find different formulations of the principle. The Cartagena Protocol's emphasis on prudential risk assessments and precaution is hard to reconcile with the cross-reference in the text to Principle 15 of the Rio Declaration. Principle 15 provides that 'where there are threats of *serious* or *irreversible* damage, *lack of full scientific certainty* shall not be used as a reason for postponing *cost-effective* measures to prevent environmental degradation' (emphasis added). This provision embodies a very weak version of the precautionary principle. Further, the reference to cost-benefit analysis is misplaced.[231] The Framework Convention on Climate Change incorporates the definition in Principle 15 with slightly different wording. The Convention on Biological Diversity, as already explained, refers to 'a *significant* reduction or loss of biological diversity' and '*lack of full scientific certainty*', while avoiding any reference to cost-benefit analysis. Finally, the World Charter for Nature only provides very vague and broad references to precaution.

Thus, from a public international law perspective, it is fair to conclude that no unequivocal and settled notion or definition of the precautionary principle exists. Rather, the precautionary principle may be defined as a constituent notion of a *transnational discourse* on socially acceptable risk.[232] Just like the AB in *EC – Hormones*, the Panel concluded that the legal status of the principle remains unsettled and refrained from taking any position or expressing any view on its status under public international law.[233] It also reiterated that the precautionary principle may not by itself 'relieve a Panel from the duty of applying the normal […] principles of treaty interpretation in reading the provisions of the SPS Agreement'.[234] This confirmed what had already emerged from the previous disputes: there is no scope for the precautionary principle to broaden the evidence-based interpretation of the SPS Agreement and rework de novo review.

[230] And particularly so if (*lato sensu*) applications of the precautionary principle beyond the specific field of risk regulation are taken into account.

[231] See above, chs 1 and 3; the pursuit of a cost-benefit effective level of protection and applications of cost-benefit analysis are diametrically opposed to the pursuit of enhanced levels of protection, consideration of OLFs and the possibility to resort to the precautionary principle. A focus on uncertainty and recourse to the precautionary principle is bound not to be cost-benefit effective.

[232] Which, in this chapter, is consistently reflected in the arguments put forward by the respondent Parties.

[233] Para 7.89.

[234] Paras 7.86 ff.

C. The Analysis of National Measures: Confirming the Irrelevance of Hazard-Related Uncertainties under Articles 5.1 and 5.7

Lastly, the Panel turned to an examination of the safeguard measures enacted by six Member States.[235] These measures prohibited the importation, marketing and cultivation of previously approved GE varieties and had been adopted on the grounds of Article 16 of the 1990 Directive or Article 12 of the 1997 Regulation.[236] As the Panel noted throughout its analysis, the procedures enshrined in the 'old' EC regulatory framework should have culminated in a decision by EC institutions to either revise the relevant EC (approval) measures or call for a termination of the national safeguard measures.[237] The Commission requested an opinion from the relevant EC Scientific Committee, with a view to assessing the scientific evidence adduced by Member States to substantiate their safeguard measures. In all cases, the EC Committee concluded that no new evidence had been produced which would invalidate the findings of the previous positive risk assessments and favourable opinions on the approval of the GE varieties.[238] However, pending reform of the governance system for GE organisms, the Commission did not take further action.[239]

As with its examination of the EC moratorium and product-specific measures, the Panel started by assessing whether the national measures qualified as SPS measures. It found that this was the case.[240] It then developed a set of preliminary considerations on the relationship between Articles 5.1 and 5.7, addressing the arguments put forward by the EC. Throughout its submissions, the EC argued that the nine national measures should have been evaluated vis-à-vis the text of Article 5.7, as they were provisional measures that Member States had enacted pending a more thorough risk assessment of the GE varieties at EC level.[241] The EC was attempting to make the *provisional* nature of a measure, rather than the notion of *scientific insufficiency*, the demarcation line for the application of Article 5.7.[242] This would have disassociated recourse to Article 5.7 from the restrictive interpretation of 'scientific insufficiency' developed by the WTO Panels and AB, sidestepping the condition that Members may only legitimately rely on Article 5.7 when evidence is quantitatively or qualitatively insufficient for the purposes of performing a sound risk assessment. On these grounds, the EC was also putting

[235] The six Member States were Austria, France, Germany, Greece, Italy and Luxembourg.
[236] Para 7.2534. The procedure was not too dissimilar to the one provided for under the safeguard clauses of the 2001–2003 legislative framework; see above, ch 4.
[237] Paras 7.2531 ff.
[238] Ibid.
[239] Para 7.2534.
[240] Paras 7.2554 ff.
[241] Paras 4.373 ff.
[242] Paras 7.2923 and 7.2924.

forward the argument that Article 5.7 is not an exception to Articles 2.2 and 5.1, but rather an autonomous right. In this sense, it contended that Articles 5.1 and 5.7 are mutually exclusive: an SPS measure may either be based on a risk assessment, pursuant to Article 5.1, or be a provisional measure, enacted under Article 5.7.[243]

Further, the EC claimed that the notion of 'scientific insufficiency' is relational. According to the EC, whether or not scientific evidence is (in)sufficient will by necessity be determined in relation to a Member's ALOP and threshold of acceptable risk; scientific (in)sufficiency cannot be analysed in a vacuum.[244] Yet again, this was an attempt to disassociate the notion of 'scientific insufficiency' from the (allegedly) 'objective' impossibility of performing a risk assessment under Article 5.1 and Annex A(4), linking it instead to a Member's ALOP. Clearly, this would have opened up space for consideration of hazard-related and risk-related uncertainties, thereby accommodating authentic precautionary risk management.

On the one hand, the Panel rejected the EC's argument on the provisional nature of SPS measures as a demarcation criterion for the application of Article 5.7.[245] On the other hand, it conceded that Article 5.7 should be 'characterised as a right and not an exception from [the] general obligation under Article 2.2'.[246] This finding has specific implications in terms of burden of proof, which is consequently bound to rest on complaining Parties.[247] However, the Panel stressed, Article 5.7 does not establish an absolute or unqualified right.[248] Rather, Members must comply with the four cumulative requirements stipulated therein. Turning to an analysis of the interconnections and relationship between Articles 5.1 and 5.7, by focusing on the text of the Agreement and the AB's previous interpretation of Article 5.7, it concluded that Article 5.7 should also be characterised as a right in relation to Article 5.1.[249]

In respect of the interpretation of 'insufficient scientific evidence', the Panel acknowledged that 'scientific insufficiency' is a relational notion. Yet, it found that the relevant relationship is the one between the available scientific evidence, on the one hand, and the possibility of undertaking a risk assessment within the meaning of Article 5.1 and Annex A(4), on the other.[250] It thus reiterated the AB's finding in *Japan – Apples* that scientific evidence will be insufficient under Article 5.7 if it 'does not allow, in quantitative or qualitative terms, the performance of an adequate assessment of risks as required [by the Agreement]'.[251]

[243] See paras 7.2930 and 7.2931.
[244] Paras 7.3226 and 7.3227.
[245] Para 7.2939.
[246] See paras 7.2969, 7.2971 and 7.2972, drawing a comparison with the relationship between Arts 3.1 and 3.3.
[247] Para 7.2976.
[248] Para 7.2973.
[249] Para 7.2997.
[250] Para 7.3234.
[251] Para 7.3233, citing *Japan – Apples* (AB), para 185.

This confirmed the irrelevance of hazard-related or risk-related uncertainties for the purposes of relying on Article 5.7. Persisting uncertainty, data gaps, limited or inconclusive scientific knowledge and the way a Member may 'subjectively' evaluate them vis-à-vis its own ALOP are irrelevant, as long as the evidence available to the scientific community is deemed 'objectively' sufficient to perform a quantitatively and qualitatively sound risk assessment. As the Panel expressly noted, a Member's ALOP will have a bearing on the selection and adoption of SPS measures[252] – after hazards and risks have been positively established. However, the Panel found that

> the definition of the term risk assessment in Annex A(4) does not indicate that a Member's [ALOP] is pertinent to an assessment of the existence and magnitude of risks. [...] We do not think that scientists need to know a Member's acceptable level of risk in order to assess objectively the existence and magnitude of a risk.[253]

As rightly emphasised, the Panel's focus on an allegedly 'objective' determination that scientific evidence is insufficient in quantitative or qualitative terms is disingenuous.[254] The notion of 'insufficiency' is by necessity open to (different) interpretation(s), just like the notions of 'adverse effects' or 'acceptable risk'. For the Panel 'to insist to the contrary is not to eschew any need for judgment, but merely to alter the identity of the party responsible for exercising it, in favour of the Panel and the scientists advising it'.[255]

At the end of these preliminary considerations, the Panel noted that it would first analyse whether national measures complied with Article 5.1. After this examination, it would move on to Article 5.7.[256] Like *EC – Hormones*, this dispute involved hazard-related uncertainties. The scientific studies and experimental evidence relied upon by Member States could neither confirm nor exclude the existence of specific hazards and risks; rather, they shed light on persisting uncertainties surrounding possible adverse effects associated with GE crops or GE food and feed. In respect of the uncertain risks posed by crop to crop gene flow, hybridisation and the pervasiveness or persistence of GE crops, the documents adduced by Member States lamented a lack of specificity in the environmental risk assessments conducted under the EC procedures, stressing how ecosystems vary from Member State to Member State and highlighting potential risks for the environment and biodiversity.[257] At a more general level, in respect of effects on non-target organisms, increased pest resistance to Bt toxin, toxicity (including the case of herbicide-resistant crops), allergenicity and spreading of antibiotic resistance, the Member States' documents pointed to data gaps and argued that

[252] See paras 7.3238, 7.3240 and 7.3242.
[253] Para 7.3243.
[254] Scott, *The WTO Agreement* (n 1) 117.
[255] ibid.
[256] See para 7.3007 (as occurred in *Japan – Agricultural Products II* and *Japan – Apples*).
[257] See, eg, paras 7.2561 ff and 7.2579 ff. On this point, see also the analysis in ch 4.

the EC risk assessments had not been sufficiently thorough and comprehensive. Notably, Member States found that potential long-term, indirect or cumulative effects had not been adequately assessed. Clearly, none of these data was embedded in a risk assessment. The studies did not provide positive, conclusive proof of specific hazards. Nor did they (or could they) provide a qualitative or quantitative evaluation of the probability of occurrence of adverse effects and their severity, as resulting from exposure to a hazard.

The Panel followed the approach of previous disputes, enquiring into the existence of a risk assessment within the meaning of the SPS Agreement and then analysing whether the national measures were based on the relevant risk assessment.[258] It first found that the original, EC-wide risk assessments and following review assessments delivered by the EC Scientific Committee[259] qualified as risk assessments.[260] Turning to an analysis of the nine national measures, it enquired whether the documents and scientific studies produced by the Member States could qualify as a 'risk assessment'.[261] In each instance, unsurprisingly, it found that this was not the case.[262]

On these grounds, the Panel then examined whether the nine national measures were based on the available risk assessments, ie the EC-wide original and review assessments for the GE varieties prohibited at Member State level.[263] Yet again unsurprisingly, it found that this was not the case. In its defence the EC argued that the national measures were compliant with Article 5.1, in that Member States had drawn their own (different) conclusions from the original (positive) risk assessments conducted under the EC approval process. From this perspective, one risk assessment may be the basis for different SPS measures and sufficiently warrant or reasonably support all of them. Clearly, the EC attempted to argue that different inferences and conclusions may be drawn from the same risk assessment, such as where the focus is on persisting uncertainty as opposed to sound scientific proof of risks.[264] The Panel rejected this interpretation and found that no rational or objective relationship existed between the positive conclusions of the EC-wide risk assessments, on the one hand, and the national bans, on the other. For this reason, it concluded that the risk assessments did not reasonably support or sufficiently warrant the national measures.

[258] Paras 7.3019 ff.
[259] ie, the further assessments delivered after the enactment of the national measures.
[260] Para 7.3027.
[261] See paras 7.3035 ff. For a partial exception, even though the studies were found not to meet all relevant requirements, see paras 7.3120 and 7.3169.
[262] At point (c) of Annex K to the Panel Report, the Panel noted that Members may conduct an 'expedited re-assessment of risk', as appropriate to the circumstances, where new or additional evidence becomes available. However, clearly, the Panel was not persuaded that the evidence produced by the Member States in this dispute met the requirements of a 'risk assessment', within the meaning of the SPS Agreement.
[263] See paras 7.3056 ff.
[264] Paras 7.3015 ff.

The Panel also added a few enigmatic considerations surrounding the requirement that an SPS measure be 'based on' a risk assessment. These seem to suggest that a Member may deviate from the positive results of a risk assessment, drawing different scientific inferences and conclusions, while still arguing that the relevant SPS measures are 'based on' that risk assessment. First, the Panel stated that Members can

> rely *in part* on an existing risk assessment which sets out a single opinion. But to the extent they *disagree* with *some* or *all* of the *conclusions* contained in such an assessment, it would [...] be necessary for Members to explain, by reference to the existing assessment, *how* and *why* they assess the risks *differently*, and to provide their revised or supplemental assessment of the risks (emphasis added).[265]

Second, it contended that

> the fact that a Member has decided to follow a precautionary approach could have a bearing on a Panel's assessment of whether an SPS measure is based on a risk assessment [...] We consider that if there are factors which affect scientists' level of confidence in a risk assessment [...] a Member may in principle take this into account in determining the measure to be applied to achieve its [ALOP]. Thus, there may conceivably be cases where a Member which follows a precautionary approach, and which confronts a risk assessment that identifies uncertainties or constraints, would be justified in adopting (i) an SPS measure, even though another Member might not decide to apply any SPS measure; (ii) an SPS measure which is stricter than that applied by another Member [...].[266]

It is impossible to square these statements with the well-established approach of the WTO Panels and AB. The best and easiest example is *EC – Hormones*. In this dispute, as already seen, the EC relied on a set of positive risk assessments; these, however, highlighted a number of persisting uncertainties. The Panel and the AB found that the EC had focused on 'theoretical uncertainty' and that the measures were not based on the relevant risk assessments. Equally, according to a footnote in the text of *EC – Biotech*, the above statements of the *EC – Biotech* Panel do not refer or apply to 'theoretical uncertainties'. Yet, it is totally unclear what uncertainties or what precautionary evaluations the *EC – Biotech* Panel was referring to; unlike other parts of the Report, the above statements do not seem to refer to consideration of the ALOP vis-à-vis the selection of SPS measures, after proving a hazard and risk. All in all, the *EC – Biotech* Panel found that the EC had failed to show that EC Member States had relied in part on the positive EC-wide risk assessments, while assessing the relevant risks differently. This, however, is quite hard to reconcile with the scientific background of the dispute.[267]

Finally, the Panel concluded by reverting to Article 5.7. Having found that both the original assessments and the review assessments conducted at EC level

[265] Para 7.3062.
[266] Para 7.3065.
[267] While the relevant EC-wide risk assessments had yielded positive results, uncertainties still persisted and had been highlighted by the Member States.

qualified as risk assessments, it concluded that the available scientific evidence was not 'insufficient' within the meaning of Article 5.7. In Annex K, the Panel emphasised that 'scientific insufficiency' includes cases of qualitative insufficiency; *quantitatively* sufficient evidence might be or might become *qualitatively* insufficient, ie unreliable for the purposes of a sound risk assessment. For instance, new or additional scientific evidence could 'negate the validity of the scientific evidence on which an existing risk assessment relied, without, however, being sufficient in quantitative and qualitative terms to allow the performance of a new risk assessment [under Article 5.1 and Annex A(4)]'.[268] Clearly, this could have occurred with the additional scientific evidence produced by Member States to justify their national safeguarding measures. However, the Panel was not persuaded that the scientific evidence adduced by the Member States had affected the validity of the EC risk assessments, making the available scientific evidence qualitatively insufficient within the meaning of Article 5.7.[269] It also reiterated that a difference exists between 'scientific insufficiency' and 'scientific uncertainty'.[270]

Against this overall backdrop, the Report drew the conclusion that all national safeguard measures were inconsistent with Article 5.7.[271] Insofar as the national measures had been found to be inconsistent with Article 5.1 and 5.7, they were also found to be inconsistent with Article 2.2.[272] This concludes the overview of *EC – Biotech*. As this sub-section has shown, the Panel Report confirmed the irrelevance of a Member's ALOP and of persisting scientific uncertainties under the SPS Agreement. Neither Article 5.1 nor Article 5.7 give Members any real margins of manoeuvre.

D. The Implications of the Evidence-Based Narrative: (Lato Sensu) De Novo Review, Regulatory Convergence and Trade Liberalisation. Can Sound Science be a Procedural Meta-Norm?

This section has provided an overview of the Panel Report in *EC – Biotech*. It has explored the Panel's interpretation of the notion of 'undue delay' and analysed its decision surrounding the applicability of the Cartagena Protocol. Further, it has explained how the Panel confirmed the narrow interpretation of Articles 5.1 and 5.7, reinforcing the evidence-based discourse underlying such an interpretation.

[268] See point (d) of Annex K to the Panel Report.

[269] For the same inference, see Scott, *The WTO Agreement* (n 1) 108, 117 and 118. As Scott noted, the Panel relied on the fact that EC Scientific Committee had found that the evidence produced by the EC Member States would not invalidate the previous EC risk assessments. See also Gruszczynski, *Regulating Health* (n 1)194 ff, emphasising that three of the experts advising the Panel had in some respects acknowledged that the available evidence was insufficient.

[270] See point (a) of Annex K to the Panel Report.

[271] Paras 7.3262 ff.

[272] Paras 7.3386 ff.

Yet again, this dispute testifies to the unbridgeable gap between evidence-based and socially acceptable risk approaches in the governance of GE organisms. The EC Member States (and EC) clearly focused on hazard-related uncertainties, as evaluated vis-à-vis the ALOP. Lack of conclusive proof of specific hazards was irrelevant to the question of the acceptability of the uncertain risks posed by GE organisms. Rather, regulators focused on the need to *dispel* scientific uncertainty in so far as technically possible, with a view to establishing that GE organisms were *safe enough* for their uncertain risks to meet the ALOP and comply with the threshold of socially acceptable risk. To some extent, this approach is also reflected in the Cartagena Protocol procedures. In a diametrically opposed way, the complaining Parties drew on evidence-based approaches and focused on sound science, ie lack of positive and conclusive scientific proof of hazards and risks. From this perspective, the EC and EC Member States had clearly failed to prove the *unsafety* of GE organisms.

The first relevant consideration pertains to the impact that the interpretation and application of the SPS Agreement in this dispute has had on the transnational debate on GE organisms. Clearly, reliance on socially acceptable risk approaches is at odds with the standard of review employed by the WTO dispute settlement organs. The option to disregard the positive results of a risk assessment and focus on persisting uncertainty, having regard to the intended level of protection and threshold of socially acceptable risk in a specific field, is irreconcilable with the Members' obligations. *EC – Biotech* has therefore considerably strengthened the transnational hegemonic narrative on the governance of the uncertain risks posed by agricultural biotechnologies, undermining counter-hegemonic discourses on socially acceptable risk. Indeed, it might not be too far-fetched to suggest that the EU institutions' evidence-based implementation of the EU regulatory framework on GE organisms, which clearly reflects a socially acceptable risk approach, has been prompted by the decision in this dispute. As anticipated in chapter four, agricultural biotechnologies have become too sensitive in transnational trade terms for the EU to stand its ground.

Second, as anticipated in the introductory section, a close analysis of this dispute sheds further light on the linkage between *lato sensu* de novo review of scientific proof of hazards and risks, transnational regulatory convergence and trade liberalisation. The text of the SPS Agreement neither mandates *lato* (or *stricto*) *sensu* de novo review nor embodies evidence-based approaches to risk regulation. In this sense, nothing would have prevented the WTO dispute settlement organs from applying a deferential standard and providing a broader interpretation of the science-based obligations. However, the SPS Agreement's turn to 'science', beyond the GATT's focus on discrimination, was intended to mark a further step in the path towards trade liberalisation.[273] In the face of scientific complexity and ubiquitous hazard-related, risk-related and methodological uncertainties, a deferential

[273] For an overview, see n 27.

standard would make virtually *any* precautionary measures compatible with the SPS Agreement, as long as the relevant procedural obligations are complied with and the SPS measures cannot be deemed arbitrary.[274] This would not respond to the SPS Agreement's overarching aim of furthering trade liberalisation. From this perspective, and taking this goal into consideration, *lato sensu* de novo review of scientific proof of hazards and risks and *stricto sensu* de novo review of the soundness or quality of scientific evidence are the only available benchmarks.

This does not mean that the WTO dispute settlement organs' interpretation and application of the SPS Agreement has sought to achieve total convergence or unconstrained trade liberalisation. On its face, the SPS Agreement allows Members to have recourse to their ALOP to enact highly protective SPS measures, after providing positive proof of hazards and risks. This power relates to the discretionary evaluation of the extent to which a risk is acceptable, after its existence has been conclusively established.[275] In this sense, the SPS Agreement does not mandate Members to rely on economic cost-benefit analysis or any 'baseline' understanding of 'adverse effects', when regulating risk.[276]

Yet, the approach of the WTO Panels and AB is somewhat ambiguous, and doubts persist as to how meaningful the notion of an ALOP is. *Stricto sensu* de novo review of the quality and soundness of the scientific evidence employed by regulating Members, in cases where hazards and risks have been established, has a twofold impact: it casts doubts on the alleged possibility of relying on minority (prudential) opinion, and undermines Members' ability to resort to their ALOP.[277] Further, the approach of the WTO Panels and AB casts some doubts on the effective possibility for regulating Members to rely on a very high (or zero risk) ALOP, after proving the existence of a hazard and risk. This partially emerged from *Australia – Salmon 21.5* and *Japan – Agricultural Products II*. *US – Continued*

[274] Ultimately, in the absence of any 'objective' and self-standing criteria of 'pure' science, review of risk regulation measures boils down to the dichotomy of deferential procedural review versus substantive review. See also Leonelli, 'Acknowledging the Centrality of the Precautionary Principle' (n 51). Throughout the years, commentators have put forward different arguments in favour of the application by the dispute settlement organs of 'intermediate' or even 'differentiated' standards of scrutiny in disputes under the SPS Agreement. For some examples, see Button, *The Power to Protect* (n 1) 222 ff; Peel, *Science and Risk Regulation* (n 1) 352 ff; J Peel, 'Of Apples and Oranges (and Hormones in Beef): Science and the Standard of Review in WTO Disputes under the SPS Agreement' (2012) 61 *International and Comparative Law Quarterly* 427, 440 ff. For an overview of different proposals and arguments, see also Button, *The Power to Protect* (n 1) 148 ff; Peel, *Science and Risk Regulation* (n 1) 347 ff. References to the 'slippery slope' of procedural versus substantive review in this chapter draw on the finding that the application of any 'intermediate' or 'differentiated' standards of scrutiny is legally impracticable in the field of risk regulation and in the face of ubiquitous uncertainties. These standards of review are also liable to produce inconsistent or arbitrary results. See for instance Leonelli, 'Acknowledging the Centrality of the Precautionary Principle' (n 51).

[275] In this sense, arguably, see paras 7.3063 and in particular 7.3065.

[276] See ch 1, section III; reference here is being made to the identification of the *legally relevant* threshold of probability of occurrence of adverse effects (and their severity) which will trigger regulatory intervention.

[277] See the analysis of *Japan – Apples 21.5* in section VI above, and *US/Canada – Continued Suspension* and *Australia – Apples* below in section VIII.

Suspension also lends itself to this interpretation. The notion of ALOP might therefore be more slippery than it first seems.

This aspect will be explored in greater detail in the next section. For the purposes of the present analysis, it is sufficient to underscore the linkage between *lato* and *stricto sensu* de novo review, regulatory convergence and trade liberalisation. This tells us something more about the hegemonic transnational narrative on GE organisms, and transnational discourses on risk governance more generally. Evidence-based approaches to risk regulation do not only foster the exercise of individual trade rights and pursue aggregate wealth maximisation, as demonstrated in chapter three. Reliance on evidence-based risk governance also provides an effective means to achieve transnational regulatory convergence, thus fostering trade liberalisation. On these grounds, as anticipated in the introductory chapter, evidence-based approaches yield a *double* economic dividend. Unsurprisingly, then, evidence-based models lie at the heart of the hegemonic transnational narrative. All in all, the evidence-based discourse *is* hegemonic *because* it yields a double economic dividend.

The final remarks on this section regard the normative aspect of enquiry. The disputes brought under the SPS Agreement and analysed in the previous sections clearly qualify as vertical regulatory conflicts, within the meaning of Conflicts Law theory. Under this theoretical framework, their successful resolution calls for the identification of a procedural meta-norm. The meta-norm shall aim to balance transnational regulatory integration and legal and value pluralism, providing a solution which will be acceptable to all parties and therefore regarded as legitimate. This lies at the heart of Conflicts Law's goal to re-politicise and re-democratise the transnational constellation, solving complex regulatory conflicts.

Can positive scientific proof of the existence of hazards and risks, as examined under *lato sensu* de novo review, qualify as a universally agreeable and therefore normatively legitimate procedural meta-norm? This question triggers some considerations. First, reference to sound scientific proof is not a *procedural* meta-norm. Indeed, as illustrated in this chapter, the standard of review employed is substantive. This is all the more true for the analysis of the 'soundness' or quality of the scientific evidence relied upon by the Parties, a criterion employed under *stricto sensu* de novo review. Second, reference to sound scientific proof can hardly qualify as a *meta-norm*. Far from being distinguished from the approaches followed by any of the Parties to the dispute, sound science is an expression of evidence-based approaches, relied upon by the complaining Parties.

Third, reference to sound scientific proof cannot provide a *universally agreeable* and *normatively legitimate solution* to transnational regulatory conflicts. Reliance on sound science is a component of evidence-based approaches. Far from being neutral and objective, as the previous chapters have demonstrated, evidence-based approaches are the expression of a specific balance between individual and collective interests; further, they come with a whole set of political, socio-economic and distributional implications. In the face of scientific complexity and multiple forms of uncertainty, sound science can by no means provide any normatively legitimate solution to transnational regulatory conflicts. Yet again, this is all the more true for *stricto sensu* de novo review. Finally, as this chapter has illustrated, the standard of review does not quite aim to *balance* transnational regulatory integration and legal and value pluralism. Rather, it aims to achieve regulatory convergence and trade liberalisation, insofar as the text of the SPS Agreement allows.

Again, this testifies to the limited ability of legal proceduralisation to solve complex transnational regulatory conflicts. The WTO dispute settlement organs have failed to identify and flesh out an adequate and viable procedural meta-norm, within the meaning of Conflicts Law theory. A procedural standard of review and a focus on reasonableness would have fulfilled the requirements of the Conflicts Law framework. Besides being a procedural criterion, reasonableness allows all Parties to draw on different models of risk governance, without imposing any specific substantive approach. In this sense, it can effectively balance regulatory integration and legal and value pluralism. Nonetheless, as observed in previous chapters, legal procedures do not exist in a political and social vacuum. Taking the material context of the SPS Agreement and its substantive goals into consideration, it is hardly surprising that the WTO Panels and AB have provided an evidence-based interpretation of the science-based obligations, opting for de novo review rather than deference. Yet again, this makes substantive analysis and substantive deconstruction all the more important to evaluate the prospects of legal proceduralisation.

VIII. Has Anything *Really* Changed Since *EC – Biotech*? Nothing has Quite Changed

Section VII has demonstrated that the interpretation and application of the SPS Agreement in *EC – Biotech* reflects an evidence-based approach; this has undermined socially acceptable discourses on agricultural biotechnologies and governance of their uncertain risks, and strengthened the hegemonic narrative on GE organisms. At a more general level, sections II to VI have shown that the interpretation of the science-based obligations of the Agreement has considerably reinforced dominant transnational discourses on sound science and evidence-based risk regulation, in so far as the WTO dispute settlement organs have conducted a *lato sensu* de novo review of scientific proof of the existence of hazards and risks or a *stricto sensu* de novo review of the soundness of the evidence relied upon.

The analysis has also illustrated the impossible quest for 'objective' and self-standing scientific criteria, within the spectrum from deference to de novo review.[278] Section VII has then emphasised that, in a context of scientific complexity

[278] See above n 274.

and persisting uncertainty, the evidence-based interpretation of the Agreement and focus on sound science approaches to risk assessment and adherence to sound science are driven by the mere need to foster regulatory convergence and trade liberalisation. On these grounds, this chapter has shed light on the connections between the hegemonic narrative on GE organisms and broader transnational discourses on evidence-based risk governance, on the one hand, and trade liberalisation, on the other.

This already answers the second, third and fourth questions underlying the application of transnational legal analysis as a methodological framework.[279] Yet, all of these questions would get a different answer if the position of the WTO dispute settlement organs had changed throughout the years. A different interpretation of the science-based obligations of the Agreement could open up spaces for the defence of socially acceptable risk approaches; the SPS Agreement system would then have a different impact on the transnational debate on GE organisms and the hegemonic and counter-hegemonic narratives. In a similar vein, the identification of different criteria, beyond adherence to sound science, could undermine the argument on the connections between evidence-based risk governance, regulatory convergence and trade liberalisation. For this reason, by way of conclusion, this section provides a brief overview of later disputes brought under the SPS Agreement. The analysis demonstrates that the arguments developed in the preceding sections are still as valid as they were at the times of *EC – Biotech*, as the prior approach was ultimately confirmed in following disputes. Overall, nothing has quite changed since *EC – Biotech*.

A. *US/Canada – Continued Suspension*

In 2003, in the aftermath of the *EC – Hormones* dispute, the EC enacted a new Directive. This relied on three new risk assessments and provided for a permanent prohibition of oestradiol-17β and a temporary prohibition for the remaining five hormones. In *US/Canada – Continued Suspension*,[280] the EC contended that the US and Canada were acting in breach of Article 22.8 DSU, insofar as the EC had removed the measure found to be inconsistent with the SPS Agreement. The respondent Parties disputed the EC's arguments.

This dispute unfolded against a very complex scientific background. The EC argued that the permanent prohibition of oestradiol-17β was based on a risk assessment, within the meaning of Article 5.1 and Annex A(4). The EC had provided in vitro proof of the genotoxicity of this hormone (hazard), relying on minority opinion to show that oestradiol-17β acted as a complete carcinogen by

[279] See above, the introductory section of this chapter.

[280] As regards the Report(s), all references in this section are made to *United States – Continued Suspension*, Panel Report (adopted 14 November 2008) WT/DS320/R, and *United States – Continued Suspension*, AB Report (adopted 14 November 2008) WT/DS320/AB/R.

exerting both tumour initiating and tumour promoting effects.[281] The respondent Parties disputed this scientific finding, arguing that the EC had failed to provide conclusive (in vivo) proof of genotoxicity. Thus, according to them, the EC had failed to prove that oestradiol-17β would have any carcinogenic effects other than in circumstances where it could exert a hormonal level on consumers. At the small levels of residues in meat, according to majority scientific opinion, oestradiol-17β could not exert any hormonal level.[282]

Drawing on the finding that oestradiol-17β is genotoxic, the EC risk assessments evaluated whether it would be possible to establish a dose-response relationship and identify a specific level of low exposure where residues of oestradiol-17β would not have tumour initiating and promoting effects. In so doing, it took account of two elements. First, the high hazardousness and DNA-damaging effects of the hormone (genotoxicity). Second, a plurality of risk-related uncertainties surrounding the hormone's bioavailability, the impact of the endogenous production of hormones in humans, cumulative and synergistic effects, confounding factors as to the development of cancer, and the possibility of abuses in the use of the hormone in growth promotion practices. In this light, it concluded that 'no quantitative estimate of risk related to residues in meat could be presented'.[283]

Having established the relevant hazard as well as the potential for adverse effects of residues of oestradiol-17β, the EC opted for a no-threshold level. Drawing on a *zero risk ALOP* for genotoxic substances, it concluded that no level of exposure to residues of oestradiol-17β would be safe enough or acceptable, and that this hormone should be banned. The respondent Parties maintained that the EC risk assessments had failed to evaluate and quantify the risks arising from the presence in meat of residues. They thus claimed that the EC had failed to conduct a risk assessment, within the meaning of the SPS Agreement.[284]

In respect of the other five hormones, the EC risk assessments could neither conclusively prove nor exclude genotoxicity (the relevant hazard). The same risk-related uncertainties surrounding exposures and probabilities applied. All in all, according to the EC, the available evidence did not allow for an adequate risk assessment. In these cases, the EC resorted to Article 5.7. International standards and MRLs for the hormones at issue existed; in fact, it is worth noting that the Codex's MRLs had been revised since the original 1998 dispute. The respondent Parties suggested that scientific evidence could hardly be 'insufficient' under Article 5.7 when international standards existed. The EC, by contrast, again put forward a relational understanding of the notion of 'insufficiency', arguing that the available evidence was insufficient to perform a definitive risk assessment for a Member applying a high ALOP of 'no risk of exposure to unnecessary additional residues [...]'.[285]

[281] See, eg, paras 7.393(d) and 7.497.
[282] See, eg paras 4.262, 4.270 and 4.313 ff.
[283] Para 7.497. See also para 4.336, on the impossibility to establish a dose-response relationship.
[284] See, eg paras 4.284 ff. and 7.490.
[285] Para 4.227.

Starting with oestradiol-17β, the Panel found that the EC had acted inconsistently with Article 5.1. More specifically, it found that the risk assessments did not comply with the requirements of Annex A(4),[286] and that the relevant scientific evidence did not support their conclusions.[287] For this reason, no risk assessment existed within the meaning of the SPS Agreement and the permanent ban was therefore not based on a risk assessment. The Panel's factual findings lend themselves to two different interpretations.

Under the first possible interpretation, the Panel conducted a *stricto sensu* de novo review of the finding of genotoxicity. In other words, it focused on the 'soundness' of the evidence on oestradiol-17β's genotoxicity and undermined the EC's ability to rely on minority opinion. As explained above, the ban largely relied on in vitro evidence of the hormone's genotoxic hazardous properties; a finding that genotoxicity has not been proved would thus produce a domino effect on the conclusions of the risk assessment.[288]

Under the second interpretation, the Panel endorsed the respondent Parties' argument that the EC had failed to address whether genotoxic effects would occur at the levels found in the hormone residues in meat. From this perspective, the EC had thus failed to evaluate the *potential for adverse effects* associated with consumer exposure to hormone *residues*, as per Annex A(4).[289] Clearly, this is a slippery slope. The EC's findings were that a no-threshold level and a zero risk ALOP should apply to highly hazardous genotoxic substances, for which no level of safe or acceptable exposure can be determined. *A fortiori*, this was found to be the case due to multiple risk-related uncertainties. In this sense, this possible interpretation of the Panel's Report is far more problematic. It suggests that the Panel supported the establishment of a dose-response relationship and the identification of a specific threshold, rather than the application of a no-threshold level; by doing so, it indirectly scrutinised the EC's zero risk ALOP, which the latter had set after the identification of a specific hazard and potential adverse effects.[290]

The AB acknowledged the flaws in the Panel's analysis of compliance with Article 5.1. Two specific points deserve attention. First, besides reaffirming the Members' right to rely on minority opinion and their need to account for potential risks as materialising under real world conditions,[291] the AB noted that Article 5.1 requires that SPS measures be based on a risk assessment; 'this does not mean that [they] have to *conform to* the risk assessment' (emphasis added).[292]

Further, it expressly recognised that 'risk assessment cannot be entirely isolated from the [ALOP]. There may be circumstances in which the [ALOP] chosen by

[286] Paras 7.485 ff.
[287] Paras 7.539 ff.
[288] See, eg, paras 7.549 ff. See also the AB Report, paras 601, 605 and 607.
[289] See, eg, paras 7.513 and 7.525.
[290] See also, although not too clearly, the AB Report, para 614.
[291] AB Report, paras 527 and 529.
[292] AB Report, para 528. The EC had put this argument forward in *EC – Hormones* and *EC – Biotech*; see sections III and VII, C, above.

a Member affects the scope and method of the risk assessment'.[293] For instance, where a Member deviates from international standards by setting a higher ALOP, it may be required 'to perform certain research as part of its risk assessment that is different from the parameters considered [...] in the [international] risk assessment'.[294] Nonetheless, the chosen level of protection 'must not affect the rigour or objective nature of the risk assessment'; nor should the ALOP 'pre-determine the results of the risk assessment'.[295] This acknowledgment that the ALOP affects the scope and methods of risk assessments conducted under Article 5.1 opens up spaces for reliance on prudential methods and recourse to precautionary risk management. Yet, this statement is hard to reconcile with the AB's insistence that the 'subjective' ALOP should not affect the (allegedly) 'objective' results of a risk assessment, ie the inferences and conclusions drawn from the available scientific evidence and the determination of the nature of 'adverse effects'. As the next section shows, these statements of principle on the impact of the ALOP on Article 5.1 turned out to be completely irrelevant in *Australia – Apples*.

Second, the AB found that the Panel had erred in the application of the standard of review. The AB held that the Panel had conducted a survey of the experts' opinions,[296] sought to ascertain whether they would have conducted a similar risk assessment,[297] and given the majority of the experts' views probative value.[298] Against this backdrop, the AB gave further directions on the applicable standard of review.[299] According to the AB's Report, a Panel reviewing consistency with Article 5.1 should first identify the scientific basis of the SPS measure. This need not reflect majority views. It should also verify that the scientific basis comes from a respected and qualified source: specifically, the views must be considered legitimate science according to the standards of the scientific community. Second, it should assess whether the reasoning articulated on the basis of the evidence is objective and coherent. Thus, the conclusions drawn must be sufficiently supported by the evidence relied upon. Finally, it should determine whether the results of the risk assessment sufficiently warrant the SPS measure.

The AB's Report carved out a quasi-procedural, rather deferential standard of review.[300] In its Report, the AB did not apply this standard, as it considered that the Panel's findings of fact were too flawed for the AB to conduct any analysis. As the next section shows, this quasi-procedural standard of review was short-lived;

[293] AB Report, para 534.
[294] ibid.
[295] ibid.
[296] AB Report, para 598.
[297] AB Report, para 592.
[298] AB Report, para 597.
[299] AB Report, para 591.
[300] For the same interpretation, see inter alia Peel (n 274) 446 ff; Gruszczynski, *Regulating Health* (n 1) 144 ff.

it was revisited in the very next dispute.[301] In fact, it is fair to say that this standard has never been applied.

Turning to Article 5.7 and the provisional ban on the other five hormones, the Panel rejected the EC's argument that the determination that evidence is 'sufficient' to conduct a risk assessment depends not only on the available data, but also on the scope and framing of the specific risk assessment and the Member's ALOP. The Panel drew on the definition in *Japan – Apples* and the findings in *EC – Biotech* to confirm an 'objective' understanding of 'scientific insufficiency'. It emphasised that while the ALOP is relevant for selecting the relevant SPS measures, the 'determination of whether scientific evidence is sufficient to assess the existence and magnitude of a risk must be disconnected from the intended level of protection'.[302]

On these grounds, the Panel examined under which conditions scientific evidence can become insufficient, and whether this can occur where international standards exist. As mentioned above in this section, the Codex had established MRLs for hormone residues; thus, the available evidence could not be deemed 'quantitatively' insufficient. Rather, it could become 'qualitatively' insufficient, ie an 'objectively' unreliable basis to perform a risk assessment, in light of new data and studies. The Panel emphasised that 'qualitative' scientific insufficiency, in the guise of 'objective' unreliability for the purposes of conducting a risk assessment, must be distinguished from scientific uncertainty.[303] The latter, the Panel alleged, should be dealt with at the risk assessment stage (eg by means of safety factors) as well as in the identification of the SPS measures meeting the ALOP.[304]

The Panel elaborated that mere hypothetical correlations, or mere suggestions that more data and evidence should be collected, will not make a successful claim that existing ('quantitatively' sufficient) evidence has become 'qualitatively' insufficient. Rather, a Member must prove that what was sufficient has become 'deficient in force, quality or amount'.[305] The Panel found that this will occur where a 'critical mass' of new evidence has developed, calling into question previous knowledge to the point that this will no longer be 'sufficient' to support the conclusions of existing risk assessments.[306] It then went on to test whether the EC had produced a critical mass of data which would make the existing evidence qualitatively insufficient, and found that this was not the case.

[301] For the view that the standard of review applied in *Australia – Apples* is irreconcilable with the findings of the AB Report in *US/Canada – Continued Suspension*, see also Peel, Of Apples and Oranges' (n 274) 451 ff; the analysis in L Gruszczynski, 'Standard of Review of Health and Environmental Regulations by WTO Panels' in G Van Calster and D Prévost (eds), *Research Handbook on Environment, Health and the WTO* (Edward Elgar, 2013); and M Du, 'Reconceptualizing the Role of Science in International Trade Disputes' (2018) 52 *Journal of World Trade* 697, 716.

[302] Panel Report, para 7.612.

[303] Panel Report, para 7.630.

[304] Panel Report, paras 7.633 ff; yet, this is irreconcilable with the Panel's own review of the EC permanent ban on oestradiol-17β.

[305] Panel Report, para 7.647.

[306] Panel Report, para 7.648.

On appeal, the EC argued that the Panel had erred in finding that 'insufficiency' was unrelated to a Member's ALOP. It also pointed out that the 'critical mass' test would make reliance on Article 5.7 virtually impossible. As soon as a 'critical mass' of evidence develops, it will be possible to conduct a new risk assessment under Article 5.1. First, the AB acknowledged that a Member's ALOP will impact on the determination as to whether scientific evidence is (in)sufficient. The AB noted that when a Member deviates from international standards and sets a higher ALOP, it will frame the scope and methodology of its risk assessment differently. As a consequence, it may have to undertake specific research, and the evidence may turn out to be insufficient for the purposes of its assessment.[307] This statement is closely linked to the AB's findings on the scope of risk assessment under Article 5.1, illustrated above. However, the AB yet again clarified that the ALOP cannot prejudice the outcome of the determination that evidence is (in)sufficient; this must remain an objective and rigorous process.[308]

Second, the threshold of a 'critical mass' of new evidence, as identified by the Panel, was deemed too high. Rather, a Member should be 'permitted to take a provisional measure where new evidence from a qualified and respected source puts into question the relationship between the pre-existing body of science and the conclusions regarding the risks', casting doubts 'as to whether the previously existing body of scientific evidence still permits of a sufficiently objective risk assessment',[309] but it is nonetheless impossible to perform a revised risk assessment. On a spectrum, this situation neither corresponds to incremental scientific developments and advances, nor requires a proper paradigm shift (development of a 'critical mass' of knowledge).[310] In this respect, the AB clarified that the possibility of conducting further research or analysing additional information to dispel persisting uncertainties does not imply that the relevant scientific evidence 'is or becomes insufficient'.[311] Science continuously evolves, and 'theoretical uncertainties' are irrelevant under the SPS Agreement.

Yet again, the AB found that the Panel's findings of fact were too flawed for it to conduct any analysis of compliance with Article 5.7. This new interpretation of Article 5.7 has never been put to the test in following disputes. The AB's decision to lower the 'critical mass' threshold and its acknowledgment that the ALOP impacts on a Member's determination that evidence is (in)sufficient comes as welcome news, from a socially acceptable risk perspective. However, the practical impact of these statements of principle is likely to be very limited.

The AB's findings are permeated by the irreconcilable tension between 'subjective' insufficiency, as appreciated vis-à-vis the ALOP,[312] and (allegedly)

[307] AB Report, para 685.
[308] AB Report, para 686.
[309] AB Report, para 703.
[310] ibid.
[311] AB Report, para 702.
[312] AB Report, paras 685 and 686.

'objective' insufficiency, ie the impossibility to perform a sufficiently 'objective' risk assessment.[313] The same tension surfaced in the AB's interpretation of Article 5.1. In the absence of any self-standing criteria of 'pure' science, squaring the circle between 'subjective' inferences vis-à-vis the ALOP and 'objective' (sound scientific) inferences is an impossible endeavour. In the context of determining scientific (in)sufficiency, decision-making will ultimately either 'subjectively' lie with the Member or 'objectively' lie with the Panel and the experts advising it.[314] In this sense, the AB's continued reference to 'objectivity' deprives the statements of principle on the impact of a Member's ALOP of any meaning.

The requirements for enacting measures to safeguard the ALOP remain exceedingly high. First, new scientific developments are needed to make a body of quantitatively sufficient scientific evidence become qualitatively insufficient, under the meaning of Article 5.7. Data gaps, the possibility of conducting further research or collecting additional data, disagreements as to the reliability of available evidence, a re-assessment of existing information and persisting hazard-related or risk-related uncertainties will not qualify as scientific insufficiency. Rather, scientific inconclusiveness as evaluated against a Member's ALOP will still qualify as 'theoretical uncertainty', or evolving science. Disputes like *Australia – Salmon*, *Japan – Agricultural Products II* and *Japan – Apples* would still yield the same results; the ALOP is ultimately irrelevant in these cases.

Second, even in cases of new scientific developments, insufficiency as evaluated vis-à-vis a Member's ALOP will not necessarily trigger the application of Article 5.7. Rather, the new information must cast doubts 'as to whether the previously existing body of scientific evidence still permits of a sufficiently objective risk assessment',[315] at an ill-defined point halfway across the spectrum of evolving scientific consensus. Yet again, the ALOP seems ultimately irrelevant.

Finally, the new evidence destabilising the previous risk assessments must not allow for the possibility of conducting a new, revised and reliable risk assessment under Article 5.1. Taking these considerations into account, the *US/Canada – Continued Suspension* test does not mark a significant turn away from the approach in *Japan – Apples* and *EC – Biotech*. Overall, the AB's reference to the impact of the ALOP on the determination of (in)sufficiency appears to be largely inconsequential.

On these grounds, it is fair to conclude that nothing has (quite) changed as a result of *US/Canada – Continued Suspension*. As this section has shown, the new interpretation of Article 5.7 has not marked any meaningful departure from the previous approach. Further, and as the next section illustrates, the 'new' standard of review and interpretation of Article 5.1 was soon revisited in *Australia – Apples*.

[313] AB Report, paras 703 and 702.
[314] See n 254 and 255.
[315] AB Report, para 703.

B. *Australia – Apples*

As Australia pointed out in its submissions, this dispute 'comes down to the degree of uncertainty that the SPS Agreement can tolerate in [a] risk assessment'[316] under the meaning of Article 5.1 and Annex A(4). New Zealand challenged the consistency with the Agreement of Australian SPS measures protecting against the potential entry, establishment and spread of a number of diseases and pests. The Australian risk assessment was semi-quantitative in nature; evidence on the relevant pathway and quantitative probabilities of entry, establishment and spread were combined in a matrix with a qualitative evaluation of the ensuing consequences. The probability values and relevant consequences were taken into account to provide a qualitative estimate of the overall risk for each pest or disease. In the presence of 'unrestricted risk', which would not meet Australia's ALOP, specific SPS measures were adopted.

New Zealand took issue with the risk assessment. First, referencing *Japan – Apples 21.5*, it argued that the assessment drew on hypothetical pathways and referred to mere 'theoretical risk'.[317] In other words, it rejected Australia's reliance on laboratory data and experimental studies on pathways. Second, it claimed that the methodological approach of the assessment was flawed in several respects. This allegedly resulted in an inflation and over-estimation of the relevant risks.[318] Australia, on its part, underlined data gaps and multiple persisting uncertainties. On these grounds, it argued that it was entitled to draw on minority opinion, resort to prudential methods and rely on prudential expert judgement in cases where data gaps were identified.[319]

The *Australia – Apples* Panel conducted *stricto sensu* de novo review, engaging in a thorough examination of the quality and 'soundness' of the Australian risk assessment. For instance, in its review of the importation steps in the case of fire blight, it found that the application of specific safety factors in the face of data gaps was not objective. Equally, the Australian choice to give more weight to a specific (prudential) body of scientific studies was considered unobjective. The Panel found that the calculated infestation rate and the exposure assessment had been over-estimated and were not objective.[320] It thus concluded that the relevant probabilities of entry, establishment and spread had been exaggerated, despite the lack of adequate scientific evidence.[321] As a consequence, overall, the Australian risk assessment could not be considered a risk assessment within the meaning of Article 5.1 and Annex A(4); nor were the measures based on a risk assessment. By implication, the Panel also found a breach of Article 2.2.

[316] *Australia – Apples*, Panel Report (adopted 17 December 2010) WT/DS367/R, para 4.444.
[317] Panel Report, para 4.385.
[318] Paras 4.385 ff.
[319] Paras 4.420 ff.
[320] See, eg, paras 7.247 ff and the relevant conclusions at 7.350 ff and 7.417.
[321] Paras 7.427 ff.

Australia – Apples must be analysed against the backdrop of the findings in previous disputes; notably, the *EC – Biotech* Panel's (somewhat vague) suggestion that uncertainties should be taken into account in the context of conducting a risk assessment under Article 5.1, rather than under Article 5.7, the AB's acknowledgement in *US/Canada – Continued Suspension* that a Member's (high) ALOP will impact on the scope and methods of risk assessment, and the AB's clarifications on the applicable standard of review in *US/Canada – Continued Suspension.* From this perspective, despite previous statements of principle, *Australia – Apples* confirms that minority opinion has a very limited role to play under Article 5.1. More specifically, the Panel took issue with Australia's recourse to prudential expert judgement, as opposed to reliance on other available data; Australia had chosen not to rely on the latter due to data gaps and persisting risk-related uncertainties. Even more clearly, this dispute confirmed that a Member's (high) ALOP and consideration of persisting uncertainties do not really have any role to play under Article 5.1. Equally, the additional notes on the applicable standard of review in *US/Canada – Continued Suspension* have proved largely irrelevant.

On appeal, Australia lamented that the Panel had erred in applying the standard of review. It noted that where a risk assessment under Article 5.1 gives rise to uncertainties, but the evidence is still 'sufficient' and recourse to Article 5.7 is foreclosed, the risk assessor should be able to rely on prudential assumptions and models.[322] After *US/Canada – Continued Suspension*, Australia claimed, the Panel should have focused on whether the risk assessment was scientifically substantiated and justifiable; it should have not enquired into its 'soundness' or correctness.[323] According to Australia's position, the AB's reference to 'whether the reasoning articulated on the basis of the evidence is objective and coherent' referred to the internal objective relationship between the scientific evidence relied upon in the risk assessment and the conclusions of the risk assessment, *not* to the objectivity or quality of the scientific evidence itself.[324] Under this interpretation, the AB's 'new' standard of review is procedural or quasi-procedural in nature.[325] On these grounds, Australia elaborated that the Panel should have asked whether the evidence 'fell within a range that could be considered legitimate by the standards of the scientific community'. Further, it should have focused on whether the alleged methodological flaws were so serious as to undermine reasonable confidence in the risk assessment.[326]

The AB took a different perspective, and ultimately reworked the *US/Canada – Continued Suspension* standard. According to the AB, the AB's Report in *US/Canada – Continued Suspension* did not set out a series of steps to be mechanically

[322] *Australia – Apples*, AB Report (adopted 17 December 2010) WT/DS367/AB/R, paras 18 ff.
[323] AB Report, para 17.
[324] AB Report, paras 18 ff.
[325] See above, the previous sub-section.
[326] AB Report, para 25. In this respect, Australia referred to the Panel's findings in *Australia – Salmon 21.5*; see section IV above.

followed; rather, it merely suggested a way to proceed in the examination.[327] In *Australia – Apples*, the AB found that a distinction must be drawn between the scrutiny of the scientific basis of the risk assessment and the scrutiny of the reasoning of the risk assessor.[328] Under the first step, a Panel should review whether the scientific basis of the risk assessment constitutes legitimate science according to the standards of the scientific community. It should also acknowledge that minority opinion may be relied upon. Under the second step, a Panel should focus on the objectivity and coherence of the reasoning of the risk assessor. In this respect, the AB indirectly suggested that a Panel should not focus on the internal objective relationship between the scientific basis of the risk assessment and the conclusions of the risk assessment, but rather on the general (ie broader scientific) objectivity and coherence of the risk assessment and its conclusions. Against this backdrop, the AB rejected the Australian 'quasi-procedural' interpretation of the *US/Canada – Continued Suspension* standard, re-injecting an element of substantive review. This betrays the spirit and the logics of the standard advocated in the previous dispute.

The AB thus concluded that the Panel had not incurred any error and upheld its findings. In respect of the Panel's review of prudential assumptions and expert judgement, it noted that '[…] scientific uncertainty does not justify a departure from [Articles 5.1 and 5.2] and, in particular, the requirement that available scientific evidence be taken into account […]',[329] persisting uncertainties or data gaps notwithstanding. As anticipated above, this dispute has confirmed the ultimate irrelevance of a Member's ALOP, persisting uncertainty and minority opinion in the context of Article 5.1. Equally, the applicable standard of review has largely remained the same. Nothing has really changed since *EC – Biotech*.

C. Following Developments Up to Nowadays

Subsequent SPS Agreement disputes, dating from the years after *Australia – Apples* until the time of writing, confirm that nothing has substantially changed in the interpretation of Articles 5.1, 2.2 and 5.7 since *EC – Biotech*. Both *US – Poultry (China)* and *India – Agricultural Products*[330] did not offer any significant new insights. In both disputes the Panel found that no risk assessment had been undertaken and that the relevant measures were therefore not based on a risk assessment.

In *US – Animals*, Argentina challenged a set of measures aimed at preventing the entry, establishment and spread of foot and mouth disease ('FMD') through trade

[327] AB Report, para 219.
[328] Paras 215 ff.
[329] Para 244.
[330] *US – Poultry (China)*, Panel Report (adopted 25 October 2010) WT/DS392/R; *India – Agricultural Products*, Panel Report (n 28); *India – Agricultural Products*, AB Report (adopted 19 June 2015) WT/DS430/AB/R.

in terrestrial animals and animal products. After finding that the relevant measures were not based on international standards within the meaning of Article 3.1, the Panel assessed whether they complied with Articles 5.7 or 5.1. In the first respect, the Panel rejected the US contention that circumstances had continuously changed in Argentina, relevant evidence was still (quantitatively) insufficient for the purposes of a risk assessment and the Argentinian application was still under review. Instead, it held that the US had not sought to obtain additional information and had failed to review the measures within a reasonable period.[331]

Turning to compliance with Article 5.1, the Panel elaborated further on the applicable standard of review by setting it within the framework of a fourfold test.[332] The first prong entails a focus on the existence of a risk assessment, within the meaning of Article 5.1 and Annex A(4). The second prong consists of an evaluation of the appropriateness of the risk assessment. This includes an examination of its scientific basis, (allegedly) bearing in mind that a Member's ALOP can influence the scope and methods of the risk assessment. The third step involves evaluating whether the scientific evidence supports the conclusions of the risk assessment. This encompasses a scrutiny of the scientific basis of the risk assessment stage as well as a scrutiny of the reasoning of the risk assessor, as identified in *Australia – Apples*. The final prong entails an examination of whether the final measure is based on the risk assessment ('rational or objective relationship'). The Panel concluded that the US interim rules, based on the Argentinian notification to the OIE, was a valid risk assessment. However, the US had failed to revise its risk assessment as circumstances changed and had thus failed to maintain measures based on a risk assessment. On these grounds, the Panel found that the US had acted inconsistently with Article 5.1.[333]

Similar considerations apply to *Russia – Pigs*, where bans targeting imports from the EU and four specific Member States (Poland, Latvia, Estonia and Lithuania) that aimed to prevent the entry, establishment and spread of African Swine Fever ('ASF') were at stake. Russia invoked Article 5.7, pointing to data gaps and claiming that evidence on the pathway for entry of ASF from each EU Member State and for each product was (quantitatively) insufficient. The Panel, by contrast, found that abundant information was available for conducting a risk assessment.[334] Equally, it dismissed Russian claims that available pertinent information indicated high risks, found that Russia had not sought information germane to the performance of a risk assessment, and further held that Russia had failed to review the measures within a reasonable period of time.[335] It also found that Russia had acted inconsistently with Article 5.1, in that it had not conducted any risk assessment.

[331] *US – Animals*, Panel Report (adopted 31 August 2015) WT/DS447/R, paras 7.288 ff.
[332] Paras 7.321 ff.
[333] Para 7.343.
[334] *Russia – Pigs*, Panel Report (adopted 21 March 2017) WT/DS475/R, para 7.672.
[335] Paras 7.677 ff.

The conclusive remarks relate to the most recent dispute, *Korea – Radionuclides*.[336] *Like US – Animals* and *Russia – Pigs*, this dispute does not show any remarkable change in the interpretation of the notion of scientific insufficiency. As already mentioned, the interpretation of qualitative insufficiency against the backdrop of a Member's ALOP, as put forward by the AB in *US/Canada – Continued Suspension*, has never been put to the test. The disputes under analysis in this section involved alleged quantitative insufficiencies, in the face of disease outbreaks or emergencies, not scientific developments and alleged qualitative insufficiency. However, it is still worth stressing that the WTO Panels and the AB have refrained from giving any relevance to the Members' ALOP, confirming the well-settled distinction between scientific uncertainty and scientific insufficiency. In this sense, these disputes align to the traditional, narrow interpretation of Article 5.7 as a 'safeguard' clause.

A set of measures enacted after the Fukushima incident were at stake in *Korea – Radionuclides*; more specifically, these measures aimed to protect against exposure to and uptake of radioactive nuclides in food. The Korean measures aimed to protect from the risks posed by low doses of radionuclides in food – notably, radiation-induced cancer. Japan challenged three specific sets of Korean measures: the 2011 and 2013 additional testing requirements, whereby certification and testing for other radionuclides was required if caesium was detected, product-specific import bans for two fish varieties from eight prefectures, and a following blanket import ban on all fishery products from the same eight prefectures. The blanket import ban was enacted after disclosure of further leaks of contaminated (radioactive) waters into the ocean in the Fukushima area.[337] Japan did not make a claim on the basis of Article 5.1; however, Korea invoked Article 5.7 and stated that an examination of the insufficiency of the evidence was relevant to the analysis of the other claims.[338]

Korea argued that available evidence on the extent of the release of radionuclides after the Fukushima incident was insufficient for the purposes of a risk assessment, particularly in respect of radionuclides other than caesium.[339] Japan claimed that Korea's choice not to consider the abundant available data did not refute its existence.[340] The Panel cited *US/Canada – Continued Suspension* and lay particular emphasis on the fact that the possibility of conducting further research or collecting further data does not 'mean that [scientific evidence] is or becomes insufficient', as the 'insufficiency' of evidence is 'not a perennial state, but rather a transitory one'.[341]

On these grounds, the Panel found that relevant scientific evidence was not (quantitatively) insufficient with respect to the 2013 additional testing

[336] *Korea – Radionuclides*, Panel Report (adopted 26 April 2019) WT/DS495/R; *Korea – Radionuclides*, AB Report (adopted 26 April 2019) WT/DS495/AB/R.

[337] Panel Report, paras 2.98 ff.

[338] Paras 7.60 ff.

[339] Paras 7.79 ff.

[340] Para 7.82.

[341] Para 7.77, citing paras 679 and 702 of the AB Report in *US/Canada – Continued Suspension*.

requirements, the product-specific import bans and the blanket import ban. With regard to the blanket import ban, more specifically, it found that Korea's concerns surrounding the further leaks were not directly related to Korea's ability to conduct a risk assessment.[342] With this finding, the Panel ultimately suggested that the evidence had not become qualitatively insufficient in light of new information and developments. Further, it found that the 2013 additional testing requirements and the blanket import ban had not been adopted on the basis of pertinent available information, that additional information had not been sought, and that the measures had not been reviewed within a reasonable period of time.[343] Korea's ALOP and the impact that this might have had for the purposes of conducting a risk assessment was not addressed anywhere in the examination of scientific insufficiency. The AB upheld the Panel's findings.

Against this overall backdrop, as anticipated earlier in this section, it is fair to conclude that nothing has really changed in the interpretation of Article 5.7 since *EC – Biotech*. The broader picture has remained largely unchanged: a Member's ALOP is ultimately irrelevant to a finding of quantitative insufficiency, and it is unclear to what extent it will support a finding of qualitative insufficiency after *US/Canada – Continued Suspension*. Similar considerations apply to Article 5.1, as developments following *US/Canada – Continued Suspension* have undermined the AB's more deferential reworking of the applicable standard of review. The interpretation of Articles 5.1, 2.2 and 5.7 still reflects the hegemonic, evidence-based narrative on risk regulation, with all the relevant consequences.

IX. Conclusions: GE Organisms, the SPS Agreement and the Evidence-Based Narrative

This chapter has interrogated the SPS Agreement as a transnationally relevant legal regime, exploring how the interpretation of the Agreement's science-based obligations has considerably reinforced the hegemonic narrative on GE organisms as well as dominant transnational discourses on sound science and evidence-based risk governance.

In order to conduct this analysis, the first sections have focused on the standard of review employed and the interpretation of the relevant provisions. The first part of the chapter has shown that an evidence-based approach is reflected in the interpretation and application of the SPS Agreement. The dispute settlement organs have consistently resorted to *lato sensu* de novo review of the existence of scientific proof of hazards and risks, or *stricto sensu* de novo review of the 'soundness' of the scientific evidence relied upon by regulating Members.

[342] Para 7.93.
[343] Paras 7.97 ff.

Hazard-related, risk-related and methodological uncertainties are ultimately rendered irrelevant within the SPS Agreement system. If a regulating Member focuses on persisting scientific uncertainty, as emerging from a positive risk assessment, it will be acting inconsistently with its obligations under Article 5.1.[344] When a regulating Member conducts a prudential risk assessment, the scientific basis of the assessment (including reliance on minority opinion) and the reasoning of the risk assessor will be exposed to *stricto sensu* de novo review of compliance with Article 5.1.[345] When persisting uncertainties or data gaps do not allow a Member to conduct a thorough risk assessment and positively prove the existence of a risk, it will be exceedingly difficult to meet the stringent conditions of Article 5.7.[346] First, the dispute settlement organs have drawn a clear distinction between quantitative insufficiency and scientific uncertainty, data gaps or evolving science. Second, it is still unclear under which conditions a regulating Member will be entitled to rely on qualitative insufficiencies. Further, some disputes have arguably blurred the boundaries between *lato* and *stricto sensu* de novo review vis-à-vis indirect review of a Member's ALOP and the SPS measures enacted to comply with it, in cases where the existence of a hazard and risk has been scientifically established.[347]

Section VII has illustrated how the SPS Agreement's interpretation has reinforced the hegemonic narrative on GE organisms, conducting a more detailed examination of *EC – Biotech*. In response to the third and fourth questions of the methodological framework, section VII has also shed further light on the hegemonic narrative on GE organisms and dominant discourses on evidence-based risk governance. The analysis of the repeated attempts to carve out an 'objective' standard of review, together with the examination of adherence by the dispute settlement organs to de novo review, has been the basis for deconstructing the linkage between *sound science approaches* to risk assessment, adherence to *sound science*, *regulatory convergence* and *trade liberalisation*. In this sense, as anticipated in the introductory section, an analysis of the SPS Agreement under the methodological category of 'legal pluralisation' is necessary to deconstruct the hegemonic narrative on GE organisms and transnational discourses on governance uncertain risks. Section VII has also developed all relevant normative considerations against

[344] See above, the analysis of *EC – Hormones*, *Australia – Salmon* and *EC – Biotech*.

[345] See above, the analysis of *Japan – Apples 21.5*, *US/Canada – Continued Suspension* (in respect of the one hormone which was permanently banned), and *Australia – Apples*.

[346] See above, the analysis of *Japan – Agricultural Products II*, *Japan – Apples*, *EC – Biotech*, *US/Canada – Continued Suspension* (in respect of the five hormones which were temporarily banned), *US – Animals*, *Russia – Pigs*, *Korea – Radionuclides*.

[347] See above, the analysis of *Australia – Salmon 21.5*, *Japan – Agricultural Products II* and *US/Canada – Continued Suspension* (in respect of the one hormone which was permanently banned); the caveat is that, in cases regarding the entry, establishment and spread of pests and diseases, the link between specific SPS measures and risk mitigation is taken into account for the purposes of demonstrating compliance with Art 5.1 and Annex A(4).

the backdrop of *EC – Biotech*. More specifically, it has pointed to the failure of the dispute settlement organs to identify a viable *procedural* meta-norm to legitimately solve vertical conflicts.

Finally, the last sections have conducted a brief examination of later disputes. The analysis has shown that nothing has really changed since *EC – Biotech*: the interpretation of the Agreement still reflects hegemonic discourses on governance of uncertain risks, with all relevant implications. This signals the increasing dominance of evidence-based approaches. The next chapter analyses this aspect in further detail by focusing on the Codex standards.

6

Legal Hybridisation: The Codex, NGO Regulatory Standards and GE Organisms. Adherence and Challenges to the Hegemonic Narrative

This chapter turns to the last constituent dimension of transnational legal analysis as a methodological framework: legal hybridisation. This involves an analysis of hybrid regulatory standards enacted by non-state actors operating *beyond* the nation-state level. For the purposes of the present enquiry into transnational narratives on GE organisms, the analysis focuses on the guidelines adopted by the Codex Alimentarius Commission (the 'Codex') and regulatory standards enacted by non-profit non-governmental organisations ('NGOs').

Starting with the standards produced by the Codex, the first relevant question is which of the two narratives is embedded in this regulatory system. At a general level, an evidence-based approach to risk governance is reflected in Codex standards, principles and guidelines. More specifically, the Codex guidelines and principles on the safety assessment of foods derived from agricultural biotechnologies reflect elements of the hegemonic narrative on GE organisms. The following question is how these guidelines and principles have had an impact on transnational debates on GE organisms, and what their transnational relevance is. The transnational impact of the Codex results from the interconnections between this standard-setting body, on the one hand, and the SPS Agreement regime, on the other. This aspect, briefly mentioned in the fifth chapter, is explored in further detail in the first section. The Codex regulatory system has thus reinforced evidence-based discourses on risk governance and the hegemonic narrative on GE organisms.

The final questions relate to how an analysis of the Codex system may uncover the goals and implications of the hegemonic narrative on GE organisms and evidence-based approaches. The analysis of the Codex confirms the link between recourse to evidence-based approaches and trade liberalisation. More specifically, the centrality of sound science and product-based approaches in the Codex guidelines on GE foods testifies to the connections between the hegemonic narrative on agricultural biotechnologies, on the one hand, and trade liberalisation, on the other. These aspects are analysed in the second section. Finally, the third section develops some brief normative considerations. It focuses on the impossibility of reconciling the hegemonic and counter-hegemonic narratives by means of procedural deliberation, referring back to the normative findings of the third and fourth chapters and echoing them.

Turning to regulatory standard-setting by non-profit NGO actors, the analysis emphasises how these hybrid standards embody a socially acceptable risk approach. NGO regulatory standards have considerably strengthened both the counter-hegemonic narrative on GE organisms and socially acceptable risk approaches, challenging the hegemonic discourse on the benefits of agricultural biotechnologies and the economic costs of precaution.

What does an analysis of NGO standards reveal about socially acceptable risk approaches and the counter-hegemonic narrative on agricultural biotechnologies, then? In this respect, the analysis focuses on the relevance of OLFs relating to consumer protection, environmental sustainability and distributional stakes, and challenges to quantitative cost-benefit analysis. Throughout the years, NGO actors have fiercely challenged all arguments on the role to be played by GE crops in tackling transnational food insecurity. Non-profit NGOs have repeatedly claimed that the development, patenting and cultivation of GE crop varieties have only benefited transnational corporations and private firms. Further, they have stressed that the public health, environmental and socio-economic 'costs' of agricultural biotechnologies are being borne by civil society. For this reason, NGOs have consistently rejected GE organisms and largely relied on alternative (food sovereignty) paradigms, putting the accent on distributional issues and questions of *access* to food.

Non-profit actors have rejected the discourse on the *benefits* ensuing from the decision to *run the risks* associated with agricultural biotechnologies. On these grounds, from a risk regulation perspective, the position of NGO actors challenges the use of cost-benefit analysis as a risk management tool. Ultimately, NGOs have challenged the assumption that aggregate wealth maximisation benefits society at large and that it should be pursued as a societal goal. Yet again, this shows that the hegemonic narrative on GE organisms and evidence-based risk governance is socially and politically constructed. The allegedly objective tenet that risks ought to be taken as long as this regulatory choice proves cost-benefit effective, and that aggregate wealth maximisation will benefit civil society, is no more than a theoretical assumption. The relevance of distributional stakes thus shines through the counter-hegemonic narrative, as defended by NGO actors. Against this overall backdrop, the sixth section sketches out some normative reflections on the impossibility of resolving diagonal conflicts, as framed under Conflicts Law theory. Finally, the conclusive section pulls together the threads of the enquiry.

I. The Codex and its Linkage with the SPS Agreement: Towards an Evidence-Based, Baseline Threshold of Safety

The predecessor of the Codex, the UN/ECE, started to operate as early as 1947. In charge of standard-setting in the field of food and agricultural products, the UN/ECE combined the predominance of the EEC/EC regional block with a close focus on public health and consumer protection issues.[1] However, the geographic scope and coverage of the organisation's standards was rather limited.[2] Three different organisations, the Codex, the International Organisation for Standardisation ('ISO') and the Organisation for Economic Cooperation and Development ('OECD') worked alongside the UN/ECE.

The Codex was established in 1963 under the auspices of the Food and Agriculture Organisation ('FAO') and the World Health Organisation ('WHO'). Its membership is open to the nation states which are either members or associate members of both parent organisations;[3] there are currently 189 members of the Codex.[4] The Codex adopts food standards, guidelines and codes of practice, which are voluntary (ie non-binding for members) in nature.[5] These cover food hygiene, labelling and presentation, methods of analysis and sampling, import and export inspection and certification as well as maximum residue limits ('MRLs') for food additives, residues of pesticides, residues of veterinary drugs and contaminants.[6] It operates through specialised committees and taskforces.[7]

The committees follow an eight-stage procedure to develop and adopt standards and guidelines.[8] The relevant regulations are then presented to the Codex plenary session. National representatives cast their vote to adopt or reject the standards or regulations. Pursuant to the Codex Procedural Manual, consensus voting should apply in both the committee and plenary sessions. However, the rules of procedure allow for voting by simple majority, on a one-country-one-vote basis, when consensus cannot be reached.[9]

[1] T Büthe, 'Institutionalization and Its Consequences: the TLO(s) For Food Safety', in TC Halliday, and G Shaffer (eds), *Transnational Legal Orders* (CUP, 2015) 266.

[2] ibid.

[3] Including the EU, given its status of regional organisation. See Codex Alimentarius Commission, *Procedural Manual*, 27th edn (Joint FAO/WHO Food Standards Programme, 2019), 128, Section I, Statutes of the Codex Alimentarius Commission, Art 2; and Section I, Rules of Procedure of the Codex Alimentarius Commission, Rule I (Membership).

[4] For more information, see the Codex's website at www.fao.org/fao-who-codexalimentarius/about-codex/members/en/.

[5] *Procedural Manual*, Section I, General Principles of the Codex Alimentarius, paras 1 (Purpose of the Codex Alimentarius), 3 and 4 (Nature of Codex Standards).

[6] *Procedural Manual*, Section I, General Principles of the Codex Alimentarius, para 2 (Scope of the Codex Alimentarius).

[7] For more information, see www.fao.org/fao-who-codexalimentarius/committees/en/.

[8] *Procedural Manual*, Section II, Elaboration of Codex Standards and Related Texts.

[9] ibid. See also *Procedural Manual*, Appendix: General Decisions, Measures to Facilitate Consensus.

The adoption of the SPS Agreement had a dramatic impact on the role and relevance of the Codex system. As explained in the fifth chapter, Article 3.1 of the SPS Agreement stipulates that Members shall base their SPS measures on existing international standards, guidelines or recommendations, except as provided for in the Agreement and Article 3.3 in particular. SPS measures conforming to international standards, guidelines or recommendations are deemed necessary to protect human, animal or plant life or health and are presumed to be consistent with the SPS Agreement and the GATT.[10] The Codex is one of the three international standard-setting organisations referred to in the Preamble, Article 3.4 and Annex A(3) of the SPS Agreement. The Agreement recognises the important contribution of international standards, guidelines or recommendations to further the use of harmonised SPS measures and thus minimise negative effects on trade.

This connection between Codex standards and the SPS Agreement regime has significantly raised the stakes for all actors involved at Codex level. This has had a number of implications. First, as highlighted by one academic commentator, the Codex is nowadays a nominally inter-governmental organisation. Throughout the years, it has developed an increasingly hybrid nature: representatives of the food industry, transnational corporations, non-profit stakeholders and technical experts have increasingly populated its national delegations,[11] which were traditionally made up of representatives from national regulatory agencies and ministries. Moreover, 237 organisations have gained the status of Codex observers. These include 16 UN organisations, 58 inter-governmental organisations and 163 NGOs.[12] Such diversification of the representatives and participants of the Codex Commission has produced inherently transnational outputs, beyond the traditional inter-governmental structure of the body or trans-governmental dynamics.

Second, the link between the Codex standards and the SPS Agreement has had a far-reaching impact on the way food safety issues are *framed* at Codex level. The Codex has been defined as the de facto TLO in the field of food safety.[13] More specifically, from this perspective, four incipient TLOs existed in this field until the early Nineties;[14] however, the SPS Agreement's express reference to the Codex standards has dramatically impacted its normative settlement, alignment and institutionalisation.[15] According to this account, then, the boundaries of the Codex TLO have come to align with the issue area of 'trade-related food safety'.[16]

[10] See ch 5, section I.

[11] See T Büthe and N Harris, 'Codex Alimentarius Commission' in T Hale and D Held (eds), *Handbook of Transnational Governance. Institutions and Innovations* (Polity Press, 2011), 219; and Büthe, 'Institutionalization and Its Consequences' (n 1) 271.

[12] See *Procedural Manual*, Section I, Rules of Procedure of the Codex Alimentarius Commission, Rule IX (Observers). See also www.fao.org/fao-who-codexalimentarius/about-codex/observers/observers/about/en/.

[13] Büthe, 'Institutionalization and Its Consequences' (n 1). On TLO theory, see ch 2, part 1.

[14] ibid 272–274.

[15] ibid.

[16] ibid 258.

In other words, Codex standards do not simply enshrine the level of food safety which is deemed most appropriate for public health and consumer protection purposes. Rather, they set a presumption that the products at stake are safe enough to be traded. On these grounds, accounts of the Codex TLO have rightly emphasised how food safety has come to be framed as 'above all a trade issue and as being among the most important non-tariff barriers for trade in agriculture'.[17]

The conclusions of this section are not dissimilar. However, focusing on transnational narratives entails drawing a preliminary distinction between the regulatory framework underlying Codex standard-setting, on the one hand, and regulatory implementation and standard-setting at Codex level, on the other. In the first respect, just like in the case of the SPS Agreement, the Codex Procedural Manual does not quite reflect an evidence-based approach. The Codex Working Principles for Risk Analysis[18] establish a clear functional separation between risk assessment and risk management,[19] and the Manual recognises that 'risk analysis is an iterative process, and interaction between risk managers and risk assessors is essential [...]'.[20] The section on risk assessment policy stipulates that constraints, uncertainties and assumptions having an impact on the risk assessment should be explicitly considered and transparently documented.[21] Risk assessment reports should then indicate any such factors and record minority opinion.[22]

Crucially, the Manual acknowledges that 'the responsibility for resolving the impact of uncertainty on the risk management decision lies with the risk manager, not the risk assessors'.[23] This statement reflects socially acceptable risk discourses.[24] It also remarks that 'precaution is an inherent element of risk analysis';[25] the degree of uncertainty and variability emerging from available scientific information and the specific characteristics of the hazard should be reflected in the risk management options selected.[26] Further, when there is evidence that a risk exists but

[17] ibid 276.

[18] See *Procedural Manual*, Section IV, Risk Analysis.

[19] ie the Codex Commission acts as risk manager, and the joint FAO/WHO expert bodies and scientific committees as risk assessors. As seen above in ch 3 and 4, this is typical of regulatory systems informed by socially acceptable risk approaches. See *Procedural Manual*, Section IV, Risk Analysis, Working Principles for Risk Analysis for Application in the Framework of the Codex Alimentarius, paras 3 and; and *Procedural Manual*, Appendix: General Decisions, Statements of Principle Relating to the Role of Food Safety Risk Assessment, para 3.

[20] *Procedural Manual*, Section IV, Risk Analysis, Working Principles for Risk Analysis for Application in the Framework of the Codex Alimentarius, para 9.

[21] ibid para 23. See also CAC/GL 62-2007, Working Principles for Risk Analysis for Food Safety for Application by Governments, para 26.

[22] *Procedural Manual*, Section IV, Risk Analysis, Working Principles for Risk Analysis for Application in the Framework of the Codex Alimentarius, para 25.

[23] ibid. See also CAC/GL 62-2007, para 28.

[24] See above ch 2, section III in particular.

[25] *Procedural Manual*, Section IV, Risk Analysis, Working Principles for Risk Analysis for Application in the Framework of the Codex Alimentarius, para 11. See also CAC/GL 62-2007, para 12.

[26] ibid para 11. See also CAC/GL 62-2007, para 12.

'scientific data are insufficient or incomplete, the [Codex] should not proceed to elaborate a standard but should consider elaborating a related text, such as a code of practice [...]'.[27]

To a certain extent, the Manual also acknowledges the role of OLFs at the risk management stage. According to The Codex Working Principles for Risk Analysis, decisions should be based on risk assessment and take into account (where appropriate) OLFs relevant for the protection of consumer health and for the promotion of fair trade practices, in accordance with the Statements of Principle Concerning the Role of Science in the Codex Decision-Making Process and the Extent to Which Other Factors are Taken into Account.[28] These Statements of Principle[29] clarify that the risk manager may identify consumer protection and fair trade OLFs and indicate how they affect the selection of risk management options.[30] The relevance of these factors at the risk management stage is thus recognised in the Manual.

Finally, the Manual does not mention cost-benefit analysis. Rather, it stipulates that the risk manager should take into account the potential advantages and disadvantages of risk management options. When making a choice among

> different [...] options which are equally effective in protecting the health of the consumer, the [Codex] [...] should take into consideration the potential impact of such measures on trade among its Member countries and select measures that are no more trade-restrictive than necessary [to achieve the level of protection deemed appropriate].[31]

This statement enshrines a necessity 'test', whereby risk management measures should not be more trade restrictive than necessary to achieve their goal. Strict proportionality, ie cost-benefit effectiveness of risk regulation, is not taken into account.[32]

Against this backdrop, the Codex Procedural Manual and relevant regulatory procedures do not quite reflect evidence-based approaches to risk governance. Nonetheless, turning to the regulatory implementation stage, Codex standards have increasingly come to align with an evidence-based *baseline* threshold of 'adverse effects' and 'food safety'; prominent examples are pesticide[33] and veterinary

[27] ibid para 10.

[28] ibid para 28. See also CAC/GL 62-2007, para 32.

[29] *Procedural Manual*, Appendix: General Decisions, Statements of Principle Concerning the Role of Science in the Codex Decision-Making Process and the Extent to Which Other Factors Are Taken into Account.

[30] ibid para 2; see also the sub-section 'Criteria for the Consideration of the Other Factors Referred to in the Second Statement of Principles', therein.

[31] *Procedural Manual*, Section IV, Risk Analysis, Working Principles for Risk Analysis for Application in the Framework of the Codex Alimentarius, para 34. See also CAC/GL 62-2007, para 38.

[32] Just like under Art 5.6 of the SPS Agreement; for a detailed overview, see J Scott, *The WTO Agreement on Sanitary and Phytosanitary Measures. A Commentary* (OUP, 2007).

[33] For a very interesting analysis, see Pesticide Action Network UK, Sustain and E Lydgate, *Toxic Trade* (PAN UK, 2020).

drug[34] MRLs. Clearly, standards will only be adopted or revised where at least a simple majority of votes is reached at Codex Commission level. In this sense, different national perspectives, approaches and goals across different food safety areas will come into play. It would then be incorrect to assume or to suggest that *all* Codex standards embody a minimum, baseline level of protection. However, as documented by the analysis of the Codex TLO, the interconnection between Codex standards and the SPS Agreement regime has resulted in intense disputes at Codex level. Controversies have arisen whenever standards are set in contested areas, and in particular where economic (transnational trade) stakes are very high.[35] In these cases, consensus voting has become marginal and the Codex Commission has increasingly resorted to simple majority voting. These trade-sensitive cases are the ones where Codex standards are most likely to align to an evidence-based baseline threshold of 'adverse effects'.

From the Codex TLO perspective, this confirms that food safety has come to be framed as 'above all a trade issue [...]'.[36] For the purposes of the present analysis, it confirms the connections between evidence-based risk regulation and the hegemonic narrative on risk governance, on the one hand, and trade liberalisation, on the other. Harmonisation of SPS measures by reference to a baseline, sound and cost-benefit effective threshold of 'safety' comes with two major economic advantages. First, insofar as Codex Members incorporate the relevant Codex standards within their national legal systems, adherence to a baseline threshold of safety relieves market actors from the costs associated with precaution and the pursuit of higher levels of protection. This point has already been illustrated in the third chapter. Second, reliance on evidence-based approaches and harmonisation by reference to a transnational baseline of safety means that stricter national or regional standards will have to be scientifically justified under the SPS Agreement.[37] Taking precautionary considerations and enhanced levels of protection as a benchmark for the enactment of Codex standards would not foster transnational trade liberalisation. Rather, it would confirm the determinations of Members with stricter standards and force other Members to raise their own standards, insofar as they seek access to these markets. In a diametrically opposed vein, relying on a transnational baseline at Codex level exposes Members with higher standards to disputes under the SPS Agreement. This encourages them to lower their standards, enabling Members with baseline standards to access their markets.

[34] See for instance the scientific and factual background in *EC – Hormones* and *US/Canada – Continued Suspension*; the rather lenient standards in place at the time of the first dispute had been revised by the time of the second dispute. In a similar perspective, see also Scott, *The WTO Agreement* (n 32) 243 ff.

[35] See Büthe and Harris, 'Codex Alimentarius Commission' (n 11) 221 ff, and Büthe, 'Institutionalization and Its Consequences' (n 1) 277 ff, making the specific example of controversies surrounding standard-setting in the case of residues of hormones in meat.

[36] Büthe, 'Institutionalization and Its Consequences' (n 1) 276.

[37] See the analysis in ch 5, section I.

This confirms the connections between evidence-based approaches to risk governance, the hegemonic narrative on uncertain risks and trade liberalisation. Codex standard-setting largely reflects evidence-based risk governance *because* this fosters the elimination of non-tariff barriers to trade and facilitates transnational market access. In this sense, the analysis of the Codex regulatory system sheds further light on the rationale and implications of evidence-based models. As the next section shows, the same is true of an analysis of the Codex guidelines on GE foods. The centrality of sound science and product-based approaches in the Codex's guidelines on GE foods testifies to the connections between the hegemonic narrative on agricultural biotechnologies, on the one hand, and trade liberalisation, on the other.

II. The Codex Principles and Guidelines on the Assessment of Foods Derived from Biotechnology

This section provides an overview of the Codex principles and guidelines on the assessment of foods derived from biotechnology, against the backdrop of the broader analysis conducted in the previous section. Unsurprisingly, the principles and guidelines reflect a sound, product-based approach, rather than precautionary process-based models. This confirms the broader findings of the previous section in the circumscribed context and field of GE foods.

The Codex principles acknowledge that the risk analysis of whole foods triggers considerations which are different in nature from the case of chemical or microbiological hazards or nutritional factors.[38] The purpose of the principles is to provide a framework for risk analysis on the safety and nutritional aspects of GE foods.[39] The principles recommend a pre-market safety assessment, designed to identify whether a hazard, other safety concern or nutritional concern is present.[40] This safety assessment is characterised by a comparative assessment of the GE food relative to the appropriate conventional counterpart, focusing on a determination of similarities and differences.[41] If a new or altered hazard, other safety concern or nutritional change emerges from the comparative assessment, the risks associated with this change should be characterised to determine their relevance to human health.[42]

[38] See CAC/GL 44-2003, Principles for the Risk Analysis of Foods derived from Modern Biotechnology, para 3.

[39] ibid para 7.

[40] Para 10.

[41] Paras 10 and 11.

[42] Para 10. See also CAC/GL 45-2003, Guideline for the Conduct of Food Safety Assessment of Foods Derived from Recombinant-DNA Plants, para 5.

As further clarified in the Codex guidelines on the safety assessment of foods derived from recombinant-DNA plants,[43] 'rather than trying to identify *every hazard* associated with a particular food, the intention is to identify *new or altered hazards relative to the conventional counterpart*' (emphasis added).[44] Indeed, the approach of the principles and guidelines is 'based on the principle that the safety of foods derived from new plant varieties [...] is assessed *relative to* the conventional counterpart [...]' (emphasis added).[45] In other words, the concept of substantial equivalence is used to structure the safety assessment of the new food by means of an identification of similarities or differences vis-à-vis the conventional counterpart.[46] The identification of differences is the factor which will trigger a risk assessment. As acknowledged in the guidelines, 'the safety assessment carried out in this way does *not* imply absolute safety of the new product; *rather*, it focuses on assessing the safety of any identified differences' (emphasis added).[47]

Clearly, the guidelines draw on a product-based model, on comparative assessment and on the general presumption of the substantial equivalence of GE organisms, as a class, to their conventional counterparts. If no new or altered hazards, safety concerns or nutritional concerns are identified, no risk assessment ensues.[48] This approach is irreconcilable with process-based models, where the general presumption of substantial equivalence of GE organisms as a class does not apply. Under these models, each and every GE variety is the object of a thorough risk assessment; comparative assessment vis-à-vis the conventional counterpart is only a starting point for a more exhaustive assessment of any potential hazards associated with the genetic engineering process.[49] Conversely, and overall unsurprisingly, the Codex principles and guidelines draw on a sound (evidence-based) scientific approach to the safety assessment of GE foods.

The rest of the guidelines provide an overview of specific factors to be taken into consideration for the purposes of the safety assessment.[50] The section on risk management within the Codex principles mentions the possibility of taking OLFs into account, cross-referencing the Codex Statements of Principle on the role of science and OLFs.[51] A brief mention is also made of uncertainties, as emerging from

[43] CAC/GL 45-2003; while these guidelines specifically relate to traditional 'GMOs', para 7 provides that they may also apply to foods obtained by different techniques.

[44] Para 4. See paras 14–17 for an acknowledgment that unintended effects may ensue from additional traits being acquired or existing traits being lost or modified (see the references to the disruption or silencing of existing genes, activation of silent genes, modifications in the expression of existing genes and formation or new or changed patterns of metabolites).

[45] Para 4.

[46] Para 13.

[47] ibid.

[48] See above, ch 3, for a description of the US product-based approach.

[49] See above, ch 4, for a description of the EU process-based approach; see also the analysis in sections I, II and V therein.

[50] See also Annexes 1 and 2 therein.

[51] CAC/GL 44-2003, para 16.

a safety assessment, and to labelling, post-market monitoring and traceability.[52] Nonetheless, for the purposes of the present enquiry, the most relevant element is the reliance on product-based models, as opposed to process-based models. As anticipated at the beginning of this section, this confirms the findings of the previous section in the circumscribed context and field of GE foods. The centrality of sound science in the Codex guidelines on GE foods, a highly trade-sensitive issue, testifies to the connections between the hegemonic narrative on evidence-based risk governance and agricultural biotechnologies, on the one hand, and trade liberalisation, on the other.

III. Normative Reflections: The Gap between Product- and Process-Based Models and the Failure of Deliberation

Can the Codex be a site of political deliberation and constructive discussion surrounding the technical, political, socio-economic and cultural factors at stake in the fields of risk governance and food safety? Do the guidelines and principles on GE foods reflect the construction of a normatively legitimate discourse on the assessment of the uncertain risks posed by agricultural biotechnologies?

The notion of 'food safety' is highly contested at the transnational level. Divergent regulatory approaches to the governance of uncertain risks, the interpretation of science through different lenses and different cultural understandings come into play. Procedurally identifying normatively legitimate solutions is therefore a very difficult endeavour. This has become all the more difficult due to the material context against which the Codex regulatory system is now set. As documented over the years, the new role of Codex standards under the SPS Agreement has resulted in disputes, negotiations and bargaining throughout the Codex standard-setting process.[53] Economic considerations, trade interests, controversy over distributional factors and the over-representation of market actors and developed countries have all undermined deliberative dynamics at Codex level.[54] The limited margins of manoeuvre to construct transnationally shared values by means of procedural deliberation have thus been further reduced by the interconnections between the Codex system and the SPS Agreement. As explained in the first section, this has made adherence to an (evidence-based) *baseline* level of safety all the more likely.

[52] ibid paras 18–21.

[53] See T Büthe, 'The Globalisation of Health and Safety Standards: Delegation of Regulatory Authority in the SPS Agreement of the 1994 Agreement Establishing the WTO' (2008) 71 *Law and Contemporary Problems* 219, 250 ff; Büthe and Harris, 'Codex Alimentarius Commission' (n 11) 221 ff; and Büthe, 'Institutionalization and Its Consequences' (n 1) 257 ff.

[54] Ibid. See also J Peel, *Science and Risk Regulation in International Law* (CUP, 2010) 286 ff; A Herwig, 'Transnational Governance Regimes for Foods Derived from Biotechnology and their Legitimacy', in C Joerges, IJ Sand and G Teubner (eds), *Transnational Governance and Constitutionalism* (Hart Publishing, 2004).

The Codex principles and guidelines on GE foods reflect this state of affairs. Procedural deliberation, as advocated under the Conflicts Law framework, should have led to the identification of a normatively legitimate solution to the clash (horizontal conflict) between product and process-based models, sound science and persisting uncertainty. Constructing a legitimate solution by means of transnational deliberative practices was bound to be a difficult endeavour in the face of the unbridgeable normative gap between substantive (evidence-based and socially acceptable risk) approaches in the field of GE organisms. This aspect has already been introduced in the final section of the third chapter.

Yet, the prospects of procedural deliberation have been further undermined by the substantive and material context within which Codex standards are now set. Unsurprisingly, the principles and guidelines on GE foods reflect an evidence-based approach and product-based models. Yet again, as emphasised in the previous chapters, this testifies to the complex dialectics of substantive and procedural factors: procedural deliberation does not exist in a political and socio-economic vacuum.

IV. Regulatory Standards Enacted by Non-Profit NGOs: Back to Socially Acceptable Risk Approaches

As explained in the second chapter, the public-private dichotomy is inherent to the nation state and to national law. By contrast, the public-private distinction gets very slippery outside the familiar boundaries of the nation state.[55] The categorisation of non-state actors as 'private' is neither particularly meaningful, nor very helpful.[56] These actors may include market, for-profit actors as much as societal, non-profit stakeholders or 'private non-competition based regulatory bodies'.[57] For the purposes of the present enquiry, the analysis will only focus on hybrid regulatory governance by a number of prominent non-profit NGOs.

The introductory section has anticipated that regulatory standards enacted by NGOs embody a socially acceptable risk approach. NGO regulatory standards have considerably strengthened both socially acceptable risk discourses and

[55] See S Cassese et al, 'The Enforcement of Transnational Private Regulation: A Fictitious Oxymoron', in F Cafaggi (ed), *Enforcement of Transnational Regulation: Ensuring Compliance in a Global World* (Edward Elgar, 2012) 331.

[56] See for instance how Abbott and Snidal have classified the actors operating within regulatory standard-setting constellations as *state*, *firm* and *NGO* actors, KW Abbott and D Snidal, 'Strengthening International Regulation Through Transnational New Governance: Overcoming the Orchestration Deficit' (2009) 42 *Vanderbilt Journal of Transnational Law* 501. Cafaggi has drawn a distinction between governmental, market/for-profit actors and civil society/no-profit actors; see F Cafaggi (ed), *Enforcement of Transnational Regulation: Ensuring Compliance in a Global World* (Edward Elgar, 2012). For a similar classification, see also D Levi-Faur, 'Regulation and Regulatory Governance' in D Levi-Faur (ed), *Handbook on the Politics of Regulation* (Edward Elgar, 2011).

[57] See the exhaustive overview in T Büthe and W Mattli, *The New Global Rulers: The Privatization of Regulation in the World Economy* (Princeton University Press, 2012).

the counter-hegemonic narrative on GE organisms, challenging the hegemonic discourse on the benefits of agricultural biotechnologies and economic costs of precaution. As the next section shows, through their stringent consumer protection, environmental and fair trade requirements, NGO standards have had a powerful impact on transnational debates, most importantly the debate on GE organisms.

The non-profit NGOs under analysis in the following section pursue a set of overlapping goals, encompassing *consumer interests*, *environmental protection* and *socio-economic justice*. In the first respect, NGOs have put food quality and consumer choice at the centre of their regulatory standards. Environmental protection goals include sustainability, biodiversity protection and limited use of pesticides and other chemicals. Fair trade and transnational redistribution lie at the heart of the social justice agenda. Regulatory standards enacted by non-profit actors thus draw on a continuum of values spanning enhanced public health and environmental protection, in accordance with the overarching tenets of the precautionary principle, and a set of relevant OLFs.

Notably, these regulatory standards categorically prohibit the cultivation and use of any GE products. Non-profit NGOs have taken a strong precautionary perspective on the uncertain public health and environmental risks posed by agricultural biotechnologies. Further, they have consistently claimed that GE organisms are irreconcilable with consumer protection goals, environmentally unsustainable and socio-economically detrimental to small-scale farmers in developed, developing and less developed countries. A socially acceptable risk approach thus shines through these standards. The uncertain public health and environmental risks posed by GE organisms are neither considered socially acceptable nor worth taking in light of persisting uncertainties, the precautionary principle and a range of relevant OLFs.

The ensuing question is how an analysis of NGO standards may shed further light on socially acceptable risk approaches and the counter-hegemonic narrative on agricultural biotechnologies. How can this part of the enquiry illuminate the rationale and implications of the counter-hegemonic narrative, as diametrically opposed to hegemonic discourses on the costs of precaution and benefits of GE organisms? This is what the next section turns to.

V. Precaution, OLFs and the Challenge to Cost-Benefit Analysis: From Agricultural Biotechnologies and Food Security to Food Sovereignty

Founded in 1972,[58] IFOAM – Organics International aims to enhance sustainable models of agriculture through a powerful regulatory governance and

[58] For more information, see IFOAM's website, in particular at www.ifoam.bio/about-us/our-history-organic-30.

meta-governance action. It includes over 800 members from 10 countries.[59] The organisation endeavours to 'build capacity to facilitate the transition of farmers to organic agriculture, raise awareness of the need for sustainable production and consumption, and advocate a policy environment conducive to agroecological farming practices […]'.[60] Food insecurity, climate change, biodiversity loss and social injustice in the farming sector are among the challenges that it seeks to tackle;[61] this is complemented by a close focus on consumer protection issues. According to IFOAM:

> unsustainable agriculture is the largest driver of biodiversity loss, it is contributing to global warming, contaminating soil, threatening rural livelihoods as well as food and nutrition security. […] The negative impacts of input-intensive or industrial agriculture on the environment and health, its inefficacy to provide a decent income for farmers, its high reliance on fossil fuels and high vulnerability to climate change all show the need for change.[62]

Guided by the Organic 3.0 strategy plan, the organisation works towards a 'widespread uptake of truly sustainable farming systems and markets based on the principles of organic agriculture'.[63]

The NGO exercises regulatory and meta-governance functions. The IFOAM's Organic Guarantee System draws a line between what is and what is not considered 'organic' by the organisation. The IFOAM Family of Standards encompasses a number of private and public (legislative or governmental) organic standards that the organisation has officially endorsed as being 'organic', based on their equivalence with the NGO's Common Objectives and Requirements of Organic Standards ('COROS'). IFOAM's COROS enable transnational equivalence assessments of organic standards and technical regulations, prior to inclusion in the IFOAM Family of Standards.[64] The Family of Standards includes three global standards (one being IFOAM's own standard) and 44 public or private standards.[65] A number of specific programmes, listed on the NGO's website, require that products be certified to one of the standards accredited and approved by IFOAM.[66] Further work is undertaken in the field of verification and certification.[67]

Organic agriculture is defined as:

> a production system that sustains the health of soils, ecosystems, and people. It relies on ecological processes, biodiversity and cycles adapted to local conditions, rather than the

[59] ibid.
[60] See www.ifoam.bio/about-us.
[61] ibid.
[62] See www.ifoam.bio/why-organic.
[63] See www.ifoam.bio/about-us/our-history-organic-30.
[64] See the data available www.ifoam.bio/our-work/how/standards-certification/organic-guarantee-system/coros.
[65] See the IFOAM – Organics International, *Family of Standards*, adopted 18 May 2020 (IFOAM – Organics International, 2020).
[66] See www.ifoam.bio/our-work/how/standards-certification/organic-guarantee-system/ifoam-family-standards.
[67] See www.ifoam.bio/our-work/how/standards-certification.

> use of inputs with adverse effects. Organic agriculture combines tradition, innovation and science to benefit the shared environment and promote fair relationships and good quality of life for all involved.[68]

The four interconnected principles of organic agriculture are identified as 'health', 'ecology', 'fairness' and 'care'.[69] First, 'healthy soils produce healthy crops that foster the health of animals and people'; thus, 'organic agriculture is intended to produce high quality and nutritious food that contributes to preventive health care and well-being'.[70] Under the second principle, ecology, organic agriculture is aligned with the cycles and ecological balances of nature and preserves biodiversity.[71] 'Fairness' puts the accent on equity, respect and social justice. The principle of 'care', finally, postulates that agriculture 'should be managed in a precautionary and responsible manner to protect the health and well-being of current and future generations and the environment'.[72] Thus, technological choices should be informed by precaution. Further, and importantly, 'decisions should reflect the values and needs of all who might be affected, through transparent and participatory processes'.[73]

The principle of care, as framed by the organisation, reflects a socially acceptable risk approach to the governance of uncertain risks. GE organisms are categorically prohibited and 'have no place in organic food and farming systems'.[74] According to the organisation, the environmental release of GE organisms has caused 'significant reduction in biodiversity, soil fertility [and] human and animal nutrition and health'. For this reason, agricultural biotechnologies are irreconcilable with the principles of 'care', 'health' and 'ecology'. Further, the reduction of consumer choice and farmer choice, contamination of GE organism-free crops, the distributional implications of coexistence[75] and increased dependency of farmers on patented seeds are found to violate the principle of 'fairness'.[76]

Drawing on an iterative socially acceptable risk approach, and taking scientific uncertainty, the precautionary principle and a whole range of OLFs into account,[77] IFOAM has thus concluded that the uncertain risks posed by GE organisms are not worth taking and should not be taken. As the NGO's position paper expressly maintains, 'deployment of genetic engineering must be based on clear evidence of its benefits',[78] and GE organisms have so far 'not contributed to the common

[68] See www.ifoam.bio/why-organic/organic-landmarks/definition-organic.

[69] See www.ifoam.bio/why-organic/shaping-agriculture/four-principles-organic.

[70] See www.ifoam.bio/why-organic/principles-organic-agriculture/principle-health.

[71] See www.ifoam.bio/why-organic/principles-organic-agriculture/principle-ecology.

[72] See www.ifoam.bio/why-organic/principles-organic-agriculture/principle-care.

[73] ibid.

[74] IFOAM – Organics International, *Position Paper: Genetic Engineering and Genetically Modified Organisms* (IFOAM – Organics International, 2016), 3.

[75] See the analysis above in chs 3 and 4.

[76] IFOAM – Organics International *Position Paper* (n 74) 4.

[77] ibid 5 and 6.

[78] ibid 4.

good'.[79] Further, IFOAM has advocated research and investment on safer and more sustainable breeding practices and methods, as an alternative to GE organisms.[80]

Fair Trade International ('FTI') has taken a similar perspective on agricultural biotechnologies. Social justice, equity and transnational redistribution lie at the heart of FTI's mission. The aim is to 'transfer wealth back to farmers and workers in developing countries'.[81] Unlike IFOAM, FTI operates across different sectors, beyond agriculture. The system relies on fair trade minimum prices, covering the average costs of sustainable production, and a fair trade (surplus) premium, used to invest in (economic, social or environmental) community projects.[82] The system is made up of FTI, acting as an umbrella NGO and entrusted with regulatory standard-setting and coordination, three regional producer networks, over 25 national fair trade organisations, and FLOCERT, the main independent certifier for products carrying the FTI mark.[83] A stringent certification and auditing system guarantees compliance and the integrity of the FTI mark.[84]

All products certified under the FTI scheme must comply with the NGO's stringent economic, social and environmental criteria. The economic criteria include the Fairtrade minimum price and Fairtrade premium. Under the social criteria, specific requirements on democratic self-organisation, participatory decision-making, transparency, non-discrimination, gender equality, freedom of association, collective bargaining rights and worker safety and health must be met. Forced labour and child labour are prohibited. Finally, the environmental criteria stress the need to adopt ecological practices; these encompass responsible water and waste management, biodiversity protection and minimal use of pesticides and agrochemicals. Organic production and certification are not required, but are promoted. Notably, FTI standards prohibit the use of any GE organisms.[85] As clearly acknowledged, the focus areas of environmental standards are: minimised and safe use of agrochemicals, proper and safe management of waste, maintenance of soil fertility and water resources, and the prohibition of GE organisms.[86]

Therefore, drawing again on socially acceptable risk approaches and taking precautionary considerations and environmental, socio-economic and distributional OLFs into account, FTI has decided to ban agricultural biotechnologies. FTI's work to contribute to the United Nations Sustainable Development Goal 2 ('end hunger, achieve food security and improved nutrition, and promote sustainable agriculture') centres on agroecological practices and the pursuit of food

[79] ibid 5.
[80] ibid 7. See also www.ifoam.bio/about-us/our-network/sector-platforms/ifoam-seeds.
[81] For more information, see FTI's website, and in particular www.fairtrade.net/about/key-benefits-of-fairtrade.
[82] See www.fairtrade.net/about/how-fairtrade-works.
[83] ibid.
[84] See www.fairtrade.net/about/certification and www.fairtrade.net/about/integrity-in-compliance.
[85] www.fairtrade.net/standard/about and www.fairtrade.net/standard/about.
[86] See www.fairtrade.net/standard/aims.

sovereignty.[87] At the heart of FTI's vision to achieve the zero hunger Sustainable Development Goal is small-scale agriculture. Capacity and infrastructure-building in developing and less developed countries, transnational redistribution and the promotion of socially and environmentally sustainable agricultural practices are seen as key to tackling food insecurity. According to FTI, GE organisms have no role to play in the achievement of any of these goals.

The Pro Terra Foundation is a non-profit organisation promoting environmentally sustainable and efficient models of agriculture throughout the supply chain (production, transport, storage, traders/dealers and industrial processing).[88] Its mission is to build a 'global network of businesses supporting more sustainable agricultural practices'.[89] These goals are complemented by a close focus on consumer demands for high levels of food quality, corporate social responsibility initiatives and concerns over 'the potential detrimental impact of herbicide-resistant, genetically modified crops on ecosystems and biodiversity […]'.[90]

The Foundation has developed a Pro Terra Standard and a Pro Terra Certification Programme. All companies certified under the Pro Terra scheme are part of the Pro Terra Network.[91] The certification scheme ensures that crops, food and feed are GE organism-free and sustainably grown and processed. The Pro Terra Standard covers the whole supply chain, from production to logistics, processing and retail. Created in 2006, the Standard's latest version (4.1) was finalised in 2019. As expressly acknowledged on the Foundation's website, the current version of the Standard focuses on rigorous non-GE organism requirements, biodiversity protection, reduced use of pesticides and fertilisers, water management, and human rights and labour law issues.[92] Again, GE organisms are rejected on public health, environmental and socio-economic grounds.

Finally, the Slow Food Movement has also taken a strong position against agricultural biotechnologies. Born in 1989 as an Italian gastronomic initiative aimed at defending regional food traditions,[93] the Movement is now a transnational network including more than 100,000 members, 1,500 food communities in over 160 countries and more than a million supporters. This grassroots association is made up of local food communities (groups of small-scale producers and stakeholders 'united by the production of a particular food and closely linked to a geographic area'[94]) and local convivia (local Slow Food chapters involved in events and projects), as well as national structures, an International Council and

[87] See below, in this section, for more details.
[88] See the Pro Terra Foundation website, www.proterrafoundation.org/.
[89] ibid.
[90] ibid.
[91] See www.proterrafoundation.org/pro-terra-networks/ and www.proterrafoundation.org/partnership/.
[92] See www.proterrafoundation.org/pro-terra-standard/.
[93] For more information, see Slow Food's website at www.slowfood.com/about-us/our-history/.
[94] See www.slowfood.com/our-network/terra-madre-network/.

an Executive Committee. It is associated with a specific logo. The Terra Madre Network, established in 2004, unites local food communities. It has now been complemented by three different networks: the Terra Madre Indigenous Network, the Migrant Network and the Youth Network. The Terra Madre Foundation, also established in 2004, supports sustainable food projects, local food communities and the growth of the network.[95]

The three interconnected principles of the Slow Food Movement are that food should be 'good' (quality, flavoursome and healthy), 'clean' (produced in such a way that it will not harm the environment), and 'fair' (accessible and socio-economically fair).[96] The full definition is enshrined in the Movement's manifesto. Slow Food promotes GE organism-free agriculture, food and animal feed. A Position Paper has expressly detailed the reasons why the organisation is against agricultural biotechnologies.[97] These include the uncertain public health and environmental risks that GE organisms may pose, the way they threaten biodiversity, increased herbicide resistance of weeds and increased pest resistance as a result of the cultivation of GE varieties, the impact of agricultural biotechnologies on small-scale conventional or organic farming due to contamination and other socio-economic issues, and food quality and food culture factors. This reflects a socially acceptable risk approach.

Unlike other NGOs, Slow Food has also emphasised questions surrounding corporate control and patents, and it has fiercely criticised discourses on the societal benefits of agricultural biotechnologies.[98] More specifically, the organisation has challenged the argument that GE organisms increase productivity and will help tackle food insecurity. The Movement's website expressly states that 'since [GE organisms] began to be marketed two decades ago, the number of starving people in the world has grown, just like the profits of the companies that produce [GE seeds]'.[99] More detailed yet similar considerations are expressed in the Movement's Position Paper, which presents a set of specific data and information prior to concluding that the 'development and production [of GE organisms] satisfy the economic interests of multinationals rather than the need to feed an expanding population'.[100]

This paves the way for a further step in the enquiry. As the concise analysis of this section has shown, regulatory standards enacted by non-profit actors reflect a socially acceptable risk approach: precautionary evaluations are complemented by a focus on consumer protection, environmental sustainability and socio-economic

[95] See www.slowfood.com/about-us/our-structure/ and www.slowfood.com/our-network/slow-food-communities/.

[96] See www.slowfood.com/about-us/our-philosophy/.

[97] Slow Food International, *Slow Food Position Paper on Genetically Modified Organisms* (Slow Food International, 2016).

[98] See www.slowfood.com/what-we-do/themes/gmos/why-we-are-against-gmos/.

[99] ibid.

[100] Slow Food International, *Slow Food Position Paper* (n 97) 5.

OLFs.[101] This results in a finding that the uncertain risks posed by GE organisms should not be taken. However, the NGOs under analysis have also more or less explicitly rejected the argument that agricultural biotechnologies can help achieve transnational food security. The specific contention that GE organisms have not helped tackle food insecurity and will not help to feed an expanding global population opens up a further angle of analysis.

As explained since the beginning of the book, the discourse on the prospective *benefits* of GE organisms and economic *costs* of precaution lies at the heart of the argument that the uncertain risks of agricultural biotechnologies *must* be taken. From this perspective, the arguments of non-profit actors shed further light on the political and social construction of the hegemonic narrative on agricultural biotechnologies. In risk regulation terms, as the remaining part of this section explains, the position of NGOs challenges the value of cost-benefit analysis as a risk management tool on distributional grounds.

Arguments surrounding the role to be played by GE organisms in tackling food insecurity originally focused on the prospects of nutritionally enhanced GE varieties and increased agricultural productivity as a result of employing GE crops.[102] However, only a handful of minimally successful nutritionally enhanced GE varieties have been developed over the years.[103] The latter element, ie increased agricultural productivity of GE crops, is still the object of high levels of controversy. This debate has gained increased visibility lately, as climate-resilient GE varieties are being developed and their adoption is advocated in the framework of climate change adaptation strategies. By contrast, non-profit NGOs argue that specific traditionally bred crops are more effective than climate-resilient GE varieties.[104] Further, these actors emphasise the need to embrace economically and environmentally sustainable models of agriculture as a way to achieve climate change *mitigation*, rather than focusing on climate change *adaptation*.[105]

This is only the latest evolution in the long-standing debate on the societal benefits of agricultural biotechnologies. Any in depth analysis of 'narratives of hunger'[106] would go beyond the scope of this book and this chapter. For the purposes of the present enquiry, and from a risk regulation perspective, it is sufficient to provide a broad picture of the relevant issues. As this section has shown,

[101] In the field of agricultural biotechnologies, see above the NGOs' references to food quality, increased herbicide resistance as a result of cultivation of herbicide resistant GE crops, increased pest resistance as a result of cultivation of pest resistant GE crops, coexistence problems and consumer and farmer choice.

[102] See inter alia M Pollack and G Shaffer, *When Cooperation Fails. The International Law and Politics of Genetically Modified Foods* (OUP, 2009).

[103] See inter alia Slow Food International, *Slow Food Position Paper* (n 97). See also data made available by the Non-GMO Project, www.nongmoproject.org/, and GM Watch, www.gmwatch.org/en/.

[104] See inter alia IFOAM – Organics International, *Position Paper* (n 74), and the websites cited in n 103.

[105] IFOAM – Organics International, *Position Paper* (n 74).

[106] See A Saab, *Narratives of Hunger in International Law. Feeding the World in Times of Climate Change* (CUP, 2019).

non-profit NGOs have consistently advocated agroecological practices, a focus on small-scale conventional and organic agriculture and capacity and infrastructure-building in developing and less developed countries as the way forward to achieve transnational redistribution and tackle food insecurity. According to NGOs, food insecurity is caused by poverty and *lack of access* to nutritious food, rather than *lack of food*; data from the FAO, cited by NGOs, shows that 'enough food to feed over 12 billion people is currently being produced'.[107] The solution thus:

> does not lie in increasing […] yields per hectare, but in a completely different system of food production, storage, distribution and access. Increasing production and consuming more energy, land and water only fuels market principles that have no place in the dynamics of the supply of means of subsistence.[108]

On these grounds, non-profit NGOs have largely embraced *food sovereignty* paradigms.[109] Pursuant to the official definition, ratified at the 1996 FAO's World Food Summit, food sovereignty is:

> the right of peoples, communities, and countries to define their own agricultural, labour, fishing, food and land policies which are ecologically, socially, economically and culturally appropriate to their unique circumstances. It includes the true right to food and to produce food, which means that all people have the right to safe, nutritious and culturally appropriate food and to food-producing resources and the ability to sustain themselves and their societies.[110]

Food sovereignty paradigms, to which NGOs refer, frame food insecurity as a question of access to food and distribution of resources.[111] GE organisms have no role to play, under these models. Rather, food sovereignty advocates have repeatedly claimed that the development, patenting and marketing of GE varieties has merely served the economic interests of transnational corporations, perpetuating inequalities and distributional conflicts across developed, developing and less developed countries. The entrenchment of agricultural biotechnologies has achieved aggregate wealth maximisation. However, it cannot possibly tackle the distributional causes of food insecurity: unequal access to food and an unequal distribution of resources. In this sense, GE organisms perpetuate a vicious circle: they are 'not a solution to the problem, but […] a further manifestation of it'.[112]

Non-profit actors have thus challenged the hegemonic discourse on the benefits of GE organisms on distributional grounds. NGOs claim that market actors

[107] Slow Food International, *Slow Food Position Paper* (n 97) 6.
[108] ibid.
[109] For a detailed analysis, see Saab, *Narratives of Hunger* (n 106). For general information, see the websites of La Via Campesina, www.viacampesina.org, and the People's Coalition on Food Sovereignty, www.foodsov.org.
[110] See Slow Food International, *Slow Food Position Paper* (n 97) 8; Saab, *Narratives of Hunger* (n 106); and the websites of La Via Campesina, www.viacampesina.org.
[111] Saab, *Narratives of Hunger* (n 106).
[112] Slow Food International, *Slow Food Position Paper* (n 97) 6.

have capitalised on the economic benefits of agricultural biotechnologies; more importantly, however, they also argue that these benefits will not spill over on consumers and farmers in developed, developing and less developed countries. For this reason, GE organisms will not tackle food insecurity and their uncertain risks are not worth taking.

From a risk regulation perspective, this argument has broader implications; it goes to the heart of cost-benefit analysis and the underlying criterion of aggregate wealth maximisation. Evidence-based models postulate that uncertain risks *must* be taken as long as this regulatory choice proves economically cost-benefit effective: cost-benefit analysis is considered an objective and universally valid risk management tool, and aggregate wealth maximisation is regarded as the overarching goal of regulation.[113] In the case of GE organisms, this is reflected in the discourse that agricultural biotechnologies yield benefits for civil society and that they are the way forward to achieve food security.[114] NGOs have put this narrative into question. By focusing on *distributional* issues, non-profit NGOs have challenged the assumption that *aggregate wealth maximisation* results in *positive spill-overs* and a *redistribution* of resources. Ultimately, these actors have challenged the assumption that aggregate wealth maximisation benefits society at large and that it should be pursued as a societal goal.

From this angle of analysis, recourse to cost-benefit analysis and reliance on the rule of aggregate wealth maximisation cannot be regarded as universally valid. The centrality of distributional stakes shines through the regulatory standards of non-profit actors. The relevant question thus becomes who is bearing the costs associated with the decision to run uncertain risks and who is reaping the relevant benefits; why are uncertain risks being taken at societal level and whether these risks are worth taking. From this perspective, in accordance with counter-hegemonic discourses, uncertain risks must be socially acceptable and the advantages and disadvantages associated with a product or process should be taken into due consideration. Ultimately, the tenet that recourse to cost-benefit analysis will benefit society at large turns out to be no more than a *value-laden* assumption.

Yet again, this shows that the hegemonic narrative on GE organisms and on evidence-based risk governance is socially and politically constructed, just like the counter-hegemonic one. On these grounds, as anticipated since the beginning of this chapter, an analysis of NGO standards sheds further light on the rationale and implications of hegemonic discourses. Further, it confirms the unbridgeable gap between hegemonic and counter-hegemonic narratives on agricultural biotechnologies. This section concludes the book's deconstruction of evidence-based and socially acceptable risk approaches to governance of GE organisms. The next section develops some brief normative considerations on diagonal conflicts. Finally, the last section pulls together the threads of the analysis.

[113] See inter alia C Sunstein, *The Cost-Benefit Revolution* (MIT Press, 2018).

[114] See ch 3 above, section VII in particular.

VI. Diagonal Conflicts and the Impossibility of Embedding Societal Standards

The successful resolution of diagonal conflict constellations, as briefly explained in the second chapter, requires societal regulatory and self-regulatory systems to be embedded within national or regional legal systems. This solution acknowledges the value of regulatory governance by societal stakeholders, and gives societal regulation recognition and institutionalisation.[115] Yet, the analysis of NGO regulatory governance provides a different overview.

Regulatory standards enacted by non-profit actors enshrine a higher level of protection than that pursued in the great majority (if not all) of regional or national legal systems. The categorical prohibition of any use of GE organisms in agriculture is one example. This triggers proper transnational diagonal conflicts. However, there is no possible way for regional or national jurisdictions to embed these societal standards. Further, and importantly, NGO actors do not really have an interest in seeing their standards recognised and institutionalised at national or regional level. What we witness is, rather, the opposite dynamic.

First, NGO regulatory standards 'compete' with national regulatory standards. For instance, IFOAM has developed its own transnational standard on organic products, which 'competes' with national or regional legislation. In a similar vein, the standards enacted by FTI or the Pro-Terra Foundation are applicable in national jurisdictions where environmental or social standards are considerably lower than those prescribed by the NGOs' accreditation system. Therefore, NGOs are autonomously acting and trading the system up.

Second, NGOs do at times perform proper meta-governance functions, accrediting and approving national or regional standards. The best example is probably IFOAM. As already explained, this NGO has set in place a system to assess the equivalence of different organic standards (the COROS criteria). The IFOAM Family of Standards includes public, legislative or governmental organic standards submitted to the organisation and officially endorsed as 'organic', based on their equivalence with the NGO's own COROS. Further, the NGO has launched several initiatives and developed regulatory toolkits to assist stakeholders with the development of standards on organic agriculture. These stakeholders include national governments in developing and less developed countries.[116] Overall, NGOs are embedding national regulation within their own governance system.

It is thus hard to identify any possible way for national or regional systems to give recognition to hybrid regulatory standards enacted by non-state actors operating beyond the nation state level. Nor is it technically possible for national or regional systems to procedurally embed these regulatory standards. Diagonal

[115] See the analysis in ch 2, part 2.

[116] For more information, see www.ifoam.bio/our-work/how/standards-certification.

conflicts between national and regional legal systems and societal regulation and self-regulation are bound to surface; however, legal proceduralisation does not offer a way forward to solve them.

VII. Conclusions: Legal Hybridisation and Narratives on GE Organisms

This chapter has turned to the last constituent dimension of Transnational Legal Analysis as a methodological framework, conducting an examination of hybrid regulatory standards enacted by non-state actors. The first three sections have focused on the Codex regulatory system, at a general level, and regulatory standards on GE foods, specifically. The analysis has shown that these principles and guidelines reflect an evidence-based approach, confirming the link between recourse to evidence-based approaches and trade liberalisation. More specifically, the centrality of sound science and product-based approaches in the relevant Codex guidelines testifies to the connections between the hegemonic narrative on agricultural biotechnologies, on the one hand, and trade liberalisation, on the other. The third section has echoed the findings of previous chapters, emphasising the impossibility of reconciling the hegemonic and counter-hegemonic narratives by means of procedural deliberation.

The remaining three sections turned to regulatory standards enacted by non-profit actors. The enquiry has emphasised how these standards embody a socially acceptable risk approach to governance of GE organisms. However, regulatory governance by NGOs opens up a further angle of analysis and lends itself to a different set of considerations. Non-profit actors have rejected the discourse on the *benefits* ensuing from the decision to *take the risks* associated with agricultural biotechnologies. From this vantage point, NGOs have challenged the use of cost-benefit analysis as a risk management tool on distributional grounds. NGOs have rejected the assumption that aggregate wealth maximisation results in positive spill-overs and a redistribution of resources, and that it should be pursued as a societal goal. This offers a different perspective on the hegemonic and counter-hegemonic narratives on GE organisms and risk governance. Yet again, it shows that *both* are socially and politically constructed. The allegedly objective tenet that uncertain risks must be taken as long as this regulatory choice proves cost-benefit effective, and that aggregate wealth maximisation will (always) benefit civil society at large, is no more than a theoretical assumption. This concludes the book's institutional analysis and deconstruction of transnational narratives. The next and final chapter pulls together the threads of the whole enquiry, focusing on the methodological, institutional and normative findings.

7

Conclusions: Transnational Legal Analysis, Transnational Narratives on Risk and the Failure of Science and Deliberation. Towards Legal Re-Materialisation?

This chapter ties together the threads of the analysis in this book, focusing on the findings of the methodological, institutional and normative strands of enquiry. Each section briefly reconstructs the analysis conducted in the book, as unfolding throughout the second, third, fourth, fifth and sixth chapters. The first section develops some final considerations on the value of transnational legal analysis as a methodological framework. The second section focuses on the institutional enquiry into transnational narratives on GE organisms and risk governance. The aim is to step back from the book's in-depth examination of discrete legal systems and provide the big picture, drawing all relevant conclusions.

The last section, which focuses on the findings of the normative strand of enquiry, raises a few final and somewhat provocative questions. Does legal proceduralisation offer a way forward to foster genuine and long-lasting agreement, at times of globalisation? What happens if, in an increasingly complex and fragmented societal landscape, legal proceduralisation and political deliberation fail to construct normatively legitimate solutions to regulatory conflicts? Can legal procedural paradigms help re-democratise an 'amorphous' World Society?[1] And if legal proceduralisation fails, what are the prospects for legal analysis to enquire into the construction of normatively legitimate discourses? Should legal analysis relinquish the distinction between law's facticity and validity, and is normative legal analysis doomed? Can *legal re-materialisation* offer a solution and pave the way for new forms of transnational normative analysis?

[1] See GC Leonelli, 'The Postmodern Normative Anxiety of Transnational Legal Studies' in P Zumbansen (ed), *The Oxford Handbook of Transnational Law* (OUP, 2021).

I. Methodology: The Value of Transnational Legal Analysis as a Methodological Framework

The first part of the second chapter has explained in detail the foundations and the rationale of the methodological framework employed in the book. As a preliminary step, the chapter has provided a brief overview of Law and Globalisation and transnational legal studies, as well as a more in-depth account of two strands of transnational legal theory: TLO and TLP theory. As the analysis of the following chapters has made clear, this is not a book about methodology or transnational legal theory. Rather, transnational legal analysis is employed as a methodological framework to deconstruct transnational narratives *from within*, *across* and *beyond* the nation state level.

The methodological framing of the notion of 'transnational law' and its application to the analysis of discrete legal systems underscores that transnational narratives do not emerge out of thin air. Rather, they are socially and politically constructed and embedded in specific legal systems. For this reason, the application of transnational legal analysis as a methodological framework postulates a focus on *transnationally relevant* legal systems. These are the norm-making sites where transnational narratives have originated and where they have been shaped, reshaped, challenged or reinforced. Indeed, from this methodological perspective, transnational narratives can only be deconstructed and explored through the identification and analysis of these legal regimes.

On these grounds, the book has used transnational legal analysis as a framework to *interrogate* regulatory systems and case law, with a view to deconstructing transnational narratives on GE organisms and risk regulation. This differentiates the application of transnational legal analysis as a methodological framework from the enquiries of both TLP and TLO theory. As explained in greater detail in the second chapter, the conceptualisation of transnational legal analysis as a methodological framework is indebted to the theorisation of transnational law as a methodological lens under TLP theory. Further, TLP theory's analysis of the evolution of societal and legal dynamics is reflected in the three constituent dimensions of transnational legal analysis as a methodological framework: extra-territoriality, legal pluralisation and legal hybridisation. In other words, as explained in the second chapter, the deconstruction and examination of transnational narratives from within (extra-territoriality), across (legal pluralisation) and beyond (legal hybridisation) the nation state level is a reflection of the evolution of law at times of globalisation and of its increasing extra-territorial impact, pluralisation and hybrid nature. However, the methodological conceptualisation of transnational legal analysis in this book goes hand in hand with a close focus on structural regulatory issues. Regulatory frameworks and case law lie at the heart of the enquiry into transnational discourses. This differentiates the application of transnational legal analysis from TLP theory, as the latter focuses on questions of agency and the triad of Actors, Norms and Processes.

In a similar vein, the methodological framework of the book is indebted to the acknowledgment in TLO theory that the nation state level and other positive legal regimes are part of the transnational picture.[2] However, yet again, the object of enquiry differs. TLO theory has focused on the analysis of discrete TLOs, framing transnational law as a specific form of socio-legal ordering. In a very different vein, transnational legal analysis as a methodological framework places the deconstruction of transnational narratives at the centre of the enquiry. This reflects an unequivocally methodological understanding of 'transnational law', which is clearly differentiated from the analysis of TLOs as 'quasi-fields' of law.

By applying 'methodological transnationalism' to a specific regulatory question within a discrete area of regulatory governance, the book shows the value of conceptualising transnational legal analysis as a methodological framework. As summarised above, transnational legal analysis is used to interrogate different regulatory frameworks and bodies of case law in transnationally relevant legal systems. A mere focus on 'beyond the state' actors and hybrid patterns of regulatory governance cannot do justice to the social construction of transnational narratives within, across and beyond the nation state level. Nor can it help explore transnational discourses and their origins. Equally, the mere identification of conflicting transnational narratives cannot possibly uncover their rationales, underlying value systems, goals and political, socio-economic and distributional implications. This can only be done through an analysis of the specific legal systems where the narratives are embedded.

The introductory section in each chapter has focused on the application of the methodological framework and relevant findings, addressing four different but interconnected questions. The first question relates to the narrative under analysis throughout the specific chapters. The third, fifth and first part of the sixth chapter have focused on the hegemonic narrative on GE organisms and risk governance. The fourth and second part of the sixth chapter, on the other hand, have turned to the counter-hegemonic narrative.

The second question focuses on the transnational relevance of the legal systems under analysis throughout the chapters; it asks why these legal systems are the object of analysis, what the transnational impact of these legal regimes has been and how the hegemonic or counter-hegemonic narratives have been constructed, reinforced or challenged within these legal systems. The US system is the legal order where the transnational hegemonic narrative on GE organisms originated. This is where the discourse on the benefits of agricultural biotechnologies and the economic costs of precaution first surfaced. Regulatory notions such as sound science or cost-benefit analysis, first developed and employed in US risk governance, have become a constituent part of hegemonic discourses on risk

[2] See also TC Halliday and G Shaffer, 'With, Within and Beyond the Nation State: The Promise and Limits of Transnational Legal Ordering', in P Zumbansen (ed), *The Oxford Handbook of Transnational Law* (OUP, 2021) as well as the first part of ch 2 for a clarification regarding the terminology of 'within, across and beyond the nation state' and similar terminology employed under TLO theory.

regulation; thus, US regulatory categories have clear transnational relevance. This reflects the logics of extra-territoriality. In an increasingly globalised world, the extra-territorial impact of national and regional legal systems has unprecedented power and reach. On these grounds, the third chapter has deconstructed the hegemonic narrative on GE organisms and risk governance *from within* the US national legal system.

The fourth chapter has turned to an analysis of EU law. This is located halfway through the dimensions of extra-territoriality, on the one hand, and legal pluralisation, on the other. Thus, from a methodological perspective, EU law has twofold transnational relevance. First, the EU legal system is the site where the transnational counter-hegemonic narrative on GE organisms has been constructed. For this reason, EU governance of agricultural biotechnologies has had an important transnational impact and EU regulatory categories have transnational relevance. Second, EU governance of GE organisms impacts on EU Member States. This adds a further layer of analysis, as the EU and EU Member State level have repeatedly clashed on regulatory implementation matters. The fourth chapter has thus deconstructed the counter-hegemonic narrative on GE organisms and risk governance *from within* the EU regional legal system and *across* the nation state (ie EU Member State) level.

The fifth chapter has focused on the SPS Agreement. The interpretation and application of the Agreement provisions has had a significant impact on the transnational debate on GE organisms, reinforcing the hegemonic narrative on agricultural biotechnologies and regulation of uncertain risks. On these grounds, the fifth chapter has examined the hegemonic narrative through an analysis of the WTO law regime, *across* the nation state level. Finally, the sixth chapter has turned to the Codex system and hybrid regulatory standard-setting by non-profit NGO actors. Both sites of norm-making have transnational relevance. In its interconnections with the SPS Agreement, the Codex system has considerably strengthened transnational evidence-based discourses on risk governance and agricultural biotechnologies. By contrast, NGO actors have directly challenged the hegemonic narrative on GE organisms and defended counter-hegemonic discourses. The sixth chapter has thus engaged in a further deconstruction of the hegemonic and counter-hegemonic narratives, *beyond* the nation state level.

The final questions addressed in each chapter bring us to the institutional enquiry of the book. What has the examination of these transnationally relevant legal systems uncovered, and how has it helped deconstruct the hegemonic and counter-hegemonic narratives on GE organisms? In other words, how has the analysis of these legal regimes shed light on the rationales, underlying value systems, goals and implications of the two transnational narratives? This third question is connected to and partially overlaps with the fourth question: how has the analysis of these legal regimes helped deconstruct transnational discourses on evidence-based and socially acceptable risk approaches to risk governance? Indeed, as explained since the introductory chapter, the hegemonic and counter-hegemonic narratives on GE organisms are informed by broader transnational discourses on the regulation of uncertain risks. The answer to these questions paves the way for an analysis of the institutional findings of the book. This is what the next section turns to.

II. Institutional Analysis: The Social and Political Construction of Transnational Narratives on GE Organisms and Risk Governance

In times of the COVID-19 pandemic, many points raised in this book have emerged with unprecedented clarity and have found some empirical confirmation in everyday life. Scientific ignorance, scientific uncertainty and the evolutionary nature of scientific knowledge and research have come under the spotlight, beyond the modernist assumption that science can provide 'sound', correct and universally valid responses. Science has a crucial role to play in the governance of uncertain risks; however, it is no silver bullet. Its limits and inherent fragility are nowadays clearer than ever. The existence and relevance of scientific pluralism is also, nowadays, clearer than ever. While any national regulatory response to COVID-19 claims to be informed by science, scientific data and scientific models diverge considerably. This results in (very) different regulatory outputs.

The inferences that regulators draw from the available evidence are also bound to vary. Variation in the extent to which regulators take persisting uncertainty into consideration reflects different value judgments and normative frames. The pandemic has reminded us that, in contexts of scientific complexity, science cannot always provide a 'correct' answer. Nor can we always assume that scientific evidence is sufficient for producing an adequate characterisation of uncertain risks.

Finally, COVID-19 has painfully shown that different regulatory responses are a consequence of the delicate balance between public health (or environmental) stakes and economic interests. The intended level of protection pursued in a jurisdiction reflects the specific balance that regulators have struck between the two. OLFs, including the impact of different regulatory options on vulnerable constituencies, are also part of the picture. And indeed, as the success of the COVID-19 vaccination campaigns has shown, the decision as to whether or not risks are worth taking is always influenced by an evaluation of the advantages and disadvantages associated with a product or process. When the stakes are high and the societal benefits of a product are clear uncertain risks will be socially acceptable even for risk averse constituencies. The positive reception of COVID-19 vaccines, notwithstanding their unprecedentedly fast development and uncertainties surrounding specific potential risks associated with vaccination, testifies to this.

This book has argued that the determination of the threshold of legally relevant adverse effects, warranting regulatory intervention, is never a matter of 'pure' science.[3] Rather, this determination results from three different factors. The first factor consists of recourse to more or less prudential approaches to risk assessment. This results in a different evidence base. The second factor consists of a regulatory focus on persisting uncertainty, as opposed to adherence to sound science, ie conclusive proof of the existence of specific hazards and risks.[4] This results in different inferences. As the book has illustrated, different normative frames come into play indirectly at this stage. Reliance on sound scientific approaches as a matter of risk assessment policy and regulatory focus on sound science are cost-benefit effective in and of themselves; they relieve market actors from regulatory burdens and economic costs, and indirectly reflect the pursuit of a cost-benefit effective level of protection. Adherence to prudential approaches and a focus on persisting uncertainties and scientific insufficiency, by contrast, indirectly reflect the pursuit of a higher than cost-benefit effective level of protection and consideration of OLFs. In other words, they embody the assumption that 'society may be willing to pay a high cost to protect an interest to which it attaches priority'.[5]

The third factor impacting on the determination of legally relevant adverse effects is the intended level of protection pursued by regulators. This comes into play *indirectly*, as the normative frame through which science is assessed and evaluated, when experts conduct their risk assessment and regulators draw all relevant inferences from the available evidence base. However, it surfaces more clearly and plays a *direct* role in cases where hazards and risks have been conclusively proven. In these cases, regulators confront the question of whether or not, or to what extent, to regulate hazardous products or processes in the face of predicted exposures. Even where faced with the same exact scientific evidence, regulators pursuing different levels of protection will draw different conclusions as to the acceptability of a risk and the threshold of risk triggering regulatory intervention.

Under evidence-based models, the intended level of protection pursued by regulators shall be economically cost-benefit effective. On these grounds, uncertain risks should only be regulated insofar as the relevant public health and environmental benefits are expected to outweigh the economic costs associated with risk regulation. Ultimately, risks will be regulated where the choice not to regulate would no longer prove cost-benefit effective. The relevant adverse effects should not be 'unreasonable' and 'excessive', taking into consideration the economic costs that risk regulation would shift onto market actors and the economic benefits that the relevant products or processes can yield.

Under socially acceptable risk approaches, by contrast, the level of protection pursued by regulators need not be cost-benefit effective; more than cost-benefit analysis may be taken into account by risk managers. Regulators may thus

[3] See n 48 in ch 1.

[4] See ch 1, section III, and ch 3, section V, for more details on sound science approaches to risk assessment and adherence to sound science.

[5] See above, ch 4.

choose to minimise exposures to hazards or determine that no level of exposure can be deemed to be 'safe'. This reflects the pursuit of enhanced levels of protection. Qualitative OLFs, including socio-economic or distributional issues, may also be taken into consideration and feed into the setting of the intended level of protection and determination of the threshold of socially acceptable risk. Further, precautionary action may be warranted when, in the face of inconclusive or insufficient scientific evidence, a risk may be too high to meet the intended level of protection. Elements such as OLFs, precaution and the pursuit of enhanced levels of protection are non-scientific in nature. However, the same is true of economic cost-benefit analysis and the pursuit of a cost-benefit effective level of protection.

On these grounds, the determination of legally relevant adverse effects in the field of risk regulation is never a mere scientific matter. The narrative on sound science disregards scientific pluralism, scientific complexity and different forms of scientific uncertainty. Further, it obscures the *normative frames* through which science is assessed and evaluated. The attacks on 'political' factors like precaution and OLFs neglect the (direct or indirect) role of *non-scientific* considerations surrounding cost-benefit effectiveness and the pursuit of a cost-benefit effective level of protection, under evidence-based models. Far from being neutral and objective, as illustrated in chapter three, the assumption that sound science approaches *must* be adhered to and sound science *must* be relied on is informed by considerations surrounding the economic cost-benefit effectiveness of risk regulation.

Against this overall backdrop, the conundrum of agricultural biotechnologies has become a lens through which to investigate the political and social construction of narratives on uncertain risks and their governance. The enquiry into the rationales, underlying value systems, goals and far-reaching implications of diametrically opposed evidence-based and socially acceptable risk discourses lies at the heart of the institutional analysis of this book.

Chapter three has deconstructed the hegemonic narrative on GE organisms and risk governance from within the US legal system, highlighting the connections between sound science approaches, adherence to sound science and the pursuit of an economically cost-benefit effective level of protection. The analysis has underscored the technocratic component of evidence-based discourses and emphasised that these approaches foster the exercise of individual, market access and trade-related rights. By focusing on aggregate wealth maximisation and by pursuing the greatest net beneficial protection of public health and the environment, evidence-based models yield considerable economic benefits. However, as the thorny issue of coexistence clearly shows, they also neglect qualitative OLFs. Further, the analysis has shown that recourse to cost-benefit analysis results in the identification of a baseline threshold of safety and the pursuit of a baseline (as opposed to enhanced) level of protection. These, however, are determined by taking a sound scientific evidence base into account; on these grounds, reliance on sound science and the application of cost-benefit analysis are liable to underestimate uncertain risks and their effects.[6]

Chapter four has turned to the counter-hegemonic narrative on agricultural biotechnologies and risk regulation, deconstructing it within the EU legal order and across the EU and Member State levels. The analysis has shed light on the central elements, implications and overarching goals of the counter-hegemonic narrative and socially acceptable risk discourses.

Chapter five has moved on to the WTO legal system, deconstructing the rationale of the hegemonic narrative by focusing on *EC – Biotech* and the specific interpretation and application of the SPS Agreement by the WTO dispute settlement organs. This chapter has shown that, in the absence of any self-standing criteria of 'pure' science, the application of *lato* and *stricto sensu* de novo review draws on the mere acknowledgment that deferential procedural review would afford Members the opportunity to defend virtually *any* SPS measure. This, however, would be irreconcilable with the rationale and overarching goal of WTO law, ie trade liberalisation. In other words, it would undermine any attempt at transnational regulatory convergence in SPS regulation. This casts further light on the implications of the evidence-based narrative on GE organisms, and risk governance more generally. Not only do evidence-based approaches, as illustrated in the third chapter, pursue aggregate wealth maximisation and facilitate the exercise of individual trade rights. As the fifth chapter shows, they are also linked to transnational regulatory convergence and trade liberalisation. This is the double economic dividend referred to in the introductory chapter.

Finally, chapter six has engaged in an analysis of hybrid regulatory standards enacted by beyond-the-state actors. The enquiry into the Codex's standards confirmed the linkage between the hegemonic narrative and evidence-based risk governance, on the one hand, and trade liberalisation, on the other. The examination of regulatory standards enacted by non-profit NGOs, by contrast, has put the counter-hegemonic narrative and distributional stakes back at the centre of the analysis.

As the institutional analysis of the book has shown, the hegemonic and counter-hegemonic narratives on agricultural biotechnologies reflect different value systems, the pursuit of different goals and a different balance between individual and collective interests. Neither evidence-based nor socially acceptable risk approaches can lay claim to neutrality or objectivity. Rather, they are informed by different normative frames and are associated with different advantages and disadvantages. Ultimately, the hegemonic narrative on GE organisms and risk regulation *is* hegemonic *because* the application of evidence-based approaches maximises aggregate wealth, facilitates transnational regulatory convergence, and fosters trade liberalisation. Consequently, the counter-hegemonic narrative is destined to remain counter-hegemonic.

[6] In this respect, see the in-depth analysis in ch 3, section VI.

The message of this book is not that uncertain risks should not be taken. Nor is it about pursuing the lowest possible threshold of risk under all circumstances. Rather, this book has argued that there is nothing objective and 'correct' in the choice to focus on what we *know*, rather than what we do *not know*. Nor is there anything objective and 'correct' in focusing on regulatory cost-benefit effectiveness, rather than pursuing enhanced levels of protection and considering different OLFs. Evidence-based models are *not* 'better' than socially acceptable risk approaches. The acritical assumption that uncertain risks must be taken, or the quest for 'pure' or 'better' science, will not bring us far. Facts and values are intertwined in the field of risk governance, and the starting point in risk regulation debates should always be a discussion about *values* and all relevant *stakes*.

Technological and scientific developments, in and of themselves, can hardly be considered inherently 'good' or 'bad'. As explained in the first and third chapters, new genome editing techniques are increasingly being employed. Their advocates have emphasised the greater precision, reliability and safety of this new generation of GE organisms.[7] This might prove to be true, dispelling persisting doubts as to the public health and environmental risks posed by agricultural biotechnologies. As new advances take place in the sector, climate-resilient GE crops might also in the future prove more effective than their conventional counterparts as a climate change adaptation strategy. Research and investment in biotech firms may then shift from herbicide-resistant and pest-resistant crops to more environmentally sustainable GE crop varieties. New and more effective coexistence strategies may be developed. The agricultural biotech sector may also open up to new actors and become more transparent. Further, public opinion could shift within jurisdictions and stakeholder groups.

All of this could happen one day, in the future; agricultural biotechnologies and their risks may then become increasingly accepted across different constituencies. The day may come when the decision to take the uncertain risks associated with agricultural biotechnologies is *not* informed by *sound science* and *economic* considerations, but draws on the acknowledgment that these risks are *socially acceptable*. For the time being, however, counter-hegemonic discourses on GE organisms and socially acceptable risk approaches have a *right* and a *reason* to exist.

III. Normative Analysis: The Failure of Science and Procedural Deliberation. Towards Legal Re-Materialisation?

The normative strand of analysis of the book has enquired into the ability of both science and procedural deliberation to generate agreement in the field of risk

[7] CRISPR-Cas9 technology, in particular; see ch 1, section I.

governance, with a view to solving regulatory conflicts. The book has argued and shown that science can hardly help generate genuine agreement. While reference to mere scientific matters *could* play a role in cases where uncertainties are very low and scientific agreement very solid, this role will be limited.

As already explained, reliance on a different evidence base and different scientific inferences reflect adherence to different approaches.[8] In controversial cases where scientific uncertainty persists, reference to mere scientific matters cannot square the circle. Sound science or the 'best' science will not necessarily yield factually 'correct' answers. Further, even in cases where uncertainties are not salient, science cannot possibly solve the value-laden conundrum of the acceptability of uncertain risks: normative considerations surrounding the intended level of protection, economic cost-benefit effectiveness and OLFs are always present in the field of risk governance. Science cannot generate genuine agreement because, in the face of scientific complexity and whenever normative perspectives differ, it cannot provide a single 'valid' and universally agreeable answer. Nor can any self-standing and objective criteria of 'pure' science be identified to solve controversies, as testified by the slippery slope of substantive (de novo) and procedural (deferential) review of risk regulation measures.[9] Even more clearly, recourse to sound science approaches and adherence to sound science cannot possibly generate agreement and provide a normatively legitimate solution to regulatory conflicts. They embody an assessment and an evaluation of scientific evidence through a specific normative frame.

Procedural deliberation provides a more promising way forward, insofar as it acknowledges the role played by normative frames and values in the evaluation of scientific evidence and in making a final decision as to whether and how to regulate risks. The book has posited that procedural struggles to mediate between different values and goals *can* work. On these grounds, the normative strand of analysis has employed the Conflicts Law framework to enquire into its potential to solve horizontal, vertical and diagonal conflicts in the field of GE organisms. However, the book has also underlined that deliberative practices do not exist in a political and socio-economic vacuum.[10] A set of *substantive* preconditions must be met for *procedural* deliberation to succeed in constructing normatively legitimate solutions.

The second part of the second chapter has provided an overview of Conflicts Law theory, paving the way for the application of the framework in the following chapters. The third chapter has sketched out some considerations on the transatlantic horizontal conflict on agricultural biotechnologies. It has highlighted the

[8] See section II above.

[9] See the analysis in ch 5; see also GC Leonelli, 'Acknowledging the Centrality of the Precautionary Principle in Judicial Review of EU Risk Regulation: Why It Matters' (2020) 57 *CML Rev* 1773, for an analysis of judicial review of EU risk regulation.

[10] See M Everson, 'The Limits to the Conflicts Law Approach: Law in Times of Political Turmoil' (2011) 2 *Transnational Legal Theory* 271.

unbridgeable normative gap between the regulatory approaches of the US and EU, and reached the conclusion that deliberation is bound to fail. The fourth chapter has analysed horizontal and vertical conflicts on agricultural biotechnologies in the EU, illustrating the gap between the approach of EU institutions and EU Member States at the regulatory implementation stage. EU institutions have drawn on an evidence-based approach; lack of conclusive, sound scientific proof of specific hazards and risks is all that they have ever taken into consideration. Further, they have consistently ignored political disagreements and societal controversies within and across EU Member States. By contrast, taking enhanced levels of protection, OLFs and the tenets of the precautionary principle into account, EU Member States and societal stakeholders have repeatedly made the point that the uncertain risks posed by GE organisms are neither socially acceptable nor worth taking. Yet again, the conflict is intractable and the normative gap too broad to bridge by means of procedural categories.

The fifth chapter has focused on the WTO dispute settlement organs' failure to carve out an adequate procedural meta-norm and construct normatively legitimate solutions to vertical conflicts under the SPS Agreement. By putting the material context of the Agreement at the centre of the enquiry, the analysis has suggested that the evidence-based interpretation of the science-based obligations is unsurprising: it perfectly responds to the Agreement's aim to facilitate transnational regulatory convergence and foster trade liberalisation. Just like deliberative practices, procedural meta-norms do not exist in a vacuum. Recourse to *lato* and *stricto sensu* de novo review must be examined in the broader context of the SPS Agreement and by taking into consideration the Agreement's overarching goals. Finally, the sixth chapter has confirmed the normative gap between diametrically opposed evidence-based and socially acceptable risk approaches and emphasised the impossibility of re-embedding hybrid regulatory systems, with a view to solving diagonal conflicts.

On these grounds, the normative analysis of the book has shown that legal proceduralisation and Conflicts Law are bound to fail in the case of GE organisms; the normative gap between hegemonic and counter-hegemonic discourses is unbridgeable. Legal procedural categories cannot possibly succeed in constructing normatively legitimate solutions and horizontal, vertical and diagonal conflicts are destined to remain unresolved. Perhaps more importantly, however, the normative analysis of the book has developed a different point. The book has suggested that the success of truly deliberative practices, the successful identification of a procedural meta-norm and the successful solution of diagonal conflicts are a *procedural* reflection of a set of pre-existing *substantive* conditions. In respect of procedural deliberation, in particular, the salient substantive precondition appears to be the existence of shared values, goals and perspectives. From this perspective, procedural deliberation and legal proceduralisation can work. However, their success largely relies on (and reflects) pre-existing substantive factors.

This has two implications. First, the struggle to *construct* normatively legitimate solutions through *procedural* legal categories should be complemented by a *substantive deconstruction* of regulatory approaches and legal systems, with a view to identifying the different perspectives involved, the values and interests at stake and the goals pursued. This can shed some light on the margins of success of deliberation and legal proceduralisation. This is the form of analysis conducted throughout the institutional strand of enquiry of the book. For example, identifying where different approaches to regulation and regulatory implementation are located on the spectrum between evidence-based and socially acceptable risk models provides indications on the prospects of deliberation between different actors. This kind of analysis has informed the enquiry into the transatlantic horizontal conflict and EU-wide horizontal and vertical conflicts. In a similar vein, an analysis of the material context of a legal system can give some hints on the potential identification of a procedural meta-norm. This deconstruction has been at the centre of the enquiry into the interpretation of the SPS Agreement. On these grounds, the deconstruction stage complements and paves the way for procedural reconstruction.

Second, this substantive deconstruction of regulatory approaches and identification of the values and interests at stake can save legal proceduralisation from the 'technocratic trap'. As noted since the first and second chapters, a focus on governance arrangements, deliberative practices and legal procedural categories can easily obscure the substantive political, socio-economic and distributional stakes underlying regulatory conflicts. In this sense, insofar as agreement is pursued as a 'goal' and the assumption is that any conflict *can* and *should* be solved, modern procedural deliberative accounts incorporate a technocratic element.[11] If the relevant substantive stakes are neglected, technocratic agreement may be mistaken for political deliberation. In a similar vein, lowest common denominator compromises may be considered an expression of deliberative practices. Transatlantic negotiations on agricultural biotechnologies or the procedural compromise underlying the 2015 EU reform offer some examples.

Against this overall backdrop, it is all the more important that procedural analysis is preceded and complemented by a substantive enquiry and deconstruction. This form of analysis can cast some light on the margins of success of legal proceduralisation, and help draw a clearer distinction between technocratic agreement and genuine deliberation. Agreement should neither be pursued at all costs, nor be framed as an overarching goal. Rather, it should build on a common ground of shared substantive values and thus reflect a fruitful mediation between all perspectives and interests at stake. Where this common ground of shared values is missing, and legal proceduralisation and political deliberation fail to construct normatively legitimate solutions, legal and value pluralism should be safeguarded. Just like in the case of GE organisms, acknowledging that there are no

[11] See Everson, 'The Limits to the Conflicts Law Approach' (n 10). See also Leonelli, 'The Postmodern Normative Anxiety of Transnational Legal Studies' (n 1).

margins to construct universally agreeable solutions is the first step to ensuring the coexistence of different discourses and approaches.

Nonetheless, this does not quite settle the post-modern normative conundrum of transnational legal studies. If legal proceduralisation fails to provide normatively legitimate solutions, and the recognition and defence of legal and value pluralism is the end point of the analysis, we are back to the starting point: the acknowledgment of legal pluralism under transnational legal theory.[12] Ultimately, this negates any normative dimension in the analysis. It also triggers a further and broader question, beyond the specific case of regulatory conflicts on GE organisms. In the face of increasing societal complexity, differentiation and fragmentation, what are the margins of manoeuvre for *modern* procedural paradigms to tackle regulatory conflicts in a *post-modern*, transnational scenario?

As suggested elsewhere, the World Society whose advent Luhmann foretold might as well be defined as an 'amorphous' World Society.[13] Economic interconnectedness and demographic, media and information flows have brought to the fore a far-reaching restructuring of societal ordering. Transnational regulatory convergence and increasing trade liberalisation have then pushed forward the neo-liberal globalisation agenda, increasingly homogenising World Society. Yet, the World Society we are living in has remained amorphous; while homogenised in several respects, it is inherently fragmented in political, socio-economic and cultural terms.[14] Therefore, as noted elsewhere, the prospects for legal proceduralisation to identify normatively legitimate solutions to highly complex regulatory conflicts and successfully construct shared principles and values appear rather bleak.[15] In the face of societal fragmentation and ubiquitous contestation over substantive values, procedural legal paradigms like Conflicts Law theory struggle to re-legitimise law through the identification of genuinely agreed political and legal solutions. Overall, as summarised in the introductory chapter, modern procedural accounts have put too much faith in the ability of rational communicative processes to construct shared substantive values and identities and underpin societal integration. In the post-modern era, these paradigms struggle in the attempt to control political and socio-economic tensions and construct legitimate solutions.

This raises the question of whether normative legal analysis is doomed in the transnational landscape. Should transnational legal theory, then, relinquish the distinction between law's facticity and validity, and limit itself to deconstructing law? Or do we find ourselves in a 'Rodrik trilemma' scenario,[16] and should we look

[12] See ch 2, part 2 and section V in particular.
[13] See Leonelli, 'The Postmodern Normative Anxiety of Transnational Legal Studies' (n 1).
[14] ibid.
[15] ibid.
[16] See the famous theorisation of the trilemma in D Rodrik, *The Globalization Paradox: Democracy and the Future of the World Economy* (Norton, 2011).

back to the nation state level? As suggested elsewhere, *legal re-materialisation* and a new focus on *purposive* forms of normativity offer an alternative way forward, paving the way for *post-modern* normative legal analysis.[17] The starting point is the acknowledgment of law's inability to construct a universally legitimate discourse in the post-modern era. Post-modern normative analysis thus 'leaves behind any claim to universality or universalisation'[18] and embarks on a less ambitious project. Just like at the times of the Welfare State,[19] law's legitimacy is assessed against the normative yardstick of specific *substantive* values, principles and goals.[20] Clearly, the relevant debates have significantly changed. For this reason, the central question becomes 'how, and under which forms, the formerly nation state based normative and political debates are likely to re-emerge at the transnational level'.[21]

A deconstruction of competing transnational narratives like the one conducted throughout the institutional analysis of this book can help identify fluid transnational stakeholder constituencies; these defend specific substantive values, refer to specific substantive principles and advocate specific regulatory approaches. In the case of agricultural biotechnologies, as the analysis has shown, these constituencies are located and operate within, across and beyond the nation state. They have relied on hegemonic or counter-hegemonic discourses on uncertain risks and defended different approaches to the governance of GE organisms, taking different perspectives and referring to different substantive values and interests. This is an example of how normative and political debates are re-surfacing at times of globalisation.

The *deconstruction* of transnational narratives can then pave the way for the *construction* of *substantive* normative arguments. Ultimately, this post-modern perspective entails taking a side in the debate and deciding where to stand. It involves constructing substantive, purposive arguments as to what approach should inform regulatory frameworks, which goals should be pursued at the regulatory implementation stage, which values should be defended, what balance should be struck between the different interests at stake and which principles should inform the solution of regulatory conflicts within, across and beyond the nation state.[22] In the case of GE organisms, for example, substantive normative analysis could involve advocating evidence-based or socially acceptable risk approaches, defending their underlying value systems, promoting their goals and putting forward specific arguments relating to how regulatory conflicts ought to be solved.

[17] Leonelli, 'The Postmodern Normative Anxiety of Transnational Legal Studies' (n 1).

[18] ibid.

[19] See ch 2, part 2 and section V in particular.

[20] Leonelli, 'The Postmodern Normative Anxiety of Transnational Legal Studies' (n 1).

[21] P Zumbansen, 'The State as Black Box and the Market as Regulator' (2009) 165 *Journal of Institutional and Theoretical Economics* 62, 67. See also Leonelli, 'The Postmodern Normative Anxiety of Transnational Legal Studies' (n 1).

[22] Leonelli, 'The Postmodern Normative Anxiety of Transnational Legal Studies' (n 1).

The re-materialisation of law and the construction of substantive normative arguments might be the only way to solve the post-modern normative conundrum of transnational legal studies. If legal proceduralisation fails in the attempt to recouple law and politics in the post-national constellation, legal analysis can still structure substantive, purposive arguments. As argued elsewhere, legal re-materialisation and post-modern normative analysis could make transnational legal studies the site of new debates and discussions between different visions for globalisation.[23] Further, they could breathe new life into politics, beyond the dichotomy of 'input' and 'output' legitimacy, the nation state and technocracy.[24]

Genuine agreement on the validity and legitimacy of law is the only way to preserve its universal recognition. However, where there are no grounds for genuine agreement, regulatory conflicts should not be solved at all costs. In fact, they are bound to re-surface. No case proves this in a clearer way than the transnational controversy on GE organisms. If legal proceduralisation fails in its struggle to safeguard law's normative legitimacy, then, all that legal analysis can do is acknowledge its own limits and put forward substantive normative arguments. In the post-modern era and in the transnational landscape, this may prove more important than ever.

[23] ibid.

[24] ibid. With regard to the EU legal order, see GC Leonelli, 'The Glyphosate Saga and the Fading Democratic Legitimacy of EU Risk Regulation' (2018) 25 *Maastricht Journal of European and Comparative Law* 582; and GC Leonelli, 'The Perfect Storm: GMO Governance and the EU Technocratic Turn' in M Peeters and M Eliantonio (eds), *Research handbook on EU Environmental Law* (Edward Elgar, 2020).

SELECTED BIBLIOGRAPHY

Abbott, KW, and Snidal, D, 'Strengthening International Regulation Through Transnational New Governance: Overcoming the Orchestration Deficit' (2009) 42 *Vanderbilt Journal of Transnational Law* 501.

—— 'The Governance Triangle: Regulatory Standards, Institutions and the Shadow of the State in W Mattli and N Woods (eds), *The Politics of Global Regulation* (Princeton University Press, 2009).

Ackerman, F, and Heinzerling, L, 'Pricing the Priceless: Cost-Benefit Analysis of Environmental Protection' (2002) 150 *University of Pennsylvania Law Review* 1553.

—— *Priceless: on Knowing the Price of Everything and the Value of Nothing* (New Press, 2004).

Adler, M and Posner, E, 'Rethinking Cost-Benefit Analysis' (1999) 109 *Yale Law Journal* 165.

—— 'Implementing Cost-Benefit Analysis when Preferences are Distorted' in M Adler and E Posner (eds) *Cost-Benefit Analysis: Legal, Economic and Philosophical Perspectives* (University of Chicago Press, 2001).

Aleinikoff, A, 'Transnational Spaces: Norms and Legitimacy' (2008) 33 *Yale Journal of International Law* 479.

Alemanno, A, 'The European Food Safety Authority at Five' (2008) 3 *European Food and Feed Law Review* 2.

—— 'The Fabulous Destiny of Bisphenol A (BPA)' (2010) 1 *European Journal of Risk Regulation* 397.

—— Annotation of Case C-77/09, *Gowan Comércio Internacional e Servicos Lda* v. *Ministero della Salute*, EU:C:2010:803, (2011) 48 *CML Rev* 1329.

—— 'Risk Versus Hazard and The Two Souls of EU Risk Regulation: A Reply to Ragnar Löfstedt' (2011) 2 *European Journal of Risk Regulation*, 169.

—— 'The Science, Law and Politics of Neonicotinoids and Bees. A New Test Case for the Precautionary Principle' (2013) 4 *European Journal of Risk Regulation* 191.

—— 'The Regulatory Cooperation Chapter of the TTIP: Institutional Structure and Democratic Consequences' (2015) 18 *Journal of International Economic Law* 625.

Alemanno, A and Wiener, JB, 'The Future of International Regulatory Cooperation: TTIP as a Learning Process Toward a Global Policy Laboratory' (2016) 78 *Law and Contemporary Problems* 101.

Anderson, C, 'Contrasting Models of EU Administration in EU Judicial Review of Risk Regulation' (2014) 51 *CML Rev* 425.

Ansell, C and Vogel, D (eds), *What's the Beef? The Contested Governance of European Safety* (MIT Press, 2006).

—— 'The Contested Governance of European Food Safety Regulation' in C Ansell and D Vogel (eds), *What's the Beef? The Contested Governance of European Safety* (MIT Press, 2006).

Archibugi, D, *The Global Commonwealth of Citizens. Towards Cosmopolitan Democracy* (Princeton University Press, 2008).

Archibugi, D, Koenig-Archibugi, M and Marchetti, R (eds), *Global Democracy. Normative and Empirical Perspectives* (CUP, 2012).

Arcuri, A, 'Law and Economics of the SPS Agreement: A Critical Perspective' in G Van Calster and D Prévost (eds), *Research Handbook on Environment, Health and the WTO* (Edward Elgar, 2013).

Avbelj, M, 'Transnational Law between Modernity and Post-Modernity' (2016) 7 *Transnational Legal Theory* 406.

Bail, C, Falkner, R and Marquard, H (eds), *The Cartagena Protocol on Biosafety. Reconciling Trade in Biotechnology with Environment and Development?* (Earthscan, 2002).

Beck, U, *Risk Society. Towards a New Modernity* (SAGE, 1992).

—— *World at Risk* (Polity Press, 2009).

Bergkamp, L and Kogan, L, 'Trade, the Precautionary Principle and Post-Modern Regulatory Process. Regulatory Convergence in the TTIP' (2013) 4 *European Journal of Risk Regulation* 493.
Berman, PS, 'From International Law to Law and Globalization' (2005) 43 *Columbia Journal of Transnational Law* 485.
—— (ed), *Oxford Handbook of Global Legal Pluralism* (OUP, 2020).
Black, J, 'The Role of Risk in Regulatory Processes' in R Baldwin and M Cave (eds), *The Oxford Handbook of Regulation* (OUP, 2010).
Blankenburg, E, 'The Poverty of Evolutionism: A Critique of Teubner's Case for Reflexive Law (1984) 18 *Law and Society Review* 273.
Bodiguel, L and Cardwell, M (eds), *The Regulation of GMOs. Comparative Approaches* (OUP, 2010).
Bourdieu, P, *Outline of A Theory of Practice* (CUP, transl. 2013).
Brownsword, R and Yeung, K, *Regulating Technologies: Legal Futures, Regulatory Frames and Technological Fixes* (Hart Publishing, 2008).
Brownsword, R, Scotford, E and Yeung, K, *The Oxford Handbook of Law, Regulation and Technology* (OUP, 2017).
Büthe, T, 'The Globalisation of Health and Safety Standards: Delegation of Regulatory Authority in the SPS Agreement of the 1994 Agreement Establishing the WTO' (2008) 71 *Law and Contemporary Problems* 219.
—— 'Institutionalization and Its Consequences: the TLO(s) For Food Safety', in TC Halliday, and G Shaffer (eds), *Transnational Legal Orders* (CUP, 2015).
Büthe, T and Harris, N, 'Codex Alimentarius Commission' in T Hale and D Held (eds), *Handbook of Transnational Governance. Institutions and Innovations* (Polity Press, 2011).
Büthe, T and Mattli, W, 'Setting International Standards: Technological Rationality or Primacy of Power?' (2003) 56 *World Politics* 1.
—— *The New Global Rulers: The Privatization of Regulation in the World Economy* (Princeton University Press, 2012).
Button, C, *The Power to Protect. Trade, Health and Uncertainty in the WTO* (Hart Publishing, 2004).
Cafaggi, F (ed), *Enforcement of Transnational Regulation: Ensuring Compliance in a Global World* (Edward Elgar, 2012).
—— 'Transnational Private Regulation: Regulating Global private Regulators' in S Cassese (ed), *Research Handbook on Global Administrative Law* (Edward Elgar, 2016).
Cassese, S (ed), *Research Handbook on Global Administrative Law* (Edward Elgar, 2016).
Cassese, S et al, 'The Enforcement of Transnational Private Regulation: A Fictitious Oxymoron' in F Cafaggi (ed), *Enforcement of Transnational Regulation: Ensuring Compliance in a Global World* (Edward Elgar, 2012).
Cata Backer, L, 'Private Actors and Public Governance Beyond the State: The Multinational Corporation, the Financial Stability Board, and the Global Governance Order' (2011) 18 *Indiana Journal of Global Legal Studies* 761.
Chalmers, D, 'Food for Thought: Reconciling European Risks and Traditional Ways of Life' (2003) 66 *ML Rev* 538.
—— 'Risk, Anxiety and the European Mediation of the Politics of Life' (2005) 30 *EL Rev* 649.
—— 'Introduction: the Conflicts of EU Law and the Conflicts in EU Law' (2012) 18 *European Law Journal* 607.
Chalmers, D, Jachtenfuchs, M and Joerges, C (eds), *The End of the Eurocrats' Dream. Adjusting to European Diversity* (CUP, 2016).
Christoforou, T, 'The Regulation of Genetically Modified Organisms in the European Union: the Interplay of Science, Law and Politics' (2004) 41 *CML Rev* 637.
—— 'The Precautionary Principle, Risk Assessment and the Comparative Role of Science in the European Community and the US Legal Systems', in NJ Vig and M Faure (eds), *Green Giants? Environmental Policies of the United States and the European Union* (MIT Press, 2004).
Codex Alimentarius Commission, *Procedural Manual*, 27th edn (Joint FAO/WHO Food Standards Programme, 2019).

—— CAC/GL 44-2003, Principles for the Risk Analysis of Foods derived from Modern Biotechnology.
—— CAC/GL 45-2003, Guideline for the Conduct of Food Safety Assessment of Foods Derived from Recombinant-DNA Plants.
—— CAC/GL 62-2007, Working Principles for Risk Analysis for Food Safety for Application by Governments.
Cotterell, R, 'Transnational Communities and the Concept of Law' (2008) 21 *Ratio Juris* 1.
Council of the European Union, *Council Document no 11226/2/09 REV 2 of 24 June 2009.*
—— *Council Document no 7153/12 of 2 March 2012.*
—— *Council Document no 10883/1/12 of 6 June 2012.*
Cremona, M (ed), *New Technologies and EU Law* (OUP, 2017).
Cremona, M and Scott, J (eds), *EU Law Beyond EU Borders: The Extra-Territorial Reach of EU Law* (OUP, 2019).
Currie, B, *Selected Essays on the Conflict of Laws* (Duke University Press, 1963).
Dąbrowska Klosinska, P, 'EU Governance of GMOs: Political Struggles and Experimentalist Solutions?' in CF Sabel and J Zeitlin (eds) *Experimentalist Governance in the European Union* (OUP, 2010).
—— 'Risk, Precaution and Scientific Complexity before the Court of Justice of the European Union' in L Gruszczynski and W Werner (eds), *Deference in International Courts and Tribunals* (OUP, 2014).
—— 'The EU and Transnational Regulation of GMOs: From Bargaining Impasse to Experimentalist Cooperation?' in J Zeitlin (ed) *Extending Experimentalist Governance? The European Union and Transnational Regulation* (OUP, 2015).
Dalhuisen, JH, 'Globalization and the Transnationalization of Commercial and Financial Law' (2015) 67 *Rutgers University Law Review* 23.
Davis, KE, Fisher, A, Kingsbury, B and Merry, SE (eds), *Governance by Indicators. Global Power Through Quantification and Rankings* (OUP, 2012).
De Sadeleer, N, *EU Environmental Law and the Internal Market* (OUP, 2014).
—— 'Marketing and Cultivation of GMOs in the EU. An Uncertain Balance Between Centripetal and Centrifugal Forces' (2015) 6 *European Journal of Risk Regulation* 532.
De Sousa Santos, B, *Toward a New Legal Common Sense: Law, Globalization and Emancipation* (Butterworths, 2002).
Djelic, ML and Quack, S, *Transnational Communities. Shaping Global Economic Governance* (CUP, 2010).
Djelic, ML and Sahlin-Andersson, K (eds), *Transnational Governance. Institutional Dynamics of Regulation* (CUP, 2006).
Dobner, P and Loughlin, M (eds), *The Twilight of Constitutionalism?* (OUP, 2010).
Douglas, M and Wildavsky, A, *Risk and Culture: and Essay on the Selection of Technical and Environmental Dangers* (University of California Press, 1982).
Dreisen, D, 'Is Cost-Benefit Analysis Neutral' (2006) 77 *University of Colorado Law Review* 335.
Du, M, 'Reconceptualizing the Role of Science in International Trade Disputes' (2018) 52 *Journal of World Trade* 697.
Dunlop, CA and Radaelli, CM (eds), *Handbook of Regulatory Impact Assessment* (Edward Elgar, 2017).
Dunoff, JL and Trachtman, JP, 'A Functional Approach to International Constitutionalization', in JL Dunoff and JP Trachtman (eds), *Ruling the World? Constitutionalism, International Law and Global Governance* (CUP, 2009).
Echols, M, 'Food Safety Regulation in the European Union and the United States: Different Cultures, Different Laws' (1998) 4 *Columbia Journal of European Law* 525.
Endres, AB, 'GMO: Genetically Modified Organism or Gigantic Monetary Obligation? The Liability Schemes for GMO Damage in the United States and the European Union' (1999) 22 *Loyola LA International and Comparative Law Review* 453.
—— 'United States Food Law Update: Labelling Controversies, Biotechnology Litigation and the Safety of Imported Food' (2007) 3 *Journal of Food Law and Policy* 253.
—— 'Coexistence Strategies, the Common Law of Biotechnology and Economic Liability Risks' (2008) 13 *Drake Journal of Agricultural Law* 115.

—— 'An Evolutionary Approach to Agricultural Biotechnology: Litigation Challenges to the Regulatory and Common Law Regimes for Genetically Engineered Plants' (2012) 4 *Northeastern University Law Journal* 59.

Endres, AB and Tarr, MN, 'United States Food Law Update: Initial Food Safety Restructuring Efforts, Poultry Production Contract Reforms and Genetically Engineered Rice Litigation' (2010) 6 *Journal of Food Law and Policy* 103.

Epps, T, *International Trade and Health Protection. A Critical Assessment of the WTO's SPS Agreement* (Edward Elgar, 2008).

—— 'Recent Developments in WTO Jurisprudence: Has the Appellate Body Resolved the Issue of an Appropriate Standard of Review in SPS Cases?' (2012) 62 *University of Toronto Law Journal* 201.

European Commission, COM(1997) 176 Final, *Commission Communication on the General Principles of Food Legislation in the European Union.*

—— COM(1997) 183 Final, *Commission Communication on Consumer Health and Food Safety.*

—— COM(1999) 719 final, *White Paper on Food Safety.*

—— COM(2000) 1 Final, *Communication from the Commission on the Precautionary Principle.*

—— COM(2002) 276 Final, *Communication from the Commission on Impact Assessment.*

—— COM(2010) 375 Final, *Proposal for a Regulation of the European Parliament and of the Council Amending Directive 2001/18/EC as Regards the Possibility for the Member States to Restrict or Prohibit the Cultivation of GMOs in their Territory.*

—— COM(2010) 380 Final, *Communication from the Commission to the European Parliament, the Council, the European Economic and Social Committee and the Committee of the Regions on the Freedom for Member States to Decide on the Cultivation of Genetically Modified Crops.*

—— COM(2015) 176 Final, *Reviewing the Decision-Making Process on Genetically Modified Organisms (GMOs).*

—— COM(2015) 177 Final, *Proposal for a Regulation of the European Parliament and of the Council Amending Regulation (EC) no 1829/2003 as regards the Possibility for the Member States to Restrict or Prohibit the Use of Genetically Modified Food and Feed on their Territory.*

—— COM(2015) 215 Final, *Better Regulation for Better Results – an EU Agenda.*

—— COM(2018) 179 Final, *Proposal for a Regulation of the European Parliament and of the Council on the Transparency and Sustainability of the EU Risk Assessment in the Food Chain.*

—— COM(2019) 640 Final, *Communication from the Commission to the European Parliament, the European Council, the Council, the European Economic and Social Committee and the Committee of the Regions. The European Green Deal.*

—— COM(2020) 381 Final, *Communication from the Commission to the European Parliament, the Council, the European Economic and Social Committee and the Committee of the Regions. A Farm to Fork Strategy for a Fair, Healthy and Environmentally-Friendly Food System.*

European Scientific Advice Mechanism, High Level Group of Scientific Advisors, *New Techniques in Agricultural Biotechnology* (2017).

European Network of GMO Laboratories, *Detection of Food and Feed Plant Products Obtained by New Mutagenesis Techniques* (2019).

Executive Office of the US President, Office of Science and Technology Policy, *Coordinated Framework for the Regulation of Biotechnology*, 26 June 1986.

—— *Update to the Coordinated Framework for the Regulation of Biotechnology*, 4 January 2017.

Executive Office of the US President, Emerging Technologies Interagency Policy Coordination Committee's Biotechnology Working Group, *National Strategy for Modernizing the Regulatory System for Biotechnology Products*, September 2016.

Everson, M, 'The Limits to the Conflicts Law Approach: Law in Times of Political Turmoil' (2011) 2 *Transnational Legal Theory* 271.

Everson, M and Joerges, C, 'Facticity as Validity: The Misplaced Revolutionary Practice of European Law' in E Christodoulidis, R Duke and M Goldoni (eds), *Research Handbook on Critical Legal Theory* (Edward Elgar, 2019).

Everson, M and Vos, E, 'The Scientification of Politics and the Politicisation of Science' in M Everson and E Vos (eds), *Uncertain Risks Regulated* (Routledge, 2009).

Fassbender, B, 'Rediscovering a Forgotten Constitution: Notes on the Place of the UN Charter in the International Legal Order' in JL Dunoff and JP Trachtman (eds), *Ruling the World? Constitutionalism, International Law and Global Governance* (CUP, 2009).
Fischer-Lescano, A and Teubner, G, 'Regime-Collisions: The Vain Search for Legal Unity in Fragmentation of Global Law' (2004) 25 *Michigan Journal of International Law*, 999.
Fisher, E, 'Drowning by Numbers: Standard-Setting in Risk Regulation and the Pursuit of Accountable Public Administration' (2000) 20 *Oxford Journal of Legal Studies* 109.
—— 'Precaution, Precaution Everywhere: Developing a Common Understanding of the Precautionary Principle in the European Community' (2002) 9 *Maastricht Journal of European and Comparative Law* 7.
—— *Risk Regulation and Administrative Constitutionalism* (Hart Publishing, 2007).
—— 'Opening Pandora's Box: Contextualising the Precautionary Principle in the European Union' in M Everson and E Vos (eds), *Uncertain Risks Regulated* (Routledge, 2009).
—— 'Framing Risk Regulation: A Critical Reflection' (2013) 4 *European Journal of Risk Regulation* 125.
Fisher, E, Jones, JS and Von Schonberg, R, 'Implementing the Precautionary Principle: Perspectives and Prospects' in E Fisher et al (eds), Implementing the Precautionary Principle (Edward Elgar, 2006).
Fisher, E, Pascual, P and Wagner, W, 'Understanding Environmental Models in their Legal and Regulatory Context' (2010) 22 *Journal of Environmental Law* 255.
Food and Agriculture Organization, *The Future of Food and Agriculture: Trends and Challenges* (FAO, 2017).
Foster, CE, *Science and the Precautionary Principle in International Courts and Tribunals* (CUP, 2011).
Francioni, F and Scovazzi, T (eds), *Biotechnology and International Law* (Hart Publishing, 2006).
Funtowicz, SO and Ravetz, JR, *Uncertainty and Quality in Science for Policy* (Kluwer, 1990).
—— 'The Emergence of Post-Normal Science' in R Von Schomberg (ed), *Science, Politics and Morality. Scientific Uncertainty and Decision-Making* (Springer, 1992).
—— 'Science for the Post-Normal Age' (1993) 25 *Futures* 739.
Geelhoed, M, 'Divided in Diversity: Reforming the EU's GMO Regime' (2016) 18 *Cambridge Yearbook of European Legal Studies* 20.
Giddens, A, *The Constitution of Society* (Polity Press, 1984).
—— 'The Globalizing of Modernity' in D Held and A McGrew (eds) *The Global Transformations Reader. An Introduction to the Globalization Reader* (Polity Press, 2000).
Graham, JD, 'Saving Lives through Administrative Law and Economics' (2008) 157 *University of Pennsylvania Law Review* 395.
Graham, JD and Wiener, JB, *Risk versus Risk. Trade-Offs in Protecting Health and the Environment* (Harvard University Press, 1995).
Grossman, MR, 'Genetically Modified Food and Feed and the US National Environmental Policy Act' (2007) 3 *European Food and Feed Law Review* 373.
—— 'Genetically Modified Crops and Food in the United States: The Federal Regulatory Framework, State Measures and Liability in Tort' in L Bodiguel and M Cardwell (eds), *The Regulation of GMOs. Comparative Approaches* (OUP, 2010).
—— 'Genetic Technology and Food Security' (2014) 62 *The American Journal of Comparative Law* 273.
Grossman, MR and Endres, AB, 'Regulation of Genetically Modified Organisms in the European Union' (2000) 44 *American Behavioural Scientist* 378.
Gruszczynski, L, *Regulating Health and Environmental Risks under WTO Law: A Critical Analysis of the SPS Agreement* (OUP, 2010).
—— 'Standard of Review of Health and Environmental Regulations by WTO Panels' in G Van Calster and D Prévost (eds), *Research Handbook on Environment, Health and the WTO* (Edward Elgar, 2013).
Habermas, J, *Communication and the Evolution of Society* (Beacon Press, 1979).
—— *Legitimation Crisis* (Polity Press, 1988).
—— 'The New Obscurity: The Crisis of the Welfare State and the Exhaustion of Utopian Energies' in J Habermas (ed), *The New Conservatism. Cultural Criticism and the Historians' Debate* (MIT Press, 1989).

—— *Between Facts and Norms. Contributions to a Discourse Theory of Law and Democracy* (MIT Press, 1996).
—— *The Postnational Constellation. Political Essays* (MIT Press, 2001).
Halliday, TC, 'Recursivity in Global Norm Making: A Socio-Legal Agenda' (2009) 5 *Annual Review of Law and Social Sciences* 263.
Halliday, TC and Shaffer, G (eds), *Transnational Legal Orders* (CUP, 2015).
—— 'Transnational Legal Orders' in TC Halliday and G Shaffer (eds), *Transnational Legal Orders* (CUP, 2015).
—— 'With, Within and Beyond the Nation State: The Promise and Limits of Transnational Legal Ordering', *University of California, Irvine Legal Studies Research Paper no 2016/59.*
—— 'With, Within and Beyond the Nation State: The Promise and Limits of Transnational Legal Ordering', in P Zumbansen (ed), *The Oxford Handbook of Transnational Law* (OUP, 2021).
Handl, G, Zekoll, J and Zumbansen, P, *Beyond Territoriality: Transnational Legal Authority in an Age of Globalization* (Martinus Nijhoff Publishers, 2012).
Harlow, C, 'Global Administrative Law: The Quest for Principles and Values' (2006) 17 *European Journal of International Law* 187.
Heinzerling, L, 'Discounting Life' (1999) 108 *Yale Law Journal* 1911.
—— 'The Rights of Statistical People' (2000) 24 *Harvard Environmental Law Review* 189.
Held, D, *Cosmopolitanism* (Polity Press, 2010).
Helfand, M (ed), *Negotiating State and Non-State Law. The Challenge of Global and Local Legal Pluralism* (CUP, 2015).
Herwig, A, 'Transnational Governance Regimes for Foods Derived from Biotechnology and their Legitimacy', in C Joerges, IJ Sand and G Teubner (eds), *Transnational Governance and Constitutionalism* (Hart Publishing, 2004).
Heyveart, V, 'The Transnationalization of Law: Rethinking Law through Transnational Environmental Regulation' (2017) 6 *Transnational Environmental Law* 205.
—— *Transnational Environmental Regulation and Governance. Purpose, Strategies and Principles* (CUP, 2018).
Hien, J and Joerges, C (eds), *Ordoliberalism, Law and the Rule of Economics* (Hart Publishing, 2017).
Höffe, O, *Democracy in an Age of Globalization* (Spinger-Verlag, 1999).
Holder, J and Lee, M, *Environmental Protection, Law and Policy* (CUP, 2007).
Howse, R, 'Democracy, Science and Free Trade – Risk Regulation on Trial at the WTO' (1999) 98 *Michigan Law Review* 2329.
Howse, R and Horn, H, 'European Communities – Measures Affecting the Approval and Marketing of Biotech Products' (2009) 8 *World Trade Review* 49.
Howse, R and Mavroidis, PC, 'Europe's Evolving Regulatory Strategy for GMOs – The Issue of Consistency with WTO Law: of Kine and Brine' (2001) 24 *Fordham International Law Journal* 317.
IFOAM – Organics International, *Position Paper: Genetic Engineering and Genetically Modified Organisms* (IFOAM – Organics International, 2016).
—— *Family of Standards*, adopted May 18 2020 (IFOAM – Organics International, 2020).
Janssen, AM and Rosenstock, N, 'Handling uncertain risks: An inconsistent application of standards?' (2016) 7 *European Journal of Risk Regulation* 144.
Janssen, AM and Van Asselt, M, 'The precautionary principle in Court. An analysis of post-*Pfizer* case law' in M Van Asselt, E Versluis and E Vos (eds), *Balancing between Trade and Risk. Integrating Legal and Social Science Perspectives* (Routledge, 2013).
Jasanoff, S, *The Fifth Branch: Science Advisers as Policy Makers* (Harvard University Press, 1990).
—— *Science at the Bar. Law, Science and Technology in America* (Harvard University Press, 1995).
—— *States of Knowledge: the Co-Production of Science and Social Order* (Routledge, 2004).
—— *Designs on Nature. Science and Democracy in Europe and the United States* (Princeton University Press, 2005).
—— *Reframing Rights. Bioconstitutionalism in the Genetic Age* (MIT Press, 2011).
—— *Science and Public Reason* (Routledge, 2012).

—— 'Epistemic Subsidiarity – Coexistence, Cosmopolitanism and Constitutionalism (2013) 4 *European Journal of Risk Regulation* 132.
—— 'A Field of Its Own: The Emergence of Science and Technology Studies', in R Frodeman (ed), *The Oxford Handbook of Interdisciplinarity* (OUP, 2017).
Jasanoff, S and Kim, SH, *Dreamscapes of Modernity. Sociotechnical Imaginaries and the Fabrication of Power* (Chicago University Press, 2015).
Jessup, PC, *Transnational Law. Storrs Lectures in Jurisprudence at Yale Law School* (Yale University Press, 1956).
Joerges, C, 'The Market Without a State? States Without a Market? Two Essays on the Law of the European Economy', *EUI Working Paper no 02/1996.*
—— 'Science and the Management of Risks to Health at the National, European and International Level – Stories on Baby Dummies, Mad Cows and Hormones in Beef' (2001) 7 *Columbia Journal of European Law* 1.
—— 'Deliberative Supra-Nationalism: Two Defences' (2002) 8 *European Law Journal* 133.
—— 'The Law's Problems with the Governance of the European Market' in C Joerges and R Dehousse (eds), *Good Governance in Europe's Integrated Market* (OUP, 2002).
—— 'Constitutionalism and Transnational Governance: Exploring a Magic Triangle' in C Joerges, IJ Sand and G Teubner (eds), *Transnational Governance and Constitutionalism* (Hart Publishing, 2004).
—— 'Constitutionalism in Post-National Constellations: Contrasting Social Regulation in the EU and in the WTO' in C Joerges and E Petersmann (eds), *Constitutionalism, Multilevel Trade Governance and Social Regulation* (Hart Publishing, 2006).
—— 'Sozialstaatlichkeit in Europe? A Conflict of Laws Approach to the Law of the EU and the Proceduralisation of Constitutionalisation' (2009) 10 *German Law Journal* 335.
—— 'The Idea of a Three-Dimensional Conflicts Law as a Constitutional Form', *ARENA/RECON Online Working Paper no 05/2010.*
—— 'Unity in Diversity as Europe's Vocation and Conflicts Law as Europe's Constitutional Form' in C Joerges (ed), *After Globalisation. New Patterns of Conflict and Their Sociological and Legal Re-Constructions* (ARENA/RECON, 2011).
—— 'A New Type of Conflicts Law as the Legal Paradigm of The Post-National Constellation' in C Joerges and J Falke (eds), *Karl Polanyi, Globalisation and The Potential of Law in the Transnational Markets*,(Hart Publishing, 2011).
—— 'Three Transformations of Europe and the Search for a Way Out of Its Crisis' in C Joerges and C Glinski (eds), *The European Crisis and the Transformation of Transnational Governance: Authoritarian Managerialism Versus Democratic Governance* (Hart Publishing, 2014).
—— 'Europe's Economic Constitution in Crisis and the Emergence of a New Constitutional Constellation' (2014) 15 *German Law Journal* 985.
—— 'Integration Through Law and the Crisis of Law in Europe's Emergency' in D Chalmers, M Jachtenfuchs and C Joerges (eds) *The End of the Eurocrats' Dream. Adjusting to European Diversity* (CUP, 2016).
Joerges, C and Everson, M, 'Reconfiguring the Politics-Law Relationship in The Integration Project Through Conflicts Law Constitutionalism' (2012) 18 *European Law Journal* 644.
Joerges, C and Glinski, C (eds), *The European Crisis and the Transformation of Transnational Governance: Authoritarian Managerialism Versus Democratic Governance* (Hart Publishing, 2014).
Joerges, C and Kjaer, PF (eds), *Transnational Standards of Social Protection. Contrasting European and International Governance* (ARENA/RECON, 2008).
Joerges, C, Kjaer, PF and Ralli, T, 'Conflicts Law as Constitutional Form in the Post-National Constellation' (2011) 2 *Transnational Legal Theory* 153.
Joerges, C and Neyer, J, 'Transforming Strategic Interaction Into Deliberative Problem-Solving: European Comitology in the Foodstuff Sector' (1997) 4 *Journal of European Public Policy* 609.
—— 'From Inter-Governmental Bargaining to Deliberative Political Processes: The Constitutionalisation of Comitology' (1997) 3 *European Law Journal* 273.

Joerges, C, Schepel, H and Vos, E, 'The Law's Problem with the Involvement of Non-Governmental Actors in Europe's Legislative Processes: The Case of Standardisation Under the New Approach', *EUI Working Paper no 09/1999*.

Joerges, C, Stråth Bo, B and Wagner, P (eds) *The Economy as Polity: The Political Constitution of Contemporary Capitalism* (UCL Press, 2005).

Joerges, C and Vos, E (eds), *EU Committees: Social Regulation, Law and Politics* (Hart Publishing, 1999).

Joerges, C and Weimer, M, 'A Crisis of Executive Managerialism in the EU: No Alternative?' in G De Búrca, C Kilpatrick and J Scott (eds) *Critical Legal Perspectives on Global Governance. Liber Amicorum David M. Trubek* (Hart Publishing, 2014).

Kahan, S, Slovic, DM et al, 'Fear of Democracy: A Cultural Evaluation of Sunstein on Risk' (2006) 119 *Harvard Law Review* 1071.

Kang, JW and Ramizo, DM, 'Impact of Sanitary and Phytosanitary Measures and Technical Barriers on International Trade' (2017) 51 *Journal of World Trade* 539.

Kelman, S, 'Cost-Benefit Analysis: An Ethical Critique' (1981) *AEI Journal on Government and Society Regulation* 33.

Kennedy, David, 'Challenging Expert Rule: The Politics of Global Governance' (2005) 27 *Sydney Law Review* 1.

Kennedy, Duncan 'Comment on Rudolph Wiethölter's Materialization and Proceduralization in Modern Law and Proceduralization of the Category of Law' (2011) 12 *German Law Journal* 474.

—— 'The Globalization of Critical Discourses on Law: Thoughts on David Trubek's Contribution' in G De Búrca, C Kilpatrick and J Scott (eds), *Critical Legal Perspectives on Global Governance. Liber Amicorum David M Trubek* (Hart Publishing, 2014).

Kingsbury, B, Krisch, N and Stewart, R, 'The Emergence of Global Administrative Law' (2005) 68 *Law and Contemporary Problems* 15.

Kjaer, PF, 'Transnational Normative Orders: The Constitutionalism of Intra- and Trans- Normative Law' (2013) 20 *Indiana Journal of Global Legal Studies* 783.

Klinke, A and Renn, O, 'A New Approach to Risk Evaluation and Management: Risk-Based, Precaution-Based and Discourse-Based Strategies' (2002) 22 *Risk Analysis* 1071.

Koskenniemi, M, 'The Fate of Public International Law: Between Technique and Politics' (2007) 70 *MLR* 1.

Koskenniemi, M and Leino, P, 'Fragmentation of International Law? Post-Modern Anxieties' (2002) 15 *Leiden Journal of International Law* 553.

Kramer, L, 'The Roots of Divergence: a European Perspective', in NJ Vig and M Faure (eds) *Green Giants? Environmental Policies of the United States and the European Union* (MIT Press, 2004).

Krimsky, S, 'An Illusory Consensus Behind GMO Health Assessment' (2015) 6 *Science, Technology and Human Values* 883.

Krisch, N, 'Global Administrative Law and the Constitutional Ambition' in P Dobner and M Loughlin (eds), *The Twilight of Constitutionalism?* (OUP, 2010).

—— 'Pluralism in Postnational Risk Regulation: The Dispute over GMOs and Trade' (2010) 1 *Transnational Legal Theory* 1.

—— *Beyond Constitutionalism. The Pluralist Structure of Postnational Law* (OUP, 2010).

Kuhn, T, *The Structure of Scientific Revolutions* (University of Chicago Press, 1962).

Lang, A, *World Trade Law after Neoliberalism. Re-Imagining the Global Economic Order* (OUP, 2011).

Lee, M, *EU Regulation of GMOs* (Edward Elgar, 2008).

—— 'The Governance of Coexistence Between GMOs and Other Forms of Agriculture: A Purely Economic Issue?' (2008) 20 *Journal of Environmental Law* 193.

—— 'Beyond Safety? The Broadening Scope of Risk Regulation' (2009) 62 *Current Legal Problems* 242.

—— 'Multi-Level Governance of GMOs in the EU. Ambiguity and Hierarchy', in L Bodiguel and M Cardwell (eds), *The Regulation of GMOs. Comparative Approaches* (OUP, 2010).

—— *EU Environmental Law, Governance and Decision-Making* (Hart Publishing, 2014).

—— 'GMOs in the Internal Market: New Legislation on National Flexibility' (2016) 79 *MLR* 317.

Leonelli, GC, 'The Fine Line between Procedural and Substantive Review in Cases Involving Complex Technical-Scientific Evaluations: Bilbaína' (2018) 55 *CML Rev* 1217.

—— 'The Glyphosate Saga and the Fading Democratic Legitimacy of EU Risk Regulation' (2018) 25 *Maastricht Journal of European and Comparative Law* 582.
—— 'GMO Risks, Food Security, Climate Change and The Entrenchment of Neo-Liberal Legal Narratives' (2018) 9 *Transnational Legal Theory* 302.
—— 'GMO Authorisations and The Aarhus Regulation: Paving the Way for Precautionary GMO Governance?' (2019) 26 *Maastricht Journal of European and Comparative Law* 505.
—— 'The Perfect Storm: GMO Governance and the EU Technocratic Turn' in M Peeters and M Eliantonio (eds), *Research handbook on EU environmental law* (Edward Elgar, 2020).
—— 'CETA and The Shifting Boundaries of The Autonomy of The EU Legal Order: Risk Regulation As a Test' (2020) 47 *Legal Issues of Economic Integration* 43.
—— 'A Threefold Blow to Environmental Public Interest Litigation: The Urgent Need to Reform the Aarhus Regulation (2020) 45(3) *European Law Review* 324–347.
—— 'Acknowledging the Centrality of the Precautionary Principle in Judicial Review of EU Risk Regulation: Why It Matters' (2020) 57 *CML Rev* 1773.
—— 'The Postmodern Normative Anxiety of Transnational Legal Studies' in P Zumbansen (ed), *The Oxford Handbook of Transnational Law* (OUP, 2021).
—— 'Judicial review of compliance with the precautionary principle from *Paraquat* to *Blaise*: quantitative thresholds, risk assessment and the gap between regulation and regulatory implementation' (2021) 22 *German Law Journal* 184.
Levi-Faur, D, 'Regulation and Regulatory Governance' in D Levi-Faur (ed), *Handbook on the Politics of Regulation* (Edward Elgar, 2011).
Livermore, MA and Revesz, RL (eds), *The Globalization of Cost-Benefit Analysis in Environmental Policy* (OUP, 2013).
Löfstedt, R, *Risk Management in Post-Trust Societies* (Earthscan, 2009).
—— 'Risk versus Hazard. Regulating in the 21st Century' (2011) 2 *European Journal of Risk Regulation* 149.
Luhmann, N, 'The World Society as a Social System' (1982) 8 *International Journal of General Systems* 131.
—— 'Operational Closure and Structural Coupling: The Differentiation of the Legal System' (1992) 13 *Cardozo Law Review* 1419.
—— *Law as A Social System* (OUP, 2004).
Majone, G (ed), *Regulating Europe* (Routledge, 1996).
—— 'What Price Safety? The Precautionary Principle and Its Policy Implications' (2002) 40 *Journal of Common Market Studies* 89.
—— 'Foundations of Risk Regulation: Science, Decision-Making, Policy Learning and Institutional Reform' (2010) 1 *European Journal of Risk Regulation* 5.
—— 'Political Institutions and the Principle of Precaution' in JB Wiener et al (eds), *The Reality of Precaution. Comparing Risk Regulation in the United States and Europe* (Routledge, 2011).
Marceau, G and Trachtman, JP, 'A Map of the World Trade Organization Law of Domestic Regulation of Goods: The Technical Barriers to Trade Agreement, the Sanitary and Phytosanitary Measures Agreement, and the General Agreement on Tariffs and Trade' (2014) 48 *Journal of World Trade* 351.
Marchant, G and Mossman, K, *Arbitrary and Capricious: The Precautionary Principle in the European Union Courts* (AEI Press, 2004).
McHughen, A and Smith, SJ, 'Regulation of Genetically Modified Crops in USA and Canada: American Overview', in CA Wozniak and A McHughen (eds), *Regulation of Agricultural Biotechnology: The United States and Canada* (Springer, 2012).
Merry, SE, 'New Legal Realism and the Ethnography of Transnational Law' (2006) 31 *Law and Social Inquiry* 975.
Osiemo, O, 'Saving Africa: the GMO Cold War and the Battle for Africa' (2018) 52 *Journal of World Trade* 143.
Parker, RW and Alemanno, A, 'A Comparative Overview of EU and US Legislative and Regulatory Systems: Implications for Domestic Governance and the Transatlantic Trade and Investment Partnership (2015) 22 *Columbia Journal of European Law* 61.

Pascual, P, Wagner, W and Fisher, E, 'Making Method Visible: Improving the Quality of Science-Based Regulation' (2013) 2 *Michigan Journal of Environmental and Administrative Law* 429.

Pauwelyn, J, 'The WTO Agreement on Sanitary and Phytosanitary Measures as Applied in the First Three SPS Disputes EC – Hormones, Australia – Salmon and Japan – Varietals' (1999) 2 *Journal of International Economic Law* 641.

—— 'Does the WTO Stand for Deference to or Interference with National Health Authorities When Applying the SPS Agreement?' in T Cottier and P Mavroidis (eds), *The Role of the Judge in International Trade Regulation: Experience and Lessons for the WTO* (University of Michigan Press, 2003).

—— 'Non-Traditional Patterns of Global Regulation. Is the WTO Missing the Boat?' in C Joerges and E Petersmann (eds), *Constitutionalism, Multi-Level Trade Governance and Social Regulation* (Hart Publishing, 2006).

Peel, J, 'A GMO By Any Other Name ... Might Be an SPS Risk! Implications of Expanding the Scope of the WTO SPS Agreement' (2007) 17 *European Journal of International Law* 1009.

—— *Science and Risk Regulation in International Law* (CUP, 2010).

—— 'Of Apples and Oranges (and Hormones in Beef): Science and the Standard of Review in WTO Disputes under the SPS Agreement' (2012) 61 *International and Comparative Law Quarterly* 427.

Pesticide Action Network UK, Sustain and E Lydgate, *Toxic Trade* (PAN UK, 2020).

Peters, A, 'The Merits of Global Constitutionalism' (2009) 16 *Indiana Journal of Global Legal Studies* 397.

—— 'Are We Moving Towards Constitutionalization of the World Community?' in A Cassese (ed), *Realizing Utopia: The Future of International Law* (OUP, 2012).

Polanyi, K, *The Great Transformation. The Political and Economic Origins of Our Time* (Beacon Press, 1944).

Poli, S, 'Continuity and Change in the EU Regulatory Framework on GMOs after the WTO Dispute on Boitech Products' (2010) 37 *Legal Issues of Economic Integration* 133.

—— 'The Member States' Long and Winding Road to Partial Regulatory Autonomy in Cultivating Genetically Modified Crops in the EU' (2013) 4 *EJRR* 143.

—— 'Scientific Advice in the GMO Area' in A Alemanno and S Gabbi (eds) *Foundations of EU Food Law and Policy. Ten Years of the European Food Safety Authority* (Routledge, 2014).

—— 'The Reform of EU Legislation on GMOs: A Journey to an Unknown Destination?' (2015) 6 *EJRR*, 559.

Pollack, M and Shaffer, G, 'Transatlantic Governance in Historical and Theoretical Perspective' in MA Pollack and G Shaffer (eds), *Transatlantic Governance in the Global Economy* (Rowman and Littlefield Publishers, 2001).

—— 'The Challenge of Reconciling Regulatory Differences: Food Safety and GMOs in the Transatlantic Relationship' in M Pollack and G Shaffer (eds), *Transatlantic Governance in the Global Economy* (Rowman and Littlefield Publishers, 2001).

—— 'Risk Regulation, GMOs and the Limits of Deliberation' in D Naurin and H Wallace (eds), The European Union Council of Ministers (Palgrave Macmillan, 2008).

—— *When Cooperation Fails. The International Law and Politics of Genetically Modified Foods* (OUP, 2009).

Popper, K, *The Logic of Scientific Discovery* (Hutchinson, 1959).

Posner, E, 'Controlling Agencies with Cost-Benefit Analysis: a Positive Political Theory Perspective' (2001) 68 *University of Chicago Law Review* 1137.

Radaelli, CM and De Francesco, F, 'Regulatory Impact assessment', in R Baldwin, M Cave and M Lodge (eds) *The Oxford Handbook of Regulation* (OUP, 2010).

Revesz, R and Livermore, M, *Retaking Rationality: How Cost-Benefit Analysis Can Better Protect the Environment and our Health* (OUP, 2008).

Rhodes, RAW, 'The Hollowing Out of the State: The Changing Nature of the Public Service in Britain' (1994) 65 *Political Quarterly* 138.

Rodrik, D, *The Globalization Paradox: Democracy and the Future of the World Economy* (Norton, 2011).

Rose-Ackerman, S, 'Precaution, Proportionality and Cost-Benefit Analysis: False Analogies' (2013) 4 *European Journal of Risk Regulation* 281.

Saab, A, *Narratives of Hunger in International Law. Feeding the World in Times of Climate Change* (CUP, 2019).

Sassen, S, 'The Embeddedness of Electronic Markets: The Case of Global Capital Markets' in K Knorr Cetina and A Preda (eds), *The Sociology of Financial Markets* (OUP, 2005).

—— *Territory, Authority, Rights. From Medieval to Global Assemblages* (Princeton University Press, 2006).

—— *A Sociology of Globalization* (Norton, 2007).

—— 'The Places and Spaces of the Global: An Expanded Analytic Terrain', in D Held and A McGrew (eds), *Globalization Theory. Approaches and Controversies* (Polity Press, 2007).

Scharpf, FW, *Governing Europe. Effective and Democratic?* (OUP, 1999).

SCHER, SCENIHR and SCCS, *Opinion on Synthetic Biology I, Definition* (2014).

—— *Opinion on Synthetic Biology II, Risk Assessment Methodologies and Safety Aspects* (2015).

—— *Opinion on Synthetic Biology III, Risks to the Environment and Biodiversity Related to Synthetic Biology and Research Priorities in the Field of Synthetic Biology* (2015).

Scott, J, 'European Regulation of GMOs and the WTO' (2003) 9 *Columbia Journal of European Law* 2013.

—— 'European Regulation of GMOs: Thinking about 'Judicial Review' in the WTO' in M Everson and E Vos (eds), *Uncertain Risks Regulated* (Routledge, 2009).

—— *The WTO Agreement on Sanitary and Phytosanitary Measures. A Commentary* (OUP, 2007).

Scott, J and Sturm, S, 'Courts as Catalysts: Rethinking the Judicial Role in New Governance' (2007) 13 *Columbia Journal of European Law* 564.

Scott, J and Trubek, DM, 'Mind the Gap: Law and New Approaches to Governance in the European Union' (2002) 8 *European Law Journal* 1.

Scott, J and Vos, E, 'The Juridification of Uncertainty: Observations on the Ambivalence of the Precautionary Principle within the EU and the WTO' in C Joerges and R Dehousse (eds), *Good Governance in Europe's Integrated Market* (OUP, 2002).

Shaffer, G, 'Transnational Legal Ordering and State Change' in G Shaffer (ed), *Transnational Legal Ordering and State Change* (CUP, 2013).

—— 'The New Legal Realist Approach to International Law' (2015) 28 *Leiden Journal of International Law* 189.

Shaffer, G and Coye, C, 'From International Law to Jessup's Transnational Law, from Transnational Law to Transnational Legal Orders', in P Zumbansen (ed), *The Many Lives of Transnational Law. Critical Engagement with Jessup's Bold Proposal* (CUP, 2020).

Shapiro, S, 'The Evolution of Cost-Benefit Analysis in US Regulatory Decision-Making' in D Levi-Faur (ed), *Handbook on the Politics of Regulation* (Edward Elgar, 2011).

Skogstad, G, 'Internationalization, Democracy and Food Safety Measures: the (Il)Legitimacy of Consumer Preferences?' (2001) 7 *Global Governance*, 293.

—— 'Contested Accountability Claims and GMO Regulation in the European Union' (2011) 49 *Journal of Common Market Studies* 895.

Slaughter, AM, *A New World Order* (Princeton University Press, 2004).

Slovic, P, *The Perception of Risk* (Taylor and Francis, 2000).

Slow Food International, *Slow Food Position Paper on Genetically Modified Organisms* (Slow Food International, 2016).

Somsen, H (ed), *The Regulatory Challenge of Biotechnology: Human Genetics, Food and Patents* (Edward Elgar, 2007).

Sunstein, C, 'Cognition and Cost-Benefit Analysis', in M Adler and E Posner (eds) *Cost-Benefit Analysis: Legal, Economic and Philosophical Perspectives* (University of Chicago Press, 2001).

—— 'Is Cost-Benefit Analysis for Everyone?' (2001) 53 *Administrative Law Review* 299.

—— *Risk and Reason. Safety, Law and the Environment* (CUP, 2002).

—— 'Beyond the Precautionary Principle' (2003) 151 *University of Pennsylvania Law Review* 1003.

—— *Laws of Fear. Beyond the Precautionary Principle* (CUP, 2005).

—— 'Precautions Against What? Perceptions, Heuristics and Culture' in JB Wiener et al (eds), *The Reality of Precaution. Comparing Risk Regulation in the United States and Europe* (Routledge, 2011).
—— 'The Storrs Lectures: Behavioral Economics and Paternalism' (2012) 122 *Yale Law Journal* 1670.
—— *Choosing Not to Choose. Understanding the Value of Choice* (OUP, 2015).
—— 'Cost-Benefit Analysis and Arbitrariness Review' (2017) 41 *Harvard Environmental Law Journal* 1.
—— *The Cost-Benefit Revolution* (MIT Press, 2018).
Teubner, G, 'Substantive and Reflexive Elements in Modern Law' (1983) 17 *Law and Society Review*, 239.
—— 'Autopoiesis in Law and Society: A Rejoinder to Blankenburg' 18 *Law and Society Review* 291.
—— 'Introduction to Autopoietic Law' in G Teubner (ed), *Autopoietic Law: A New Approach to Law and Society* (Walter De Gruyter, 1987).
—— 'The Two Faces of Janus: Rethinking Legal Pluralism' (1992) 13 *Cardozo Law Review*, 1443.
—— *Law as An Autopoietic System* (Blackwell, 1993).
—— 'Global Bukowina: Legal Pluralism in the World Society' in G Teubner (ed), *Global Law Without a State* (Aldershot, 1997).
—— 'Fragmented Foundations: Societal Constitutionalism Beyond the Nation State' in P Dobner and M Loughlin (eds), *The Twilight of Constitutionalism?* (OUP, 2010).
—— *Constitutional Fragments. Societal Constitutionalism and Globalization* (OUP, 2012).
Thaler, RH and Sunstein, C, *Nudge. Improving Decisions about Health, Wealth and Happiness* (Yale University Press, 2008).
Trubek, D and Santos, A (eds), *The New Law and Economic Development. A Critical Appraisal* (CUP, 2006).
Twining, W, *General Jurisprudence. Understanding Law from a Global Perspective* (CUP, 2009).
US Advisory Committee on Biotechnology and the 21st Century Agriculture, *A Framework for Local Coexistence Discussions. A Report of the Advisory Committee on Biotechnology and the 21st Century Agriculture (AC21) to the Secretary of Agriculture*, December 8, 2016.
US APHIS, Proposed Rules, *Movement of Certain Genetically Engineered Organisms*, 84 FR 26514-26541, Docket No APHIS-2018-0034, June 6 2019.
US FDA, *Statement of Policy – Foods Derived from New Plant Varieties*, Final, May 1992.
US National Academies of Sciences, Engineering and Medicine, *Genetically Engineered Crops: Experiences and Prospects* (National Academies Press, 2016).
US National Research Council, *Risk Assessment in the Federal Government: Managing the Process* (National Academies Press, 1983).
—— *Introduction of Recombinant DNA-Engineered Organisms into the Environment: Key Issues* (National Academies Press, 1987).
—— *Field Testing Genetically Modified Organisms: Framework for Decisions* (National Academies Press, 1989).
—— *Science and Judgment in Risk Assessment* (National Academies Press, 1994).
—— *Science and Decisions: Advancing Risk Assessment* (National Academies Press, 2009).
US President, 46 FR 13193-13198, Executive Order 12291 of 17 February 1981, *Federal Regulation* (US National Archives).
—— 58 FR 51735-51745, Executive Order 12866 of 30 September 1993, *Regulatory Planning and Review*.
—— 76 FR 3821-3823, Executive Order 13563 of 18 January 2011, *Improving Regulation and Regulatory Review*. – 76 FR 41587-41588, Executive Order 13579 of 11 July 2011, *Regulation and Independent Regulatory Agencies*.
—— 82 FR 9339-9341, Executive Order 13771 of 30 January 2017, *Reducing Regulation and Controlling Regulatory Costs*.
—— 84 FR 27899-27902, Executive Order 13874 of 11 June 2019, *Modernizing the Regulatory Framework for Agricultural Biotechnology Products*.
M Van Asselt and E Vos, 'The Precautionary Principle and the Uncertainty Paradox' (2006) 9 *Journal of Risk Research* 313.

—— 'Wrestling with Uncertain Risks: EU Regulation of GMOs and the Uncertainty Paradox' (2008) 11 *Journal of Risk Research* 281.
Van Asselt, M, Versluis, E and Vos, E (eds), *Balancing between Trade and Risk. Integrating Legal and Social Science Perspectives* (Routledge, 2013).
Van Asselt, M, Vos, E and Rooijakers, E, 'Science, Knowledge and Uncertainty in EU Risk Regulation' in M Everson and E Vos (eds), *Uncertain Risks Regulated* (Routledge, 2009).
Vattimo, G, *La Fine della Modernitá* (Milano, 1991).
—— *A Farewell to Truth* (Columbia University Press, 2010).
Vig, NJ and Faure, M (eds), *Green Giants? Environmental Policies of the United States and the European Union* (MIT Press, 2004).
Vogel, D, *Trading Up. Consumer and Environmental Regulation in a Global Economy* (Harvard University Press, 1997).
—— 'Trade and Environment in the Global Economy: Contrasting European and American Perspectives' in N Vig and M Faure (eds), *Green Giants? Environmental Policies of the United States and European Union* (MIT Press, 2004).
—— *The Politics of Precaution. Regulating Health, Safety and Environmental Risks in Europe and the United States* (Princeton University Press, 2012).
Vos, E, 'The EU Regulatory System on Food Safety: Between Trust and Safety' in M Everson and E Vos (eds), *Uncertain Risks Regulated* (Routledge, 2009).
—— 'Responding to Catastrophe: Towards a New Architecture for EU Food Safety Regulation?' in CF Sabel and J Zeitlin (eds) *Experimentalist Governance in the European Union* (OUP, 2010).
Wagner, W, Fisher, E and Pascual, P, 'Misunderstanding Models in Environmental and Public Health Regulation' (2010) *NYU Environmental Law Journal* 293.
Walker, N, *Intimations of Global Law* (CUP, 2015).
Walker, VR, 'Keeping the WTO From Becoming the World Trans-Science Organization: Scientific Uncertainty, Science Policy and Fact-Finding in the Growth Hormones Dispute' (1998) 31 *Cornell International Law Journal* 251.
—— 'The Myth of Science as a 'Neutral Arbiter' for Triggering Precautions' (2003) 26 *Boston College International and Comparative Law Review* 197.
—— 'A Default-Logic Model of Fact-Finding for United States Regulation of Food Safety' in M Everson and E Vos (eds), *Uncertain Risks Regulated* (Routledge, 2009).
Weiler, JHH, 'The Community System: The Dual Character of Supranationalism' (1981) 1 *Yearbook of European Law* 257.
—— 'The Transformation of Europe' (1991) 100 *Yale Law Journal* 2403.
Weimer, M, 'Applying Precaution in EU Authorisation of Genetically Modified Products – Challenges and Suggestions for Reform' (2010) 16 *European Law Journal* 624.
—— 'What Price Flexibility? The Recent Commission Proposal to Allow for National Opt-Outs on GMO Cultivation Under the Deliberate Release Directive and the Comitology Reform Post-Lisbon' (2010) 1 *European Journal of Risk Regulation* 345.
—— 'Risk Regulation, GMOs and the Challenges to Deliberation in EU Governance: Politicisation and Scientification as Co-Producing Trends', in C Joerges and C Glinski (eds) *The European Crisis and the Transformation of Transnational Governance* (Hart Publishing, 2014).
—— 'Risk Regulation and Deliberation in EU Administrative Governance – GMO Regulation and Its Reform' (2015) 21 *European Law Journal* 622.
—— *Risk Regulation in the Internal Market. Lessons from Agricultural Biotechnology* (OUP, 2019).
Weimer, M and Pisani, G, 'The EU Adventures of "Herculex". Report on the EU Authorization of the Genetically Modified Maize 1507' (2014) 5 *European Journal of Risk Regulation* 208.
—— 'Expertise and Justification. The Contested Legitimation of the EU Risk Administration' in M Weimer and A de Ruijter (eds), *Regulating Risks in the European Union. The Co-Production of Expert and Executive Power* (Hart Publishing 2017).
Wiener, JB, 'Whose Precaution After All? A Comment on the Comparison and Evolution of Risk Regulatory Systems (2003) 12 *Duke Journal of Comparative and International Law* 207.

—— 'Convergence, Divergence and Complexity in US and European Risk Regulation', in NJ Vig and M Faure (eds) *Green Giants? Environmental Policies of the United States and the European Union* (MIT Press, 2004).

Wiener, JB et al (eds), *The Reality of Precaution. Comparing Risk Regulation in the United States and Europe* (Routledge, 2011).

Wiethölter, R, 'Proceduralization of the Category of Law' in C Joerges and D Trubek (eds) *Critical Legal Thought: An American-German Debate* (Nomos, 1985).

—— 'Justifications of a Law of Society' in O Perez and G Teubner (eds), *Paradoxes and Inconsistencies in the Law* (Hart Publishing, 2006).

—— 'Proceduralization of the Category of Law' in C Joerges, D Trubek and P Zumbansen (eds) 'Critical Legal Thought: an American-German Debate. An Introduction at the Occasion of Its Republication in the German Law Journal 25 Years Later' (2011) 12 *German Law Journal* 466.

Winickoff, D et al, 'Adjudicating the GM Food Wars: Science, Risk and Democracy in World Trade Law' (2005) 30 *Yale Journal of International Law* 81.

Wozniak, CA and McHughen, A (eds), *Regulation of Agricultural Biotechnology: The United States and Canada* (Springer, 2012).

Wozniak, CA et al, 'An Introduction to Agricultural Biotechnology Regulation in the US' in CA Wozniak and A McHughen (eds), *Regulation of Agricultural Biotechnology: The United States and Canada* (Springer, 2012).

Wüger, D and Cottier, T (eds), *Genetic Engineering and the World Trade System* (CUP, 2008).

Wynne, B, 'Uncertainty and Environmental Learning: Reconceiving Science and Policy in the Preventative Paradigm' (1992) 2 *Global Environmental Change* 111.

Zeitlin, J (ed) *Extending Experimentalist Governance? The European Union and Transnational Regulation* (OUP, 2015).

Zhao, J, 'Towards State Avoidance of Conflicts Between the SPS Agreement and the Cartagena Protocol on Biosafety: a Fresh Perspective' (2019) 53 *Journal of World Trade* 625.

Zumbansen, P, 'Sustaining Paradox Boundaries: Perspectives on the Internal Affairs in Domestic and International Law' (2004) 15 *European Journal of International Law* 197.

—— 'Niklas Luhmann's Law as a Social System' (2006) 15 *Social and Legal Studies* 453.

—— 'Law After the Welfare State: Formalism, Functionalism and the Ironic Turn of Reflexive Law' (2008) 56 *American Journal of Comparative Law* 769.

—— 'The State as Black Box and the Market as Regulator' (2009) 165 *Journal of Institutional and Theoretical Economics* 62.

—— 'Transnational Legal Pluralism' (2010) 10 *Transnational Legal Theory* 141.

—— 'Neither Public Nor Private, National Nor International: Transnational Corporate Governance From a Legal Pluralist Perspective' (2011) 38 *Journal of Law and Society* 50.

—— 'Lochner Dis-Embedded: The Anxieties of Law in a Global Context' (2013) 20 *Indiana Journal of Global Legal Studies* 29.

—— 'Law and Legal Pluralism: Hybridity in Transnational Governance', *CLPE Research Paper no 42/2013.*

—— 'Why Global Law is Transnational' (2013) 4 *Transnational Legal Theory* 463.

—— 'The Incurable Constitutional Itch: Transnational Private Regulatory Governance and the Woes of Legitimacy' in M Helfand (ed), *Negotiating State and Non-State Law. The Challenge of Global and Local Legal Pluralism* (CUP, 2015).

—— 'Theorizing as Activity: Transnational Legal Theory in Context', in C McCrudden, U Baxi and A Paliwala (eds), *Law's Ethical, Global and Theoretical Contexts. Essays in Honour of William Twining* (CUP, 2015).

—— 'Where the Wild Things Are: Journeys to Transnational Legal Orders, and Back' (2016) 1 *UC Irvine Journal of International, Transnational and Comparative Law* 161.

—— *The Many Lives of Transnational Law. Critical Engagement with Jessup's Bold Proposal* (CUP, 2020).

—— 'Manifestations and Arguments: The Everyday Operation of Transnational Legal Pluralism' in PS Berman (ed), *Oxford Handbook of Global Legal Pluralism* (OUP, 2020).

—— (ed), *The Oxford Handbook of Transnational Law* (OUP, 2021).

INDEX

www.ingramcontent.com/pod-product-compliance
Lightning Source LLC
Chambersburg PA
CBHW071303180926
51613CB00001B/112
9781509937387